PERSPECTIVES IN WEB COURSE MANAGEMENT

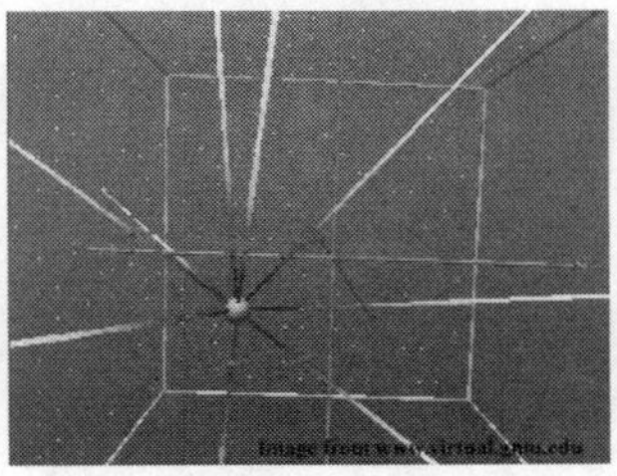

PERSPECTIVES IN WEB COURSE MANAGEMENT

Bruce L. Mann,
Contributing Editor

Canadian Scholars' Press Inc. Toronto 2000

Perspectives in Web Course Management
Bruce L. Mann, Contributing Editor

First published in 2000 by
Canadian Scholars' Press Inc.
180 Bloor Street West, Suite 1202
Toronto, Ontario
M5S 2V6

CSPI acknowledges the financial support of the Government of Canada through the Book Publishing Industry Development Programme for our publishing activities.

DISCLAIMERS

First, some of the information has been provided by external sources. Every reasonable effort has been made to locate copyright holders. The contributing editor welcomes any information concerning copyright holders. Some documents or graphical elements are subject to the copyright at another source. Please note that some restrictions on the reproduction of such documents or graphical elements may apply. Although every effort has been made by the authors and editor to ensure the accuracy, currency, and reliability of the content, they can accept no further responsibility in this regard.

Second, the authors and editor have no control over accessibility to remote sites, and are not responsible for the changing information found at the sites. The inclusion of hyperlinks or screen captures does not constitute unconditional endorsement by the authors and editor.

Third, where legislation has been reproduced, the authors and editor assume no responsibility for any discrepancies that may have been transmitted with the electronic version.

Canadian Cataloguing in Publication Data

Main entry under title:

Perspectives in Web course management

Includes bibliographical references
ISBN 1-55130-143-1

1. Computer managed instruction. 2. World Wide Web (Information retrieval system). 3. Internet (Computer network) in education. 4. Education, Higher – Computer-assisted instruction. I. Mann, Bruce Leslie, 1950- .

LB1044.87P47 2000 378.1'734467 C00-931758-9

Managing Editor: Ruth Bradley-St-Cyr
Marketing Manager: Susan Cuk
Copy Editor: Lu Cormier
Page layout: Brad Horning
Cover design: Renné Benoit

00 01 02 03 04 05 06 6 5 4 3 2 1

Printed and bound in Canada by AGMV Marquis

TABLE OF CONTENTS

PREFACE

I think it fair to say that none of the authors in this book believe in a "total solution" to learning over the Internet, as some Web software companies would have us believe. We all know that the provision of Web management software in no way guarantees critical thinking; that the current status of online collaborative social learning in no way matches the variety of interactions in seminars and tutorials. We already know that self-paced learning has had a long history of student attrition due to the huge motivational investment required on the part of the student.

That said, most of us also believe that Web course management systems have the potential to offer some of us in higher education a new means of self-expression and new opportunities for student engagement with our course material, but our curiosity about the systems is rivalled only by our pedagogical skepticism in using them. It is in this context of doubt and self-doubt that we share our perspectives of Web course management, including issues of instructional development, professional development, and current methods of assessing student learning in higher education and training situations.

World Wide Web

Originally intended as a way of displaying graphical images on the Internet, the World Wide Web is the brainchild of Tim Berners-Lee at CERN, a European laboratory for particle physics. The World Wide Web, also known as WWW, 3W, or simply "the Web," is a network of computer servers on the Internet that provides information and clickable text links called *hypertext* on pages called *Web pages*. Although Web browsers can display plain text, most Web pages are written in a computer language known as *HTML*. Using HTML computer language and the principle of hypertext linking, Web pages can connect to specific Web-compatible files on the same server, or on servers located throughout the world.

Web Course Management Systems

Several Web-based products offer educators design tools for managing their Web courses online. Since these tools are customarily grouped together, interact under a course name, and are protected by a password, they can be considered a system: a Web course management system (WCMS). Since most Web courses interact with systems outside of the course, they can also be considered open systems. These are a sample of comprehensive WCMSs and some of the companies' claims for their use in education.

WebCT (Goldberg, 1997) was developed in 1996 at the University of British Columbia, Canada. WebCT purports to facilitate the creation of Web-based educational environments, presumably by nontechnical users. WebCT claims to enable the development of entire online courses, or to simply publish materials that will supplement existing courses. Results of a recent study (Mann, Chapter 1), however, showed that educators with knowledge of instructional design but limited technical knowledge of WebCT needed more technical and design assistance than currently offered in their Web tools and contextualized help.

LearningSpace from the Lotus Corporation (1998) was developed for creating and delivering education and training. LearningSpace purports to combine "total solution" distance learning with a collaborative, educator-facilitated environment to match the benefits of face-to-face classroom discussion. The developers aspire to provide course creation and management tools to create a place where people can train and learn together.

The developers of **TopClass** at WBT Systems (1997) in San Francisco, California, believe that their product can manage course delivery and support training and education over the Internet and campus intranets. TopClass utilizes templates and built-in threaded discussion capabilities that apparently will permit educators with little programming expertise to create online courses. Like the other programs of this type, TopClass claims to be able to support collaboration, and to manage all students, educators, and assigned course material on the server.

Virtual-U was developed by Harasim and Calvert (1997) at Simon Fraser University, Canada. The developers suggest that their system will inspire educators to customize their Web course design, delivery, and enhancement. Virtual-U is described as a user-friendly, flexible, and dynamic learning environment that also purports to require no programming knowledge to operate. Learners electronically submit their assignments, and educators organize and comment on submissions. The components of Virtual-U include a group conferencing system, a course structuring tool, a grade book, and system administration tools.

Not all Web course management systems are as large and inclusive as the ones described above. The following systems have fewer features. Notably, however, the number of educational claims remain the same, and some profess even more benefits than their larger competitors.

WebFuse (Jones, 1997) is an Australian Web publishing tool, originally designed to help build Web sites at Central Queensland University. WebFuse claims to help authors create effective Web sites with a minimum of technical knowledge.

WebTeach (Hughes, 1995) is another Australian product that claims to facilitate discussions and use familiar classroom teaching strategies within their virtual classroom. WebTeach does not focus on supporting the development and uploading of Web pages; it also does not focus on student administration.

Zebu is designed by Centrinity (1999) in Canada. Zebu is supposed to arm teachers with the tools necessary to help students create dynamic online collaborative products, whether among students in class or with a class in another part of the world.

eWeb (ECT Inc, 1997) is an American product for delivering training, test preparation, and pre-certification evaluation. Apparently, using eWeb learners can study and practise until they learn the material. eWeb can be used on the job, or within any organization that places a value on knowledge and competence.

Web Course in a Box by MadDuck Technologies (1996) in Richmond, Virginia, even claims to have been "the first Web course management system." This is a curious appropriation given the relative infancy of Web browsers and the much longer history of command-line Internet systems such as PARTIcipate (see CoNet, 1998) introduced in 1981, and CoSy (see Softwords, 1995) initiated in 1985.

This is only a sampling; there are many other Web course management systems—large and small, expensive and cheap. During the late 1990s and into 2000, educators continue to struggle with decisions about which system to implement in their courses and how best to use it. Consultants are hired and money spent to compare these systems directly.

One method of comparing Web course management systems is embodied in an online Web site: The Comparative Analysis Web Tool (CAWT) developed by Dr. Bruce Landon of Douglas College in British Columbia, Canada (see Figure P.1 on page x). Dr. Landon's CAWT focuses on technical specifications, instructional design values, media capabilities, tools, ease of use, potential for collaboration and connectivity, and contact information. His original research model allows quick access to the Web-based data; manipulation of values to best suit specific institutional needs; ability to expand the site to include more applications over time; and a model for other quantitative research projects.

It is from within this climate of pedagogical uncertainty over Web course and management systems that the writing of this book began. Some chapters describe Web course development tools or development efforts at particular institutions. Others are theoretical, offering models or commenting on the current state of the art. Whereas no attempt was made to select authors by their country of origin, the perspectives from three countries are represented in this book; namely, Australia, Canada, and the United States. I spoke with most of the authors personally, and discovered that they each had an interesting story to tell. Undoubtedly you have some stories of your own to tell as well. I welcome your comments.

Figure P.1
The Comparative Analysis Web Tool (CAWT)

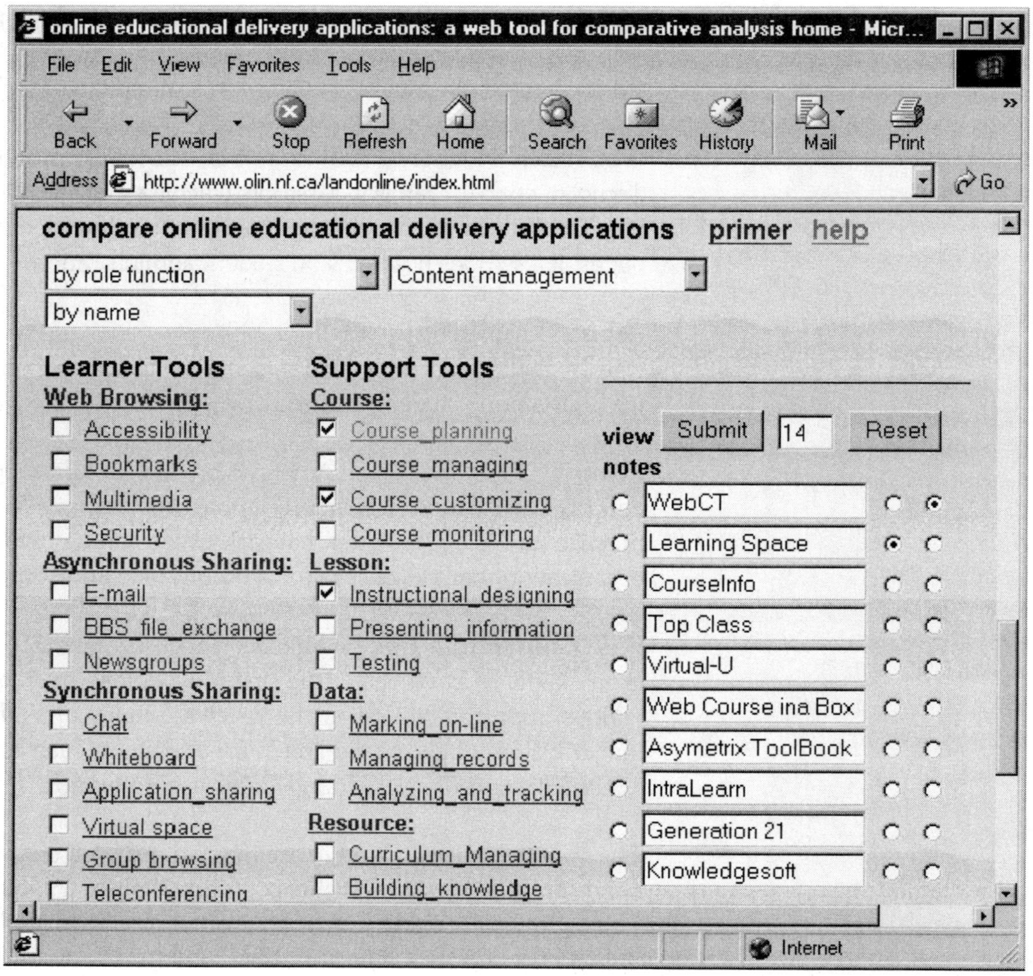

Acknowledgements

I wish to thank all of the authors here for contributing to this volume. I would also like to thank Dr. Jack Wayne and Ruth Bradley-St-Cyr at Canadian Scholars' Press for liking the idea and managing the project; graduate students Beth Power, Ju Wang, and Jianping Cui for their careful reading of the manuscript; Lu Cormier for her patience and tireless copy editing; and Brad Horning for his patience and tireless design and layout. Last, but not least, I wish to thank my wife and confidant, Diane Mann, for her continued support throughout the project.

Bruce L. Mann

References

Centrinity. 1999. *Zebu*. Computer program. Toronto: Centrinity Software Inc. (http://www.centrinity.com/products/zebu)

CoNet. 1998. *Background to PARTIcipate*. (http://fox.co.net/participate/parti.html)

ECT Inc. 1997. *eWeb*. Salem, Oregon: Education Communication Technologies, Inc. (http://www.ewebsite.com/default.html)

Goldberg, M. 1997. "Communication and Collaboration Tools in WebCT." Proceedings of the Conference Enabling Network-Based Learning, Espoo, Finland, May 28–30. (http://homebrew.cs.ubc.ca/Webct/docs)

Harasim, L., and T. Calvert. 1997. *Virtual-U*. Vancouver: Simon Fraser University. (http://virtual-u.cs.sfu.ca/vuweb/VUenglish/index.html)

Heylighen, F. 1999. *Stochastic. In Principia Cybernetica Web: A Web Dictionary of Cybernetics and Systems*. (http://pespmc1.vub.ac.be/ASC/Stochastic.html)

Hughes, C. 1995. *WebTeach*. Professional Development Centre, University of New South Wales, Sydney, Australia. (http://www.pdc.unsw.edu.au/webteachdemo/welcome.html)

Jones, D. 1997. *WebFuse*. Faculty of Informatics and Communications, Central Queensland University, Rockhampton, Queensland, Australia. (http://webfuse.cqu.edu.au/Information/What/#do)

Landon, Bruce. 1999. The Comparative Analysis Web Tool. British Columbia: Douglas College. (http://www.onlin.nf.ca/landonline/index.html)

Lotus Corporation. 1998. *Lotus LearningSpace*. The Lotus Corporation. (http://www.lotus.com/home.nsf/tabs/learnspace)

MadDuck Technologies. 1996. *Web Course in a Box*. Richmond, Virginia. (http://www.madduck.com/)

Mann, B. 1998a. "Instructional Design for Online Learning: A Case Study of WebCT Developers." *Universities in a Digital Era: Transformation, Innovationn and Tradition*. Proceedings of the Seventh Annual EDEN Conference, University of Bologna, Italy, June 26.

Softwords Research International. 1995. "What is CoSy?" (http://www.swifty.com/SRI/cosy400/cover.html)

WBT Systems. 1997. *TopClass*. WBT systems. (http://www.wbtsystems.com/index.html)

CONTRIBUTORS

Angela Benson (University of Georgia, U.S.A.)

Angela Benson is a doctoral candidate in Instructional Technology at the University of Georgia and the author of a book of fiction called *Telling the Tale*, through Berkeley Publishing. The book was developed from an online writing course called Romance in Color, which Angela has taught for the past few years. A recent article published in *Open Learning Systems News* recounts her experiences with the different delivery modes of the course. Angela also writes articles on Web-based learning, including "Evaluating Web-Based Training: Seven Lessons from the Field" for *Technical Training* and "Pedagogy and Policy in the Age of the Wired Professor: A Case Study of Teaching Spanish-Language Online" for *T.H.E. Journal*. Angela currently serves as Chair of the Graduate Student Committee of the American Educational Research Association (AERA). Her research interests are in the areas of distance learning, technology integration, and instructional design.

Gary Boyd (Concordia University, Canada)

Gary Boyd is Professor of Educational Technology at Concordia University. A geophysicist by training, Gary was a Scientific Officer in charge of ALERT in the Northwest Territories in the 1950s, a Lecturer in Physics at Royal Roads Military College, and a post-doctoral fellow on the Incoherent Backscatter Radar Project at the University of Western Ontario in the 1960s. Since joining Concordia in 1968, he has been co-founder of several core elements of the graduate programs in Educational Technology, and is currently the Director of the doctoral program in Educational Technology at Concordia University in Montréal, Canada. Dr. Boyd specializes in Educational Cybernetics, maintaining memberships in many prominent associations, including AMTEC, CIPTE, CADE, the American Society for Cybernetics, the International Society for Systems Sciences, IEEE (life member), Computer Society ACM, AERA, and ALT-UK.

Robert Bracewell (McGill University, Canada)

Robert Bracewell is an Associate Professor in the Department of Educational and Counselling Psychology, McGill University. Robert received his PhD from the University of Toronto. His research interests focus on the mastery of ill-structured tasks, and include such topics as the incorporation of information and communication technologies into instruction.

Nada Dabbagh (George Mason University, U.S.A.)

Nada Dabbagh is Assistant Professor of Instructional Technology at George Mason University, with interests in the design and evaluation of Web-based instruction, problem generation and representation in problem-based learning, and the contextualization of instruction through constructivist learning environments. Nada was recently awarded a technology fellowship from the Center of Instructional Advancement and Technology at Towson University, where she designed and developed a problem-based learning environment that exposed the students to the contextual and problem-solving nature of instructional design. This research effort is ongoing, with the goal of building a Web-supported database of problem-based case scenarios to support the teaching and learning of instructional design through authentic contexts. Currently, she is working on evaluating the pedagogical effect of traditional courses that have been redesigned for online delivery using Web-based course authoring tools. Nada recently published an article and a book chapter that articulate her findings on this issue.

André Durette (Laurentian University, Canada)

André Durette is the Counsel, Intellectual Property for the School of Graduate Studies and Research at Laurentian University in Sudbury, Canada. Initially trained in Molecular Biology and Genetics, André was called to the bar in Ontario. He then engaged in a litigation practice in his hometown of Sudbury, in Northern Ontario. Loving legal analysis, but finding himself disenchanted with the confrontational lifestyle of a litigator, André sought a career in nontraditional practice. After a short stint teaching in a wired community college, he found a home advising and supporting the corporate affairs of the Mining Innovation, Rehabilitation, and Applied Research Corporation (MIRARCO), a recently incorporated initiative affiliated with Laurentian University of Sudbury, bringing academic research and industry closer together. While still continuing to support MIRARCO, André now spends most of his time advising and supporting Laurentian University in intellectual property and technology transfer matters as Counsel, Intellectual Property.

Allan Ellis (Southern Cross University, Australia)

Associate Professor Allan Ellis is the Director of Research and Postgraduate Programs in the School of Social and Workplace Development at Southern Cross University, Australia. Allan is Co-chair of the AusWeb Conference series, which commenced in 1995, and is currently Chair of the Geneva-based International World Wide Web Conference Committee. Since June 1998 he has been the Academic Coordinator of the School's SaWD Online project, which involves the development of a full, twenty-four course, Web-based undergraduate degree program.

Tony Fetherston (Edith Cowan University, Australia)

Tony Fetherston is a Senior Lecturer in the School of Education at Edith Cowan University, Perth, Western Australia. His current interests include the use of new technologies in primary and secondary schools to enhance teaching and learning and the evaluation of the use of these technologies. His other interests include pedagogy, science education, and education research methods.

Adam Finkelstein (McGill University, Canada)

Adam Finkelstein is currently a Lecturer and doctoral candidate in the Department of Educational and Counselling Psychology, and Royal Bank graduate student fellow at the Centre for University Teaching and Learning, McGill University. His major concentration is in computer applications in education and instructional psychology. His area of research includes the psychological implications of virtual reality, the implementation of technology in education, and instructional design issues for online learning.

Terry Gandell (McGill University, Canada)

Terry Gandell is an Assistant Professor at the Centre for University Teaching and Learning (CUTL) and Associate Member in the Department of Educational and Counselling Psychology, McGill University, where she received her PhD. Terry's current interests are in the evaluation of teaching and learning and the use of technology in higher education. This is an extension of her past research work investigating telecommunications to deliver literacy instruction to adults with severe disabilities. Her work and research at the CUTL currently concentrates on the effective use of technology in teaching and learning, with a particular focus on the interactive features of the Web and their uses to enhance learning.

Susan Gibson (University of Alberta, Canada)

Susan Gibson is an Associate Professor in the Department of Elementary Education at the University of Alberta. Her specialization area is Social Studies curriculum and instruction. Susan's research focuses on the integration of technology in Social Studies and the role of technology in Teacher Education. In a related article with Nina Nocente, Dr. Gibson wrote on teachers' perspectives and students' attitudes toward computers in social studies education in *Computers in the Schools*. Together with Dianne Oberg, Dr. Gibson has begun a three-year SSHRC-funded (Social Sciences and Humanities Research Council of Canada) study of Internet use in schools. For further reading on this topic, see their article entitled "What's Happening with Internet Use in Alberta Schools?" in the *Alberta Journal of Educational Research* and two studies of teacher learning about Internet use, published in the *International Journal of Educational Leadership in Learning*.

Marc Glassman (Memorial University of Newfoundland, Canada)

Marc Glassman is Associate Professor of Education at Memorial University, and the Principal Investigator representing Memorial in the Canadian SchoolNet Grassroots Project. This project concerns the theoretical contexts and in-school factors that contribute to the successful and sustained use of innovative ICT-based pedagogical practices. Marc is also developing a province-wide professional development Web site on literacy for teachers throughout the province of Newfoundland and Labrador. Dr. Glassman's work includes the development and implementation of undergraduate and graduate Web courses, and the creation of online textbooks and multimedia formats to enhance the learning experience of his students. A sixth Web course is under development, with the possibility of it being offered "on demand." In this way, students can register and take an undergraduate course at times that are convenient for them, rather than at times bound by the traditional semester format.

Pamela Havice (Clemson University, U.S.A.)

Pamela Havice is a Visiting Assistant Professor of Counseling and Educational Leadership at Clemson University, Clemson, South Carolina. Pamela coordinated and directed distance learning continuing education opportunities for health professionals prior to her arrival at Clemson University. She is currently teaching students in the Masters of Counseling in Student Affairs program and is an integral part of developing distance learning courses for the Counseling program. Dr. Havice's research and publication record focuses on distance education and presentation skills. She is a member of the American Association of Adult and Continuing Education.

William Havice (Clemson University, U.S.A.)

William Havice is a Professor of Technology and Human Resource Development at Clemson University, Clemson, South Carolina. Bill teaches and advises students in the Masters of Human Resource Development program, teaching courses in instructional materials development. He is currently on the Board of Directors for the International Technology Education Association and has earned the honour of Distinguished Technology Educator (DTE). Dr. Havice's primary areas of research include Web-based distance learning applications, multimedia, and hypermedia. He is currently involved with the development of an online graduate program in human resource development at Clemson University. He is a member of the American Association of Adult and Continuing Education.

Rod Heimpel (University of Toronto, Canada)

Rod Heimpel is Assistant Professor of French, University of Toronto. His principal research interests are French nineteenth- and twentieth-century literature, literary and cultural theory, computer-assisted instruction, and the relation between pedagogy and technology. Rod's doctoral dissertation (University of Toronto, 1996) will be published by the Presses Universitaires du Nouveau Monde in 2000 under the title *Généalogie du manifeste littéraire*. Since joining the faculty of the Department of French in 1996, Dr. Heimpel has been involved with several initiatives. As Webmaster, he manages the Web site of the Department of French (http://www.chass.utoronto.ca/french) and has designed many important Web sites, including Web courses. Dr. Heimpel has also developed curriculum on New Media and Technology, and has recently published articles on Web-based language learning centres and the pedagogy of technology (TEXT Technology, 1998) and the ideological underpinnings of electronic publication (TEXT Technology, 1999). These articles have been co-published online by Computing in the Humanties Working Papers (1998/1999) at http://www.chass.utoronto.ca/epc/chwp .

Clint Isbell (Clemson University, U.S.A.)

Clint Isbell is a Professor of Technology and Human Resource Development at Clemson University, Clemson, South Carolina. Clint teaches and advises students in the Masters of Human Resource Development (HRD) program, teaching courses in needs assessment, instructional system design, and evaluation of Training/HRD Programs. He is Past President of the Carolinas Society for Training and Development. Dr. Isbell's primary areas of research include Web-based distance learning applications and evaluation of training/HRD programs. He is currently involved with the development of an online graduate program in human resource development at Clemson University.

Diane Janes (University of British Columbia, Canada)

Diane Janes is a Project Manager and Instructional Developer in Distance Education and Technology at the University of British Columbia. In addition to her courseware development in the areas of the Health Sciences, Education, Intercultural Studies, and the Plant Sciences, Diane is a member of the core design team and an instructor for the Certificate in Technology-Based Distributed Learning, a series of five Web-based graduate-level distance education courses launched internationally in the fall of 1997. She has been teaching and facilitating online distance education courses since 1992. She holds an M.Ed. in Educational Technology and is presently pursuing a PhD at UBC. Her current research area is faculty development for online teaching.

James Kerr (Brock University, Canada)

James Kerr is an Associate Professor in the Faculty of Education, Brock University, St. Catharines, Ontario, where he has held various positions since 1987. James teaches in the Math/Science/Technology area of pre-service education. His research and teaching interests are in technological competencies for teacher education and the effective use of instructional technologies in the classroom. Jim has been a member of the Educational Computing Organization of Ontario since its inception. He has offered online course components to over 400 students. Because of his primary responsibility for academic computing innovation, Jim has collected a wide variety of e-toys, including a global positioning system, digital camera, electronic memo pad, data link watch, and a host of computers, from Vic 20s to the most recent model. All of this equipment helps to keep him on the verge of bankruptcy and drives his wife crazy. In the past three years Jim has collaborated with Coral Mitchell on several projects related to instructional technologies. They have tracked the implementation of Web-based instruction in three different university courses and have presented the results at regional, national, and international conferences. Their most comprehensive work to date (other than the one in this text) is a paper, co-authored with Tony DiPetta, entitled "The Frontier of Web-Based Instruction, or How Several Faculties of Education and Individual Faculty Members Came to Understand and Love (or Hate) Web-Based Course Delivery in Late 20th Century Ontario: A Drama in Three Acts." Coral and Jim both serve on the Brock University Task Force for Instructional Technologies, where they steadfastly insist that teaching and learning, rather than technology, remain the central concern in the debate.

Joe Luca (Edith Cowan University, Australia)

Joe Luca is Lecturer in the Department of Multimedia at Edith Cowan University, Australia, and specializes in project management methodology for multimedia development and online delivery of educational materials. Before joining the university, Joe was Multimedia Project Manager in a commercial environment. He was the Managing Director of New Media Management Pty. Ltd., which specializes in project management of the development of multimedia product and online educational material. Dr. Luca's publications include *Project Management for New Media*, a book used by final-year university students and the multimedia industry, and a book chapter on "A Project

Management Model for New Media Development" used by first-year university students. Joe Luca can be reached at j.luca@cowan.edu.au.

Bruce Mann (Memorial University of Newfoundland, Canada)

Bruce Mann is Associate Professor of Education at Memorial University and the editor of this book. Bruce's work on Web course management includes recent articles in *Australian Educational Computing* (1999) and in *The Bulletin* of the *Canadian Society for the Study of Higher Education* (1999), and an experiment with Ed Brown concerning the effects of pre-computer Web site framing on student recall and knowledge restructuring for the *International Journal of Telecommunications in Education*. Dr. Mann is currently completing an experiment on divided attention in multimedia learning with Paul Newhouse, Jeremy Pagram, and Alistair Campbell at Edith Cowan University in Australia, and writing a book on the critical competitors in educational computing for Althouse Press.

Dave Mason (Ryerson Polytechnic University, Canada)

Dave Mason is currently a Professor at Ryerson Polytechnic University in Toronto, Canada. He is a PhD candidate in Computer Science at the University of Waterloo, and obtained his M.Sc. from the University of Toronto. Dave's research interests are in computer science education, programming languages, and gender issues in computer science. He is a co-founder of the WICS (Women in Computer Science) project, which is addressing issues about girls' and women's opportunities in computer science. He has published many papers, which can be viewed on the Web at http://www.sarg.ryerson.ca.

Lynn McAlpine (McGill University, Canada)

Lynn McAlpine is an Associate Professor at McGill University. She is appointed to the Department of Educational and Counselling Psychology, and is the Director of the Centre for University Teaching and Learning (CUTL). Lynne has had a long-term interest in the instructional uses of technology, beginning with a master's degree in the field twenty-five years ago. She has used WebCT as an instructor, and sits on several university committees concerned with the educational uses of new technologies. She is also a researcher involved in the Tele-learning Centres of Excellence grant. A recent joint publication explored how generic instructional design guidelines can be modified for online learning.

Rory McGreal (TeleEducation New Brunswick, Canada)

Rory McGreal is the Executive Director of TeleEducation New Brunswick, a province-wide distributed distance learning network. As the principal leader of the TeleCampus initiative, he is responsible for creating an online virtual campus with courses available on the World Wide Web. With the support of Industry Canada and other sponsors, his team has created a comprehensive online database of more than 20 000 courses. Rory has worked in Canada as a teacher and teacher representative, and abroad in the Seychelles, the Middle East, and Europe as a teacher, ESL technological training coordinator, instructional designer, language and computer laboratory coordinator, and educational adviser. Rory served on the provincial Task Force on the Information Highway and on the federal Learning and Training Working Group for the Information Highway Advisory Committee. Presently he is on the the Education Steering Committee for CANARIE Inc., the Board of Directors of the Tele-Learning Research Network, Le centre international pour le développement de l'inforoute en français, the International Nursing Institute of Canada, and the Irish Centre for Distance Education Research and Applications. Before joining TeleEducation NB, he was responsible for the expansion of Contact North (a distance education network in Northern Ontario) into the high schools of the region. Dr. McGreal's main interests focus on the implementation and development of distributed learning systems. He has written articles and book chapters on topics such as distributed learning environments, the economic development role of distance education, and Web course design. He is the lead author of "Learning on the Web," an online instruction guide for teachers.

Coral Mitchell (Brock University, Canada)

Coral Mitchell is an Associate Professor in the Faculty of Education, Brock University, St. Catharines, Ontario. Coral has been a faculty member at Brock University since 1995, with experience in pre-service and graduate education. Her teaching and research interests are in the area of educational change. In recent years she has explored the ways in which the infusion of technology is changing the contexts and contents of teaching and learning. Coral has collaborated with Jim Kerr on several projects related to instructional technologies, and they have both served on the Brock University Task Force for Instructional Technologies. Although not a complete Luddite, Coral is definitely technologically challenged.

Dianne Oberg (University of Alberta, Canada)

Dianne Oberg is an Associate Professor in the School of Library and Information Studies and the Department of Elementary Education at the University of Alberta. Dianne's major teaching area is Teacher-Librarianship. Dr. Oberg's research focuses on issues related to school library program implementation. See her related article with J. Henri, "Changing Concerns in Distance Education for Teacher-Librarianship" in *Education for Information*.

Renata Phelps (Southern Cross University, Australia)

Renata Phelps is a Lecturer in the School of Education at Southern Cross University in Australia. Renata has a BA in Library and Information Science and a masters degree in Distance Education. Renata has worked as senior Research Assistant with the School of Social and Workplace Development and later as Project Manager for the SaWD Online project during its first six-month phase. During this time, Renata was involved in promoting a collaborative action learning approach to staff development. More recently, she has been focusing on Web-based instructional design and in experimenting with innovative and flexible approaches to teaching through lecturing in several Web-based courses. Renata is currently conducting PhD research, investigating the influence of individual learning styles on the technological capability of pre-service teacher education students.

Lynne Schrum (University of Georgia, U.S.A.)

Lynne Schrum is Associate Professor in Instructional Technology at the University of Georgia. Her research interests are in the areas of online and distance learning, technology integration, and ethical uses of information technology. Lynne is the immediate Past President of the International Society for Technology in Education (ISTE) and has been an international researcher and keynote speaker for the last several years. The chapter co-authored with Angela Benson for this book was drawn from a case study of an MBA program published in the *Journal of Asynchronous Learning Environments*. Dr. Schrum's other recent works include an article with Zane Berge in the *Canadian Journal of Educational Communication*, on creating student interaction within the educational experience, and a chapter about online education as an emerging pedagogy in B. Cahoon's book about adult learning and the Internet, published by Jossey-Bass.

Richard Seltzer (Internet Consultant, U.S.A.)

Richard Seltzer graduated from Yale in English in 1969, and has a masters in comparative literature in Russian, French, and German from the University of Massachusetts. After nineteen years with Digital Equipment (now Compaq), Richard now works as an independent Internet speaker, writer, and consultant. Based on his experience both at Digital and with the BandR Samizdat Express, he is frequently called upon to speak and write about the Internet and where it is headed. His books include *Shop Online the Lazy Way* (1999) and *The AltaVista Search Revolution* (1994). In 1994, he received the first Internet Marketing Award at Internet World for his video *A Glimpse of the Future*. His article "Reinventing Publishing in a Global Electronic Mall" was published in the handbook *The Electronic Publishing Business and Its Market* (1998), and he hosts "Business on the World Wide Web,"one of the longest-running chat programs on the Web. Some of his other publications include *The Name of Hero* (1981); a collection of children's stories, *Now and Then and Other Tales from Ome* (1976); and *The Lizard of Oz* (1974), which will soon be released by EBooks Multimedia as an interactive CD-ROM for children.

Cynthia Weston (McGill University, Canada)

Cynthia Weston is an Associate Professor at the Centre for University Teaching and Learning and Department of Educational and Counselling Psychology, McGill University. Her work focuses on teaching and learning in higher education. Cynthia's previous research investigated the influence of different strategies of formative evaluation on improving the effectiveness of instructional materials. Her current research, funded by the Social Sciences and Humanities Research Council of Canada, focuses on reflection as a formative process in teaching development. The research team is building a model of reflection and investigating the function of reflection in improving teaching.

Laura Winer (McGill University, Canada)

Laura Winer is Assistant Professor of Educational Psychology at McGill University. Laura has worked extensively on the application of new technologies to education, including a project of the Tele-Learning National Centres of Excellence on developing instructional design principles for collaborative tele-learning. She was the Director of the Vitrine 2001 project of APO Québec, the Québec Centre for Research on Educational Computing from 1986 to 1991. Dr. Winer is currently Assistant Professor in the Centre for University Teaching and Learning of McGill University. Recent publications include a chapter on "Canadian Tele-Learning Experiences: Applications, Issues, and Questions," in *Information, Innovation and Impacts* by J. de la Mothe and G. Paquet, eds.; a chapter with N.J. Rushby and J.A. Vázquez-Abad, "Emerging Trends in Instructional Interventions," in *Handbook of Human Performance Technology* by H.D. Stolovitch and E. Keeps, eds.; and a chapter with J. Bourdeau and J.A. Vázquez-Abad on "Information and Communication Technologies for Generating and Disseminating Know-How" in *REDES* (Revista de estudios sociales de la ciencia), special issue.

Denise Woit (Ryerson Polytechnic University, Canada)

Denise Woit is currently an Associate Professor at Ryerson Polytechnic University in Toronto, Canada. Denise achieved her PhD in Computer Science from Queen's University and her masters degree from the University of Waterloo. Her research interests are in computer science education, software reliability and testing, and gender issues in computer science. Dr. Woit is a co-founder of the WICS (Women in Computer Science) project, which is addressing issues about girls' and women's opportunities in computer science. She has attained a number of research grants, which support her work in education and reliability. Copies of her papers are available on the Web at http://www.sarg.ryerson.ca.

Part A

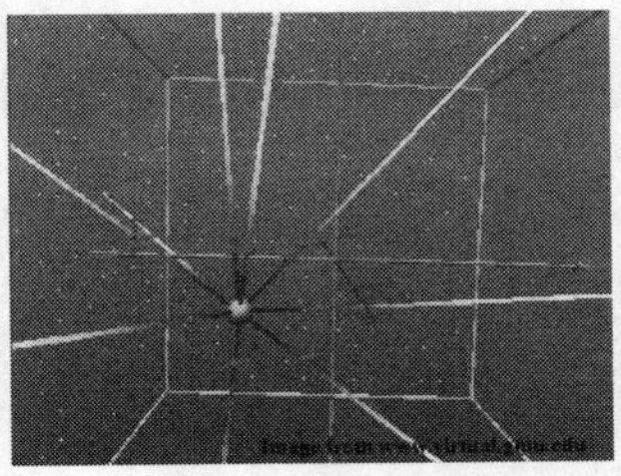

Theories and Models of Web Course Management

CHAPTER 1

Phase Theory: A Teleological Taxonomy of Web Course Management

Bruce Mann
Memorial University of Newfoundland
Canada

Phase theory is introduced as a teleological taxonomy of Web course management systems such as WebCT (Goldberg, 1997), TopClass (ECT Inc, 1997), Virtual-U (Harasim and Calvert, 1997), LearningSpace (Lotus Corporation, 1998). Phase theory is based wholly on the educator's intuition, personal preferences, and prior educational experiences with Web course tools. Central to phase theory is the view that educators learn to manage their Web courses in phases.

Phase Theory Assumptions

A theory is properly grounded when its assumptions provide its context, rationale, and legitimacy in empirical research and expert opinion. Like other recent theories of technology-based teaching (Gunawardena, Lowe, and Anderson, 1997; Kearsley and Schneiderman, 1998; Mayer, 1997), the assumptions and principles of phase theory are presented in a conceptual framework. In this light, three assumptions for a phase theory of Web course management are presented:

Assumption I. The need, timeliness
Assumption II. Web course management systems
Assumption III. Instructional design

Assumption I: The Need, Timeliness

One of the most important assumptions for considering a new theory is its timeliness. Is this the right time for this particular theory? Is the field overloaded with new theories, or is there a reported need for alternative ways of conceptualizing things—a new theory? At the present time, there appears to be a need for a new theory of Web course management; a descriptive framework of expert opinion and research-based principles. "There is a need for more new instructional theories…to offer guidance on how distance learning technologies can be used effectively," (Reigeluth and Squire, 1998, p. 46) to reflect the current increased emphasis on alternative perspectives in the field (Richey, 1997).

Assumption II: Web Course Management Systems

Prevalence of Tools

Colleges, universities, and training organizations around the world that aspire to offer students a Web-supported, on-site, and by-distance education will continue to use a Web course management system (see, for example, ECT Inc, 1997; Goldberg, 1997; Harasim and Calvert, 1997; Lotus Corporation, 1998; WBT Systems, 1997). Stand-alone Web pages, organizational e-mail, chat, and listservs will continue to play a supporting role.

Suspect Claims

Recent claims have been made that Web course management systems should be considered suspect, including the following:

- The claim that the tools and help offered in current Web course management systems can enable designers or instructors with little or no technical preparation to customize, design, deliver, and enhance education or training delivered over the World Wide Web;
- The claim that the capability of combining online collaborative interaction matches the benefits of face-to-face classroom discussion.

Assumption III: Instructional Design

Limited Use

Despite their longevity, familiar ID models and theories (for example, Dick and Carey, 1996; Gagne, 1985) are too static (Boshier, Mohapi, Moulton, Qayyum, Sadownik, and Wilson, 1997), inert (Yang, Moore, and Burton, 1995), and unusable (Wild and Quinn, 1998) for prescribing the conditions of interactive learning for all learners in all settings.

ID models and theories are often based on psychological and educational theories that some believe are simply too broad in scope and too rigid for delivering instruction on hypermedia systems like the Web (Tergan, 1998). Also, "instructional design (ID) procedures often don't work" (Winn, 1997, p. 36). For these reasons, ID models and theories are rarely used with contemporary authoring, multimedia, and hypermedia systems, and when they are used, they are regularly misapplied (Gros, Elen, Kerres, Merrienboer, and Spector, 1997).

Prevalence of ID

Educational institutions will continue to offer training in instructional design. Departments and institutions of distance education will continue to employ people trained in current models and theories of instructional design to deliver instruction in a variety of formats, including the World Wide Web.

Phase Theory Principles

Theories are meant to explain something or to help us understand the way things are within a certain domain (Wilson, 1997). Phase theory is intended to help distance educators understand the way things work for Web course management. Following are the seven principles of phase theory:

1. Descriptive theory
2. Teleological taxonomy
3. A three-concept cluster
4. Phasing
5. Origin
6. Principles rather than templates
7. Principles rather than assistance

Principle 1: Descriptive Theory

Phase theory is a descriptive theory of professional development of Web course management, not a decision theory of instructional development per se.

> Descriptive theories are useful for understanding why a design theory does or does not work, and in areas where no design theories exist, it can help a practitioner to invent new methods or select known instructional methods that might work. (Reigeluth, 1997, p. 43)

Descriptive theories are different from decision or prescriptive theories (Simon, in Reigeluth, 1997; Smith and Ragan, 1999). Whereas prescriptive or decision theories attempt to offer a means to accomplish given ends (for example, Bonk and Cummings, 1998; Maddux and Johnson, 1997; Mikovsky, 1998; Riley, 1998; Wilkinson, Bennett, and Oliver, 1997), descriptive theories attempt to describe how things function. Similarly, phase theory is different from decision theories of instructional design such as Gagné's (1985) events of instruction.

Unlike theories that invariably revert to systematic procedures of instructional design, phase theory descriptions assist practitioners to determine their own inventions or selection of known instructional methods to use with Web course management systems. Bannan-Ritland and associates (1998), for example, recommended an interesting framework for Web-based instruction that reverted to principles of instructional design.

> However, these categories and components do not in and of themselves guarantee good instruction since it is obviously the instructional design methods which ultimately determine the site's effectiveness in producing effective learning. (Bannan-Ritland et al., 1998, p. 80)

Despite current perceptions that decision theories of instructional design often do not work (for reasons stated earlier in the assumptions section), some authors are still reluctant to relinquish methods of systematic instruction for interactive multimedia environments like the Web. Phase theory purports to provide educators with a descriptive theory of professional development of Web course managers.

Principle 2: Teleological Taxonomy

In theory construction, taxonomic classification is a way of organizing concepts that allows for grouping by pre-identified categories. The classifications in phase theory are both taxonomic and teleological, based on a critical realist approach to Web course management (described later). Taxonomic classifications require division into groups based on shared characteristics.

> A taxonomy consists of systems of categories constructed to fit empirical observations so that relationships among categories can be described. (Seels, 1997, p. 15)

The phases in this taxonomy, to a greater or lesser extent, utilize the features provided in a Web course management system for the purpose of managing teaching and learning.

The taxonomy is also teleological insofar as the phenomena in each phase are discussed in pragmatic terms, according to its intended purposes instead of observed behaviours (empiricist) or postulated causes (rationalist). The phasing teleology includes initial insight; the inherent awkwardness of competitive elaboration; the apparent re-socialization effect during phasing in and out; and, of course, the different ontological characteristics of management in each phase.

The teleology of the "lesson enhancement" phase, for example, is the enhancement of print-based or lecture-based lessons to provide a collaborative environment, a means of self-expression, or a means of assessing students. The teleology of the "resource-based teaching and learning" phase is the storing and retrieving of materials that provide content, support a learning activity, support a learning process, or build on other resources. The teleology of the "learning environment" phase is the creation of a virtual reality interface that maintains the Web-dependent inquiry environments for learners' knowledge construction.

Recent observations of college participants (Mann, 1998a, and reported earlier in this paper) greatly informed the revisions to the three-category system (that is, lesson enhancement, online resource-based learning, and online learning environment). To some extent, the questions of taxonomic classification are questions of schema. It can be expected that the schemata will limit the taxonomic structure we eventually accept. In this way, taxonomies stimulate further research, which will test the categories used, summarize knowledge, and allow predictions and comparisons that one would not think of without them (Seels, 1997).

Principle 3: A Three-Concept Cluster

A theory is a cluster of concepts organized together to form a whole.

> Not all concepts in a cluster are precisely defined; in fact usually key concepts—the ones most central to the theory—are not operationally defined, but instead maintain a flexibility and fluidity so they can be used in a variety of ways in addressing different problems. (Wilson, 1997, p. 22)

Phase theory clusters three concepts together as professional development for educators:

Phase 1: Lesson enhancement
Phase 2: Online resource-based teaching and learning
Phase 3: Online learning environments

Resource-based learning and learning environments already have well-established precedents in education. Relative to the others, lesson enhancement is a new concept. The three phases are explained below:

Phase 1: Lesson Enhancement

Lesson enhancement is the initial phase of Web course management. Decisions about lesson enhancement tend to be intuitive rather than empirical or theoretical; initial ideas stochastic and idiosyncratic. Usually with help from the resident technologist, the Web course designer will decide to introduce the Internet or Web-supported material as extracurricular activities to enhance the curriculum. Three types of lesson enhancement are categorized for this phase, as follows: immersive collaborative environment, online self-expression, and online lesson assessment.

Immersive Collaborative Environment (ICE)

An immersive collaborative environment is one way an educator or distance developer can initiate lesson enhancement with students. An ICE can be any combination of threaded, electronic bulletin boards, newsgroups, and chat rooms supported by the Web course management system. The goal of an ICE is to "significantly enhance the instructional capability of a Web course from a mere text and resource delivery to a dynamic, evolving interaction concerning instructional content" (Bannan-Ritland, Harvey, and Milhelm, 1998). Most of the Web course management packages can provide these capabilities. Figure 1.1 shows a typical WebCT bulletin board collaboration.

There are several principles associated with maintaining an ICE:

Prep time The preparation time required for an ICE is about twice the amount required for a conventional course, and the maintenance is at least double the time. The rewards are (1) twice the engagement by about a third of the students; (2) about twice the number of students engaged; (3) twice the student time on task; and (4) about twice the quality of student work from about a third of the students.

Dribble files Web course management systems will maintain a log or dribble file of students' messages read and new postings.

Effort Students will work only as hard in an ICE as they perceive their instructor to be working. If students are given to believe that the commitment is less than originally stated, students will assume the standard has dropped, and they will drop the quantity and quality of their postings accordingly.

Communication Although an ICE is a "media mix" (Mann, 1997) of both writing and speaking, the mental activity more closely resembles that of associating ideas during a telephone conversation than revising paragraphs in an essay. Therefore,

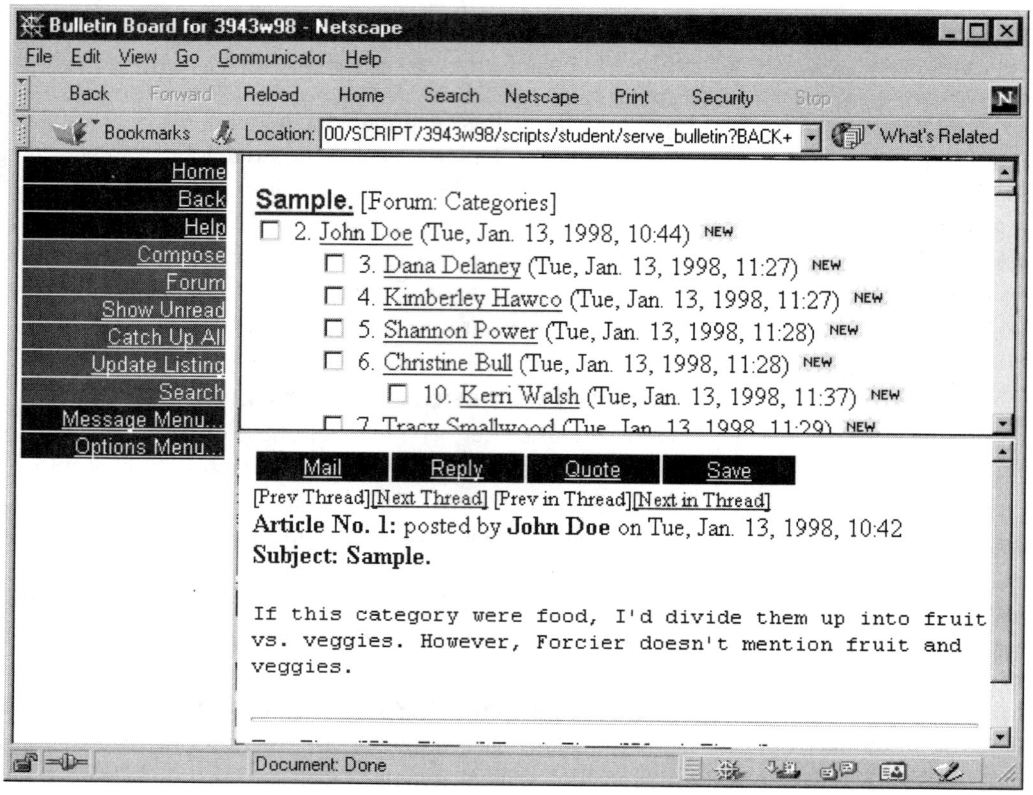

Figure 1.1 Online collaboration using a bulletin board system

Mann, Education 3943, 1997 (see Credits)

students who prefer to express themselves verbally—by argument or debate—are favoured in an ICE over the literate souls with a passion for creative writing.

Skills transfer There are many similarities between the bulletin boards, newsgroups, and chat rooms provided in the Web management systems and those offered by public Web sites. Therefore, students who browse and post messages to bulletin boards, newsgroups, or chat rooms in public Web sites will have an advantage in an ICE over students who do not.

Team-like environment Bulletin boards, newsgroups, and chat rooms are team-like, interactive environments. Students who thrive in an interactive environment (for example, a sports team or debating club) are favoured in an ICE over those who work better individually.

Incremental interaction An ICE requires consistent commitment from the instructor and tutors to ongoing engagement with students online. Immersive collaboration means student immersion, not instructor immersion. A wise Web course manager increases the amount of student interaction incrementally. Requesting too much online too fast will overwhelm and tire both the moderator and the audience, throwing them both out of phase with the content. Staying in-phase means getting a best student opinion, satisfactory summary statement, or group consensus before giving a moderator's view.

Engagement An ICE increases the engagement of some students with the course content. However, there will always be those who lurk but do not post, and those who neither read nor post, for whatever reason.

Democratic process ICE values all students' opinions equally. Provision for anonymous postings in the software can maximize the effects of this attribute.

Typing ability Those who like to type or can type quickly become more visible than those who cannot or do not wish to type.

Personality/writing differences In a face-to-face lesson, extrovert personalities tend to dominate discussions while the shy, quiet types stay hidden in the background. In the case of online ICE, natural-born writers take the stage from natural-born talkers.

Online Self-Expression

Like creative writing, Web site development can be a medium of self-expression and of public scrutiny. One way that a designer can initiate Internet experiences with students is to integrate graphics, text, a sound prompt, and video clips to enhance instruction.

Separate Course Web Sites

Increasing numbers of distance educators, instructors, and students are designing separate course Web sites. Graphics, sound, and other files are added appropriately to complement the text as extracurricular activities to enhance instruction. Web page development requires authoring in HTML (Hyper Text Markup Language). Although Web site editors are not absolutely necessary for creating a home page, they simplify the process of creating HTML documents by automating the coding. They also allow the user to easily preview their work (Tanner and Hood, 1997). The rapid prototyping capability of HTML qualifies it as developmental software for use in educational settings.

Student Presentation Areas

Web course management systems can support student groups and allow the designer to designate group membership by creating student presentation areas. As an alternative, these systems can divide the class into groups, given the desired group size. Each group is provided with a presentation area to publish their projects. The presentation areas are access-controlled: An area can be edited only by group members, but can be viewed by any member of the class. The designer can also edit the content in the presentation area. Groups can also have access to dedicated bulletin-board fora for collaboration.

Online Lesson Assessment

An instructor can choose to enhance a lesson with an assessment feature. Lesson assessment can be maintained for groups or individuals by (1) setting up and maintaining discussion topics in a computer conference or chat room; (2) monitoring student participation throughout the conference in accordance with current issues (Boshier, Mohapi, Moulton, Qayyum, Sadownik, and Wilson, 1997); and (3) assigning grades based on an analysis of the textual output (Gunawardena, Lowe, and Anderson, 1997). Figure 1.2 shows a typical online assessment using a quiz tool.

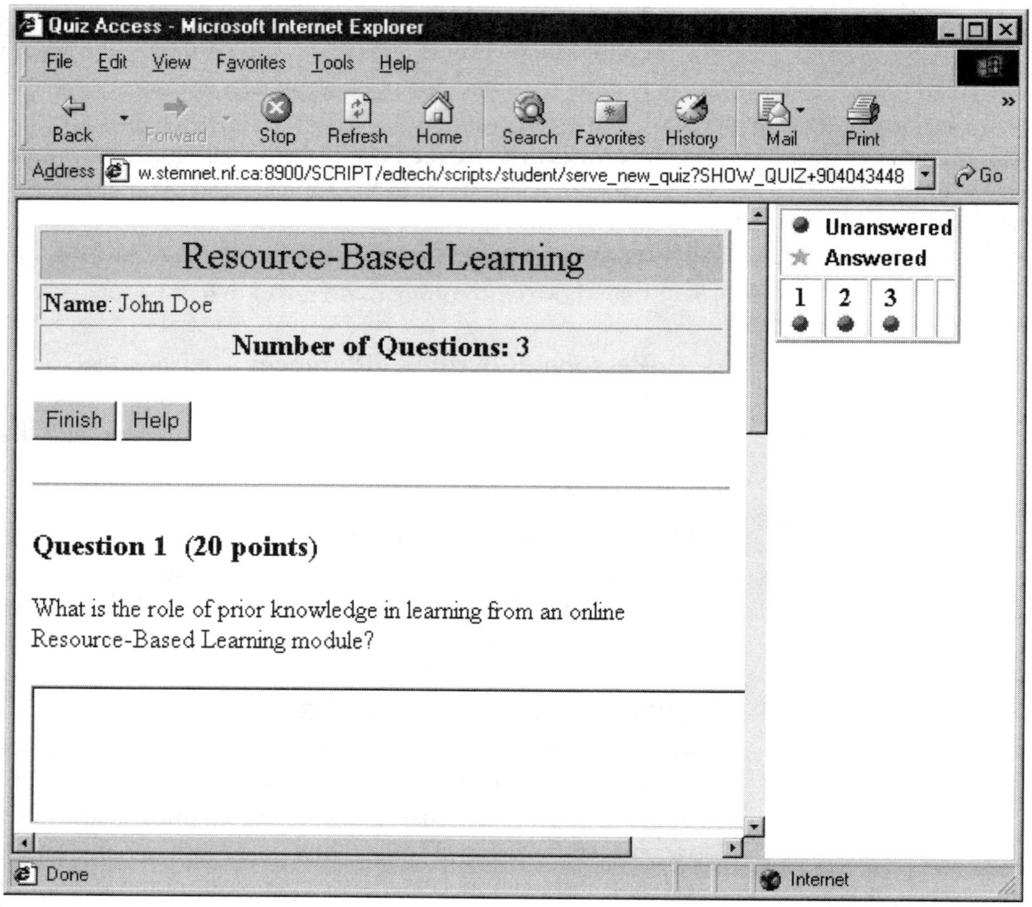

Figure 1.2
Online assessment using a quiz tool

Mann, Education 3943, 1997 (see Credits)

Online Individual Assessment

Lesson assessment of individual students can be achieved with timed, online quizzing and marking. Web course management systems permit several types of questions—multiple choice, matching, short answer, paragraphs, and calculations—and will automatically mark each of these question types, except for the paragraph and short answer. Each student can view his or her own marks as entered by the designer, or as generated by the online quiz auto-marking mechanism. An explanation can accompany each answer indicating why the chosen answer was correct or incorrect and perhaps supplying hints or extra information.

Online Group Assessment

The course manager can enhance a lesson by relying on a conventional Web course management system to quiz or survey the students in a course automatically.

Quizzing student knowledge. The course manager may use up to four different question types to quiz students automatically; namely, multiple choice, matching, short answer, and calculation questions. Only the "paragraph" question type requires subjective assessment by a tutor or course manager.

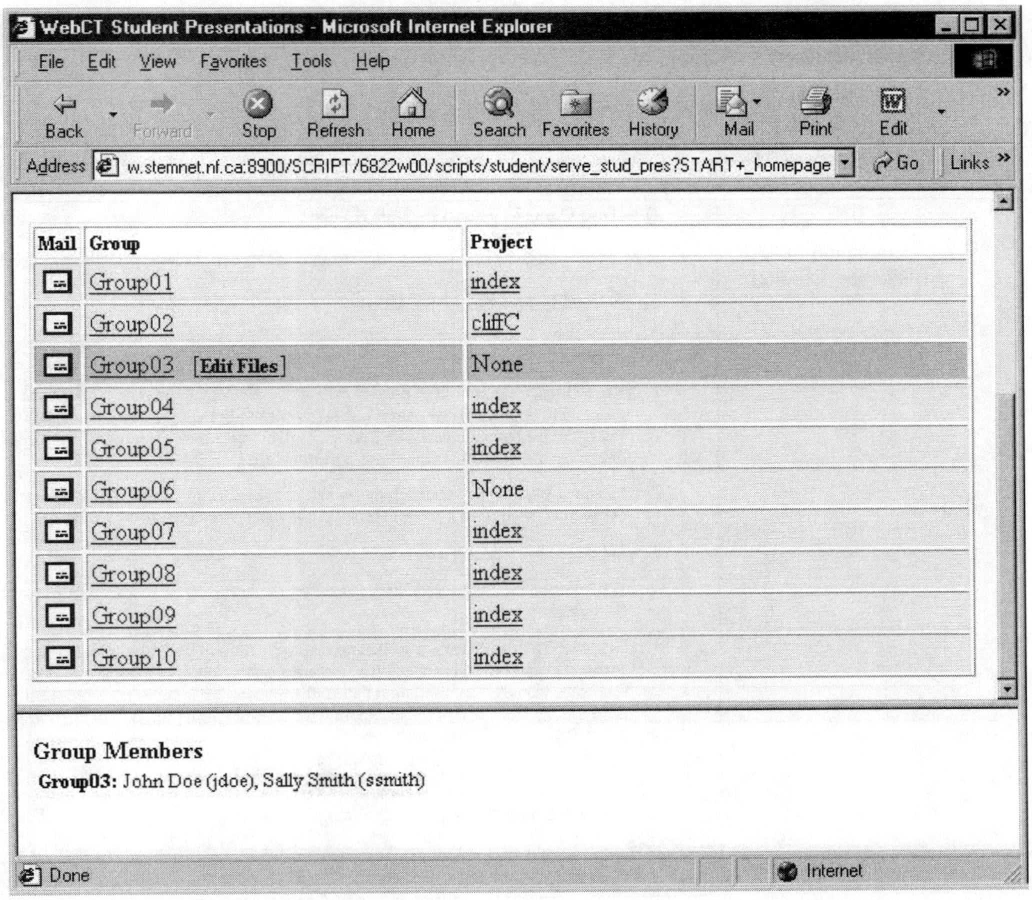

Figure 1.3 Uploaded group assignments

Mann, Education 6822, 1997 (see Credits)

Surveying student opinion. Arguably the best kind of online assessment, however, is the use of a conventional survey tool to enhance grading validity and reliability of student assignments. First, students group up using a grouping capability offered in the software. Next, students work collaboratively on a project or issue using mail and bulletin board tools. Then, they upload their group project into a common file area where other students can view the group's project. Students within the group can edit their own work, and view the work of other groups in the class. Once all the group work has been uploaded, the students vote on each group's presentation using the survey tool.

"Voting" in this sense means "assigns a mark." Individual students view each group's uploaded presentation in WebCT by clicking Index in the Project column, as shown in Figure 1.3. The illustration shows the list of group assignments of seventeen students in a recent graduate course as they were displayed in the WebCT Presentation area. Once individual students view each group's uploaded assignment, they assign a mark and add a justifying comment for each group, using the survey tool. The instructor also assigns a mark and adds a justifying comment for each group. Then, the instructor concatenates the marks and justifying comments of the instructor and individual students, as shown in Figure 1.4.

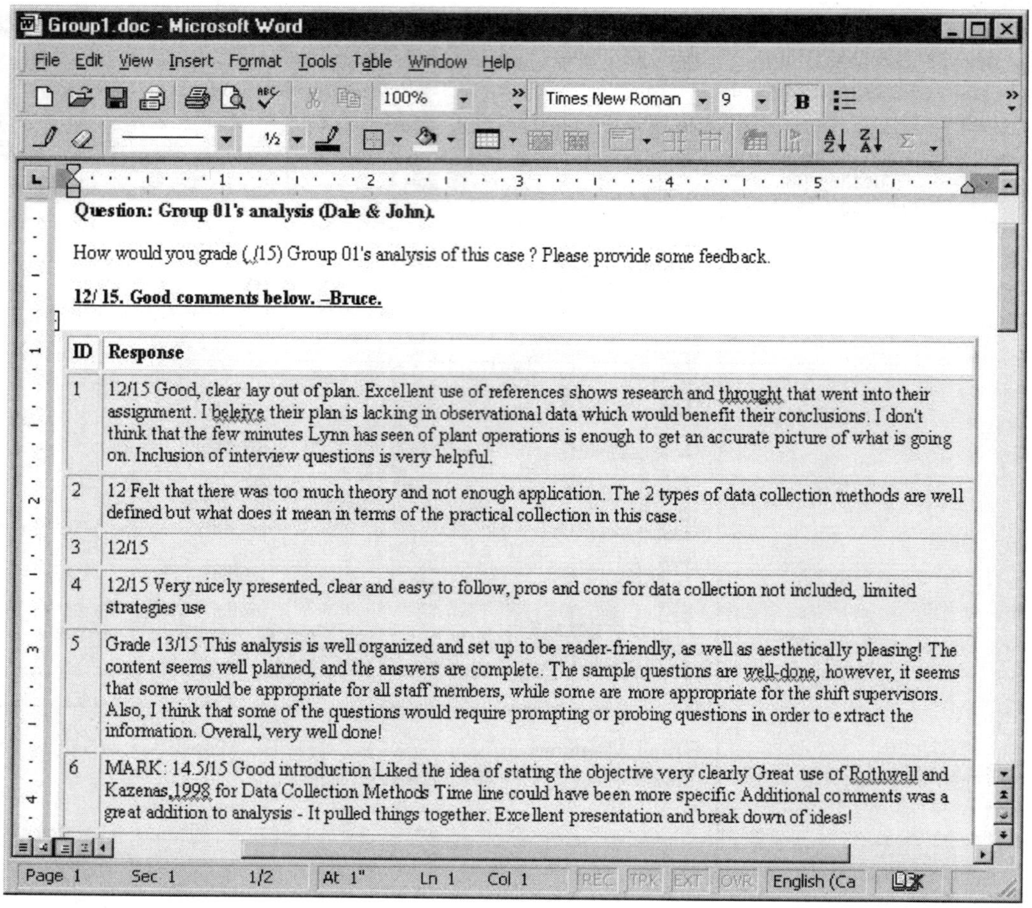

Group1.doc - Microsoft Word

Question: Group 01's analysis (Dale & John).

How would you grade (_/15) Group 01's analysis of this case ? Please provide some feedback.

12/ 15. Good comments below. –Bruce.

ID	Response
1	12/15 Good, clear lay out of plan. Excellent use of references shows research and throught that went into their assignment. I beleive their plan is lacking in observational data which would benefit their conclusions. I don't think that the few minutes Lynn has seen of plant operations is enough to get an accurate picture of what is going on. Inclusion of interview questions is very helpful.
2	12 Felt that there was too much theory and not enough application. The 2 types of data collection methods are well defined but what does it mean in terms of the practical collection in this case.
3	12/15
4	12/15 Very nicely presented, clear and easy to follow, pros and cons for data collection not included, limited strategies use
5	Grade 13/15 This analysis is well organized and set up to be reader-friendly, as well as aesthetically pleasing! The content seems well planned, and the answers are complete. The sample questions are well-done, however, it seems that some would be appropriate for all staff members, while some are more appropriate for the shift supervisors. Also, I think that some of the questions would require prompting or probing questions in order to extract the information. Overall, very well done!
6	MARK: 14.5/15 Good introduction Liked the idea of stating the objective very clearly Great use of Rothwell and Kazenas,1998 for Data Collection Methods Time line could have been more specific Additional comments was a great addition to analysis - It pulled things together. Excellent presentation and break down of ideas!

Figure 1.4 Separate marks and justifying comments for Group 01

Mann, Education 6822, 1997 (see Credits)

The instructor examines the marks and justifying comments, and determines the final mark and justifying comment for each group. The final mark is determined from the mid-point between the instructor's assigned mark and the median mark (average vote), in this case, of all seventeen students' assigned marks for Group 01. Based on previous experience, the instructor's vote will conform in most cases to the median vote cast by students.

Finally, the instructor pastes the entire results page (including the final mark and justifying comment) into a word processor, and attaches it to each student's e-mail in that group. In a few cases, where students cannot read the RTF (rich text format) file, the text is pasted into the e-mail buffer.

In sum, lesson enhancement describes the educator's initiation into Web course management. Planning to use Web course tools judiciously will keep Web course management problems to a minimum. For example, planning two or three weeks rather than twelve weeks of student postings, or one or two instead of five or six problem-based learning activities, can keep the lesson enhancement phase just that: enhancement. The lesson enhancement phase can be adequately defined by phrases, such as sharing opinions, interacting with students, socializing, socialization, and perhaps even social learning.

Figure 1.5
Student hits using a profiling tool

Mann, Education 3943, 1997 (see Credits)

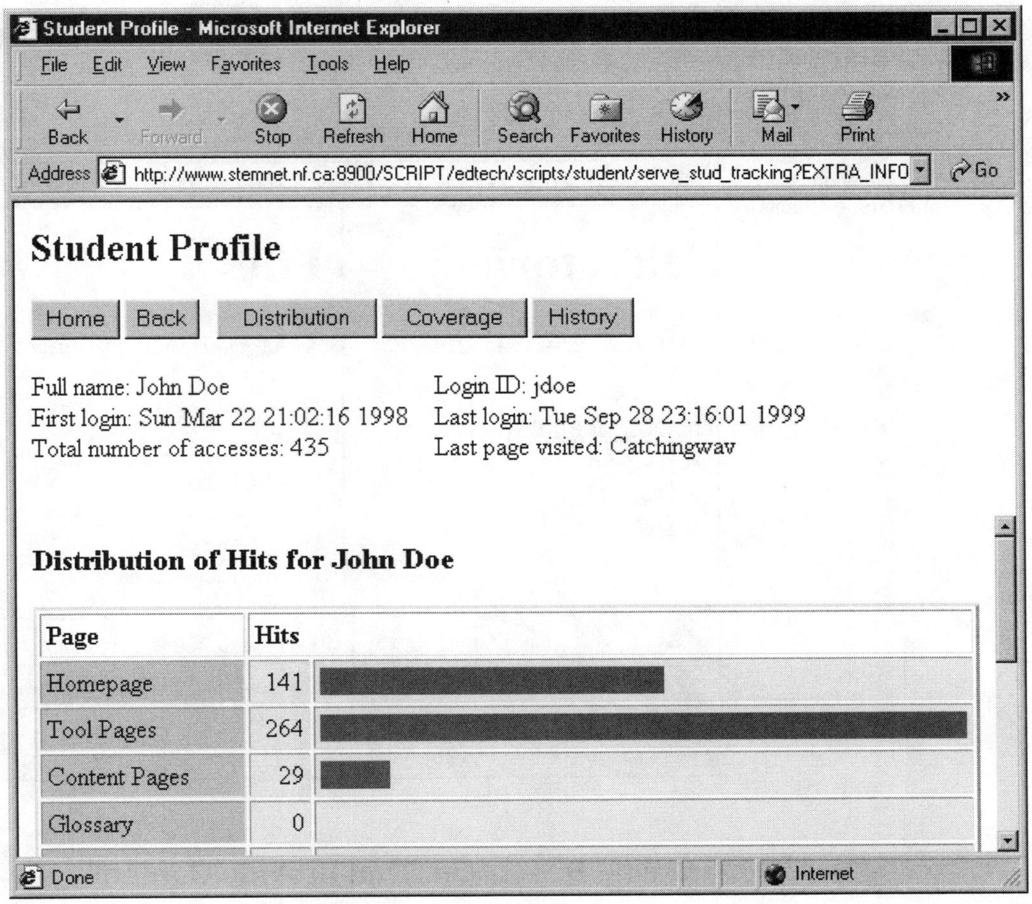

Phase 2: Online Resource-Based Teaching and Learning

Online resource-based learning is the next phase of Web course management. "Resources" can take any audiovisual form—text, pictures, or video clips—and any knowledge type—declarative, procedural, or strategic—for subsequent retrieval by students. The mindset for online resource-based learning is similar to that of storing and retrieving materials in a media repository or school library. Figure 1.6 shows a typical listing of files in a Web course.

The following online classification has been adapted from a taxonomy of conventional learning resources developed by Parsons and Gibbs (1994):

- Online resources that provide content
- Online resources that support a learning activity
- Online resources that support a learning process
- Online resources that build on other resources

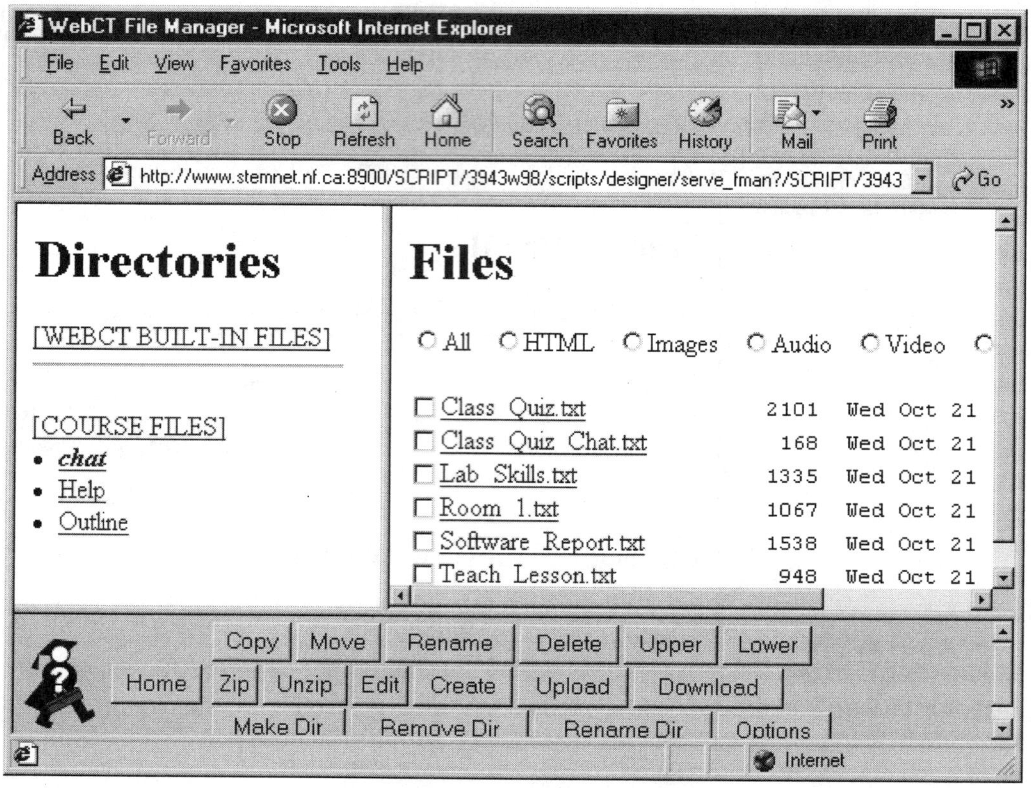

Figure 1.6 Files listed in a file manager

Mann, Education 3943, 1997 (see Credits)

Online Resources That Provide Content

Notes Online lecture notes or full-text articles are provided by the instructor, and can be a useful resource for students.

Reader An online reader is a collection of copyright-cleared materials assembled in a duplicated pack to provide the core reading material for the lesson; it usually consists of chapters, articles, and extracts from nonbook sources.

Resource pack An online resource pack is a set of readings assembled at little cost by the course manager. Copyright problems can be avoided with proper clearance from the publisher or author. An online pack may include data, maps, photographs, video and audio clips, slides, or curriculum-related software.

Online Resources That Support a Learning Activity

Manual An online manual simply explains how to do things. Manuals can be used for a variety of purposes, such as explaining skills and procedures that are normally explained face to face.

Laboratory guide Online laboratory guides contain background theory that would otherwise be presented in lectures. Such guides can become too prescriptive, leaving students little to do except follow instructions. Well-developed guides, however, have an appropriate balance of information.

Seminar guide Conventionally, seminars explore topics introduced in lectures and supported by the reading list for the lesson as a whole. Online seminar guides go further, providing additional material to help students prepare for seminars.

Fieldwork guide A special aspect of the online fieldwork guide is the *trail*, which takes students along a carefully planned route designed to maximize what can be seen and provides photographs, diagrams, and text to illustrate important points. Different student groups can even be given a fieldwork guide that takes different approaches to the same site, and can later be asked to compare their experiences and observations.

Project facts guide A good way to start writing an online project facts guide is to list all the requests students make for information and assistance during work on the project, and then to write down useful responses to these requests.

Work placement guide Some of the guidance and advice that would normally be delivered face to face can be replaced by written instructions. A work placement guide can also prompt students to prepare thoroughly for a visit from a VIP, making the best possible use of their time.

Figure 1.7 shows a typical online resource that supports a learning activity.

Online Resources That Support a Learning Process

Skills guide The typical skills guide is a how-to resource that explains how to use the library, write lab reports or essays, work in groups, give seminar presentations, and so on.

Skills profile A skills profile can come in many different forms, but commonly includes lists of key or transferable skills. As with a skills guide, a profile makes little impact unless it is linked to the formal curriculum.

Student log An online student log is similar to a diary. Logs help students to structure and reflect on their learning, and may encourage them to record ideas raised by practice for discussion with other students at a later date.

Online Resources That Build on Other Resources

Textbook study guide An online textbook study guide is designed to help students use their textbooks effectively. This guide contains brief overviews, and questions to be answered by reading selected sections of the textbook. Sometimes it can be much quicker and cheaper to write a textbook study guide around a good textbook than to attempt to write comprehensive learning materials from scratch.

Figure 1.7
An online project facts guide

Accoll Arts, 1999 (see Credits)

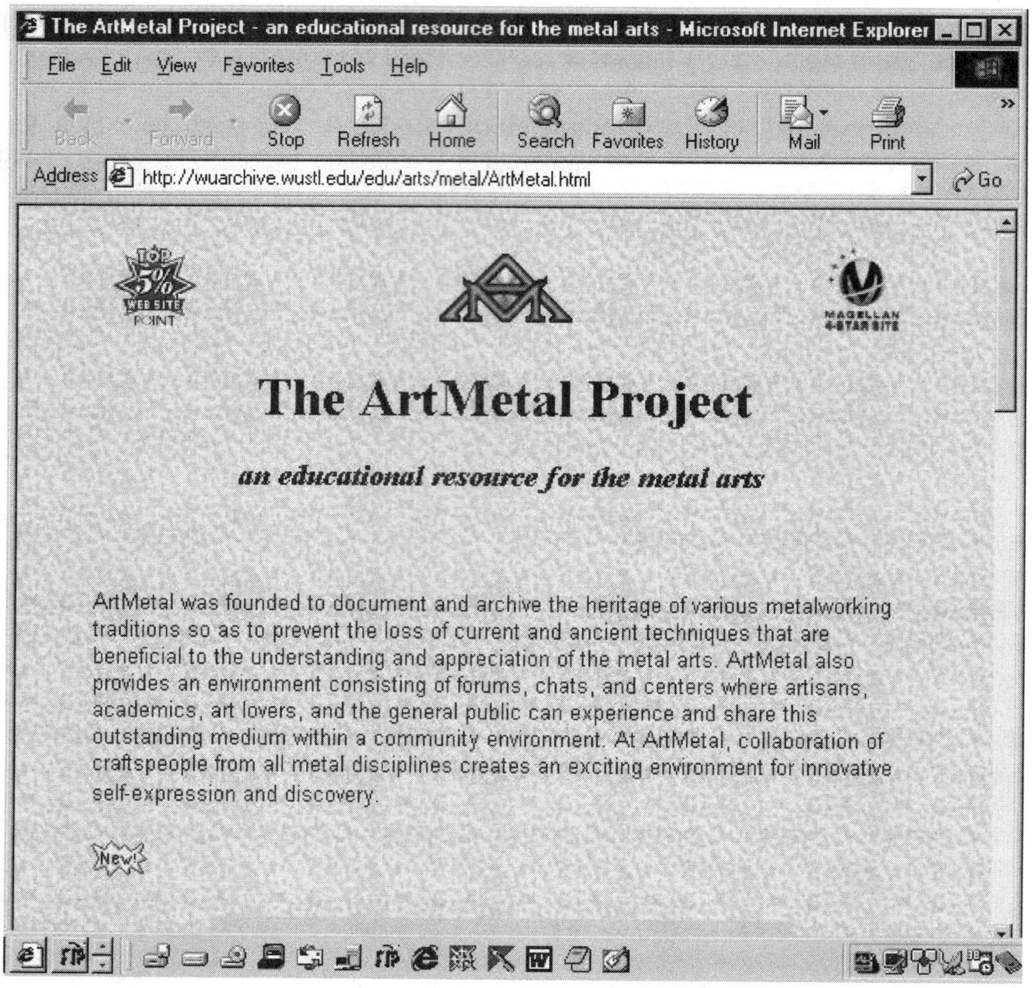

Reading guide An online reading guide usually looks like an extended reading list, with annotations, advice, abstracts, suggestions for alternatives to key texts, and so on. It provides information to help students find relevant reading resources or suitable alternatives, and to make appropriate use of them. Students find frank, subjective comments more helpful than neutral descriptions. They also appreciate detailed information about which parts to read and which to skip.

Lesson outline An online lesson outline (or lesson guide) is designed to help students select and exploit a range of other resources effectively and operate independently within a lesson.

In sum, four types of resources that have been classified as general patterns for online resource-based learning may require a redefinition of pedagogical goals, a restructuring of curricular offerings, provision for instructor training and support material, and sufficient online tools for the collection of student data. Terms such as stockpiling, massing, stacking, accessing, and accumulating might well define the linguistic framework of the online resource-based learning phase.

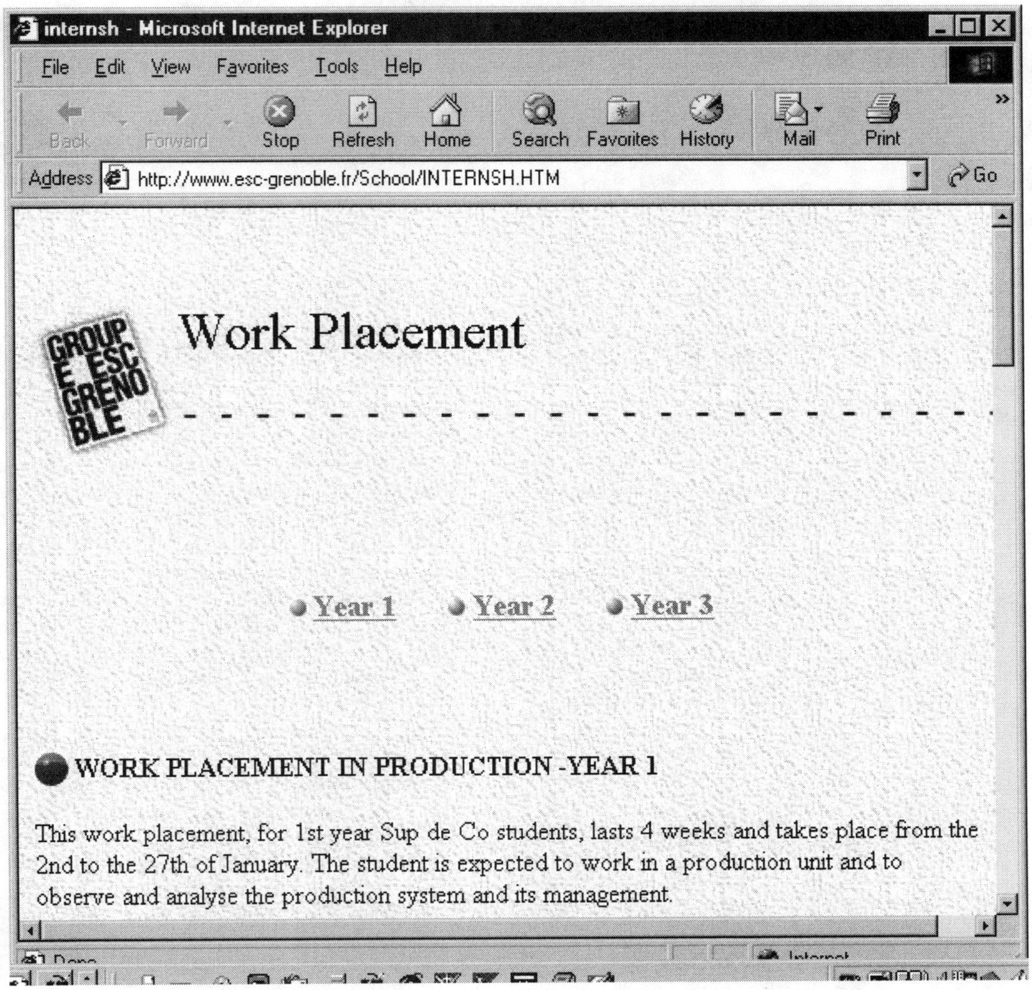

Figure 1.8
An online work placement guide supports a learning activity

ESC Group, 1999 (see Credits)

Phase 3: Online Learning Environments

An online learning environment is the third phase of Web course management. A learning environment is a virtual space where learners work together and support one another as they use a variety of tools and information resources in pursuit of learning goals and problem-solving activities (Wilson, 1997). In general, six components comprise the learning environment (adapted from Perkins, 1991):

1. Information banks (for example, an encyclopedia);
2. Symbols pads (for example, a note pad area);
3. Construction kits (for example, DreamWeaver and Flash-It, Netbook and SpeakEasy);
4. Phenomenaria (for example, ScienceSpace);
5. Online microworlds (for example, Biology-Guided Inquiry Learning Environment, Collaborative Notebook);
6. Virtual environments (for example, SIBLE and SSciVEE).

Learning environments apply principles of cognitive psychology to the Web course. This is particularly true of learning projects characterized by an active or collaborative

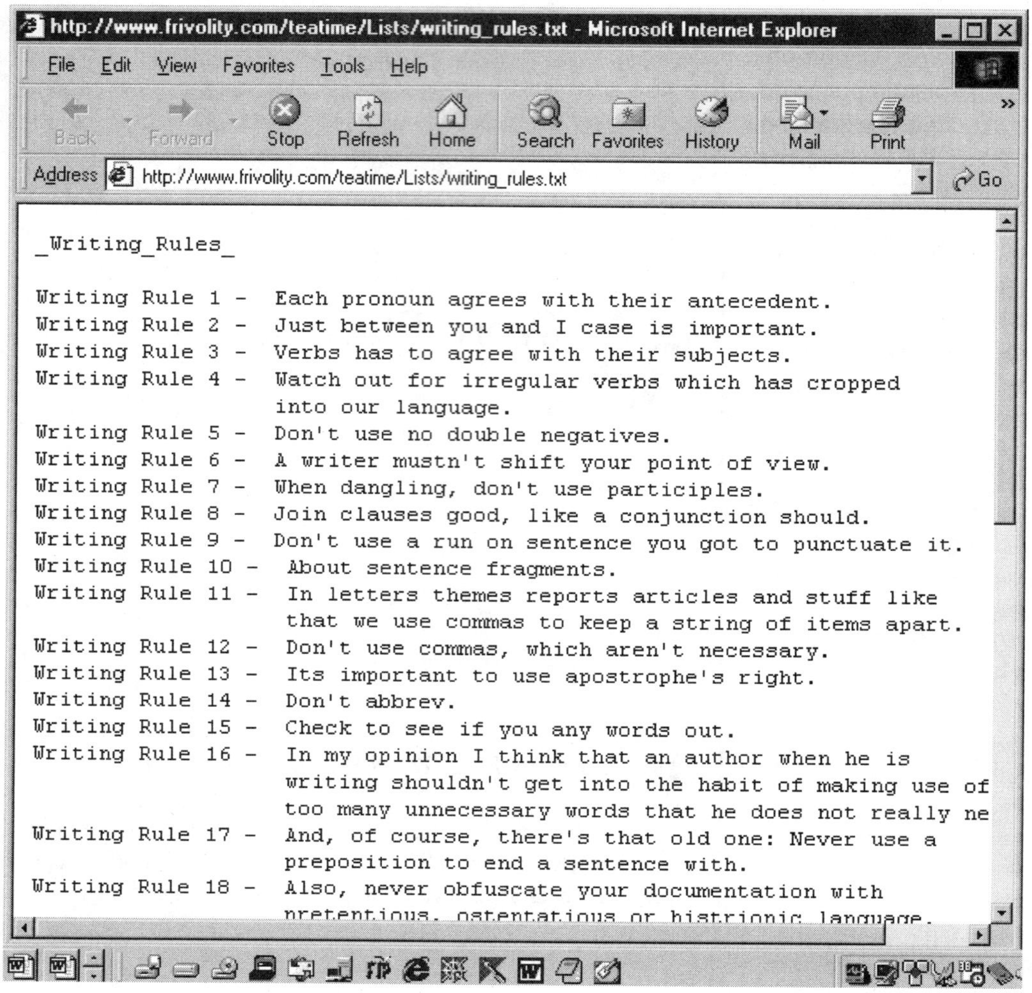

_Writing_Rules_

Writing Rule 1 - Each pronoun agrees with their antecedent.
Writing Rule 2 - Just between you and I case is important.
Writing Rule 3 - Verbs has to agree with their subjects.
Writing Rule 4 - Watch out for irregular verbs which has cropped into our language.
Writing Rule 5 - Don't use no double negatives.
Writing Rule 6 - A writer mustn't shift your point of view.
Writing Rule 7 - When dangling, don't use participles.
Writing Rule 8 - Join clauses good, like a conjunction should.
Writing Rule 9 - Don't use a run on sentence you got to punctuate it.
Writing Rule 10 - About sentence fragments.
Writing Rule 11 - In letters themes reports articles and stuff like that we use commas to keep a string of items apart.
Writing Rule 12 - Don't use commas, which aren't necessary.
Writing Rule 13 - Its important to use apostrophe's right.
Writing Rule 14 - Don't abbrev.
Writing Rule 15 - Check to see if you any words out.
Writing Rule 16 - In my opinion I think that an author when he is writing shouldn't get into the habit of making use of too many unnecessary words that he does not really ne
Writing Rule 17 - And, of course, there's that old one: Never use a preposition to end a sentence with.
Writing Rule 18 - Also, never obfuscate your documentation with pretentious, ostentatious or histrionic language.

Figure 1.9 Writing Rules is an online skills guide

Melissa Binde, *Writing Rules*, 1999 (see Credits)

learning approach (Bissell, Manring, and Rowland, 1999). The following stills of ScienceSpace's Worlds are taken from the project's server. The physical interface to the virtual worlds is typical of current high-end virtual reality. The hardware includes a Silicon Graphics reality engine, coupled with a head-mounted binocular display; an orientation and position sensing system with a 3-Ball sensing unit (similar to a 3-D mouse); stereo sound; and a custom vest that delivers haptic sensations. This physical interface enables course managers to immerse the students in a 3-D visual, auditory, and tactile virtual world.

This virtual reality interface has the potential to complement existing approaches to science instruction by creating inquiry environments for learners' knowledge construction. The focus here is on meaningful learning that is active and involves the students in learning by discovery.

By becoming part of the phenomenon (for example, a student becomes a point mass, undergoing collisions in a frictionless artificial reality), learners gain direct experiential intuitions about how the natural world operates, and increased understanding of scientific principles most salient to learners' senses (Salzman, Dede, and Loftin, 1996).

Figure 1.10
Selecting tools within NewtonWorld's 3D menu-accessing learning environment

Chris Dede, Project ScienceSpace, 1999 (see Credits)

Figure 1.11
The learning environment of PaulingWorld's 3D ball-and-stick representation of a molecule

Chris Dede, Project ScienceSpace, 1999 (see Credits)

Figure 1.12
The learning environment of MaxwellWorld's 3D single-charge with field lines

Chris Dede, Project ScienceSpace, 1999 (see Credits)

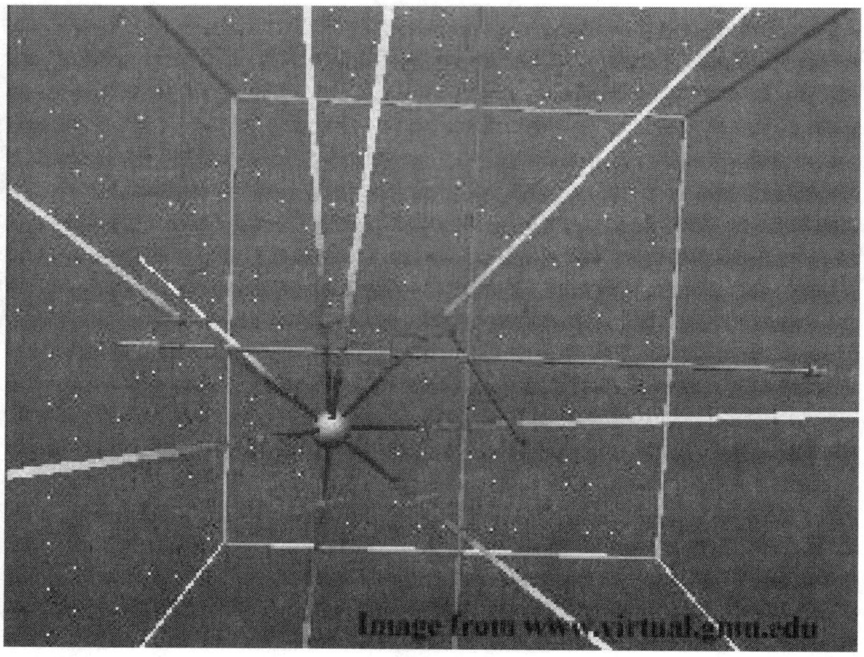

Several Web sites characterize meaningful learning by the design of the subject matter. "Living History" projects, for example, teach history through a student's re-enactment of historical events (Bissell, Manring, and Rowland, 1999) through role-playing, simulation, and re-enactment. A good annotated listing of examples is provided at the University of Saskatchewan School of Education Web site. The learning environment phase may be adequately defined by such terms and phrases as exploring, experimenting, constructing, and knowledge transforming.

Principle 4: Phasing

A *phase* is defined in the Merriam Webster Dictionary (1998) as a distinguishable part in a course, a development, or a cycle (for example, still in the early phases of her career). Phasing, or working in and out of phases, is determined by personal preference, intuition, and a kind of self-testing called *competitive elaboration* (Julnes and Mark, 1998). Competitive elaboration adheres to an emergent realist philosophy (Mark, Henry, and Julnes, 1997; Henry and Julnes, 1997), which incorporates elements of constructivism and empiricism. Together they appear to constitute phasing in and out of Web course management patterns in the following three ways:

The Initial Insight

First, the educator develops an initial insight for a new pattern of Web course management (say, an ICE to support problem-based print material). In thinking about the purpose of the insight, the educator develops one or more explanatory accounts of the pattern, which subsequently define the phase.

Alternative Insights

Next, competitive elaboration occurs when the educator's initial insight and explanatory accounts of the pattern become susceptible to an alternative purposeful insight (say, a quiz to support the problem-based print material). These competing insights are "critical competitors" (Mann, 1998b), creative alternatives that may add value and provide comparable or even better patterns of Web course management. The strength and plausibility of each insight can be tested by adding a comparison (say, level of student support) that places them into competition. The outcome of the competition determines a candidate pattern of Web course management, and even a possible change in phasing status.

Patterns Are Tested

Before the decision is made to adopt one insight over the other, the new pattern is tested as warranted action of a self-evaluative activity. The resulting decision then guides the development of more adequate insights and explanatory accounts (Julnes and Mark, 1998). Notably, only the explanatory accounts of the purposeful insights that define a phase are distinctive; the tasks are not. So educators working in different phases of Web course management can be performing similar tasks and testing similar insights for different purposes. For example, uploading files is common to all phases but explains nothing of the purposeful insights that define a particular phase per se. Furthermore, predictability and generalizability of explanatory accounts of purposeful insights that define a phase are not given a high priority at this early stage of the research; hence the rationale for implementing a pre-experimental (for example, case study) research design. In this way, educators can use competitive elaboration to consider and rule out alternative patterns and their insights.

Principle 5: Origin

The observation that educators gradually implement educational telecommunications in stages originated with Schrum and Berenfeld (1997), first as an extracurricular activity, then for uploading resources to be used by students, and lastly, for tutoring students in discrete computer-mediated communication modules. Whereas the cumulative and developmental nature of this version seems correct, the "stages of educational telecommunications" were deemed to be too inflexible and task-oriented for a theory of Web course management, reminiscent theories, and models of instructional design. So the "stages of educational telecommunications" were replaced with the three-phase schema for assimilating information about Web course management (that is, lesson enhancement, online resource-based learning, and online learning environment).

Principle 6: Principles Rather Than Templates

Phase theory is different from design templates. There are two types of templates in current use: information templates and instructional design templates. Information templates sometimes have instructional benefit for some users, but they are not instruction, despite the labelling. A *template* can be introduced to students in a nonconstructive manner, as a vessel into which the proper amount and type of information content is poured by the teacher; or the template may be used to promote constructive thinking.

For example, Gregory and Brown (1997) described how to develop a Web site utilizing a template for writing HTML. Hergert (1995) created a modular multimedia attitude assessment system from a template developed with authoring software.

However, phase theory is more personalized than information guidelines or templates. To some extent, phase theory re-socializes educators to consider their own personal knowledge and experiences that may be pertinent to Web course management. The developmental and, to some extent, cumulative and subsumptive nature of the phases distinguish this theory from ergonomic guidelines and templates for structuring information.

Principle 7: Principles Rather Than Tools

Phase theory is different from authoring assistance offered by some software developers. Zhao (1998) described the development of an integrated Web-based educational environment using eWeb (ECT Inc, 1997) for educational activities in a range of organizational and theoretical contexts over the Internet. Ward and Tiessen (1997) described the theory-based authoring kit ALiVE!, which consists of resource management and collaboration and coordination tools for schools. Undoubtedly, teachers could make good use of such programs. This approach relegates the educator to a facilitator position. In phase theory, approaches are used that retain the responsibility and authority for using or not using tools, for the nature and level of student interactions, and for the presentation of content with provision of feedback to the educator. But unless program copies and recipes for their use are provided to schools, teachers are unlikely to know where and how to acquire and use them. According to phase theory, the educator becomes more or less of a facilitator, depending on the phase they choose to adopt.

Conclusion

This chapter described a theoretical framework about how people work and think with a Web course management system. Using this framework, they invent new methods or select known instructional methods to help them achieve their aims. One future direction would be to implement phase theory as an instructional strategy to train novice Web managers.

Credits

Figure 1.1. "Online Collaboration Using a Bulletin Board System." In B. Mann. Education 3943. Unpublished Web site. St. John's, NF: Memorial University, 1997.

Figure 1.2. "Online Assessment Using a Quiz Tool." In B. Mann. Education 3943. Unpublished Web site. St. John's, NF: Memorial University, 1997.

Figure 1.3. "Uploaded Group Assignments." In B. Mann. Education 6822. Unpublished Web site. St. John's, NF: Memorial University, 1997.

Figure 1.4. "Separate Marks and Justifying Comments." In B. Mann. Education 6822. Unpublished Web site. St. John's, NF: Memorial University, 1997.

Figure 1.5. "Online Display of Student Hits Using a Profiling Tool." In B. Mann. Education 3943. Unpublished Web site. St. John's, NF: Memorial University, 1997.

Figure 1.6. "Files Listed in File Manager." In B. Mann. Education 3943. Unpublished Web site. St. John's, NF: Memorial University, 1997.

Figure 1.7. "Online Resource That Supports a Learning Activity." ArtMetal Website. Accoll Arts, 1999. Used with permission.

Figure 1.8. "Another Online Resource That Supports a Learning Activity." ESC Group, France, 1999. Used with permission.

Figure 1.9. "An Online Resource That Supports a Learning Process," *Writing Rules*. Melissa Binde, 1999. Used with permission.

Figure 1.10. "Selecting Tools Within NewtonWorld's 3D Menu-Accessing Learning Environment." In Chris Dede's Project ScienceSpace, George Mason University. 1999. Used by permission.

Figure 1.11. "PaulingWorld's 3D Ball-and-Stick Representation of a Molecule." In Chris Dede's Project ScienceSpace, George Mason University. 1999. Used with permission.

Figure 1.12. "MaxwellWorld's 3D Single-Charge with Field Lines." In Chris Dede's Project ScienceSpace, George Mason University. 1999. Used with permission.

References

Bannan-Ritland, B., D. Harvey, and W. Milheim. 1998. "A General Framework for the Development of Web-Based Instruction." *Educational Media International* 35(2), 77–81.

Bissell, J., A. Manring, and V. Rowland. 1999. *Cybereducator: The Internet and World Wide Web for Education*.

Boettcher, J., and P. Cartwright. 1997. "Designing and Supporting on the Web." *Change* 29, 10.

Bonk, C., and J. Cummings. 1998. "A Dozen Recommendations for Placing the Student at the Centre of Web-Based Learning." *Educational Media International* 35(2), 82–87.

Boshier, R., M. Mohapi, G. Moulton, A. Qayyum, L. Sadownik, and M. Wilson. 1997. "Best and Worst Dressed Web Lessons: Strutting Into the 21st Century in Comfort and Style." *Distance Education* 18(1), 327–349.

Dick, W., and L. Carey. 1996. *The Systematic Design of Instruction* (4th edition). New York: HarperCollins.

ECT Inc. 1997. *eWeb*. Salem, Oregon: Education Communication Technologies, Inc. (http://www.ewebsite.com/default.html)

Gagné, R. 1985. *The Conditions of Learning*. Chicago: Holt Rinehart and Winston.

Gardner, H. 1999. "Multiple Approaches to Understanding." Pp. 89-89 in *Instructional Design Theories and Models: A New Paradigm of Instructional Theory*, ed. C.M. Reigeluth. Mahwah, New Jersey: Lawrence Erlbaum Associates.

Goldberg, M. 1997. "Communication and Collaboration Tools in WebCT." Proceedings of the Conference Enabling Network-Based Learning, Espoo, Finland, May 28–30. (http://homebrew.cs.ubc.ca/Webct/docs)

Gros, B., J. Elen, M. Kerres, Merrienboer, and M. Spector. 1997. "Instructional Design and the Authoring of Multimedia and Hypermedia Systems: Does a Marriage Make Sense?" *Educational Technology*.

Gregory, G., and M. Brown. 1997. "World Wide Web Page Design: a Structured Approach." *Journal of Interlibrary Loan* 7(3), 45–59.

Gunawardena, C., C. Lowe, and T. Anderson. 1997. "Analysis of a Global Debate and the Development of an Interaction Analysis Model for Examining Social Construction of Knowledge in Computer Conferencing." *Journal of Educational Computing Research* 17(4) 397–431.

Harasim, L., and T. Calvert. 1997. *Virtual-U*. Vancouver: Simon Fraser University. (http://virtual-u.cs.sfu.ca/vuweb/VUenglish/index.html)

Henry, G., and G. Julnes. 1997. *Values and Realist Evaluation: New Directions for Program Evaluation*. San Francisco: Jossey Bass.

Hergert, 1995. "Two Applied Revisions of a multimedia tool: Assessing Attitutdes Toward Computer Technology and Cultural Diversity." Annual conference of the International Visual Literacy Association. Tempe, Arizona, October 12–16. ED380092.

Jonassen, D., K. Peck, and B. Wilson. 1999. *Learning with Technology: A Constructivist Perspective*. New Jersey: Merrill Prentice Hall.

Julnes, G., and M. Mark. 1998." Evaluation as Sense Making: Knowledge Construction in a Realist World." *New Directions for Evaluation* 78, 33–52.

Kearsley, G., and B. Schneiderman. 1998. "Engagement Theory: A Framework for Technology-Based Teaching and Learning." *Educational Technology* September–October.

King, K. 1998. "Course Development on the World Wide Web." *New Directions for Adult and Continuing Education* 78, 25–32.

Lotus Corporation. 1998. *Lotus LearningSpace*. The Lotus Corporation. (http://www.lotus.com/home.nsf/tabs/learnspace)

Maddux, C., and L. Johnson. 1997. "The World Wide Web: History, Cultural Context, and a Manual for Developers of Educational Information-Based Web Sites." *Educational Technology* 37, 5–12.

Mann, B. 1997. "Shifting attention in Multimedia: Stochastic Roles, Design Principles and the SSF Model." *Innovations in Education and Training International* 34(3), 174–187.

Mann, B. 1998a. "Instructional Design for Online Learning: A Case Study of WebCT Developers." *Universities in a Digital Era: Transformation, Innovation and Tradition*. Proceedings of the Seventh Annual EDEN Conference, University of Bologna, Italy, June 26.

Mann, B. 1998b. "Motor Learning, Metacognition and Teacher Competencies: Critical Competitors in Educational Technology." *The Morning Watch: Educational and Social Analysis* 25, 3–4.

Mark, M., G. Henry, and G. Julnes. 1997. *A Realist Theory of Evaluation Practice: New Directions for Program Evaluation*. San Francisco: Jossey Bass.

Mayer, R. 1997. "Multimedia Learning: Are We Asking the Right Questions?" *Educational Psychologist* 32(1), 1–19.

Merriam Webster Dictionary. 1998. "Phase." (http://www.m-w.com/dictionary.htm)

Mikovsky, E. 1998. "Techniques for Distance Learning Instruction." *Media and Methods* 34, 24.

Morrison, G., D. Lowther, and L. DeMeulle. 1999. *Integrating Technology into the Classroom*. New Jersey: Merrill Prentice Hall.

Ohl, M., and M. Cates. 1997. "Applying Metaphorical Interface Design Principles to the World Wide Web." *Educational Technology* 37, 25–38.

Oliver, K., G. Wilkinson, and L. Bennett. 1997. "Evaluating the Quality of Internet Information Sources." *Information Selection University of Georgia* ED412927.

Parsons, C., and G. Gibbs. 1994. *Lesson Design for Resource-Based Learning*. Oxford: Oxford Brookes University Press.

Perkins, D. 1991. "What Constructivism Demands of the Learner." *Educational Technology* 9, 19–21.

Reigeluth, C. 1997. "Instructional Theory, Practitioner Needs and New Directions: Some Reflections." *Educational Technology* January–February.

Reigeluth, C., and K. Squire. 1998. "Emerging Work on the New Paradigm of Instructional Theories." *Educational Technology*.

Reynolds, J. 1998. "What the Instructional Designer Needs to Know About HTML." *International Journal of Instructional Media* 25(2), 161–169.

Richey, R. 1997. "Agenda-Building and Its Implications for Theory Construction in Instructional Technology." *Educational Technology* January–February.

Riley, P. 1998. "Designing, Developing and Implementing WWW-Based Distance Learning." *Journal of Interactive Development* 10(4), 18–23.

Salzman, M. C., C. Dede, and B. Loftin. 1996. "ScienceSpace: Virtual Realities for Learning Complex and Abstract Scientific Concepts." Pp. 246–253 in *Proceedings of IEEE Virtual Reality Annual International Symposium*. New York: IEEE Press.

Schrum, L., and B. Berenfeld. 1997. *Teaching and Learning in the Information Age: A Guide to Educational Telecommunications*. Needham Heights, Massachusetts: Allyn and Bacon.

Seels, B. 1997. Taxonomic Issues and the Development of Theory in Instructional Technology. *Educational Technology*. January–February.

Smith, P., and T. Ragan. 1999. *Instructional Design* (2nd edition). Toronto: Maxwell Macmillian.

Stake, R. 1994. "Case Studies." Pp. 236–247 in *Handbook of Qualitative Research*, ed. N. Denzin and Y. Lincoln. Thousand Oaks, California: Sage Publications.

Tanner, D., and J. Hood. 1997. "Tips and Guidelines for Building a Web Site." *Music Educators Journal* 84, 22–28.

Tergan, S. 1998. "Misleading Theoretical Assumptions in Hypertext/Hypermedia Research." *Journal of Educational Multimedia and Hypermedia* 6(3/4), 257–283.

Ward, D., and E. Tiessen. 1997. "Adding Educational Value to the Web: Active Learning with Alive! Pages." *Educational Technology* September–October.

WBT Systems. 1997. *TopClass*. WBT Systems. (http://www.wbtsystems.com/index.html)

Wild, M., and C. Quinn. 1998. " Implications of Educational Theory for the Design of Instructional Multimedia." *British Journal of Educational Technology* 29(1), 73–82.

Wilkinson, G., L. Bennett, and K. Oliver. 1997. "Evaluation of Criteria of Quality for Internet Resources." *Educational Technology* September–October.

Wilson, B. 1997. "Thoughts on Theory in Educational Technology." *Educational Technology* January–February.

Winn, W. 1997. "Advantages of a Theory-Based Curriculum in Instructional Technology." *Educational Technology* January–February.

Yang, C., D. Moore, and J. Burton. 1995. "Managing Lessonware Production: An Instructional Theory with a Software Engineering Approach." *Educational Technology Research and Development* 43(4), 60–70.

Zhao, Y. 1998. "Design for Adoption: The Development of an Integrated Web-Based Education Environment." *Journal of Research on Computing in Education* 30(3), 307–328.

CHAPTER 2

Creating a Nexus Between Tele-Teaching and Tele-Learning

Marc Glassman
Memorial University of Newfoundland
Canada

There is a group dynamic that occurs in a synchronous "face-to-face" university classroom environment (Johnson and Johnson, 1975). At times, this dynamic is an appropriate and authentic method of teaching. However, the prosaic nature of how we have viewed this sort of academic interaction up to the present has both literally and virtually opened the door to the creation and implementation of dynamic Web courses. This chapter discusses the links between tele-learning and tele-teaching, and also recounts the rites of passage, both intentional and unintentional, in the creation and implementation of three university-level Web courses.

Background

Many have questioned the validity of a university experience that has students learning via a direct lecture-based form of communication by a professor, also known as "the sage on the stage" (Hullfish and Smith, 1961; Moffett, 1968; Rogers, 1969; Hirst and Peters, 1970; Becker and Gersten, 1982; Joyce and Calhoun, 1998). Personally, I have learned a great deal in just this sort of format, and have even utilized this pedagogy for part of my teaching career. However, I have begun to question and rethink this form of instructional design and professional development.

During the 1980s, the Faculty of Education at Memorial University of Newfoundland became a leader in distance education utilizing a province-wide teleconference system. I had the opportunity to develop three undergraduate courses for this system, which were offered twenty-one times during the period (between 1981 and 1991). The synchronous nature of teleconferencing required that the students register at one of the thirty-eight teleconference sites located throughout the province of Newfoundland and Labrador. In a Canadian province three times the size of the state of California, this form of distance education was considered vital in providing pre-service and in-service teachers opportunities to take university courses as a means of fulfilling degree requirements or for professional development. The seeds of my understanding on the development and implementation of distance education courses were sewn during this ten-year period.

Yet it would be 1996 before they would germinate into the early design of a Web course.

With encouragement from the Dean of the Faculty of Education at Memorial, I created my own Web page (http://www.ucs.mun.ca/~glassman). I wanted to provide my students with some insight into who I was as a professor and a person. Also, if the truth were known, I did not want to be considered an "information technology Luddite." This Web site initially became the conduit for my course outlines.

One day, a student who was scheduled for surgery asked me if I could put certain of my class notes and lectures onto my personal Web site. It was at this point that I realized the potential for Web-supported course material. I created a dedicated Web site for each of the undergraduate and graduate courses I taught. I included hyperlinked course outlines, class notes/lectures, diagrams/charts, writing guidelines for assignments, and other Web sites of relevance to the course. Based on the immediate positive responses from my students, I discovered a pedagogy appropriate to both the current technology and my personal style of teaching.

I once saw a bumper sticker that read "Students need to help their teachers find the on-ramp to the information highway." My students helped me see and understand the potential for Web-supported course material, and now I was ready to journey into cyberspace with the creation of a self-contained, nonlinear tele-teaching/tele-learning environment.

With the approval of the Dean and technical support from Memorial University's School of Continuing Studies, I began the creation of a *mediacentric* classroom environment, which utilized the potential of multimedia and computer technology to deliver my message.

Tele-Teaching

I focused on specific pedagogical concerns in the creation of my initial Web course, "Current Approaches to the Teaching of Reading in the Primary and Elementary Grades." The *transmissional* model of instruction, where content is the primary focus, was a teaching strategy I was using less and less often. Lecture notes had been uploaded onto the faculty's server for my Web-supported courses, and students could download these notes either prior to or after in-class discussions on their content. In my on-campus courses, I was effectively utilizing the *transactional* model of instruction, where interaction is the focus of the presentation of selective content (Routman, 1991; Graves, Watts-Taffe, and Graves, 1999). However, I saw the inherent need to implement a *transformational* model of instruction, with its focus on a holistic, interdisciplinary curriculum and a social identity structure based on each student's own learning style. I did not want to create a tele-learning environment that had a format founded on a sense of social Darwinism, where only the technologically fittest students survived. I wanted to develop a course where active involvement in the synthetic process of knowledge construction and the analytic process of understanding could be experienced by all, with each person enabled to achieve their personal potential (Lefrancois, 1991).

This tele-teaching experience needed to become a guided discovery into learner-centred instruction. To accomplish this task of creating a self-contained, nonlinear tele-learning environment, I was forced to consider the paradox of *time/space binding*. The asynchronous nature of this course required a format that enabled active online involvement from persons physically removed from my location. Support services to assist any one learner had to be built into this system. These support services took the following forms:

- Detailed prerequisites were provided prior to student registration in the course, as a fail-safe measure to inform students of the technological necessities of the course (for example, access to e-mail, an Internet service provider [ISP] account, a VCR, and a word processing program with attachment capabilities).
- Specific online instructions provided information on how to access, register for, and successfully log on to the AltaVista Forum (AVF) component of the course.
- Specific finder-friendly hyperlinked navigational icons were provided to assist each learner in their journey through the various components of the Web course (for example, a glossary was created for the various terms that were utilized throughout the online manual, with links embedded within the online text to easily navigate from the text to the glossary and back to the text).
- Direct e-mail contacts on a daily basis were established during the first week of the course, to ensure that any technical problems could be overcome immediately. Frustration on the part of students is the death of any distance educational format.

At the core of this tele-teaching experience was the necessity to create instructional content that had relational value when compared to a traditional on-campus course. It was important that the tele-learner feel a real sense of involvement and accomplishment from the onset to the conclusion of the experience, and that they feel their involvement worth the effort.

Tele-Learning

I make a distinction between tele-teaching and tele-learning. In tele-teaching, the instructor designs experiences that will enhance a learner's knowledge and understanding via an analytical and critical engagement with various mediums. This cannot take the form of impositional teaching, which is the direct teaching of some form of knowledge without regard for the learner. The effective tele-teacher needs to "think like a tele-learner," envisioning as many potential problems and frustrations as possible in order to offset or alter those negative factors. As well, the tele-teacher needs to consider what I call the *addendum factor*. A classic line from the Broadway play "Oliver" best sums it up: "Please, sir. I want some more." An efficient tele-learning environment will contain components of what an instructor considers to be needed by a learner, along with components of what learners perceive as being relevant.

The tele-learning experience, if designed well, provides self-paced independent learning with remote feedback and assistance. However, tele-learners need to fully understand their role in this new teaching/learning experience. Tele-learners must assume some responsibility for their own learning. A sense of autonomous individuality and a unique form of self-affirmation needs to be present in each learner. Such learners must work well alone, due to the flexible asynchronous schedule of this experience. The intrinsic motivation of these learners must be strong enough to overcome a potential sense of virtual abandonment. The tele-teacher can provide "scaffolding," with clear-cut directions and electronic feedback (that is, e-mail guidance), but the emphasis is on a learner-centred experience.

Convergence

During the winter semester of 1997, Ed. 3510/3520, "Current Approaches to the Teaching of Reading in the Primary and Elementary Grades"—the first totally Web-based undergraduate course through the Memorial University Faculty of Education—went online, with an initial enrollment of twenty-nine. This brought together the various relevant elements of a traditional teaching/learning experience within a technology-based distance-learning environment. The course combined an online textbook (that I authored) to supplement a traditional textbook (Blount, 1994), along with a two-hour videotape, e-mail, and an interactive discussion component on the AltaVista Forum (Digital, 1996).

The online textbook that I had written specifically for this distance education format provided the specific theoretical information and practical instructional techniques that I would share with these students if they were taking this as an on-campus course. This information was collated around the four current approaches of reading/writing instruction that comprised the focal points for the course (that is, the Literature-Based Curriculum, the Writing/Reading Connection, the Integrated Thematic Curriculum, and Computer-Managed Instruction). This was to be a nonlinear, inter-textual experience for the tele-learners since they were required to relate this online material to teaching/learning in the real-world classroom.

The AltaVista Forum assisted me in my role as an instructional facilitator. I attempted to maximize student interactions with an asynchronous reflective format. I posed questions on the AVF that were to be answered by the tele-learners. These questions were specific, but open-ended, to help create a risk-taking online environment where students felt that they were able to express their thoughts freely. Initially, I used a Socratic questioning technique, providing positive feedback with each of their responses and then posing additional questions for their reflection. In each of these individual responses I made reference to the comments of other students, encouraging inter-student commentary and replies. Eventually, this interaction came about naturally, with students freely commenting on the replies made by each member of this virtual cyber family. Students posed their own questions and this added greatly to the interactive reflection. I provided a specific site on the AVF for exchanges of a non-academic nature. This site, the Café Chez Marc, was a "meeting place" where the participating students exchanged views on such diverse topics as the state of the Newfoundland economy, trends in school fashions, the weather, and the Stanley Cup.

I posted e-mail office hours when students could send me a question and expect a fairly instantaneous reply. However, I found that students were e-mailing me their questions at almost every hour of the day. I attempted to access my e-mail from home each night at 8 p.m.; and at midnight, for those who posted their messages late at night or read my replies very early in the morning.

The videotape contained a collection of what I considered to be ten effective educational CD-ROMs, and was professionally produced by the Centre for Academic and Media Services at the University. As I utilized each educational CD, the images and sounds on the screen of the computer monitor were fed directly into a video camera along with a voice-over to describe the strengths and weaknesses of each CD from an educational frame of reference.

Assignments—such as the Web learning logs, the interdisciplinary literature-based unit, a reflective final, and the qualitative participation on the AltaVista Forum—were submitted in a variety of ways. The assignments (other than the AVF interactions) could be submitted in hard-copy form via mail or hand delivered to my office, or electronically in the form of an e-mail attachment. Students submitted sample drafts of their writing online, and I commented on these drafts via e-mail attachments the same day they were received. Thus, just as a student on-campus could come in to see me for specific guidance on an assignment, the Web-based student could also access me and receive feedback, albeit in a virtual format.

Eureka

At the conclusion of this course, I realized that I had discovered a way to deliver university-level courses utilizing the Web in a pedagogically appropriate manner. From this experience came the impetus to create three additional Web courses. To supplement Ed. 3510/3520, which is intended for undergraduate students enrolled in our primary/elementary education program, I created another undergraduate Web course intended for students enrolled in our intermediate/secondary school program (Ed. 4350, "Content Area Reading in the Intermediate and Secondary Schools"). To provide options for our graduate students, I created two Web-based graduate courses in the area of literacy (Ed. 6641, "Writing in the Primary, Elementary, and Secondary Schools" and Ed. 6647, "The Diagnosis and Assessment of Reading and Writing Difficulties"). By the end of the 1998–99 academic year, there had been total enrollments of 136 students for these five Web courses. Each of the five were offered at least once during the 1999–2000 academic year, and can be accessed at http://www.mun.ca/educ/fac_Web/distmain.html.

The three additional Web courses have a structure that is similar to my initial course; but taking into account a totally different content, there will be technologically significant additions to each of these courses in the near future. I intend to apply PDF formatting for the online supplementary textbook, streaming video, CD-ROMs, and I Pen Pro editing pad.

Using an Adobe Reader, students will be able to download and print a formatted personal copy of the online supplementary textbook for off-line reference. The streaming videos provide demonstrations and simulations that are best understood if they are seen and heard, rather than merely read in text form. Thus, any student can at any time observe these demonstrations and simulations (for example, how to administer and analyze a miscue analysis form of oral reading proficiency). By using basic technology, the streamed videos are accessible to the vast majority of tele-learners (for example, for those using a 28.8 modem and a Pentium or mid-range 486 PC with a soundboard and good video card). An alternative to the streamed video would be the creation of CD-ROMs containing the same content. I Pen Pro is an electronic "touchpad" that allows a person to edit an e-mailed message or attachment. A student might e-mail an assignment, and I would provide specific and direct citations and commentary prior to e-mailing it back to the student. This assessment would be provided in much the same manner as it would be if the assignment were submitted to me on paper.

Future Considerations, or "I like WebCT, but they like the AVF"

Since interactivity is a vital component of Web courses, the format for this interaction is of great importance. Although WebCT provides an instructor greater flexibility and options for the creation and delivery of course content, AltaVista Forums are somewhat simpler for the student. This view came from a random sampling of my Web-based students who have taken courses on- and off-campus using both formats. Such student considerations must be taken into account, since the distance from the professor can be either an isolating factor or an asset. Isolation occurs when a student does not experience a sense of connection to the professor or the course content, and feels that he or she has no way to rectify the situation. However, this distance can be an asset when experiences from a variety of locales are shared in an asynchronous manner in an easy-to-access format. According to my students, the AltaVista Forum has a more intuitive feel than does the WebCT format; it is easier to access and utilize as a communication tool.

Excelsior

Having been born and raised in New York City, I learned early on in public school that the motto of the State of New York is "excelsior" (that is, "always upward"). It is only now that I understand the complexity of that term. Because of my experiences, from my first teleconference course back in the winter of 1981 to the e-mail note I received from a student I had never met, telling me how great it was to be able to take my course online, I now have a sense of the meaning of this continual upward momentum. What made that e-mail so significant was that the student who wrote the note was located in Nain, Labrador. The distance between St. John's, where I was located, and Nain, where she was taking the course, is comparable to the distance between New York City and Chicago.

When I consider the link between tele-learning and tele-teaching, I envision an environment with a revised paradigm of the teacher and learner. In this environment, the use of instructional technology "re-places" (as opposed to replaces) the teacher and the learner. In this zone of possibilities, both the teacher and learner are actively involved in a process of re-inventing their roles in the instructional/learning encounter.

References

Becker, W., and R. Gersten. 1982. "A Followup of Follow Through: The Later Effects of a Direct Instruction Model." *American Educational Research Journal* 19(1), 75–92.

Blount, R.H. 1994. *Implementing Literature-Based Instruction and Authentic Assessment*. Grand Rapids, Michigan: T.S. Dennison.

Digital Equipment. 1996–98. *AltaVista Forum*. Digital Equipment Canada.

Graves, M., S. Watts-Taffe, and B. Graves. 1999. *Essentials of Elementary Reading*. Boston: Allyn and Bacon.

Hirst, P., and R. Peters. 1970. *The Logic of Education*. London: Routledge and Kegan Paul.

Hullfish, G., and P. Smith. 1961. *Reflective Thinking: The Method of Education*. New York: Dodd, Mead and Company.

Johnson, D.W., and F. Johnson. 1975. *Joining Together: Group Theory and Group Skills*. Englewood Cliffs, New Jersey: Prentice-Hall.

Joyce, B., and E. Calhoun. 1998. *Learning to Teach Inductively*. Boston: Allyn and Bacon.

Lefrancois, G. 1991. *Psychology for Teaching*. Belmont, California: Wadsworth, Inc.

Moffett, J. 1968. *Teaching the Universe of Discourse*. Boston: Houghton Mifflin Company.

Rogers, C.R. 1969. *Freedom to Learn*. Columbus, Ohio: Charles Merrill.

Routman, R. 1991. *Invitations: Changing as Teachers and Learners K–12*. Toronto: Irwin Publishing.

CHAPTER 3

Managing Staff Development for Web-Based Teaching: A Four-Stage Model and Its Application

Allan Ellis and Renate Phelps
Southern Cross University
Australia

The development and delivery of Web-based courses involves more than the development of technical skills. For academics to successfully make the transition to become online teachers or learning facilitators they need to challenge their pedagogical approaches and previous teaching practices. Web-based teaching requires new and innovative approaches to the presentation of material, student/teacher dialogue, group interaction, and assessment. From a management perspective, it also necessitates attention to issues concerning academic work practices. Web-based development and delivery brings together teams of people, each with unique skills, into a course design, development, and delivery team. For best results, these challenges and changes require a focused and structured approach to staff development.

As a framework for managing staff development, a four-stage model is proposed for the delivery of information and skills training in a relevant and timely fashion while maintaining motivation and seeking to modify academic workplace practices. These four stages can be conceptualised as

Stage 1 The provision of background information and the development of motivation and enthusiasm;
Stage 2 Maintenance of commitment and the initial development of Web-based materials;
Stage 3 Delivery, revision, refinement, and extension;
Stage 4 Mentoring and self-direction.

This paper discusses these stages and illustrates them through a discussion of the changes being implemented in the School of Social and Workplace Development (SaWD) at Southern Cross University as staff develop an undergraduate program of study for Web-based delivery.

The Need for Planned and Structured Staff Development

The transition to Web-based teaching within any college, university, or commercial training organisation involves significant challenges to the skills and knowledge of staff, their visions of the future of educational delivery, and the official policies and resourcing of the organisation. This may include changes in workload allocation, professional recognition, and reward (Coaldrake and Stedman, 1999). Initially, Web-based delivery of units was pioneered by "online mavericks" (Ellis and Phelps, 1999). However, increasingly, as Web-based course delivery becomes more widespread and accessible, less technologically literate staff will inevitably become involved in both development and delivery of Web-based units. These trends in development have presented, and are presenting, unique difficulties that require substantial staff development initiatives (Ellis, O'Reilly, and Debreceny, 1998).

There are vast differences between individually driven initiatives and the systems change required to move an entire organisation's staff toward Web-based delivery. To date these issues have been scarcely discussed in the literature (Bruce and Desloge, 1999). Academic organisations are faced with considerable challenges, not only in terms of training and staff development, but also with regard to philosophy and ideological beliefs, motivation, culture change, and challenges to staffing roles and structures (Ellis and Phelps, 1999). As stated by Bruce and Desloge (1999, p. 143), "educational institutions need to create the right pre-conditions—in terms of both technical and pedagogical support and staffing and hardware infrastructure" for Web-based development to be successful.

Web-based delivery initiatives must be regarded as a staff development exercise and approached from that perspective. There are a number of key areas that need to be addressed through planned and structured staff development programs, and each is equally important. These are as follows:

- Pedagogy
- Work practice
- Technological skills
- Policy, infrastructure, and resourcing

Attention to any one of these areas at the expense of the others may be detrimental to the overall success of Web-based teaching initiatives.

Most organisations moving into the area of Web-based course provision are likely to do so in an incremental fashion that will involve working with mostly existing academics who have a wide range of prior knowledge and expertise and who come forward as waves or small subgroups of the overall teaching staff. Rarely will the staff of an entire organisation attempt to shift to the Web-based mode of delivery in a single move. Consideration of each of the four stages mentioned above needs to be made within the context of a transitional model.

Before examining each of these stages, we will first provide some context for the key areas of staff development mentioned above. We will then present the four-stage model, indicating how each of the key areas can be addressed in each stage. Finally, we will illustrate the application of this model within the context of a specific course development project within the university.

Pedagogy

Unlike the conditions for teachers outside universities and colleges, there is no requirement for academics at university or college level to hold formal qualifications in teaching and learning. In fact, such qualifications are quite rare, particularly in disciplines that, in themselves, are not concerned with teaching or training. Without additional stimulus or staff development, instructors are likely to perpetuate the teaching approach they are most familiar with.

From the way academic careers have traditionally evolved, it is reasonable to conclude that the majority of teaching academics gained their formal qualifications from traditional on-campus, face-to-face teaching. A much smaller number would have had experience with the off-campus, distance education mode of teaching, and only very few would have had online learning experience (Ellis and Phelps, 1999).

Web-based development and delivery requires new pedagogical approaches, challenging previous practices with regard to the presentation of material, student/teacher dialogue, group interaction, and assessment. These challenges are not entirely new. They are similar to the challenges academics face when they make the transition from face-to-face modes of delivery to the traditional print-based distance education. Just as distance education increased the visibility and accountability of teaching practices so too does Web-based teaching and learning, a notion discussed most recently by McDonald and Postle (1999).

In organisations where traditional print-based distance education has emerged as an accepted and widespread mode of delivery, staff have already been led to challenge traditional pedagogical approaches. While many of these experiences do, of course, carry across to the Web-based teaching environment, Web-based developments require quite a different shift in pedagogical design. It is also worth noting that many organisations that have not been involved in system-wide adoption of distance education are now adapting directly to the Web-based delivery environment. The staff development required in these organisations will be considerably different.

Work Practice

If existing academics are being asked to develop and deliver new Web-based materials, then the support process must involve change management. Academics will probably need to give up certain activities in order to do others if they are not to become overloaded. They will also need to integrate their new tasks into the existing demands of their current role. If academics are moving to conduct all teaching and learning in a Web-based mode, then the change issues will be somewhat different from the issues for academics who are required to teach in both traditional face-to-face and online modes. In the latter case, opportunities to develop core materials once, then adapt minimally for delivery in either mode, will be a major issue. In rare cases academics may be required to teach across all three modes; face-to-face, paper-based distance education, and Web-based education.

Further, issues relating to work practices are frequently of primary concern to academics faced with making the transition to Web-based teaching. As documented by Bruce and Desloge (1999), there may be widespread apprehension regarding the time-consuming nature of development and delivery, fear of computers and of redundancy, and issues relating to "de-skilling."

Web course development thus requires careful attention to academic work practice issues, perhaps in a way that previous teaching modes never have. These issues include ongoing maintenance and updating, student expectations of teaching staff (particularly with regard to contact and response times), and student support issues, including technical support. More than ever before, collaborative relationships must come to bear on the teaching process, and with these changes, added staff and policy development with regard to work practices.

Technological Skills

Development of Web-based teaching and learning materials must occur within the current framework of the organisational policies and resourcing. For example, if the organisation has adopted a campus-wide course management shell, the staff must learn the features and idiosyncrasies of either a commercial product (for example, WebCT, LearningSpace, TopClass, or one of the other hundred or so products that exist worldwide) or the resident Web course management system.

Choices regarding the type of media and software adopted and how this media is used will, of course, be important issues of debate undertaken during staff development processes, and will involve input from a wide range of individuals, from academics to instructional designers and technical staff. It is not the focus of this chapter to explain these technologies, but rather to discuss the strategies employed to manage these adoption processes.

Information technology (IT) staff and other non-academic staff who will play a role in providing technical support to both academics and students will also need to develop an understanding of what academic staff are trying to achieve pedagogically so that they are able to provide appropriate technical support and advice.

Policy, Infrastructure, and Resourcing

The need for organisational policies, infrastructure, and resourcing in any system-wide transition to Web-based teaching is, of course, essential. It is beyond the scope of this chapter to discuss these needs in detail, and every organisation will develop a unique response in each of these areas. Instead this chapter will focus on the need that exists for organisational managers, policy makers, and executives to also receive staff development as part of the four-phase transitional model.

This need for staff development at management level is frequently overlooked. It is often assumed that policy makers and financial planners have the knowledge, understanding, and subsequent values to successfully manage the change process. This is not always the case. For Web-based teaching to be successful it must have institutional support for overall policies, strategic plans, and resourcing (for areas such as hardware and software), including course management software, network infrastructure, training, and marketing. Institutional policies should also address workload issues, and this may include addressing concerns voiced by academic unions. In Australia these issues are being taken up by the National Tertiary Education Union (NTEU, 1999).

There is a significant trap that organisational managers are investing in new technology on the premise that its implementation will lower faculty/student ratios (Putterill, 1999). Such fallacies can be circumvented through accurate understanding and clarification of motivations at this early stage.

The Theoretical Foundation to the Model

The proposed model of staff development is founded on the principles of action research and action learning. The role that action learning and action research can play in both staff development and organisational change has been well documented in the literature (Zuber-Skerritt, 1991; 1993; 1996; Limerick, Passfield, and Cunnington 1994; Bourner and Flowers, 1999). Web course development, more so than either face-to-face or distance education modes, demands a team approach to both course development and ongoing delivery, with specialists such as instructional designers, programmers, graphic designers, librarians, copyright officers, network technicians, and computer help-desk staff all playing important roles.

Since action research involves "team research by practitioners into their own practice, rather than by specialists on their behalf" (Zuber-Skerritt, 1991, p. 113), it is an appropriate methodology to support problem solving and collaboration in online projects, where a well-documented theoretical framework has yet to be developed.

Action learning entails a simple but effective cyclical structure, which involves participants in planning, acting, observing, and reflecting. In the proposed model, the cycles of action learning occur both between the four stages and within each individual stage.

A Model of Staff Development in Web-Based Teaching

Staff development for Web-based teaching should be viewed as an incremental process involving the four stages mentioned earlier (Ellis, 1999). The aim of each stage is illustrated in Table 3.1.

The nature of the material that needs to be presented or made available at a given stage will be discussed in detail below. However, it is essential that this development be customised on the basis of the individual academic's prior knowledge and experiences, the specific demands of individual projects, and the organisational context in which the development occurs.

Stage 1: Background Information, Motivation, and Enthusiasm

A particular focus in these initial stages will be enhancing awareness of the Web as a potential teaching and learning environment. The provision of print-based literature is particularly beneficial (for example, Laurillard 1993; Mason 1994; Alexander 1995; Smith 1995; Bates 1995; Boalch 1996; Arnold 1997; Brown and Thompson, 1997; Rossiter, 1997; Haughey and Anderson 1999; Chambers, 1999). Initial materials in paper-based format can be studied and summarised using existing skills and available resources. While the content may be challenging, the form of the study materials is traditional and acceptable.

It is also essential that academics have opportunities to make personal contact with "pioneers" or "online mavericks." Aside from the opportunities for sharing pedagogical ideas and experiences, this is an important opportunity for discussing work practice issues. This type of contact can be facilitated through informal lunchtime presentations and demonstrations on current online activities within the organisation and seminars by visiting staff members on projects and activities occurring in other organisations. Staff should begin to develop an awareness and understanding of the demands of Web course

Table 3.1 Aims of staff development stages

Stage	Aims
Stage 1 Background information, motivation, and enthusiasm	• To raise the interest and increase the motivation of individual academics to know more about the general issues involved in teaching and learning online. • To provide individual academics with a basic set of up-to-date hardware and software tools for Internet/Web access and at least preliminary courseware development. • To provide notes and one-on-one or small-group training sessions that cover the skills needed to access the Internet, manage e-mail, search the Web, bookmark sites, and develop simple Web pages using a basic HTML editor.
Stage 2 Commitment and development	• To provide focused support for the academics who have indicated that they are ready to learn more and to commit to a clearly defined online teaching and learning project. • To develop a sense of ownership of the technology. • To create a community of developers to facilitate sharing experience and ideas, collaborative blueprint development, and mutual assistance with technology/pedagogy. • To develop all the materials necessary to deliver a course (or class) on the Web.
Stage 3 Delivery, revision, refinement, and extension	• To encourage critical analysis of current approaches and practices. • To further develop and extend the instructor's knowledge and skills through revision and refinement of existing materials.
Stage 4 Mentoring and self-direction	• To assist academics to consolidate their own learning. • To acknowledge and reward exemplary practice. • To facilitate the transfer of learning, experience, and enthusiasm to others.

development and delivery and the transitional process involved in moving from paper-based to Web-based resources (Ellis, Wildman, and O'Reilly, 1996; Pickett and Shea, 1999).

As stated by Salter, Hansen, and Davies (1999, p. 1605), "staff are likely to benefit by actively experiencing online skills as a learner and...those who have positive experiences and have adequate support are more likely to integrate technology into their own teaching." Encouraging academics to gain experience learning via the Web might involve introducing them to Web sites that provide resources for teaching and learning (for example, East Anglia Polytechnic, 1999; The NODE, 1999b; EDUCAUSE, 1999). In addition there are Web-based, self-paced courses available that provide excellent general instruction in the design, development, and delivery of materials (for example, TeleEducation NB 1999a; Southern Cross University 1999b; Schlegel 1999). Some academics may even wish to explore the possibility of formal accredited awards in the area of distance education, flexible delivery, or Web-based teaching and learning. Many awards are available at certificate, diploma, and masters levels at various universities around the world (for example, The Open University in the United Kingdom, Athabasca University in Canada, and the University of Southern Queensland in Australia). Studying online, even if it only involves a small self-paced course, puts academics into the role of being a student, and this experience can provide invaluable insights that can be applied in the later stages when the academic is designing, developing, and delivering materials. Perusing examples of Web courses in their disciplinary area can also be advantageous. The extent to which study materials are freely accessible before paying enrolment fees varies from organisation to organisation; however, there is an increasing array of material freely available (TeleEducation NB, 1999b).

Some initial technical skill development will also occur during this first phase. This will include assisting individual staff members to acquire appropriate hardware and basic software to access the Internet and the World Wide Web from their office and from home. It might include the use of laptop computers that allow dial-in access while travelling. Depending upon the individual academic's experience and skill base, it may be appropriate to provide some initial one-on-one assistance in setting up their Internet connection and basic software (Web browser, the necessary plug-ins, e-mail, and related utilities). Providing a bookmarked set of Web resources in their discipline or interest area can also be motivational.

During this stage some academics may begin early experimentation such as introducing small Web course support pages to existing courses or using e-mail discussion lists for external students. Some may even move some of their course material online, purely as a supporting resource.

Notably, at this stage, it is important to provide training only in areas that the academic is ready to utilise immediately. The most difficult aspect of staff development processes is managing the timeliness of learning opportunities. There is a fine balance between exposing staff to technological possibilities and overwhelming them with technology that they cannot immediately use. Although demonstrations may occur of various specific technologies, such as course management software, it is not yet appropriate to give staff the hands-on training.

While the provision of basic equipment and sufficient information and training to operate it effectively are essential at this stage, the development of enthusiasm and motivation should also be regarded as a major goal. High levels of motivation will support the more detailed and complex learning that will need to occur in later stages.

Policy, infrastructure, and resource development will also need to begin during Stage 1. The success of Web-based developments will be enhanced if upper-level managers develop an understanding of, and demonstrate a commitment to, such initiatives as they play a crucial role in the culture-change process. This can be achieved through contact with online pioneers, as well as networking with other organisations' representatives. In this first stage, lobbying and application for support and resourcing for online development will begin to occur.

Stage 2: Commitment and Development

The second stage represents a landmark in both individual and organisational commitment to Web-based development and delivery. This stage involves focused, specialised technical skill development—for instance, in the use of the organisation's course management shell (for example, WebCT, LearningSpace, TopClass)—and HTML editor software. It may also be necessary to teach the use of other related tools, for example, those that might be used to create digital audio or video resources that can be linked into the course shell. A useful Web resource on this topic is the NODE multimedia online primer (The NODE, 1999b).

This type of training is usually undertaken in small groups and at set times, and the skilling of cohorts of academics from a single organisational unit will enable peer support and ongoing assistance. Training will usually involve both academics and administrative staff. It is important not to overwhelm academics with technical information. Too much detail can create as many problems for the academic/learner as too little. Training needs to be linked to application and practice and to incorporate sufficient time to integrate newly learned skills with existing skills. These are key principles for any successful adult education.

An important objective throughout this training is to ensure that the technology is comprehendible in educational terms and that it is intuitive or easy in skill terms. The focus must remain on teaching and learning, not on the mastery of a particular piece of software. In this sense it is important that technical skill development is soundly integrated with discussion of pedagogical issues. One way of ensuring this occurs is to structure the formalised stages of course blueprint development prior to, and concurrently with, technical skill development.

Academics may continue to engage in many of the staff development activities mentioned in Stage 1, such as examining examples of online courses and regularly reviewing the literature; however, in Stage 2 their efforts will begin to be more focused. They will examine pedagogical ideas, content structure, and instructional designs in a more critical manner, searching for ideas most adaptable to their own courses. It is most beneficial at this stage to encourage staff to begin the process of developing their own course blueprints, and forming small support groups that meet formally or informally to discuss their blueprinting ideas.

During this stage, academic release time may be necessary to support and encourage academics to engage in staff development as well as the development of new material concurrent with their normal teaching and research loads. To expect the latter to occur without the former may negate the motivation and enthusiasm built up in Stage 1 and would not achieve the expected output. Even if this release time is notional and does not fully compensate staff, it nevertheless signifies the organisation's commitment to this stage of Web-based materials development.

Academics often work in isolation when they prepare face-to-face course materials or undertake research. Those who have been involved in preparing distance education materials are likely to be familiar with a team-based approach. By its nature, Web course development requires a team-based approach that brings together many support staff.

Structuring staff development activities to create opportunities for academics to share their development experiences will create a community of developers and will support and facilitate the exchange of ideas, collaborative blueprint development, and mutual assistance with technological and pedagogical issues.

Stage 3: Delivery, Revision, Refinement, and Extension

Pedagogically, Stage 3 involves supporting academics to review and modify the material they developed in Stage 2 on the basis of the experience and feedback provided by testers and/or the first intake of real students. As a basic exercise this means correcting any errors and amending any procedures that did not perform as expected. A second round of delivery and evaluation can then follow. As the cycles of reflective learning progress, academics will be able to refine existing materials or develop new materials that are more sophisticated and involve more complex teacher-student and student-student interactions, or perhaps include collaborative projects or peer review.

During this stage further technical skill development will also be progressing. This might involve advanced training, such as introducing academics to synchronous chat or perhaps the use of audio or video in their teaching. By this stage it would be expected that academics would initiate at least some of this advanced technical training based on their own teaching experiences and the demands of students.

Delivery of courses in a Web-based environment will raise workplace issues such as the acceptable student load per academic, acceptable time in responding to student e-mails, the acceptance or otherwise of collaborative student work, and the admissibility or otherwise of online assessment.

Delivery of courses also has implications at a technical level. This will involve student dial-in access and the availability of help-desk services. Overall this places increasing demands on the IT infrastructure of the organisation, which need to be addressed through adequate forward planning and resourcing. A particular staff development issue is the training of help-desk staff in the course development shell as well as any more advanced technologies being adopted by academic staff (for example, streaming video) so that help-desk staff can be responsive to student and academic needs.

Stage 4: Mentoring and Self-Direction

Stage 4 involves acknowledging the academic's new skills and expertise. This can be achieved by offering them the opportunity to mentor and initiate staff development for academics who are new to the Web-based development environment. Mentoring also provides a means to consolidate learning. Mentoring provides a number of rewards for the mentor, including a sense of pride and achievement (Watt, 1996). For the best performers, acknowledgment via a teaching-excellence award or similar reward would provide organisational and peer recognition. Financial support to attend conferences and seminars would be another tangible way to demonstrate support for achievements.

In this stage, trained and experienced academics are themselves a resource that can be used in the future as one1 of the input elements to the staff development component of new Web-based teaching projects. The expectation is that academics will have largely become self-directed in keeping up to date with technical developments and pursuing new and creative ways of using Web-based technology in their teaching. The latter will require ongoing resourcing (for example, new software) if maximum benefits are to be gained.

In the area of work practices, it is becoming evident that the ability to teach online in a Web-based environment creates opportunities to work away from campus. This ability, in turn, creates opportunities to attend conferences and participate in research projects that would previously have been impossible using the face-to-face mode.

Staff Development for Web-Based Delivery: A Case History

In this section, the four-stage model of staff development has been used to guide the transition to Web course development and delivery at Southern Cross University (SCU). A case history is presented of one particular school at SCU. First, we provide a brief history and background to the developments within the School of Social and Workplace Development (SaWD). Then, we summarise, through the use of a matrix (Figure 3.1), the activities that occurred in each of the four stages according to the key areas of pedagogy, work practices, technological skills, and policy, infrastructure, and resourcing.

The School of SaWD has long demonstrated an innovative and responsive approach to its course development at SCU, being an early adopter of paper-based distance education materials in the early 1990s. The School saw the move to Web course delivery as an essential response to changes in University provision, both nationally and internationally, as well as a responsive development to cater to the needs and demands from its existing and future student base. Members of the School of SaWD have a wide variety of expertise and experience in Internet technology, ranging from one academic who is well recognised in the field internationally to those with some expertise and some novices (Dunn and Wallace, 1998).

Early moves to develop Web-based materials at SCU were primarily driven by "online mavericks," and two such individuals emerged within the School of SaWD. These early initiatives have been described by Ellis, Wildman, and O'Reilly (1996) and Debreceny and Ellis (1996). In the early days of experimentation with online teaching and learning there was a dearth of documented experience in online delivery. Online initiatives were usually initiated by individuals rather than schools or faculties.

Throughout 1996 and 1997, the School began to develop its postgraduate program for Web-based delivery, involving some of the less technologically experienced academics. A significant number of academics underwent staff development exercises such as basic HTML editing. The Technology in Teaching and Learning (TiLT) Unit, which had been established at SCU to support Web-based development, was given the responsibility for converting all postgraduate units to HTML as a precursor to Web course delivery. Academics also initiated various approaches, such as offering discussion lists to project-based students, translating hard-copy study guides directly into hypertext with links to

Figure 3.1 The four stages and four key issues of staff development activities

Figure 1: The intersection of each of the four stages with each of the four key issues maps the type of staff development activities that were undertaken in the School of SaWD.

	Pedagogy	Work Practices	Technological Skills	Policy and Infrastructure
Stage 1: Background Information, Motivation and Enthusiasm	• Early experimentation by "online mavericks" is observed by peers • Several staff study via the Web • Observing and discussion • Conference attendances • Workshops and presentations by invited "experts" • Sharing literature • Early experimentation with basic online learning including moving text based units onto Web with Discussion Lists • Reflection on student feedback • Reaching shared understanding regarding nature of online learning • Viewing and discussing examples of Web-based courses. • Realisation of limitations of these early approaches	• Realisation of workload issues from early experimentation, through networking and through literature • Discussion of potential work load issues in staff meetings	• One-on-one and small group skill development • Training and increased use of Internet technologies (Web and e-mail) • Hardware (laptop) and software purchases (Web authoring tools) • Set up PPP remote access • Some staff training in HTML Editor software	• Establishment of TiLT Unit • Upgrading of network • Survey of student groups regarding technology access • Senior Executives network and become enthusiastic and supportive • Initial development of an application for funding as an Innovations and Development initiative • Recognise the potential benefits of adopting an organisation wide solution such as a single course management shell • Discuss copyright issues and invite specialist speakers.
Stage 2: Commitment and Development	• Discussing innovative assessment approaches • Collaborative blueprint development • Sharing literature	• Project Management including resource allocation, timeline management • Formalisation of action and collaborative learning models • Development of School policies, for instance strategies for containing/minimising workload	• Discussions with IT staff regarding networks, servers, IT Web publishing policies • Examination and discussion of available technologies (video, audio, HTML Editors • Training in use of specific technologies such as sound file production, HTML editors and course management shell	• Trialing Course Management Shell [note that this should have occurred in Stage 1 however circumstances meant that this important stage was delayed to the long-term detriment of the project] • Strategic Online Teaching Plan developed • Copyright clearance policies and strategies adopted
Stage 3: Delivery, Revision, Refinement and Extension	• Correction of any minor errors that slipped through the test phase • Re-writing of sections indicated as needing attention (e.g. through student feedback) • Upgrading sections to build additional opportunities for interaction by introducing more sophisticated use of technology	• Issues of consolidating multi-mode teaching commitments	• Try out new software purchases • Exploration of the use of new media e.g. streaming video • Adding additional features such as synchronous chat sessions	• Development of guidelines and policies for Web-based teaching • Strategies for institution wide information management
Stage 4: Mentoring and Self-Direction	• Papers begin to be published • Presentations at workshops and conferences in areas such as collaborative assessment • Experienced academics work with novice academics.	• Work practice issues for staff moving into mentoring roles (e.g. secondment to the Teaching and Learning Unit)	• Nominations for Teaching Awards • Exploration of further technology • Experimentation with teaching via the Web while off campus (e.g. travelling overseas)	• Refinement of policies and acceptance as University Wide policy

electronic resources, and offering optional assessment tasks through online asynchronous discussion lists (Dunn and Wallace 1998). These authors further elaborate on the views of current practitioners and report on an evaluation of postgraduate units taken by practitioners from public and private spheres that were offered with an online option for the first time in 1998. After these initial developments, staff realised the limitations of the approach employed in this early phase of development. Their level of pedagogical input had been minimal and their subsequent feeling of ownership of the product limited.

These early experiences provided a critical insight into the workload issues associated with Web course development and delivery. Although staff enjoyed these initial experiences, the number of students who opted for online assessment was small and workloads were disproportionately high (Dunn and Wallace, 1998).

In 1998 the School received an innovations and development grant for a major project (SaWD Online) to develop an undergraduate program of study for Web course delivery. This marked the end of Stage 1 of the School's development and the transition to Stage 2. This specific project has been reported in greater detail elsewhere (Ellis and Phelps, 1999; Ellis, 1999; McMurray and Dunlop, 1999). This second phase of development was philosophically and ideologically different from earlier Web-based initiatives in the following ways:

- It focused on development of a full online degree, necessitating involvement of all academic staff, not just the most technologically literate.
- Our definition of Web-based development entailed full redesign of units, not just Web mounting or Web enhancing of existing paper-based external materials.
- It represented more than simply technological enhancement of teaching; it was a student-focused pedagogically sound redesign.
- It entailed changing work practices for *all* staff within the School, both academic and administrative.
- It involved a concerted attempt to address issues of policy development, both within the School and within the University.

The approach aimed to combine the best features of internal study with the best features of external study and to supplement this with new and innovative teaching and learning approaches made possible by online technologies. Initial meetings in relation to the SaWD Online Project involved the majority of staff within the School, both administrative and academic. From these initial meetings arose much of the shared understanding about the values, motives, and philosophical and ideological foundations upon which the project was founded. Although not all staff within the School continued with regular involvement in this early phase of development, all were aware of the activities of the core project team and continued to receive feedback at various staff meetings. Staff also participated in policy and work practice decisions arising from the first phase of development. Both full-time and part-time staff maintained a regular monitoring/observation of the progress of the project, knowing that they would, in the near future, be developing courses themselves. Dissemination of information was facilitated via a discussion list and project home page.

Action research and change-management issues during this stage of development were documented by McMurray and Dunlop (1999). These authors stated that it is "important that those responsible for the practice of the action maintain collaborative control of the process" (p. 3). Staff development workshops were held weekly, and these were opportunities for staff to learn together, to challenge each other's designs, and to share resources, ideas, and frustrations. Each smaller unit development team also met separately to develop blueprints and to produce the design and develop the material.

There was immense value in this collaborative approach, including the cross-fertilisation of ideas and experiences. In particular, the group developed a sense of cohesiveness and were extremely supportive as development progressed. Sharing blueprints was seen as beneficial for most of the staff involved and, from a project management perspective, ensured that deadlines were maintained.

Perhaps the biggest advantage at this point in the development was the level of commitment from the staff. All staff were extremely enthusiastic about involvement in the project. Enthusiasm was maintained, at least initially, through the team-based collaboration.

A major issue to emerge was the importance of staff being involved in policy decisions and of these decisions being made in a timely and efficient manner so that development progress would not be delayed. Ownership, of both process and product, was an important issue. As reported by McMurray and Dunlop (1999, p. 4) "many academics, accustomed to exercising autonomy with respect to developing and delivering learning materials, openly resisted the role the Information Technology department of the university assumed in making decisions that were often seen as having pedagogical overtones." Other issues and policy implications were also identified and reported by Ellis and Phelps (1999).

Following these developments, staff were more aware of the time-consuming nature of online development; "it takes as much time as you can give it" was one academic's comment. A number of academics felt, on reflection, that a faculty retreat would be an effective forum for development, with all relevant staff away from their day-to-day routines and able to devote solid time to design and development. This tactic would also create a good opportunity for team collaboration and ready access to all individuals in the various roles. It was important for the instructional (or educational) designer to foster staff development and promote innovative design developments, particularly through cross-fertilisation. This concept is not by any means new, and has been described in the early distance education literature (Kember and Mezger, 1990).

As staff move through the fourth development stage, they began to document their learning experiences. Parry and Dunn (1999), for instance, reported on the interactive design features of two Web courses and the importance of assessment in reinforcing certain learning values. Staff also examined the approaches adopted by their students to these design features and explained how online learning fostered meaningful approaches to learning tasks.

Conclusions

Web-based teaching is an emerging form of education that requires academics to learn new skills, and organisations to provide new forms of infrastructure and new support. If the transition from traditional face-to-face teaching or paper-based distance teaching to Web-based teaching is to be successful, careful planning and management of the transition process is needed. Furthermore, in environments with a strong demand for limited resources, it is important to deliver just what is needed at the exact time it is needed—nothing more and nothing less.

In this chapter, a four-stage model of staff development was proposed, and key issues were discussed that provided a project management framework founded in principles of action learning. This model identified various training requirements, and resource and support structures that are needed at different stages in the transition process. This case history illustrated the kinds of activities and responses likely to occur when the model is applied to a real situation within the context of the actual resources and goals of a specific organisation.

References

Alexander, S. 1995. "Teaching and Learning on the World Wide Web." Pp. 93–100 in *AusWeb95: Innovation and Diversity: The World Wide Web in Australia,* eds. R. Debreceny and A. Ellis. Proceedings of AusWeb95: The First Australian World Wide Web Conference. Ballina: Southern Cross University Press. (http://www.scu.edu.au/ausweb95/papers/education2/alexander/)

Arnold, M. 1997. "Using the Web to Augment Teaching and Learning," Pp. 37–41 in *ASCILITE 97: What Works and Why?, Proceedings of the 14th Annual Conference of the Australasian Society for Computers in Learning in Tertiary Education, December 8–10*, eds. R. Kevill, R. Oliver, and R. Phillips. Perth: Curtin University of Technology. (http://www.curtin.edu.au/conference/ASCILITE97/papers/Arnold/Arnold.html)

Bates, A.W. 1995. *Technology, Open Learning and Distance Education*. London: Routledge.

Boalch, G. 1996. "WWW as an Educational Support Medium: An Australian Case Study." Pp. 197–204 in *AusWeb96: Landscaping the Web, Proceedings of AusWeb96: The Second Australian World Wide Web Conference*, eds. R. Debreceny and A. Ellis. Ballina: Southern Cross University Press. (http://www.scu.edu.au/sponsored/ausweb/ausweb96/educn/boalch/paper.html)

Bourner, T., and S. Flowers. 1999. "Teaching and Learning Methods in Higher Education: A Glimpse of the Future." (http://www.bbk.ac.uk/Learning/ASD/bourne.htm)

Brown, A., and H. Thompson. 1997. "Course Design for the WWW: Keeping Online Students Onside." In *ASCILITE 97: What Works and Why?, Proceedings of the 14th Annual Conference of the Australasian Society for Computers in Learning in Tertiary Education, December 8–10*, eds. R. Kevill, R. Oliver, and R. Phillips. Perth: Curtin University of Technology. (http://www.curtin.edu.au/conference/ASCILITE97/papers/Brown/Brown.html)

Bruce, N., and P. Desloge. 1999 " 'Don't Forget the Teachers!': Evaluating the Impact of IT Integration into a University Curriculum." Pp. 143–148 in *WebNet 99: World Conference on the WWW and Internet*, eds. P. de Bra, and J. Leggett, Honolulu, Hawaii, October 24–30, AACE.

Burnett, D. 1999."Pedagogical Alternatives for Web-Based Instruction." Paper presented at AusWeb99. (http://ausweb.scu.edu.au/aw99/papers/burnett/)

Chambers, M. 1999. "Design as Learning, Design as Teaching: Embedding Pedagogy in Web-Based Course Design." Pp. 1217–1218 in *WebNet 99: World Conference on the WWW and Internet*, eds. P. de Bra and J. Leggett, Honolulu, Hawaii, October 24–30, AACE.

Coaldrake, P., and L. Stedman. 1999. "Academic Work in the Twenty-First Century: Changing Roles and Policies." Occasional Paper Series, Higher Education Division, Department of Education, Training and Youth Affairs. (http://www.deetya.gov.au/highered/occpaper/99H/academic.pdf)

Debreceny, R., and A. Ellis. 1996. "Developing and Implementing Information Technology in Teaching and Learning: A Critical Success Factors Perspective." Pp. 149–161 in *13th Annual Conference of the Australian Society for Computers in Learning in Tertiary Education, University of South Australia*, eds. A. Christie, P. James, and B. Vaughan, Faculty of Health and Biomedical Sciences, University of South Australia.

Dunn, L., and M. Wallace. 1998. "How Does Online Learning Affect the Acquisition of Vocational Knowledge?" Pp. 56–64 in proceedings of papers presented at the 6th International Conference on Post-Compulsory Education and Training, Centre for Learning and Work Research, Faculty of Education, Griffith University, December.

East Anglia Polytechnic. 1999. "Flexible Learning and Higher Education Resources." (http://bridge.anglia.ac.uk/www/flexi.html)

EDUCAUSE. 1999. "Transforming Education Through Information Technologies." (http://www.educause.edu/)

Ellis, A. 1999. "Instructor Support for Web-Based Courseware Development and Delivery." Unpublished manuscript. Southern Cross University.

Ellis, A., M. O'Reilly, and R. Debreceny. 1998. "Staff Development Responses to the Demand for Online Teaching and Learning." Paper presented at ASCILITE 98. (http://cedir.uow.edu.au/ASCILITE98/asc98-pdf/ellis0005.pdf)

Ellis, A., and R. Phelps. 1999. "Staff Development for Online Delivery: a Collaborative Team-Based Action Learning Model." Accepted for presentation and publication at ASCILITE99, December. (http://www.tals.dis.qut.edu.au/ascilite99/)

Ellis, A., P. Wildman, and M. O'Reilly. 1996. "Migrating from Paper-Based Course Materials to Interactive Web-Based Multimedia Courseware." Pp. 345–354 in *1996 IEEE International Conference on Multi Media in Engineering Education, University of Melbourne, 3rd-5th July*, ed. M. Aldeen. New Jersey: IEEE.

Gilbert, C. 1996 "Teaching and Learning on the Web at Queensland University of Technology." In *AusWeb96: Landscaping the Web, Proceedings of AusWeb96: The second Australian World Wide Web Conference*, eds. R. Debreceny and A. Ellis. Ballina: Southern Cross University Press. (http://www.scu.edu.au/sponsored/ausweb/ausweb96/educn/gilbert/paper.html)

Haughey, M., and T. Anderson. 1999. *Networked Learning: The Pedagogy of the Internet*. Toronto: McGraw-Hill Ryerson.

Kember, D., and R. Mezger. 1990 "The Instructional Designer as a Staff Developer: a Course Team Approach Consistent with the Concerns-Based Adoption Model." *Distance Education* 11(1), 50–70.

Laurillard, D. 1993. *Rethinking University Teaching: a Framework for the Effective Use of Educational Technology*. London: Routledge.

Limerick, D., R. Passfield, and B. Cunnington. 1994. "Transformational Change: Towards an Action Learning Organisation." *The Learning Organization* 1(2), 29–39.

Martyn Wild, M., and A. Omari. 1996. "Developing Educational Content for the Web: Issues and Ideas." In *AusWeb96: Landscaping the Web, Proceedings of AusWeb96: The second Australian World Wide Web Conference*, eds. R. Debreceny and A. Ellis. Ballina: Southern Cross University Press. (http://www.scu.edu.au/sponsored/ausweb/ausweb96/educn/wild/)

Mason, R. 1994. *Using Communications Media in Open and Flexible Learning*. London: Kogan Page.

McDonald, J., and G. Postle. 1999. "Teaching Online: Challenge to a Reinterpretation of Traditional Instructional Models." (http://ausweb.scu.edu.au/aw99/papers/mcdonald/paper.htm)

McMurray, D.W., and M.E. Dunlop. 1999. "The Collaborative Aspects of Online Learning: A Pilot Study." Paper presented at The Sixth International Literacy and Education Research Conference on Learning, Penang, September.

The NODE. 1999a. *Learning Technologies Network: Supporting Informed Decision Making in a Connected World*. (http://node.on.ca/)

The NODE. 1999b. *Multimedia Online: Primer*. (http://node.on.ca/tfl/primers/multimedia/)

NTEU. 1999. "Teaching Online." (http://www.csu.edu.au/special/NTEU/online_guid.html)

Parry, S., and L. Dunn. 1999."Benchmarking as a Meaning Approach To Learning In Online Settings." Paper presented at the 4th Northumbria Assessment Conference, Assessment for the Learning Society, University of Northumbria, U.K., September.

Pickett, A., and P. Shea. 1999. "The Evaluation of Faculty Development and Course Design at the SUNY Learning Network." Pp. 143–148 in paper presented at WebNet 99: World Conference on the WWW and Internet, eds. P. de Bra and J. Leggett. Honolulu, Hawaii, Oct 24-30, AACE.

Putterill, M. 1999. "Brighter, Bolder, But Is It Better? The Perennial Course Design Dilemma." Presentation at the 1999 AusWeb Conference. (http://ausweb.scu.edu.au/aw99/papers/putterill/paper.html)

Rossiter, D. 1997. *The Digital Edge?: Teaching and Learning in the Knowledge Age*. Brisbane: QUT Publications and Printery.

Salter, G., S. Hanson, and P. Davies. 1999. "Increasing the Adoption of Online Teaching by Modelling Good Practice." Pp. 1605–1606 in *WebNet 99: World Conference on the WWW and Internet*, eds. P. de Bra and J. Leggett, Honolulu, Hawaii, October 24–30, AACE.

Schlegel, K., ed. 1999. "EduWeb. Using the Web for Learning: Theory, Practice, Media and Interaction." (http://netcity.netspot.com.au/eduweb/)

Slay, J. 1999. "Creating an Online Learning Environment: Issues in Academic Staff Development." Paper presented at AusWeb99. (http://ausweb.scu.edu.au/aw99/papers/slay2/paper.html)

Smith, T. 1995. *Why the Web?* Preliminary Research Report. Seven Hills, New South Wales: PICA.

Southern Cross University. 1999a. *Southern Cross University Online Learning Strategic Plan, Final Report*. Lismore: Southern Cross University.

Southern Cross University. 1999b. "Staff Development Online." Southern Cross University. (http://www.scu.edu.au/services/tl/sdonline/intro.html)

TeleEducation New Brunswick. 1999a. "Learning on the Web: a Self-Directed Online Course for Educators." (http://tenb.nbcc.ca/lotw/)

TeleEducation New Brunswick. 1999b. *Database of Online Courses*. (http://courses.telecampus.edu/)

Watt, L.D. 1996. *A Guide to Mentoring*. Melbourne: National Staff Development Committee for the Australian National Training Authority.

Wild, M., and A. Omari. 1996. "Developing Educational Content for the Web: Issues and ideas." Paper presented at AusWeb96. (http://www.scu.edu.au/sponsored/ausweb/ausweb96/educn/wild/paper.html)

Zigarnin, P., K. Blanchard, and D. Zigamin. 1985. *SLII: a situational Approach to Managing People: Module III: Diagnosis*. Escondido, California: Blanchard Training and Development.

Zuber-Skerritt, O. 1991. "Action Research as a Model of Professional Development." Pp.112–135 in *Action Research for Change and Development*, ed. O. Zuber-Skerritt. Aldershot: Avebury.

Zuber-Skerritt, O. 1992. *Professional Development in Higher Education: Theoretical Framework for Action Research*. London: Kogan Page.

Zuber-Skerritt, O. 1993. "Improving Learning and Teaching Through Action Learning and Action Research." *Higher Education Research and Development*, 12(1), 45–58.

Zuber-Skerritt, O. 1996. "Emancipatory Action Research for Organisational Change and Management Development." Pp. 83–104 in *New Directions in Action Research*, ed. O. Zuber-Skerritt. London: Falmer Press.

CHAPTER 4

Design for a Managed Web Learning Environment

Tony Fetherston
Edith Cowan University
Australia

Until we gain control of the direction of change needed in the use of the World Wide Web; until we fully understand what the Web is; until we know the specific skills required of students and teachers; and until lecturers stop relying on their own judgements about the students in front of them, then the Web should not be used in university education. It is at once a threat to instructional systems and an exciting new tool for learning.

There is a growing interest in university systems worldwide about how best to use the Internet as part of teaching and learning processes. McKenzie in 1996 (p. 30) wrote that "before schools invest millions of dollars to provide access to the World Wide Web (Web) they would be wise to stop and ask 'Why?'" The answer to the question requires some understanding of what using the Web in teaching involves.

Using the Web to Teach

The use of the Web in university teaching will contribute directly to the development of information-handling key competencies but will also validate these competencies as being of educational value. To successfully incorporate the Web into teaching, however, will require change in pedagogical practice by lecturers. For example, lecturers may need to have knowledge of several topics and skills across several disciplines to adequately support students' understanding of material gathered from the Web. This is because the organisation of material on most Web sites does not follow organisation by discipline. Personal change will be required by some lecturers who use the Web to provide a context in which their students will turn data gathering into meaningful information, and lecturers may need to adopt a constructivist approach to their teaching to help their students to develop concepts and meaning.

An obvious feature of the use of the Web for learning purposes is that it allows students to communicate with a wider audience than their immediate peers. This potential expands their learning network. The lecturer may be relied on less frequently. Expanding the learning network enables problems to be studied in greater depth and complexity than the traditional lecture and tutorial format allows. Ideally, Web-based learning has the potential to allow classes to emphasise process as well as product. Authentic activities can be set and understandings sought, rather than content recalled. Learning networks on the Web have the potential to deliver answers at the time they are needed, especially if mentor relationships are encouraged. Expertise from far outside the school walls can be shared. In these ways, the role of the lecturer as the fount of knowledge can be decreased and replaced by authentic networking activity for the development of new understanding.

At present, the use of the Web in universities can be seen to market drive the pedagogy, rather than the reverse. Some are skeptical of academics who suggest that the use of the Web may have learning benefits; they believe instead that this contributes to "technology fever" (Noble, 1997). Recently, Fetherston (1999, p. 394) stated that "it is timely then to examine the role of the Web in moves towards better teaching and learning for internal and external students at university." Clearly the use of the Web in university teaching presents many challenges to existing systems. Fetherston (1999, p. 395) enunciated some of the challenges:

- To begin regarding the use of the Web not as a delivery medium, but as a teaching and learning tool;
- To equip our tertiary students with the conceptual models and practical skills to enable them to participate in the (Web) community;
- To implement technical capabilities to bring about meaningful learning;
- To use the Web for good assessment;
- To use the Web to encourage good learning behaviours in students;
- To assist lecturers with changing their usual practice.

Good instructional design of material presented or delivered through the Web is required to meet the above challenges. It is likely that lecturers themselves will have to be closely involved in the instructional design process, since few universities possess the infrastructure to be able to meet the demand for courses to be delivered through the Web. Consequently, lecturers will have to gain a good working knowledge of instructional design principles or a systematic model that can be implemented. It is highly likely that lecturers will be using one of the many integrated Web management systems that are designed to manage learning on the Web.

In the remainder of this chapter I describe a very practical approach to assist university teachers in adapting to the use of any of the management systems designed for handling instruction via the Web. Most of these systems contain facilities for delivering text, audio, and video through Web browsers. They also include threaded e-mail discussion with links to external e-mail providers, and many have synchronous chat areas. Almost all provide many tracking functions so that lecturers can see which students have taken tests and submitted assignments, and which pages on the site have been visited and how often, for example.

Considerations

Before teachers begin to design materials, they need to consider the following factors. First, there is little compelling evidence that the use of the Web in a classroom leads to better learning, yet there is little evidence to the contrary: that it leads to worse learning! So why should lecturers bother to incorporate it into their teaching? Following are some suggested reasons:

Figure 4.1
A simple overview
of mediation
in learning
(Fetherston, 1998)

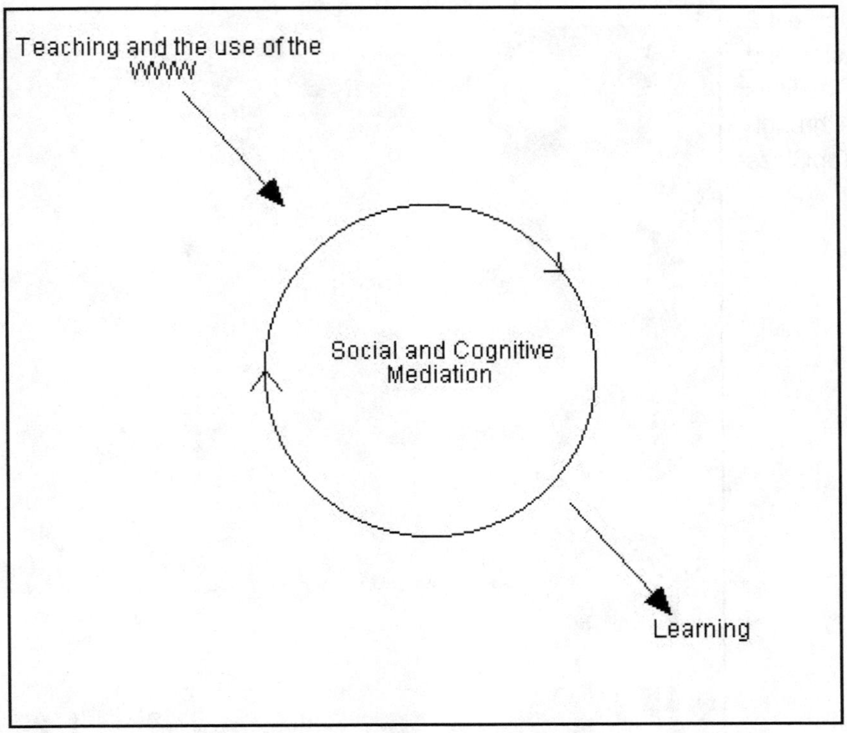

- To provide variety for students;
- To provide a context for students to learn information-handling skills;
- To widen the classroom, allowing communication with a wider range of people;
- To give students an audience for their writing;
- To build research skills in students;
- To promote active learning and an authentic context for learning;
- To provide a problem-solving context for learning.

A second main consideration is that the systems mentioned above are only *delivery systems*. The system by itself provides little in the way of the social and cognitive mediation so necessary for learning.

The use of different media can assist with the mediation process in learning. But before this can occur, careful instructional design is necessary to maximise the opportunities provided by these systems.

A third consideration is that the use of these systems should either support teachers in their usual approach or assist them with the change process. This means that should a teacher adopt a student-centred, constructivist approach to teaching then that same approach should be reflected in the use of the Web managed system. If a teacher is exploring different approaches, then the use of these systems can assist the change or provide the catalyst for further change.

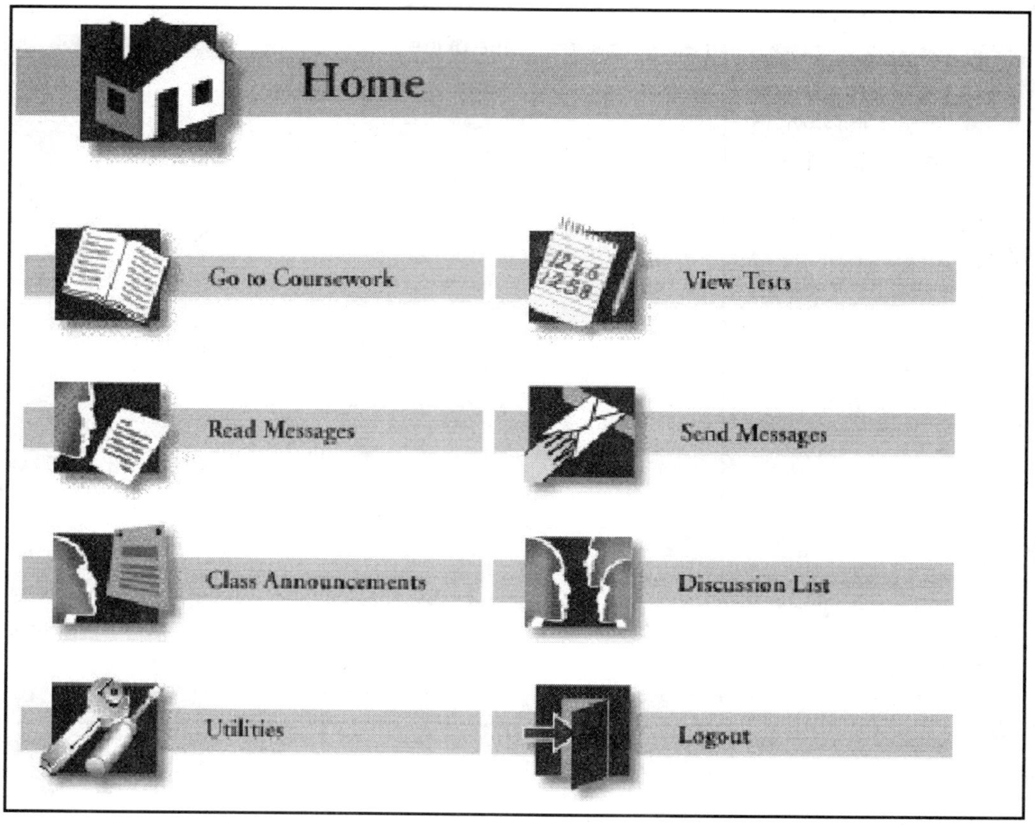

Figure 4.2 Discussion and e-mail facilities available through TopClass

E-Mail

Integrated course management systems like TopClass (WBT Systems, 1998) allow students, once enrolled in a course, the opportunity to participate in asynchronous chat through a discussion list and e-mail facilities.

If this chat feature can be incorporated into a course, then students will immediately begin talking about the course, and this, in itself, may be an advance over usual practice! A second advantage is that an instructor can view and participate in the discussion and thereby gain a better picture of student understanding of material covered. The following two messages from a student discussion in a beginning instructional design course illustrate this point; both reveal a lot about what the students understand:

> The authenticity of the setting was relatively good. From the lay of the land to the sound effects of approaching ships, one could genuinely become immersed in the task at hand. The time factor and budget considerations added to the realism. However, whether or not this (authentic setting) is a prerequisite to the game being effective in learning terms is a debatable point. Perhaps this relies more on the imagination, attitude and need of the end user?

And a reply from another student:

> Well Karen, I also agree that the setting was relatively authentic albeit a very simplified version of reality. This authenticity is a very helpful

> thing, the "prettiness" of the product placing it in a realm that is easily relatable for the learner. By this I mean that an assortment of facts and figures placed on the screen would have eventually been understood and may have said everything that the program says pictorially, it would not have been a very user-friendly set-up. At least through the use of snappy graphics and sounds, the user is able to relate to what his decisions are doing and the influence he/she is having over their "city." Therefore the authenticity, or "prettiness," of the product does indeed affect the learning process, in a positive way.

Understandings are really only revealed using these kinds of facilities when the question or task has a degree of openness. In other words, when the question requires only a yes or no response, then that is all that will be received. With care, tasks or questions can encourage extended responses, and such responses are more likely to lead to higher order learning. For example, the messages above were posted in response to a set of five questions, the last of which was: "How authentic is the setting? How authentic does it have to be to be effective in learning terms?"

Sometimes instructors make postings compulsory by allocating marks to the quantity of the posts or by using simple marking schemes for the perceived quality of the postings. Automatic marking applications can be used when allocation of marks is based only on the quantity of chat.

Any allocation of marks in an assessment-led system will encourage the type of content in the e-mail that will gain the most marks. This means that students may be inhibited in revealing their true understandings, thoughts, beliefs, and attitudes in such a structure; therefore, the usefulness of the discussion for the assessment of students' understandings is decreased. Compare the following two e-mails produced for marks in a postgraduate course with the two above, which were not produced for assessment:

> Your article explores a very important and relevant issue. I can see how peer assessment would be beneficial, in that it would develop a person's ability to self-assess and assess others. This is of course a very important skill in the workforce.

And the following message:

> After reading your summary, I can see how qualitative studies and the gathering of data in your case study, can be repeated in action research that uses other forms of multimedia. You did well to interpret such a vast array of information.

These two e-mails reveal little of these students' understandings and clearly are designed with the instructor, and marks, in mind.

Most instructors who use discussion lists soon realize that it is a double-edged sword. Without careful planning and structuring of the task, it is possible that instructors will be flooded with e-mails to respond to or evaluate. In the situation where students must post an e-mail to obtain marks, many of the postings are low level and of little educational benefit. Students often either paraphrase an idea from a text or paper or add a "me too, that was great" comment to a previous posting. For example:

> I also acknowledge the importance of the www as a learning tool.
>
> Hopefully, teachers will one day make more use of the Internet.

So how can we get more out of this system, in education terms? First, if postings are compulsory then procedures need to be designed to raise the quality of the postings and decrease the quantity. Second, procedures should focus on using the list to encourage higher order learning. Here are some techniques that may be useful in bringing about these results.

One useful technique is to split the class into groups; instead of receiving e-mail from each individual you receive e-mail only from the groups. Structure the groups so that they fit your learning objectives, and structure the task so that the students within the group mediate and engage in the task.

The students do not have to meet in the same room at the same time, since applications like TopClass can organise this in virtual fashion. Let each member of the group know everyone else's e-mail address on TopClass so that they can correspond that way. Set the task and then ask each student to chat about this task within their group using the e-mail facilities. After a period of time, for example, the time between lectures in the subject, ask one student to post a consensus view from the group onto the class discussion list. This would be the first publicly visible (to the whole class) posting and should be of reasonable quality because the act of coming to a consensus forces revision of views and necessitates discussion. Then, each group could be asked to compare their posting with another group's posting and to describe and explain any commonalities and differences. This process of social negotiation of knowledge is a constructivist approach and is more likely to lead to good conceptual development and higher order learning.

In well-ordered domains like science and mathematics we require students to construct "correct" knowledge; in other words, knowledge that is regarded by those in the profession as "true." In these domains, instructors may be surprised at the understandings expressed via discussion lists, since often they are far from true! To a certain extent these lists mimic what happens in face-to-face communication among students when they discuss lectures; the ideas presented in these sessions are also often far removed from scientific acceptability. It is important that the ideas expressed in the list are accepted as students' own ideas and not evaluated as right or wrong. Such evaluation may hinder the open nature of the communication.

However, any misconceptions displayed in postings need to be addressed, and one way for the instructor to respond to a set of incorrect ideas is by posting a response that is couched in effective learning principles: "Newton might disagree with you about the direction that gravity is acting in this situation. For example, see (the text) on page.... How does this idea compare to your idea? Which one do you think would work better in the case of a falling apple?" This approach accepts the student's idea and forces comparison of that idea with correct notions and allows further dialogue to proceed.

Another good technique to increase the quality of exchanges on discussion lists is to ask a student (or preferably a group) to explain an idea to another group. This forces the teaching group to come to an understanding of the material themselves, to clarify that understanding among themselves, to compare their understanding with accepted ideas in the profession, and then to organise a logical presentation of that idea to someone else. Much good learning can result from this process, and most of the learning occurs in the group that was asked to explain the concept. The other group should respond to the original group until the original group is confident that the other group also understands the concept.

Presentation tools or even more sophisticated multimedia authoring systems can be used to advantage here for the presentation to the other group. Finished products can be mounted through TopClass, thus becoming available to other students in the course. If this process is adopted, it is important that the group explaining the idea does check their understanding with the accepted version, either through text or with the instructor; otherwise this becomes an excellent technique for propagating misconceptions.

In summary, the e-mail and discussion sections of TopClass can be used to good learning advantage if we implement processes that concentrate on the quality of ideas rather than the quantity.

Video

With some Web applications such as RealPlayer, RealProducer (Real Products, 1999), and QuickTime (Apple Computer, 1999) that permit streaming, it is now possible to deliver audio and video over the Internet at reasonable speed through modems. Using server solutions, live audio and video over the Internet is produced at viewable quality. This makes it possible for lectures to be delivered live to distance education students, and for lectures, tutorials, and demonstrations to be recorded and stored on a server to be accessed anytime by students.

The event must first be recorded, then digitised—converted to digital format. This is done either by computer or directly by the recording device such as the latest versions of video cameras. After the audio or video is digitised and stored on a computer, it is then compressed. The compression process "squashes" the size of the file and allows transmission over the relatively slow modem connections. The process can reduce the size of the file enormously, but also reduces the quality of the file. Once the file is compressed, it can be made available through Web pages or as a direct download. When it is downloaded, the file must be uncompressed through proprietary software before it can be played. Compression software often resides as a "plug-in" on common Web browsers and is invoked automatically when the file starts to download. A player appears on the screen with controls for volume, backwards, forwards, and stop, much like a usual video player.

The ability to deliver such content in useable form forces us to address the question of how best to use it for learning purposes. A decision to use video could be made simply because the instructor wants to show how something works or moves or to show something that would ordinarily not be visible because it is too small, too far away, or moves too fast. "Video can be more engaging and motivating than text and can display human behaviour" (Horton, 1997, p. 21). The benefit in learning terms is directly related to the quality of the video that can be delivered, so it is worth investing time and effort to capture good quality video in the first instance before the "massaging" occurs to place it online.

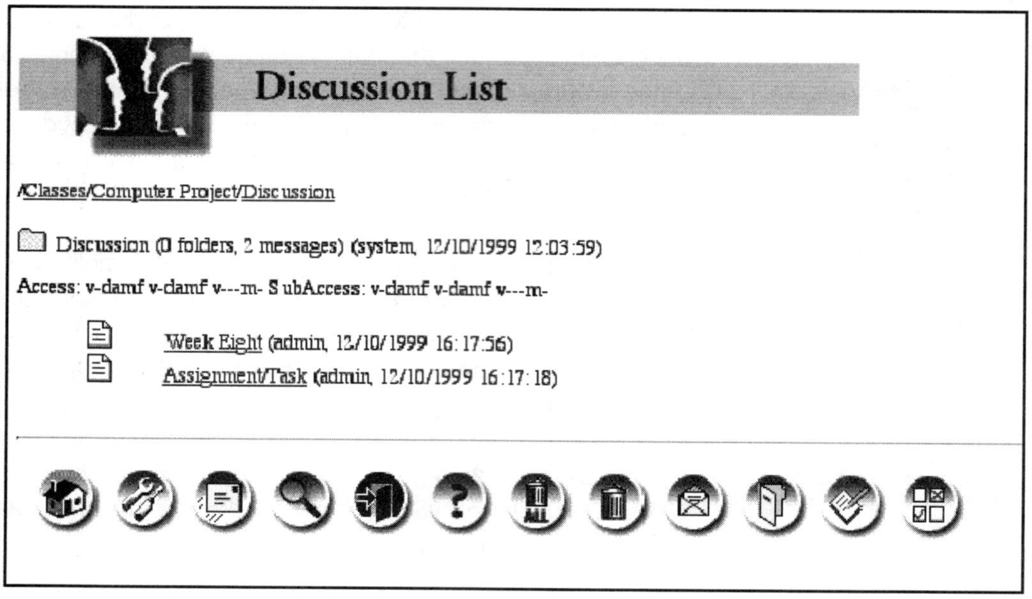

Figure 4.3 TopClass screen shot shows a posting to start a threaded discussion (Week Eight)

Videos of lectures can provide a convenient alternative for students but, like e-mail, it is an asynchronous communication. Students do not have the chance to ask questions of the lecturer, a situation that may also be true in most large lectures. The technology in this area is evolving very quickly and there are products being developed at the moment that will allow students to ask questions directly. However, if lectures are delivered without interaction, students should always be provided with some forum that allows them to clarify ideas and understandings constructed from the lecture.

The convenient way to do this with products like TopClass is through the e-mail feature or discussion list. Probably the best format is the discussion list, since it organises the questions automatically into topics (threads) and makes all questions publicly available for all other students. This is important because one student's question will likely be considered by other students as well. Preparation for a discussion can be made before the lecture by posting an e-mail to the discussion list to start the thread.

If the lecturer is aware of common topics of concern, each of these topics can form separated threaded discussions. The advantage of this threaded system is that the questions and answers can remain very readily available to students for revision purposes or to check growing understandings, and they are available if the lecture is ever repeated for review by students.

Video is not always necessary. In many cases, audio may be sufficient. For example, in one unit, we began to discuss the requirements for a forthcoming assignment. Distance education students were taking the same unit, and I surmised that they would also be asking similar questions. Using a normal audio recorder and external microphone, it was possible to record the students' questions and my answers. After digitising, this recording was mounted on a page in TopClass. It was then available for students throughout the remainder of the course.

It is possible with these technologies to stream not only speech but also music (in stereo), including live concerts and other forms that can be converted to digital format and played with appropriate software.

Video can be useful in situations that are difficult or dangerous to replicate for students, or for items that are too small or occur too quickly for students to see otherwise. It can also be used to tremendous advantage for distance education students by recording seminars of visiting fellows, special seminars, graduate presentations, and the like, provided copyright hurdles can be overcome. These can also be streamed live using the appropriate server software.

Text

The mounting of text onto pages in systems like TopClass is probably the most common method of delivering a Web course. These Web pages may contain administrative content or learning material, and are usually composed of a mixture of text and graphics. Text Web pages are almost always transmissive in nature; that is, they "transmit" to the student content that is deemed essential to the course. The unstated assumption is that the student who reads the pages will also learn the material, but constructivist approaches to learning tell us that more than passive reception is required to engender learning.

The careful design of Web pages is required to encourage participation and engagement. Learning is also encouraged by the thoughtful use of questions, discussion pages, and e-mail, and by requiring students to explicate their understanding. Authentic tasks can be effective for structuring all of the subsequent learning. These tasks mimic real world challenges and provide a focused context for student learning.

Unfortunately, platforms like TopClass, being mostly delivery mechanisms, do little to enhance interactivity in the pages presented. This means that it is not usually possible to accept student responses to presented pages; it is also usually not possible to give feedback or suggest future learning directions based on a response from a student. There are technical ways around this, mostly by constructing interactive learning material with programs like Director (Macromedia, 1999) and then using the specialist saving functions to save it as a Shockwave (Macromedia, 1999) file. This compresses the file and allows it to be delivered through a Web page; this means that it can be delivered through TopClass, providing access to ancillary functions like e-mail and discussion lists. Again, these pages must be carefully designed to encourage interactivity and learning.

Conclusion

I have discussed several practical ways in which a Web management tool such as TopClass can be used to assist lecturers to manage their courses over the Internet. Most lecturers will use systems such as these as entry points for the incorporation of the Internet into their teaching programmes. The successful use of these tools will depend, to a large extent, on their willingness to adapt to change, on their preparedness to take a risk with these new technologies, and, of course, on the availability of the technology. As lecturers begin to use these systems, they will encounter the very practical problems and issues addressed above, and they will also begin to address more fundamental issues. They will encounter instructional design challenges; and to meet these challenges, lecturers will need to reflect on their ideas about how people learn. University systems will need to be sensitive to this change process and provide appropriate support, from practical, technical help to expertise in instructional design and access to a range of pedagogical approaches upon which lecturers can model successful practice.

References

Ackerman, E. 1996. "Perspective Taking and Object Construction: Two Keys to Learning." Pp. 25–35 in *Constructionism in Practice: Designing, Thinking, and Learning in a Digital World*, eds. Y. Kafai and M. Resnick. New Jersey: Lawrence Earbaum Associates.

Apple Computer. 1999. *QuickTime*. (www.apple.com)

Archee, R., and A.H. Duin. 1995. "The Web and Distance Education: Convergence or Cacophony?" Paper presented at the AUUG '95 and Asia-Pacific Web '95 Conference and Exhibition, Sydney, Australia.

Baird, J.R., and J.R. Northfield. 1992. *Learning from the Peel Experience*. Melbourne: Monash University.

Brown, J.S., A. Collins, and P. Duguid. 1989. "Situated Cognition and the Culture of Learning." *Educational Researcher* 18(1), 32–41.

Dillenbourg, P., and D. Schneider. 1995. "Collaborative Learning and the Internet." (http://tecfa.unige.ch/tecfa/tecfa-research/CMC/colla/iccai95_1.html)

Duffy, T.M., and D.H. Jonassen. 1992. "Constructivism: New Implications for Instructional Technology." Pp. 1–16 in *Constructivism and the Technology of Instruction: a Conversation*, eds. T.M. Duffy and D.H. Jonassen. Hillsdale, New Jersey: Lawrence Erlbaum Associates, Inc.

Eklund, J., P. Brusilovski, and E. Schwartz. 1998. "A Study of Adaptive Link Annotation in Educational Hypermedia." In *Proceedings of ED-MEDIA/ED-TELECOM 98*, eds. Ottman and Tomek. Charlottesville: AACE.

Fetherston, T. 1998a. "A Socio-Cognitive Framework for Researching Learning with IMM." *Australian Journal of Educational Technology*.

Fetherston, T. 1998b. "Using Interactive Multimedia for Assessment." In *Proceedings of ED-MEDIA/ED-TELECOM 98*, eds. T. Ottmann and I. Tomek. Freiburg, Germany.

Fetherston, T. 1999. "Pedagogical Challenges for the Web." Presented at ED-MEDIA/ED-TELECOM 99. Seattle.

Horton, W. 1997. "Mew Media: An Assay for Managers." *Performance Improvement* March, 18–22.

Macromedia. 1999. *Macromedia Director*. Macromedia software.

Macromedia. 1999. *Shockwave*. (www.macromedia.com)

McKenzie, J. 1996. "Making Web Meaning." *Educational Leadership* 54(3) 30–32.

McMahon, M. 1997. "Social Constructivism and the World Wide Web: A Paradigm for Learning. (http://www.curtin.edu.au/conference/ASCILITE97/papers/Mcmahon/Mcmahon.html)

Noble, D.D. 1997. "The Overselling of Educational Technology." *Educational Leadership* 54(3) 18–23.

Real Products. 1999. *RealPlayer*. (www.real.com)

Real Products 1999. *RealProducer*. (www.real.com)

Shymansky, J., and W. Kyle. 1992. "Establishing a Reform Agenda: Critical Issues of Science Curriculum Reform." *Journal of Research in Science Teaching* 29(8), 749–778.

Smith, P.L., and T.J. Ragan. 1992. *Instructional Design*. New York: Macmillan.

Walker, R.A., and P.E. Lambert. 1996. "Designing Electronic Learning Environments to Support Communities of Learners: A Tertiary Application." (http://walkerr.edfac.usyd.edu.au/henresite/aare/AARE-paper-.html)

WBT Systems. 1998. *TopClass*. Dublin: WBT Systems.

CHAPTER 5

Appropriate Use of the Web in Teaching Higher Education

Terry Gandell, Cynthia Weston, Adam Finkelstein, and Laura Winer
McGill University
Canada

In this chapter, we propose two ways to consider the appropriateness of using the Web in teaching in higher education. First, we discuss the extent of use of the Web in terms of relevance to explicitly stated learning goals and impact on student learning. We begin with a concern for professors who have become disillusioned with technology because it hasn't had the impact they wished, or because the time and effort invested hasn't paid off in terms of student learning. By building on the work of others, and providing some new tools, we attempt to show that the time and effort invested in technology can pay off if the instruction is planned to capitalize on Web features that facilitate specific types of student learning. Thus, the significance of this chapter is distinguishing between intentional and appropriate use of the Web for achieving learning goals and other uses that may be nice but not necessarily required or appropriate for the desired student learning.

Appropriate Use of the Web in Teaching

Use of the World Wide Web is growing exponentially with each passing month (Datamonitor, 1999). Many students are benefiting from the Web and are requesting that it be used in courses (Brown, 1999). Some professors are feeling pressured by the administration, their colleagues, or their students to start incorporating new technologies into their teaching. This paper proposes a framework for the novice and experienced Web user in which features of the Web can be used to achieve different types of student learning.

Many professors put a tremendous amount of time and effort into developing Web pages or incorporating the Web into their teaching. It is not unusual for some professors to become disillusioned with the technology when it does not have the desired impact. In order to be worthwhile in terms of student learning, incorporation of the Web must be planned to capitalize on features that facilitate specific types of learning.

Using the Web in teaching means many things to many people. For some instructors, it means using a bulletin board to post information. For others, it means delivering an entire course via telecommunications. Some researchers have presented categories or classification systems for using the Web. For example, Harasim's (1995) classification of the use of the Web relates to the way instruction is delivered to the student; that is, online or mixed mode. Bates (1997) classified the Web by making analogies to traditional teaching strategies. For example, he compares postings to a lecture model, computer mediated communication to a seminar model, and CD-ROM simulations to problem solving. Laurillard (1993) categorizes features according to the type and function of the particular media: hypermedia, interactive media, adaptive media, and discursive media. For example, she describes interactive media as technology that permits students to interact with peers (for example, e-mail) or material (for example, databases), and adaptive media as technology that has the added capability to adapt or respond to a student's input (for example, a tutorial).

The two tools we present in our framework extend previous work by helping to distinguish two aspects of appropriate Web use that are important for understanding and successfully applying the Web in teaching in higher education. By "appropriate" we mean use of the Web that (a) has an impact on student learning, (b) is relevant to explicitly stated learning outcomes, and (c) is matched to the types of learning desired. We will begin by looking at the appropriateness in terms of two linked factors: impact and relevance. For example, a professor may use the Web in a way that has an impact on student learning in a general sense (learning to communicate via e-mail), but is not relevant to the learning outcomes of the specific course (the use of e-mail is not an explicit course learning goal nor is it evaluated). Once extent of use is determined, we then consider the appropriateness of specific features of the Web to types of learning. For example, a professor may use the Web in a way that is relevant to learning outcomes and explicitly stated, but is not matched to the types of learning desired and therefore is not likely to help students achieve the learning outcomes.

Extent of Appropriate Use of the Web

Extent of Web use can be described in terms of the impact it has on learning relevant to the course. We categorize extent of use according to the relevance and importance of learning goals appropriately addressed. Table 5.1 presents five categories that represent a continuum of extent of use: minimal, supplemental, integral, central, and exclusive.

Table 5.1 provides a tool professors might use when considering this relationship of extent use. Often professors use the Web as a value-added option, thinking that it will have an impact on student learning; however, upon consideration, they may discover that it has not been very useful. Examining the extent of use of the Web in terms of relevance and impact on student learning may ultimately save time, effort, and resources. The five categories are explored below.

> By **minimal**, we mean a use of the Web that is neither relevant nor necessary to achieve any explicitly stated course learning goals and therefore has no impact on course-related learning. The way in which the Web is used may still have an impact on non–course-specific student learning (for example, being able to post a course outline; or management/administrative tasks that provide convenience, such as electronic submission of assignments). However, these uses are not relevant to explicitly stated course learning goals and therefore, according to the categories presented, the extent of use is minimal for achieving student learning.

Table 5.1
Extent of appropriate use of the Web

Relevance to learning goals	Impact on achieving student learning goals
Minimal	none
Supplemental	not much
Integral	a fair amount
Central	quite a bit
Exclusive	a great deal

Supplemental use of the Web means use that is relevant but not necessary to achieve a few explicitly stated course goals; therefore, it would not have much impact on related student learning. Examples of supplemental use are providing online texts that can be downloaded and read off-line, or adding hot links to references that are additional but not required reading for the course.

Integral use of the Web means use that is relevant and contributes to achieving some of the learning goals in the course and thus could have a fair amount of impact on student learning. Examples include a group report following an online discussion on a given topic, which is part of the student's grade; or online practice quizzes with tutorials that help students review concepts covered in class.

Central use means Web use that is relevant and necessary to achieve most learning goals in the course, and the Web used in this way would have quite a bit of impact on student learning. Examples of central use include some course objectives that can only be achieved by using the Web, such as assignments requiring online collaboration or access to distant information sources such as online databases.

Exclusive use means that Web use is both relevant and necessary for achievement of all learning goals; the Web used in this way would therefore have a great deal of impact on student learning. An example of this is a distance education course conducted solely via the Web and not available in a face-to-face format.

Professors may find these categories to be a useful tool for determining the extent to which use of the Web currently addresses student learning and whether this matches their expectations. A professor with limited experience using technology may find it useful to begin using the Web in a minimal way and work toward using it in a more integral way, if this is appropriate for the learning goals of the course.

Professors are sometimes surprised to find that their use of the Web is less strongly linked to their learning goals than they imagined. They would like their use of the Web to more directly address their learning goals. If this is the case, the professor can decide which learning goals might be appropriately addressed using the Web and which Web features would best suit those learning goals. We turn to this in the next section.

Matching Features of the Web to Types of Learning

In addition to cultural and institutional pressures to increase the use of technology in teaching and learning, there are sound pedagogical reasons for using the Web in teaching. Most importantly, it offers excellent opportunities for students to actively engage in the learning task through interactive features such as online discussion, practice and feedback, and simulations, all of which enhance a student's ability to construct knowledge and consolidate learning (for example, McKeachie, 1994).

In the previous section we discussed appropriate use of the Web in terms of the impact and relevance to student learning. We will now explore the concept of appropriate use through matching types of learning to Web features, some of which facilitate active learning better than others. Figure 5.1 presents one way of thinking about the correspondence between features of the Web and their suitability to the types of student learning desired.

Second, we explored the match between Web features and types of student learning desired. Figure 5.1 provides another tool that might help professors assess the suitability of Web features for use in their teaching. Those features that provide mostly text and one-way communication (for example, content presentation) are most appropriate for gaining knowledge (for example, factual information). Those features that provide interaction with other participants in the teaching-learning process or with the content (for example, online discussion and simulations) are more appropriate for higher level learning, such as understanding and thinking.

Features

We use the term *features* to refer to Web capabilities that can be used as teaching strategies. The vertical axis of Figure 5.1 identifies six general features: content presentation; searchable information; information exchange; guidance, practice, and feedback; discussions; and simulations.

Content presentation is the capability of the Web to present static information; that is, one-way communication not intended for interaction. For example, some professors use bulletin boards and postings of course outlines, graphics, course notes, and references as a strategy for transmission of general information or facts when interaction is not necessarily required.

Searchable information is the capability of the Web to present libraries, databases, or collections of static information that can be explored using key words or other searching mechanisms to identify and select desired items. For example, professors often require students to search the ERIC database to find current articles relating to a specific topic. Another teaching strategy is to encourage students to search keywords of course notes to highlight the importance of particular themes throughout a course.

Information exchange is the capability of the Web to support unguided two-way synchronous or asynchronous communication. For example, professors may incorporate e-mail and chat rooms to allow students to ask questions of their professors or peers and to informally discuss topics of interest.

Figure 5.1
Matching Web features to types of student learning

Adapted from Cranton and Weston, 1986

→ Types of Learning / ↓ Features of the Web	KNOWING (e.g., memorize, list, define)	UNDERSTANDING (e.g., explain, identify, classify)	THINKING (e.g., analyze, evaluate, synthesize)
Content Presentation (e.g., course outline, course notes references, demos)	yes	maybe	no
Searchable Information (e.g., articles, journals)	yes	maybe	no
Information Exchange (e.g., e-mail)	yes	maybe	maybe
Guidance, Practice & Feedback (e.g., quizzes, self testing, exercises, Q&A)	yes	yes	yes
Discussions (e.g., on-line conferences, listserve, video-conferencing)	no	yes	yes
Simultations (e.g., interactive tutorials, models, labs)	no	maybe	yes

Guidance, practice, and feedback are the various ways in which a professor can guide students to actively engage in practicing skills and concepts while receiving an evaluation of some kind (for example, correct, incorrect, branching back to appropriate text, explanation, hint). For example, professors may insert questions within course notes to focus students' thinking and then, for comparison, provide students' responses from the previous year. They may also provide tests or quizzes that can be self-corrected or links to feedback describing why a particular answer was correct or incorrect. Another possibility is to provide hyperlinks from a student's incorrect answer to course notes, references, or posted material where this concept was originally discussed.

Discussion refers to a structured group online discussion or conference, usually mediated through text and/or video. We see two things that differentiate discussion from information exchange (the third feature, above). First, a discussion is more formal and structured; students usually need to join a conference and focus on defined topics. Second, discussion allows for multi-way synchronous or asynchronous communication; in other words, it supports discussion among many participants. Third, discussion may require a moderator to increase effectiveness. For example, professors may use a computer conference or online discussion group to provide a forum for students to interact with each other, exchange ideas, collaborate on projects, and discuss readings.

Simulations, in this context, are interactions with a computer program, where the student can act upon information provided by the computer, and the program can respond to information provided by the student with varying degrees of sophistication. For example, in a lab simulation students input a value for a given variable and the program responds by demonstrating the effect of their input (for example, results of blood levels based on the amount of anticoagulant administered virtually). A more sophisticated simulation might include an intelligent tutor that provides problem-solving opportunities and adapts to the level of student performance by varying the level of subsequent tasks (for example, if the patient blood levels become too thin, the program might branch to a review of that particular medication or to a problem solving exercise asking for diagnoses as to why the recommended dose was failing in this particular patient).

Types of Learning

The horizontal axis of Figure 5.1 presents three types of learning in the cognitive domain: knowing, understanding, and thinking (LaSere Erickson and Weltner Strommer, 1991). *Knowing* is defined as committing information and concepts to memory and being able to recall them when needed. *Understanding* is characterized by the ability to see relationships between specific instances and more general ideas or to name the concept exemplified in particular examples. *Thinking* requires transforming, combining, and creating beyond what currently exists, such as solving problems, drawing conclusions, making recommendations, and critiquing arguments.

Particular teaching strategies can facilitate achievement of certain types of learning (for example, McKeachie,1994; Weston and Cranton,1986). Weston and Cranton (1986) provide a matrix that analyses the relationship between traditional teaching methods and how they support different types of learning. For example, less interactive teaching strategies such as a lecture can be appropriate for conveying facts and basic information associated with the knowledge type of learning. More interactive strategies that actively engage students are required to facilitate higher levels of learning such as analysis and synthesis associated with thinking. Their analysis pre-dated Web-based teaching strategies; however, the relationship between instructional strategies and types of learning achieved applies equally to using the Web in teaching.

Correspondence of Features and Types of Learning

In Figure 5.1 the correspondence between features of the Web and the three types of learning is indicated in terms of appropriateness: usually appropriate, possibly appropriate, or not usually appropriate. It should be noted that these categories are not discrete, and the appropriateness must always be assessed in context. Three examples are presented.

Content presentation is usually an appropriate strategy for facilitating knowing because it easily presents factual information that you might expect students to memorize or acquire as background for further learning. It can be appropriate for facilitating understanding, depending on how the content presentation is used in the instruction; for example, where study questions are presented online and students use them to guide their reading. Content presentation is not usually an appropriate strategy for facilitating thinking because it is one-way communication that does not normally require the student to actively engage and apply the information being presented.

Discussion is usually an appropriate strategy for facilitating thinking (for example, analyzing, evaluating, synthesizing). For example, online discussion can provide the student with the active engagement and practice required to develop thinking skills. On the other hand, online discussion is not usually the most appropriate strategy for helping students to gain basic knowledge because discussion is not typically either efficient or effective for transmitting facts and encouraging memorization.

Online simulation is usually appropriate to help students develop thinking skills; for instance, when problem solving is required. It is not usually appropriate to develop knowledge, which can be more easily and efficiently developed with other traditional and online content presentation strategies.

There are two main points we would like to make about the above figure. First, as you move down the left side of the figure, from content presentation to simulation, the interactivity of the Web feature increases and therefore the potential for achieving higher levels of learning increases (compare Laurillard,1993).

Second, as you move down the left side of the figure, the time, effort and resources required to create and maintain the instruction also increases. Therefore, it is important to ask whether it is worth the time to create and maintain the instruction in terms of the type of learning you are trying to achieve. For example, putting a course outline on the Web requires some front-end time and limited amounts of time for maintenance, but has little impact on explicitly stated learning outcomes. On the other hand, online discussion requires a fair amount of time to structure and set up initially and can take a significant amount of time to monitor and maintain, depending on the role a professor chooses. However, online discussion can have a significant impact on learning when structured so that it is relevant to achieving course learning goals.

Summary

Use of the Web is growing exponentially and many students are benefiting from Web-based courses. At the same time, professors are feeling pressured to incorporate new technologies into their teaching. This chapter presented a framework for the novice and experienced Web user to help distinguish between intentional and appropriate use of the Web for achieving learning goals and other uses that may not be appropriate. Two ways of considering the appropriateness of the use of the Web in teaching in higher education were proposed. First, five categories were discussed to help determine the extent of use of the Web desired, in terms of relevance to explicitly stated learning goals and the impact on student learning. Second, we provided a tool to help determine the match between Web features and types of student learning desired. The classification and chart have been offered here as tools to help guide professors' thinking about how to use the Web more effectively in their teaching.

References

Bates, A.W. 1997. "Restructuring the University for Technological Change." Paper presented to the Carnegie Foundation for the Advancement of Teaching: What Kind of University?, Vancouver, British Columbia.

Brown, D.G. 1999. "83 Professors Assess the Impact of Technology on Learning." *Journal for Computer Enhanced Learning* 99 (1), 55–74.

Cranton, P., and C. Weston. 1986. "Developing the Instructional Strategy." Pp. 79–135 in *Planning Instruction for Adult Learners*. Toronto: Wall and Thompson.

Datamonitor, 1999. "Online Population to Top 300 Million by 2005." NUA Internet Surveys. (http://www.nua.ie/surveys/?f=VSandart_id=905354807andrel=true)

Harasim, L. 1995. *Learning Networks: A Field Guide to Teaching and Learning Online*. Cambridge, Massachusetts: MIT Press.

LaSere Erickson, B., and D. Weltner Strommer. 1991. *Teaching College Freshmen*. San Francisco, California: Jossey-Bass.

Laurillard, D. 1993. *Rethinking University Teaching: A Framework for the Effective Use of Educational Technology*. London: Routledge.

McKeachie, W.J. 1994. *Teaching Tips: Strategies, Research and Theory for College and University Teachers*. Lexington: D.C. Heath and Co.

Weston, C., and P.A. Cranton. 1986. "Selecting Instructional Strategies." *Journal of Higher Education* 57, 259–288.

CHAPTER 6

Toward the Webversity: Managing to Clone Scholars and Researchers via the Web

Gary Boyd
Concordia University
Canada

> Technology is, after all, the transformation of the world through thought, and as such essential and inescapable.
>
> —Israel Scheffler (1991)

Managing to clone our academic selves as scholars and researchers as well as innovative workers engaged in worldwide networks of communication and practice is the essence of our academic way of being in the world. This way of being and becoming is one which many of us believe to be one of the highest achievements of personkind. The academic and professional enterprise is an eternal widening and deepening, self-correcting, autopoietic conversation. Consequently, serious faculty will look at any attempts to reform higher education for greater cost-effectiveness in terms of how beneficial the changes are likely to be. Will innovative, reflective practitioners still be sent out into other walks of life? Will critical and creative scholars and researchers be cloned? It would be a tragic waste of our capabilities if we did nothing more than train and accredit various professionals. This is not, as it may appear to some, just a matter of elite versus mass interests. The interests of the masses can be well served by critically reflective practitioner-researchers if they share their findings with society at large. Also, as Antonio Gramsci insisted, the exploited need access to the most potent education that they can get if they are to overcome miserable situations.

Traditional technologies supporting the ongoing re-creation of our learning and teaching have included speech, writing, transport, money, printing, mail, and more recently radio, telephone, and television. Now with the Internet—and especially with the World Wide Web—we have a new global technology encompassing all of those older technologies. If we can manage it appropriately, the Web is capable of sustaining and enlarging the eternal conversation of scholarship, research, and innovative practice far beyond past dreams.

The Current Situation

The current situation is one where information and telecommunication technology has become cheap enough and ubiquitous enough to appreciably change the ways in which knowledge is developed and shared all over the planet. Since the Web appears cost-effective to governments, administrators, and corporations, so too, now for the twenty-first century, we in the universities are also being faced with the challenge of managing to clone our best scholar-researcher-practitioner selves and our research conversation communities via the Web. Some of us see this as a wonderful opportunity; others as an impossible proposition, or perhaps as merely a dreadful imposition, imposed by the global corpocracy and myopic, opportunistic politicians.

The Web is viewed as a major educational opportunity by the great technical and scientific societies such as the Institute of Electrical and Electronics Engineers (IEEE) http://www.ieee.org/; the Association for Computing Machinery (ACM) http://www.acm.org ; the American Psychological Association (APA) http:// www.apa.org/; the American Educational Research Association (AERA) http://www.aera.net/; and the Association for Education Communications and Technology (AECT) http://www.aect.org. These "Webscieties" are not only selling documents online but also conducting special-topic courses for their members. They are managing to clone some of their own researcher-engineer scholars online—in parallel, if not in competition, with universities.

Concerns

My main concern is the tragic failure that may result from success. Educational technologists have too frequently tended to assume that learners' reproduction of knowledge and skills (that is, the achievement of behavioural objectives, which can be easily measured) is what education is about. They (we) have sought cost-effective and efficient means to produce such objectively measurable results for as wide a range of learners as possible. This is not at all bad, as far as it goes. But it does not go very far toward scientific and epistemological progress. Such progress arises from propagating the "tacit knowledge" (Polanyi, 1958) and sophisticated mutually critical self-improving ways of being in the world together, which characterize excellent scholars and researchers, and knowledge-developing engineers, physicians, teachers, lawyers, and others. In 1973, I made a case for the re-creation of the university as a more transparent institution with its scholarly and research work as open as possible to the public, and especially to potential students, through electronic access. I also argued that initiation of scholars and researchers through critical dialogue should be protected and supported electronically. Not until people have exhibited serious work and commitment online should they be allowed to clutter up face-to-face seminars. And for those people who need hand-holding and live personal encouragement, perhaps this service could be provided informally and voluntarily by employers, friends, and family.

Others have realized that much has gone wrong with the evolution of higher education in the twentieth century (for example, Archer, 1984). Their prescriptions vary greatly across a spectrum, from "community of scholars" through Warfield's (1990–1999) "great university" to Sir John Daniel's "mega universities." Warfield's "Wandweaver" proposal (http://www.gmu.edu/departments/t-iasis/wandwaver/wandw.htm), for example, is particularly attractive from the standpoint of cloning scholar-researcher-innovator actors. In particular, "Horizon College" for progressive innovation separates the cloning of researchers and the generation of innovative knowledge into a new type of college, distinct from conventional standardized professional accredited instruction faculties.

More broadly, the concern is that meritocratic scholarly communities and research societies, often in conjunction with practising professionals, have evolved very fine and intellectually potent ways of learning collectively. This should not be lost just because cost-effective, accessible, basic professional training and accreditation have become higher priorities than the guardianship of our historic and evolving cultural, scientific, medical and engineering achievements. The life forms of "pure science" and "pure scholarship" are really (sometimes) very meaningful in sustaining both our desire and our ability to survive well and long together as the crew of spaceship Earth.

The Core Argument

"Ours the Task Eternal" is the motto of Carleton University, where I first was acquired by the academic way of life, and it nicely encapsulates the concern that most of us share for re-creating much more than mere facts and skills in our present and future generations of students. Most serious academics wish to clone onto their best students their way of being in the world as a scholar or researcher. This is a matter of passing on tacit knowledge as well as attitudes, commitments, and styles of enquiry and debate, not only delivering facts and skills. Our work is mostly the propagation of academic and professional "memeplexes" or "self-plexes." Ideally, what we should want to—and do need to—propagate is the evolving, "transvidual," distributed-processing memeplex of coherent and tested knowledge generation (science-ing) and using. But actually what we usually try to propagate is as much of our own personal self-plex (self as scholar-researcher-practitioner meme-complex) as possible.

We find it imperative to clone our academic selves for two reasons. The first reason is that all human beings quintessentially are evolved in an attempt to propagate large parts of not only merely our genetic identities, but also our psychocultural (memetic self-plex) identities via the young and other suitable humanimal hosts (Boyd, 1984). (Even many businoids are as interested in producing more businoid self-plexes as they are in acquiring monies.)

The second reason is that we want and need our best students to become participants in self-critical, empirically validated, transvidual learning conversations; that is to say, who we are, and who we want and need our best students to become.

In my view, the object of it all is to improve the viability and extend the coverage and creativity of scientosophic scholarship and research, which can be the best possible sort of loving human life form so far devised. For a good view of how something like this might be done, see Duchastel's work (1977).

How to Cybersystemically Manage the Scholar-Researcher-Practitioner Cloning Enterprise via the World Wide Web

Cloning scholar-researcher-practitioners via the Web is by no means impossible to manage, if the aspects to be cloned are chosen somewhat more abstractly and flexibly than some would wish. Indeed, if we are to realize the new global growth possibilities and opportunities for success opened up by the Web, then not only the academic personae/self-plexes but also teaching-learning actions and the social communion processes of the great research societies (Webscieties) and the universities have to be transformed a good deal. Some of the needed changes I will sketch here, based on my own understanding of the credibility, status, conjectures and refutations, knowledge development, games, leagues of science, and scholarship, and based upon my own online teaching experience and the literature. My prescription is also based upon fundamental cybersystemic "communicontrol" understandings.

The Eight Crucial Sets of Systemic Variables to Be Managed

What has to be co-managed on the Web to clone our academic selves? There are four paired sets of variables to be managed. These are illustrated schematically in Figure 6.1 and explained below.

I The evolving *goals* variables paired with…
II The *controls* variables (the means cannot be separated from the ends: the rules of the Relevant Credibility Status games and their enforcers).
III The participants' *psychostructure* variables paired with their…
IV *Sociostructure* variables (for example, who we are and how we interrelate over time in our Websciety).
V *Mathemata* variables (or stuff to be learned): ACKS = attitudes, Commitments, Knowledge Skills to be acquired/constructed, paired with the requisite variety of…
VI *Illustrata* variables (such as metaphors, narratives, images, working models, sample problems, simulations) needed to explain, illustrate, and help reconstruct, and internalize them.
VII The *media* variables (for example, signal to noise ratio, bandwidth, modality, reciprocity, speed, coverage) paired with the time-space and budget.
VIII *Context boundaries of accessibility* variables of the venture.

All of the important parameters and variables in each of these four paired sets of variables must be carefully considered and managed. They must be wisely chosen, courageously negotiated, continually monitored, and formatively evaluated on an ongoing basis to attain success in the scholar-researcher community cloning process on the Web. Let us look at each of these classes of variables in turn to see how they need to be specified to clone scholar-researcher-practitioners.

Managing Goals (I) and Needed Controls (II)

In general, what is required to manage the goals of cloning academic and reflective-practitioner-researcher personae and their life-world, is to arrange romantic portrayals and engaging performances that seduce enrollees to suspend their disbelief and lead them to becoming acolytes who unreservedly participate in practicing the new roles and new language and new ways of thinking for just long enough so that the new persona becomes added to their own stable. This may sound like dreadful indoctrination, and indeed it would be, were it not for the mutually critical, thoughtful conversation that is the central activity of this way of life.

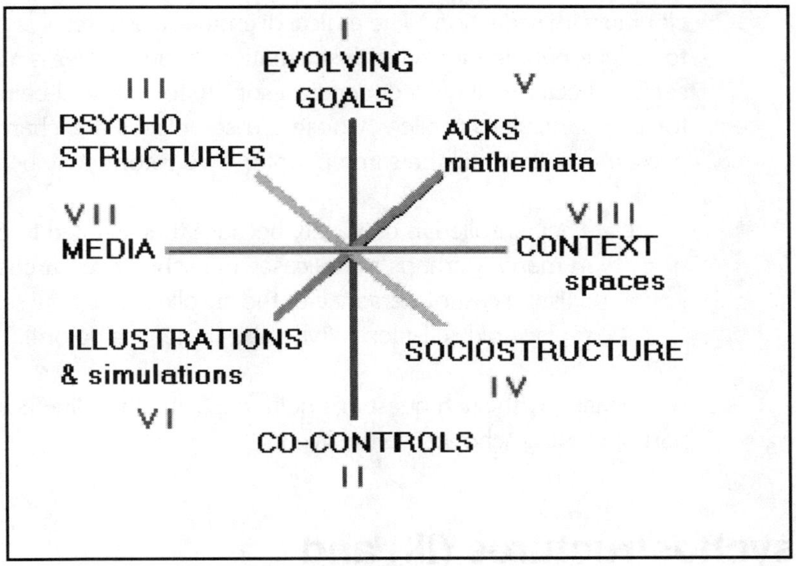

Figure 6.1 System variable classes (after H. Frank)

Parts of our academic heritage (for example, scholasticism) and many recent fads are bad; even evil (hope-destroying). Probably the worst thing is that teachers have secure, well-paid jobs that they cannot afford to leave despite the belief that they have no vocation for teaching, at least not for teaching bureaucratically assigned curricula to enrollees who cannot possibly be made to embody the parts of their once academic/professional selves which they most valued and once hoped to clone.

Then too, many scholars and researchers have strangely mutated to meet fashionable respectability (for example, postmodern or quantitative). For the first half of the twentieth century, psychologists devolved into rigorous behaviourism and are only now mutating into cognitivism. Historians and geographers disciplined themselves quantitatively to become social scientists; political economists split their mindset into those of political scientist and econometrician. ("Anything which calls itself a 'science' is not!") Antiquarian conservators and appreciators of literature aspired to deconstructionist fashion. Arguably, none of these self-plexes should be cloned.

Managing Cloning Through Negotiation?

Why not manage cloning by just negotiating with the enrollees to commit their time to becoming scholar-researcher professionals? This can be, and is, done. But it does not work as rationally or ethically as one might think. Until they have experienced the new way of being in the world they cannot knowledgeably decide whether they want it or not. There is no substitute for the experience of immersion. Afterward, the new ways can be knowledgeably rejected if they don't satisfy. However, scholar-researcher self-plexes are different from most others that people acquire because a central part of their ways of being in the world is (ideally) the habit of skeptical criticism of anything that might seduce and addict us.

Can we honestly manage to use romance and intellectual seduction to induce people to become rational skeptics? Can we indoctrinate people to be immune to indoctrination? Well, yes, perhaps we can, and do, and have done so since Socrates. Should we manage cloning with seduction? The ethical dilemmas are unresolved. Is it even ethical or moral to seduce people into self-transformation? One answer is Yes, if the result is good for society, because all of us depend on society for our well-being. But how can it be good for the particular enrollees whose old self-plexes are changed into real student self-plexes? Are they still the same people? Two retorts may be made:

1. They enrolled in university because they wanted to be changed.
2. In many, perhaps most, cases the scholar-researcher self-plex is added to the existing cast of personae of the enrollee. The new self-plex does not kill off and replace old self-plexes (who she or he was before).

Dealing with such questions quite explicitly in online conversation is an important part of cloning scholars via the Web.

Selecting Psychostructures (III) and Managing Sociostructures (IV)

In selecting psychostructures, as Biggs (1978) and Entwistle (1988) have established, higher-education students (in a given course at least) may be fairly categorized as functioning as either: personal meaning (deep) seekers, reproductive (surface) learners, or grades-game players (intent on getting a good grade by any means). At first glance one might think that only the deep learners are suitable carriers for cloning academic ways of being. However, many academics, scholars, and researchers (at least by title) are not driven by deep curiosity and reverence for knowledge, but are mainly reproducers of facts, techniques, and academic language, or are game players. For them, perhaps even the reproductive surface learners and gamesters have potential for self-plex cloning.

Managing sociostructures for scholar cloning at the macro level is best achieved by the great scientific and professional societies such as The Royal Society (TRS). At the micro level in universities and Webversities, managing sociostructure is a matter of appropriate selection of study-group members. If you allow or encourage self-selection of partners or debate-team members, this may set up a barrier against learning new ways of being in the world because those who know each other will reinforce old habits. One big advantage of the Webversity is that fewer students are already settled into relationships with one another. I have found over ten years of teaching with computer-mediated conferencing (CMC) that trios and even quartets are preferable to dyads because of the vulnerability of dyads when one member drops off-line, as frequently happens. Also, there is more likely to be a requisite variety of complementary personae, perspectives, and skills in trios or quartets, say, than in dyads. With students of similar age and background, larger groups than four should be avoided (given our existing tools) because the pervasive "normal" peer cohort way of life is more likely to dominate and exclude the scholar-researcher way of life. Small groups can and should be feeding into larger conferences of groups with varied perspectives and skills.

ACKS/Mathemata (V) and Illustrata (VI)

The essential attitudes of scholars and researchers include the following: (1) curiosity; (2) reverence for the ongoing scientosophic mutually critical learning conversations and for those who seriously pursue them; an attitude of openness to correction, and of openness to re-framings and re-naming, in the light of new tools, facts, arguments, and needs is crucial; (3) the most essential commitment is one of high quality attention-time; a few hours a day for one's lifetime will do!; (4) the knowledge to be acquired depends on the state of knowledge in the field, and the entry knowledge profile of the learner; the skills to be acquired similarly depend on the state of the art and entry-level skills of the learners; however, metacognitive skills for managing learning conversations with oneself and others are of great importance.

Media (VII) and Context (VIII): Environment—Managing to Have the Essential Media, Essential Space, and Place

Regarding the use of appropriate media, Webversity and Webscicty application software is needed. These media should be designed to support discourse that promotes Habermasian ideal nondominative understanding (Boyd, 1987; Habermas, 1985). Habermas demonstrates that in order for communication to promote understanding, five conditions must be met:

1. Serious intent;
2. Respect for the moral and ethical norms of the community;
3. Factual correctness;
4. Logical, or at least rationally, plausibly correct reasoning;
5. Exclusion of threats and promises (including stylistic threats and aesthetically seductive intimations); critical whistle blowing must be encouraged and protected.

To Habermas' desiderata I would add the prerequisites of good signal-to-noise ratios and ways of ensuring the classical Greek virtue of moderation. Flame wars and spammings are educatively unproductive. Pseudonymity and the ability to delay and censor, on the one hand, and the potential to appeal to a higher court on the other, are easy to provide only through computer-mediated communications, and make CMC the best, if not the only, possible medium for Habermasian ideal discourse. However, at present I know of no CMC/Webversity system with the kind of intelligent agents, stratified levels of discourse, and discourse-access arbiters that are required to achieve the ideal. Nevertheless, at modest cost, these capabilities could be added to any good Webversity application such as SAVIE (http://www.savie.qc.ca/), Virtual-U (http://virtual-.cs.sfu.ca/), FirstClass (http://wwwfirstclass.com) or Web-CT (http://www.webct.com/). Moreover, we need Webversity/Webscicty applications designed as helpful guides (paths), gracious and dignified "virtual places," and indeed as producers, since the co-evolution of tools is necessary to the evolution of knowledge.

The most important class of producers are learner-modifiable modelling workbenches (for example, applications such as the University of Colorado AgentSheets Simulation Construction Toolkit (http://www.agentsheets.com/behavior-exchange.html); the dynamic simulation modelling tool, or Stella (http://www.hps-inc.com). The Webversity needs to become—or to affiliate with businesses to become—the application software provider (ASP) for such producer applications for all of its students.

I have suggested that a desirable, if not absolutely necessary, complement to our work on the Web would be a regular (but not actually on the Web at all) place and time for traditional ritual/liturgical academic celebrations. Since we learn with our viscera and our noses and our dancing marching bodies, not just with our brains, these B-2-B-2-B (body-to-body-to-building) events could even include public parades. The celebrations could be held at traditionally appropriate local places around the world, such as campiversities outside regular semester times. Such gatherings and celebrations are needed not only for the romance, to sustain the desire, but also to give the local publics opportunities to feel that the great knowledge enterprise belongs to them too. A world university day, perhaps called "WUNDAY," would be a good idea. WUNDAY would be a day for parading together students and faculty from the heritage campiversities as well as those of the new Webversities. The summer schools of the U.K. Open University, which provide hands-on and B-2-B laboratory and workshop experiences, also seem to be a very desirable if not an indispensable component for cloning proto-researchers. (However, as far as I know, they do not as yet involve parades and public celebrations in the various venues or Milton Keynes.)

Conclusion

My general conclusion is that inclusive, equitable, progressive re-creation—not cloning—of academic scholar-researchers and reflective professionals probably can be done, and should be done, via the Web, but only when the Web is augmented with some intensive face-to-face group work at frequent occasions. It should be done because it can ameliorate life. There is so much wasted time and effort and misbegotten misery arising among both students and faculty. Some new source for hope is essential in our frequently overcrowded, underfunded colleges and universities. New avenues of opportunity are needed for the many young would-be scholars and researchers who cannot arrange the time or funding to attend colleges and laboratories, and who need new avenues of opportunity. Of course, much more developmental research is required to ensure that re-creating (let us now more accurately and responsibly say "re-creating" rather than "cloning") the new scholar-researcher, through Webversity ventures, constitutes an improvement for all stakeholders. Universities not only should, but must, live in a symbiotic relationship with government and business, as well as, of course, religious and ethnic collectives and should also contribute in many ways to helping the three billion people on Earth who live on less than two dollars per day.

References

Archer M.S., ed. 1984. *The Sociology of Educational Expansion*. Cupertino, California: Sage (ISA Book Series).

Biggs, J.B. 1978. "Individual and Group Differences in Study Processes. *British Journal of Educational Psychology* 48, 266–279.

Boyd, G.M. 1973. "Educational Technology and the Re-Creation of the University." *McGill Journal of Education* 8(2), 169–175.

Boyd, G.M. 1984. "Autonomy, Intervention and Selective Self-Reproduction." Pp. 547–551 in the Proceedings of the Society for General Systems Research Conference, New York.

Boyd, G.M. 1987. "Emancipative Educational Technology." *Canadian Journal of Educational Communications* 16(2), 168–173.

Boyd, G.M. 1993. "Educating Symbiotic P-Individuals Through Multi-level Conversations." *Systems Research* 10, 113–128.

Boyd, G.M. 1993. "Home Page" (http://alcor.concordia.ca/~boydg/drboyd.html)

Blackmore, S. 1999. *The Meme Machine*. Oxford: Oxford Univ. Press.

Bruffee, K.A. 1999. *Collaborative Learning* (2nd edition). Baltimore: Johns Hopkins University Press.

Cude, W. 1987. *The Ph.D. Trap*. WestBay, Nova Scotia: Medicine Label Press.

Duchastel, P. 1997. "A Web-Based Model for University Instruction." *Journal of Educational Technology Systems* 25(3), 221–228.

Entwistle, N. 1988. *Styles of Learning and Teaching*. London: David Fulton Publishers.

Frank, H. 1969. *Kybernetik Grundlagen der Padagogik*. Baden Baden: Agis Verlag.

Frye, N. 1976. "The University and Personal Life." Chapter 2 in *Spiritus Mundi: Essays on Literature Myth and Society*. Toronto: Fitzhenry and Whiteside.

Grint, K. 1997. *Fuzzy Management: Contemporary Ideas and Practices at Work*. Oxford: Oxford University Press.

Habermas, J. 1985. *The Theory of Communicative Action*. Boston: Beacon Press.

Halsey, A.H. 1984. "Who Owns the Universities?" *New Society* 68(1119), 177–190.

Halsey, A.H., and M.A. Trow. 1971. *The British Academics*. London: Faber and Faber.

Haskins, C.H. 1923. *The Rise of the Universities*. Ithaca, New York: Cornell University Press.

Polanyi, M. 1958. *Personal Knowledge*. Chicago: University of Chicago Press.

Scheffler, I. 1991. *In Praise of the Cognitive Emotions*. New York: Routledge.

Tether D.C.B., ed. 1982. *Towards the Community University: Case Studies of Innovation and Community Service*. London: Kogan Page.

Warfield, J.N. 1990. "Cybernetics, Systems Science, and the Great University." *Systems Research* 7(4), 287–294.

Warfield, J.N. 1992. "Some Magnificent Academic Trusels and Their Social Consequences." Prepared for presentation at the Annual Meeting of the Association for Integrative Studies, Pomona, California, November 19–22. (http://www.gmu.edu/departments/t-iasis/paper/p3.htm)

Warfield, J.N. 1999. "The Wandwaver Solution: Creating the Great University." (http://www.gmu.edu/departments/t-iasis/wandwaver/wandw.htm)

Part B

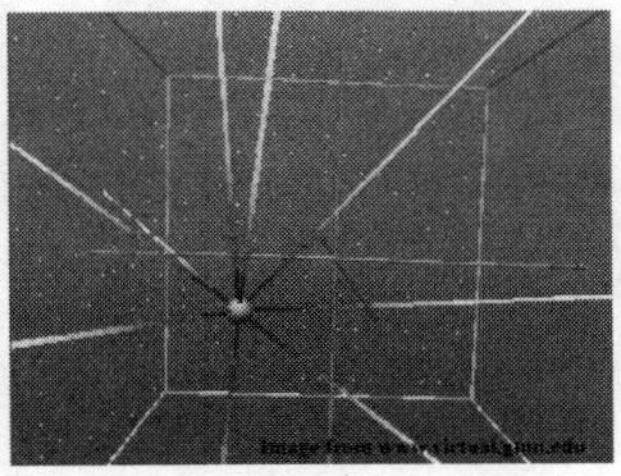

Web Course Ownership

CHAPTER 7

Why Didn't the Walls Come Tumbling Down? An Outsider's View of Online Distance Education

Richard Seltzer
Internet Consultant
U.S.A.

Back in October 1993, when the first Web browsers became generally available, it looked like the Internet would change everything. And visions of paradise danced in our heads. In the arena of education, we expected the following to happen:

- Internet-style sharing on a larger scale;
- Vast amounts of information immediately available for free to anyone, anywhere;
- Students and teachers connecting with one another, teaching one another regardless of institutional walls and geography;
- Courses of all kinds available online to anyone, anywhere.

In brief, we would have

- Libraries without walls
- Schools without walls
- Walls without walls

The teaching profession would be changed.

Lectures and class discussions—important spontaneous aspects of education—would be captured, saved, and searchable; that key question, that key insight that comes unexpectedly as teachers and students interact. You would no longer have to count on the note-taking skills of students to capture and preserve the insights of a Socrates or a Richard Feynman. The volume of educational content would expand enormously.

Publication and, hence, reputation and tenure would no longer remain in the hands of a few commercial publishers who get their content for free from professors seeking reputation and tenure; who sell subscriptions at enormous prices to college libraries; and who take forever to produce their print publications, slowing the pace of research.

Professors would become like consultants, available for assignments—at competitive prices—from several different institutions at the same time.

Where Are We Now?

Now, six years later, what actually happened? Yes, there has been some progress:

- Many courses and degree programs are available online.
- New institutions that focus on distance learning flourish.
- Sometimes you can get credit at one institution for courses taken at others.
- There are much richer offerings for continuing education.

But six years is an eternity on the Internet, and I, for one, was hoping for more. While some resources are available for free to anyone, many institutions limit access to their faculty and paying students. Yes, many courses are available online, but for the most part, institutions continue to offer courses that are meant to mimic old-style education—with credit hours and degrees. And they still typically serve up learning in large-size semester or quarter-long chunks. And students in one class still typically have little interaction with students in others, much less with students from other institutions.

A lot of interaction takes place online instead of in physical classrooms and, hence, it could be readily captured, preserved, made searchable. But for the most part, the content is not valued. It is treated as transient and disposable. Chat transcripts are not preserved. There is no audio or video archive.

A number of official refereed journals have migrated to or been started on the Web. The Internet is used for pre-publication comment and spreading the word about research before print publication. But change has come slowly. And the traditional publications—whether distributed in print or electronically—still command a high level of respect and are still tied into the tenure process.

Work completed for distance learning is considered "teaching" not "publication." Therefore, the more time you devote to developing and delivering online courses and perfecting the art of doing that well, the less time you have left for activities that would help you get tenure.

While they don't value this material for purposes of tenure, many schools claim ownership ("work for hire") of the class materials that their teachers create for online learning. Not only can you not make that material available to the general public, but furthermore, when you leave the school, you can't deliver that course anymore. Contracts of many schools prevent you from teaching online courses for any other institution.

What happened (or what didn't happen)?

As usual, we see an enormous gap between what's technologically possible and what actually happens; a gap between what you see in labs, on the news, and in trade shows, and in what becomes widely adopted and changes how we learn and work and live. It's the age-old gap between the possible and the real. Consider these statements:

- Only what people actually use will change how we learn and work and live.
- Technology stimulates the imagination.
- Marketing changes the world.

What Are the Barriers to Change in Distance Education?

There are static barriers to change—the human barriers of habit, regulations, and industry practice (including "standard" contracts). There are also dynamic barriers—they are the cost barriers: where technology drives down costs, which opens business opportunities; business drives volume, which drives costs far lower, which opens new opportunities. The human barriers to change in distance education are normal, natural, essential elements of everyday reality. You may love to teach, but you don't teach just for the love of it. You need income and security and predictability. You need to be able to build a stable career and help put food on the table for yourself and your family.

Education is a business, not a charity. It depends on tuition fees, salaries, and contracts. How people value the work, and the cost they are willing to pay, depend on accreditation, course credits, degree programs. And career advancement and security depend on systems of rewards and recognition, with promotions and tenure. There's a lot of inertia there, a lot of resistance to change, and that's not a bad thing. Just don't expect miracles; don't expect radical change from schools that in many ways still closely resemble the Renaissance institutions they are descended from.

But while the human barriers are static, the cost barriers are dynamic. And thanks to the combination of technology and business, change is coming to education—just not as fast as folks like me might have dreamed of. As an example, let's look at audio/video storage costs. Six years ago storage cost was prohibitively high for large-scale archiving of audio and video. My dream of saving lectures and even class discussions didn't make economic sense. And, of course, back then, you couldn't easily search audio and video files, as you can today.

But thanks to advances in technology, the cost has been declining rapidly. Now the possibilities are becoming very interesting. That new PC you are tempted to buy probably has more than 10 gigabytes of storage. And business factors are likely to accelerate the rate of change. For instance, digital storage is becoming so cheap that over the next few years it's likely to replace videotape for saving and retrieving television programs in the home. We already see ads for such units that sell for about $500. If such an application takes off, the increased volumes could drive down the price of consumer-quality disk drives in general (like the use of transistors in portable radios drove down the price of transistors back in the 1950s.) Very soon, what sounded utopian will begin to be practical.

So what's the next-generation audio/video opportunity? We'll see increasing bandwidth on campus with gigabit Ethernet. Bandwidth for remote students will also increase, with DSL (digital subscriber line) and cable replacing dial-up. Searchable digital audio and video based on voice recognition (as Virage does today) will become commonplace. Chat applications will automatically save transcripts, organize them in threads of discussion, and embed them in forums for further discussion (as SiteScape does today). We'll see opportunities to integrate audio/video content with text—to make it all searchable, and to make it easy for us to comment on.

Meanwhile, not-so-formal education— continuing education—is flourishing on the Web, where the goal is to learn something useful and practical, rather than to earn a degree, tenure, or to publish on the Web or in academic journals; and where the focus is on tutoring, mentoring, expertise, and learning styles.

Expert Web Sites

Recently, several companies launched "expert" sites on the Web. Part of their rationale is that people can't find answers with search engines. This is due in large part to the fact that people new to the Internet don't know how to use search engines, and don't know about the other free resources available on the Internet and how to get the most out of them. And they come to the Internet with the expectation that you have to pay to get quality information.

Companies are setting up databases that match up the people with questions and the people who have the knowledge and experience to answer them. This is an interesting alternative model for learning and for earning.

If your contract prohibits you from teaching distance education courses for other educational institutions, does it prohibit you from private tutoring? Probably not. Does it prohibit you from consulting? Probably not. Does it even foresee the possibility of you getting paid for providing answers, information, and instruction online in small chunks, to random customers? Probably not. Following are some recent startups:

> **Tutor.com** provides Web-based referral services for "supplemental education." Basically, they run a matching service for physical-world, face-to-face tutoring.
>
> **EXP.com** (formerly known as Advoco) allows visitors to post questions and advisors to respond describing their service and proposing a schedule and cost. For now, the company seems designed for business-related questions that require significant effort to answer.
>
> At **Inforocket.com**, visitors post questions, and people with answers bid for the opportunity to answer it. The questioner picks the winner and pays when an acceptable answer is delivered on time.
>
> **ExpertCentral.com** handles questions of all kinds, many for free, matching people who have questions with experts who should have answers. The experts decide on a case-to-case basis whether to charge and how much to charge.

These businesses all go to the heart of the Internet experience—connecting people to people, rather than documents to documents. This is another way of learning, another way of teaching, in a very informal context; one step beyond newsgroups, e-mail distribution lists, and bulletin board forums.

Today, well-established Web-based services strive to help you find the place to find the people with answers, who are willing to share their expertise in the old pre-Web Internet style. **Deja.com** does this for newsgroups, **Liszt.com** for distribution lists, and **Forum One** for forums. These startups provide the place with the experts and answers; they do not just point you somewhere else. These startups are geared to Internet newcomers, for users who

- Don't know how to use search engines;
- Don't know about or understand free Internet services;
- Distrust the value and quality of anything that is free.

And you thought that commerce might corrupt the Internet style of sharing? You thought it was crass to ask for payment? Believe it or not, in many cases, these people would rather pay. They'll value the answers more if they have to pay for them.

Where Is Online Distance Education Headed?

So where does this take us? I see a new utopia in the works—a more practical, doable vision of where distance education is headed. I see an emphasis of matching people to people for learning and earning, in the style of these startups. Databases will help match people with people as the basis for paid online tutor and mentor services, without institutional boundaries.

So try out those new sites and maybe make a few dollars today, while you figure out how to adapt that model to be effective for education. And spread the word—make sure your department head signs up as an expert, too. That's your best insurance against the creation of new restrictive policies and contract terms; get the decision makers involved on a personal basis, and self-interest will work on your side.

At the same time, I hope and expect to see more reciprocal agreements to expand academic sharing. We have plenty of examples of grassroots sharing over the Internet: documents freely published on the Web, e-mail distribution lists (DEOS) and newsgroups, Global Learn Day, MOO-based classrooms.

Course material, courses themselves, and class-style access to professors are typically limited to students of a particular institution. Is that truly necessary? Or is it a matter of inertia? Consider interlibrary loan programs as an example of how institutions can share their intellectual property for the benefit of all. Why not negotiate similar reciprocal agreements for sharing distance learning resources and even people? This could include course materials, controlled access to particular teachers as online guest lecturers, plus audio/video of lectures and class discussions.

Let's imagine that costs drop to the point where it becomes relatively inexpensive to save lectures and course discussions in audio and maybe video form and to make those digital files searchable. Then give millions of students around the world the right to search in this way and to access the files that match. Demand from a single institution would probably not be enough to justify the effort—who aside from the students in the class would be interested? Yes, it would help those who couldn't attend that particular lecture. Yes, it would make it easier to review for exams, even without notes of the lectures. But that's still providing information for very few people per gigabyte or even terabyte of storage. But when those files might be accessed by students from other institutions, the equation changes. This would allow people the opportunity to save, index, and share spontaneous educational content: transient Web content such as chat; transient classroom content such as the lecture that is delivered from rough notes; and the unexpected classroom exchange.

We also can expect to see more alternatives to traditional publishing: not only will traditional paper text be placed on the Web, but the Web will also be treated as a different medium entirely, and it will be used differently. Remember that copyright covers the particular expression of your ideas, not the ideas themselves. So in learning to adapt ideas to a new medium new opportunities are opening up for selling your writing. Your college may have locked up the copyright on your online teaching materials "work for hire." But you may be paid for different expressions of those same thoughts. As an example of this direction, take a look at **Learnlots.com**. They are repackaging tutorial content for the Web, in easily digestible pieces called "learnlets"—little chunks of instruction that take no more than a few minutes to read and absorb; and interrelated in series.

Meanwhile, we need to institutionalize and reward Web-based academic functions. Much of the work that is necessary for the success of a distance education program is not valued at all by the administration today. It's work that you are supposed to just fit in somehow. The things you do to make your course easily accessible over the Web, the time you put in for online interaction with students, the research to track down and make accessible useful online resources, is just taken for granted. Print publication counts toward tenure. Online activities count for zilch.

The people who perform important functions to create Web-based instruction should be given important titles and be paid commensurate with the value of what they do; they should also have their workloads adjusted so that they can give these activities the right kind of attention.

Consider the model of **About.com** (formerly The Mining Company). Their guides organize resources relating to a particular subject, and answer questions, and in the process they build personal reputation. Imagine formalizing such a role within a department. The online guide for molecular biophysics at your school might help your school develop an international reputation in that field by serving as a guide not just for your school, but also for students and faculty elsewhere. Consider also the example of **iSyndicate.com**, which distributes Web content (for a price) across a variety of commercial Web sites. The writer gets paid. And the Web sites get content that their visitors are interested in.

Why not syndicate course modules in a similar way? Not entire courses—that would be more a distance education clearinghouse kind of operation, such as Western Governance. Rather, syndicate one lecture or a few interrelated lectures, or even discrete elements of a single lecture or class experience. Imagine that you as a teacher or administrator are trying to put together all the pieces you need for a distance education class. You could search the Web content to find pieces that you need to complete or enhance a course you plan to offer. Or if you are a creative distance education teacher, you could have your materials and your time (as guest lecturer) offered in this mode.

In this case, you would probably be prevented by contract from listing your own material and your own services as an individual and from being paid as an individual. But your institution might want to list you, and you would be paid for your work and your services, or would qualify for reciprocal benefits from the other institution. Suddenly distance education ceases to be just another form of teaching that, strangely, most colleges have never valued. Rather it becomes a way to enhance the reputation of the institution and the department and to generate new revenue or other benefits for them.

You might think of this scheme as "educational outsourcing." You can mix and match to build/enhance an online course: focus on what you do best and outsource the rest. At the same time, your college offers your services in this mode, with prices determined by demand, which depends on reputation. Then the quality of your teaching becomes a source of additional revenue for your institution, and your cross-institutional work builds your reputation and that of your institution/department. Over time, distance education gradually becomes a key factor in tenure decisions.

Summary

Very interesting opportunities are opening up—opportunities that could greatly change how people teach and learn, and how they are paid for their teaching. It will take a lot of creativity and effort on the part of many people to make this practical utopia a reality—but it can be done. Spread the word and help change the world.

CHAPTER 8

Legal Perspectives in Web Course Management

André Durette
Laurentian University
Canada

This chapter is concerned with the legal aspects of Web-based education. The work is presented from a Canadian perspective, though readers are inevitably referred to several American sources. The author attempts to provide practical information for institutions offering courses over the Web, while also addressing some fundamental questions about the administration of such courses.

This paper does not present an exhaustive statement of the law on the topics it touches upon. Readers should seek legal opinions from counsel from their respective jurisdictions on any specific questions of law.

Introduction

Much has been written on the legal aspects of the Web. One notices very early on when reviewing these materials, however, that until legislative and judicial developments catch up, there will continue to be a level of uncertainty in this area. Making matters worse, not every jurisdiction treats the law related to cyberspace uniformly, making it hazardous to rely on judicial pronouncements or legislative acts made outside one's borders. Trying to fully understand the repercussions of the transnational aspects of exchanging information over the Internet can therefore overwhelm Web-course managers, faculty, students, and university administrators alike.

Copyright

Although many people remember the beginning of the Web infiltrating our daily lives, the oldest among us cannot remember a world devoid of copyright. Copyright laws have certainly developed over time and they vary among jurisdictions. In an attempt to keep up with the technology, amendments or entirely new statutes are either being newly introduced or newly applied and interpreted to deal with the ever-increasing power of the Internet. Yet, despite the novelty of mass digital exchange, anyone sufficiently familiar with the Web who takes a conservative, common sense approach to traditional copyright can generally keep to the right side of the law. Those who insist on testing the limits of copyright on the Web, however, face a multitude of challenges and must revisit issues that were once settled in the pre-Internet world.

Online Course Ownership

The Web brings more than just technical questions to the management of online courses. Universities might ask themselves more fundamental questions. How, for instance, should the traditional university activities be balanced against the opening of the new educational markets through online courses? Suddenly, geographic barriers matter less to the business of education, and colleagues, within and among universities, can increasingly become either partners or competitors in new ventures. The traditional educational market, though not necessarily larger, is becoming more fluid. The technology increases the capacity for entrepreneurial faculty and universities to offer courses to new or nontraditional markets, and also to further compete for existing markets. This new activity is at least partially economic in nature, and where there is money involved, there inevitably follows the potential for dispute: Who owns or controls the intellectual capital (the ability to develop courses offered over the Web) and the revenue from these new activities? The ability to offer courses on the Web is therefore applying new pressures for shaping the rights and roles of faculty and universities.

What Is Copyright and How Does It Relate to Courses Offered on the Web?

A Bundle of Exclusive Rights

Simply put, a copyright owner has a bundle of exclusive rights, and anyone who purports to exercise one of those rights regarding a work without the copyright owner's consent is infringing that copyright. The bundle of rights provided by the *Copyright Act* that relates to Web courses includes the following rights:

1. To produce or reproduce the work or any substantial part thereof in any material form (s. 3(1));
2. To perform the work or any substantial part thereof in public, where merely communicating to the public by means of telecommunication is not alone deemed to be a performance (ss. 3(1) and 2.3);
3. To publish an unpublished work or any substantial part thereof, where publication means, among others, making copies of a work available to the public (ss. 3(1) and 2.2(1)(a));
4. To produce, reproduce, perform or publish any translation of a work (s. 3(1)(a));
5. To convert a dramatic work into a novel or other non-dramatic work (s. 3(1)(b));
6. To convert a novel, another non-dramatic work or an artistic work into a dramatic work, by way of performance in public or otherwise (s. 3(1)(c));
7. To make any sound recording, cinematographic film or other contrivance of a literary, dramatic or musical work by means of which it may be mechanically reproduced or performed (s. 3(1)(d)). Presumably such "contrivance" includes digital media files;

8. To reproduce, adapt and publicly present any literary, dramatic, musical or artistic work as a cinematographic work, where such a work presumably includes digital media files (ss. 3(1)(e) and s. 2, definition of "cinematographic work");
9. To communicate any literary, dramatic, musical or artistic work to the public by telecommunication (s. 3(1)(f));
10. To present an artistic work created after June 7, 1988, other than a map, chart or plan, at a public exhibition, for a purpose other than sale or hire of the work (3(1)(g)). This provision is generally meant to ensure that no one displays an art work at, say, an art exhibition, without first securing the permission of the artist. The exception for sale or hire is created so that an art dealer authorized to deal with a work need not obtain the artist's permission to display the work for that purpose (For Web courses, one could envisage an artist's or author's right being infringed should a Web course containing an art work be delivered or displayed in a public environment, such as perhaps a university open-house or a trade show.);
11. To rent out a computer program or a sound recording in which a musical work is embodied (ss. 3(1)(h) and (i)). (This might be important if a course is rented out with the underlying software needed to drive it.);
12. To authorize any of the above (s. 3(1)).

In a nutshell, if a person does not own copyright in a work or if he or she does not have the permission from the copyright owner, then that person cannot perform any of the above activities with the work without infringing the copyright, subject to the exceptions described below.

Subsection 3(1)(f), the *communication by telecommunication provision*, is probably the most important provision for Web courses. The act of communicating, under the *Copyright Act*, excludes merely acting as a conduit for such communication by providing the equipment necessary for another person to communicate (s. 2.4(1)(b)). The services of Internet service providers or of any other person or corporation that provides the hardware, software, and generally all Internet and intranet means for such communication is therefore likely excluded from the *Copyright Act* in this limited respect.

Subsection 3(1)(f) talks about communications made "to the public." No one today will seriously contest that making material available over the World Wide Web without restriction amounts to anything less than communication made to the public. One might propose, however, that a Web course is not normally delivered to the general public, but only to a limited and known subset of the public—that is, students enrolled in the course—as enforced by password-secured access. Though Canadian judicial pronouncements are scarce on this point, the Federal Court of Appeal has stated that telecommunication is made to the public if it is made openly and without concealment to a sufficiently large number of persons (*Canadian Cable*, 1993). Unfortunately, no Canadian court has apparently specified the minimum number of persons required. Therefore, the matter remains uncertain (Racicot, Hayes, Szibbo, and Trudel, 1997).

Interestingly, the North American Free Trade Agreement (NAFTA) has an intellectual property provision defining "public" as follows (art. 1721(1)):

> ...any aggregation of individuals intended to be the object of, and capable of perceiving, communications or performances of works, regardless

> of whether they can do so at the same or different times or in the same or different places, provided that such an aggregation is larger than a family and its immediate circle of acquaintances or is not a group comprising a limited number of individuals having similarly close ties that has not been formed for the principal purpose of receiving such performances and communications of works.

Though the *Copyright Act* has not been amended to incorporate this NAFTA provision, it has been suggested that this definition would nevertheless be persuasive in a Canadian court (Racicot et al., 1997). Thus, the Web course manager is advised to treat courses offered to even a very small number of persons as if it was offered to the public for the purpose of setting policy to avoid infringement. The fullest extension of this argument would be to treat a course offered to a single person as communication to the public for the purpose of identifying possible copyright issues.

Also, one should note that special exceptions are made for educational institutions and that these exceptions do not appear to cover Web courses. Legislators have considered educational exceptions when they made amendments related to them, and as Racicot et al. suggest, those exceptions were intended to be exhaustive. At minimum, the educational exceptions fail to cover Web courses, and these Web courses therefore do not benefit from any enhanced exemption beyond what is clearly stated in the *Copyright Act*. The conclusion for Web course managers is that all such courses should be treated as vehicles for potential copyright infringement. This conclusion is consistent with similar conclusions drawn for bulletin board systems, a close kin to Web courses (Racicot et al., 1997).

How Does Copyright Arise?

For copyright to arise, one need only be a Canadian or a citizen of any of a number of countries having signed applicable treaties, and to have authored an original work that is fixed—for example, printed on paper, recorded onto a CD, or stored on a computer's hard drive (Kratz, 1998). Although it can be useful to do so, it is not necessary to file any registration or to affix any formal notice in order for copyright to arise in Canada (*Berne Convention*, art. 5(2)).

Registration of copyright with the Canadian Intellectual Property office (CIPO) is optional, although it is an inexpensive and advisable measure since it provides evidence of copyright ownership (*Copyright Act*, s. 53) as well as a rebuttable presumption of copyright (*Circle Film Enterprises Inc. v. C.B.C.*, 1959). The application for registration may be downloaded from the CIPO Website at http://strategis.ic.gc.ca/sc_mrksv/cipo/.

Affixing a notice of copyright—for example, © year of first publication, copyright owner's name—prominently on a work (for example, on the title or welcome page of a Web course) provides an additional optional tool for claiming copyright over a work. No registration is required before placing the notice, so the notice in the above format should be affixed to works as a matter of practice. This notice is not required for protection of copyright within countries that have signed the Berne Convention (over a hundred countries, including Canada, most if not all of Europe, Australia, and the United States). The notice is mandatory, however, for protection in the very few countries that have not signed the Berne Convention, but that have signed the Universal Copyright Convention (UCC). In addition, inserting the notice helps to remind users of copyrighted material that the Web is not a medium without rules, and that thoughtlessly copying material may attract liability.

Canadian authors and publishers should be aware that first or simultaneous publication of a work in the United States, where simultaneous means within ninety days of publication in Canada, may cause the work to be considered an American domestic work for the purpose of copyright protection in that country (*Copyright Act* (U.S.), ss. 101 and 104). This result would mean that reliance on the Berne Convention for automatic protection without formalities might not be enough, and that the copyright owner would need to comply with the more complex U.S. copyright procedures in order to secure protection (Kratz, 1998).

Copyright generally ends on December 31 of the year that is fifty years after the death of the work's author. In the case of joint authors, the time starts running after the death of the last surviving author. There are other special provisions for timing, but fifty years from the date of first creation of the work is the shortest term of protection (*Copyright Act*, ss. 6–12).

Moral Rights

The *Copyright Act* provides certain rights termed "moral rights" for the author of a work (ss. 14.1 and 28.2). Moral rights generally last as long as the copyright. What makes moral rights special, however, is that they can only be vested in the author, regardless of who owns the copyright.

Generally, moral rights include the right of integrity of the work, meaning that the work cannot be distorted or mutilated to harm the reputation or honour of its author. The work should also not be used in association with any product, service, cause, or institution where such association would have a negative effect on the author's reputation. Another basic moral right is the right to be associated with a work by name or by pseudonym, or alternatively, the right to remain anonymous, at the author's option. Moral rights are therefore meant to enhance or protect the reputation of authors, even where copyright has been contracted away from them. These rights are very real and must be observed.

It is impossible to sell or give moral rights to another, but an author's waiver of any or all such rights is enforceable under normal circumstances. Wherever possible, it is therefore in the interest of the owner of the copyright (if other than the author) to negotiate a waiver of all or most moral rights by all authors in order to maximize the flexibility for the use of the work. The converse is true for the authors, in that they may wish to retain moral rights in order to exercise some limited control over the use of the work after contracting away copyright. (Authors would rarely agree to waive the right of being recognised as the author of a work.)

International Protection

Canada has signed a number of treaties that extend copyright to authors from numerous other countries in exchange for the protection of the copyright of Canadians in those countries. For instance, the WIPO Copyright Treaty (1996) deals with the strengthening of copyright protection in a digital environment. The treaty compels members of the World Intellectual Property Organization (WIPO) to protect works made available to the public by telecommunication. The WIPO treaty updates the Berne Convention, which provides reciprocity of copyright protection without the requirement of formalities between signatory countries. Under NAFTA, Canada, the United States, and Mexico must adhere to the Berne Convention (art. 1701(2)(a) and (b)). The U.S. has therefore signed onto the Berne Convention effective in 1989, ensuring uniform copyright protection for Canadians in that important market.

Copyright Infringement

Web course managers should consider infringement of copyright in two contexts: infringement of copyright in the Web course by third parties and, conversely, infringement by the Web course of any third party's copyright.

External vs. Internal Rights

A well-developed Web course might encompass many types of content, each of which may be subject to its own peculiar copyright issues. There are often many contributors, and each individual contribution may or may not have copyright attached to it, or capable of attaching to it, prior to finding its way into the Web course. The entire course—that is, the entire portion that can be experienced by students—should be treated as a single whole for the purpose of claiming copyright against the rest of the world. If it is the intention to eventually break the course up into discrete units that may or may not remain associated with the original whole, then any such unit should also be reviewed for individual copyright capacity and ownership.

A distinction must be drawn for the management of copyright between the owner of the Web course and the rest of the world; and between the owner of the Web course and the owner/creator of its individual contributions. Authors of individual parts of the Web course whose individual contributions amount to copyrightable material may have copyright and moral rights (described above) in these contributions. Also, contributing authors may wish to use parts or all of the works of other external authors as part of their contribution to the Web course. This could be as "apparently" insignificant as borrowing an icon.

The Web course manager should ensure that contributors disclose what portions, if any, of their contributions are not original, and also whether any third party has any rights over any of the material. (For example, if a work was published elsewhere, the publisher of that work often owns the copyright in the work.) Except for material that is clearly covered by the fair dealing (fair use in the U.S.) or other defence to copyright infringement (see below), any material in which third parties may have rights must be covered by adequate contracts, licences, permissions, or assignments with the respective copyright owners covering all applicable rights before the Web course is "published." Similarly, the rights in all of the original works contributed directly must be captured in contracts and assignments with the respective authors. In some cases, such as professional Web course developers, their employment or consulting contract will hopefully cover this issue. The Web course manager should ensure that this is the case, and if possible, he or she should keep a copy of any such contract on file and review it periodically to ensure it continues to meet current needs.

Exceptions

For Web courses, there are two main types of exceptions (uses that do not infringe copyright) that are of most interest. The first exception, fair dealing, is universal and therefore applies to everyone. The second exception applies only to educational institutions of all levels in Canada, as well as to a select group of nonprofit organizations.

Fair Dealing

The *Copyright Act* provides that activities for the purpose of research or private study do not infringe copyright (s. 29). Of some relevance also to Web courses is the exception for criticism or review. This type of exception has the minimal onus of providing the source and generally the name of the author of the work (s. 29.1). These few lines of the *Copyright Act* have been supplemented with some judicial interpretation of the otherwise rather vague words "fair dealing."

As a starting point, *Zamacois v. Douville and Marchand* (1943) tells us that the copying of an entire work, in that case a newspaper article, is not fair dealing. A much less intuitive result came from the *Breen v. Hancock House Publishers Ltd.* (1985) decision, where the Federal Court held that copying twenty to thirty pages of a thesis by the author's professor into the latter's own work was also not fair dealing, despite the fact that the copied work represented a small fraction of an otherwise extensive original work. As a result, it is likely accurate to state that Canadian courts have found the fair dealing exception to be rather narrow. After all, the "rationale for the exception is to permit limited private use or quotation of a copyright work provided that such use does not compete with the interest of the copyright owner" (Racicot et al., 1997, p. 285), as has just been done in this sentence.

Some attempt has been made to introduce an American doctrine into Canada, being the parody defence. Some defendants in infringement suits would like to import the doctrine into Canada's criticism exception. In other words, the defendant pleads that he or she copied significant portions of a copyright work in order to criticize through the medium of parody or satire. This was attempted in the *Michelin v. C.A.W.* (*Cie Generale*, 1996) case, where the Michelin Tire Company took offence to the Canadian Auto Workers Union's organizing leaflet, which featured a smiling Michelin Tire Man stomping on a worker. The court in that decision did not recognize the parody defence, and found that the union had infringed Michelin's copyright in its logo.

Contrast the *Productions Avanti Ciné-vidéo Inc. v. Favreau* (1997) decision of the Québec Superior Court, a few months after the Michelin decision. The Québec court accepted the parody doctrine when it allowed its use by a defendant alleged to have infringed the copyright in the plaintiff's television program series. The defendant had produced an erotic parody version of the program.

A Web course manager would be well advised not to rely on parody as a fair dealing defence under the criticism heading until further judicial pronouncements clarify the matter.

A recent and helpful general pronouncement on the use of fair dealing comes from *Allen v. Toronto Star Newspapers Ltd.* (1997). In that case, the copying of a magazine cover was held to be fair dealing based on a purposive approach. Instead of restricting itself to a mechanical calculation of the extent to which the allegedly infringing work copies from the original, the court looked at the purpose of the copying. In that case, the copy essentially supported a story on current news, a purpose that was held to be different from the purpose of the original work. Though the case is mentioned here as a general help for understanding fair dealing, the reader should nevertheless use this precedent cautiously since the exception relates to news reporting, which now forms its own separate category of fair dealing. Also, the fair dealing aspect was not the only reason given for dismissing the case, and might even have played a secondary role in the decision.

Use of the extensive American precedents applying the fair use defence is of little assistance in Canada (*Cie Generale*, 1996). The full extent of the defence of fair dealing law is therefore not known.

Exceptions for Educational Institutions

The educational institution exceptions of the *Copyright Act* impose the condition that the excepted activity must not be carried out for gain, although cost recovery is allowed (s. 29.3(1) and (2)).

Subsection 29.4(1)(a) allows handwritten reproduction of copyrighted material, such as on blackboards. Some daring person might try to argue before a judge that this exception should permit the use of "smart" boards that allow the digitization of handwritten dry erase board notes, or scanned flip chart notes, or again of a digital pen that allows one to record freehand writing. This argument can be made, but its success is dubious, and a Web course manager would be advised not to rely on this exception unless a court decision supports it or unless the section is amended accordingly. In any event, this exception is restricted to use on the premises of the institution, and therefore it could likely only be applied to a Web course that is offered over a local intranet only; that is, of course, subject to an institution convincing a judge that the school exists in cyberspace, and that therefore the premises are wherever the student is logged in.

Subsection 29.4(1)(b) is a little more useful for Web courses, in that it permits the copying of material for projection with an overhead projector "or similar device." Whether it is too much of a stretch to say that a scanned image embedded into a Web course is a projection of that one authorized copy, one cannot say for certain. There is a fairly strong negative argument in that multiple copies are made when more than one student views the image at once. Also, a plain reading of the section suggests that the legislators probably did not contemplate digital copies, though this factor alone is not necessarily fatal. It might be appropriate to work around this problem by having the Web course software programmed to prevent access to any unlicensed copyright work by more than one student at a time. This is not a certainty, nor has it been judicially tested to this author's knowledge. Besides, there is here the same problem about the use being restricted to the institutional premises. The lowest-risk advice remains that only authorized (licensed or permitted) material should be displayed in the Web course.

Subsection 29.4(2) is the "reproduction for examination" provision. This exception specifically addresses the use of telecommunication for communicating an unauthorized work without infringement, provided that it is required for a test or examination. Unfortunately, the limitation says clearly that the copy must be located on the premises of the institution, thereby eliminating any off-campus use. The specific language in this subsection, compared to the lack of mention of telecommunication in the earlier sections, casts a doubt to stretching the interpretation of subsections 29.4(1)(a) and (b) to cover Web courses. Still, there does not appear to be a binding decision on this point.

As if trying to use the above exceptions with a Web course was not challenging enough, subsection 29.4(3) is an exception to the exceptions found in s. 29.4(1)(b)—copying for projection—and s. 29.4(2)—examinations. It appears that if a work that would avoid having to use these exceptions for copying is commercially available, then the exceptions are not available to avoid infringement. For example, if you needed to copy an image from paper to acetate or to a digital medium for use on a projector, and if that same or equivalent image is commercially available already on the desired medium, then making the copy yourself is now an infringement (no longer excepted).

Section 2 defines "commercially available" as follows:

> in relation to a work or other subject matter
>
> (a) available on the Canadian market within a reasonable time and for a reasonable price and may be located with reasonable effort, or
>
> (b) for which a licence to reproduce, perform in public or communicate to the public by telecommunication is available from a collective society within a reasonable time and for a reasonable price and may be located with reasonable effort.

The reader is given no guidance as to what "reasonable" means, but presumably this will be determined by circumstances and common sense, as decided by a judge if necessary.

Other Exceptions

A Web course manager is encouraged to look at all of the exceptions to infringement if he or she is ever required to offer a course where not all of the contents are authorized for telecommunication to the public. These exceptions to infringement can be found from s. 29 to s. 32.2 of the *Copyright Act*.

One of those additional exceptions warrants a mention here: the "incidental inclusion" exception found at s. 30.7. This is a general exception that applies to anyone. This exception forgives the incidental inclusion of copyright work into another work without authorization. The trouble with this exception is that it cannot be used deliberately. This exception is therefore not a planning tool, but might be a defence for an innocent mistake. A prudent Web course manager should hopefully never find him- or herself in a position of clinging to this section after the fact in the hope of escaping liability in an infringement action. Reckless or willful blind inclusion will not likely be viewed as incidental.

Remedies for Infringement of Copyright or Moral Rights

The infringement of copyright and moral rights may both be remedied in civil court by the use of injunctions: to stop the infringement, damages; to pay for losses incurred by the plaintiff resulting from the infringement, and accounts; for the defendant to disgorge moneys unjustly earned as a result of the infringement (*Copyright Act*, s. 34).

Two new sections of the *Copyright Act* have come into force October 1, 1999, and these add a radical twist to infringement actions. Statutory damages are now available (s. 38.1). These range between $200 and $500 where the court is satisfied that the defendant was unaware of the infringement, and otherwise between $500 and $20 000, "as the court considers just." Statutory damages remove the arduous task of proving damages or of the forensic evidence required for an accounting. The factors to consider in determining the amount within the range that the defendant should be made to pay are not related to the amount of money made or lost, but rather to the good or bad faith of the defendant, to the conduct of the parties during the court procedures, and to the need to deter others from infringing copyright. There is also authority to order less than the minimum amount in special cases where the statutory damages are grossly disproportionate to the infringement. Also, collective societies, such as CANCOPY, can only access a modified version of statutory damages where the range is between three and ten times the unpaid royalties. In both cases, exemplary damages may still be awarded over and above ordinary damages as before.

Section 38.2, also newly in force, effectively eliminates statutory damages exposure for educational institutions, libraries, archives, and museums and limits awards instead to the amount of royalties that the institution should have paid to an authorized collective, or an amount determined by tariff. In either case, this damage amount only applies where the collective society is authorized, or the tariff provides for the payment of royalties, for a work of the category that was infringed, and copying of that general nature and extent is covered by the society collective's agreement or the tariff. It appears that if the type of work is not covered by a collective or tariff or the type of copying is not ordinary, then the educational institution may face either statutory damages exposure or else ordinary damage assessment, depending on how these new provisions are interpreted. It is therefore in the Web course manager's interest to remain abreast of what types of works and copying the collective societies are authorized to deal with. In any event, knowing this is essential since any gap in coverage by these collective societies requires direct licensing from copyright owners or, where these are not known, from the Copyright Board.

The last type of remedies is found under the criminal provisions in ss. 42 and 43 of the *Copyright Act*. Rather than benefit an aggrieved copyright owner directly, these remedies deter infringement through the threat of fines and imprisonment.

Who Typically Owns the Copyright in the Web Course?

Why even ask the question? Traditionally, ownership of the materials necessary to offer a course was rarely questioned. Faculty would normally produce their own materials for the courses they teach in class. They then typically interpret these materials to offer lectures and run seminars, adapting their offering to the general flow of the course as it progresses. Now, however, the Web makes it feasible for a person or a group of persons to develop a course that can be offered over the Web at any time by a person not at all involved in the course development. In effect, a Web course can be a stand-alone product, with varying amounts of student-instructor interaction possible. Even if universities attempt to retain traditional values in education, there is no doubt that the ability to break down a program into modules or courses that can be purchased from internal or external professional course developers has the potential to bring commercial issues and franchise values into university education.

The Case of Arthur Miller

Arthur Miller might be considered a "legal celebrity." He has had regular public exposure for twenty years through television appearances on "Good Morning America" and "Court TV" among others, as well as in numerous newspaper columns (Leigh Bureau, 1999). He has also served (or is serving) as Commissioner, United States Commission on New Technological Uses of Copyrighted Works. A professor at Harvard since 1971, teaching copyright law and civil procedure, among other courses, Miller is also the Co-Director of Harvard's Berkman Center for Internet and Society. The latter centre offers online courses, some of which are intended for current or future consumption by law students (Johnson, 1999).

Miller is at the centre of a controversy over the ownership of intellectual capital as it relates to online courses. According to the *Wall Street Journal*, he has videotaped some lectures specifically for use by the Concord University School of Law, an online university, to offer a civil procedure course (Marcus, 1999). Harvard, meanwhile, reportedly leases to other universities a CD-ROM version of a civil procedure course offered by Miller. Harvard, according to the same article, wants Miller to end his arrangement with Concord.

Apparently, Harvard's policies do not permit professors to teach at other institutions during the academic year. Miller seems to have gotten around this by taping his lectures over the summer break (Marcus, 1999). He also apparently has no interaction with the students at Concord, making it difficult for Harvard to claim that he is actively teaching there. A Concord student confirmed this point:

> Prof. Miller does not interact directly with the students at Concord. We cannot e-mail him, call him on the phone or ask him questions. Nor does he ask specific questions of any particular student. To my knowledge he does not know our names or even the number of students who are hearing his lecture. He does not provide us with tests nor does he grade us. (Komito, 1999)

Concord's courses normally allow interaction between professors and students through online discussion forums (Johnson, 1999). The different mode of presentation in Miller's case is presumably rooted in the restrictions imposed by his contract with Harvard. The incentive for Concord to accommodate such limits arguably stems from Miller's very high profile, being a draw for attracting students. In other words, Concord may be gambling that the disadvantage of offering Miller's course in a noninteractive (at least with Miller) format will be offset by the additional students drawn to the school by the public and professional reputation of this distinguished lecturer. Concord certainly took pains to advertise Miller's role as lecturer and as a member of the school's board of faculty advisers (Wilson, 1999).

No doubt, Harvard wishes to reap benefits from its investment in and affiliation with Miller. (Of course, Miller has undoubtedly benefited from this relationship as well.) Though this may not be Harvard's intention, Johnson (1999) has suggested that technological developments might tempt "[p]restigious law schools [to] use the technology to establish classroom-free 'branches,' forcing many schools out of existence."

This writer is not suggesting that Miller, Concord, or Harvard is acting improperly or with less than honourable motives. The point belaboured here is that these parties each have valid economic interests at stake, and that the proven intellectual capital that Miller represents is the subject of overlapping and potentially conflicting claims. Miller, who probably understands the issues better than most, identifies the key question as follows: "[H]ow much of Arthur Miller does Harvard own?" (Marcus, 1999).

The writer expands on the question to ask, "How much of Arthur Miller can anyone own, control, assign, licence, waive, pledge, or promise to stakeholders?" The question can undoubtedly be answered in as many ways as there are ways to manage traditional university intellectual capital.

Works for Hire

The *Copyright Act* provides in s. 13(1) that the author of a work is the first owner in the copyright. If, however, the author created the work under a contract of service or apprenticeship, and if the work was made in the course of employment, then it is the employer who is the first owner of the copyright unless there is an agreement that sets out differently (s. 13(3)).

The courts have interpreted the relationship between a person and an employer on numerous occasions to try to determine whether a person is hired under a contract *of* service (an employee) or a contract *for* service (an independent contractor). If the author fits under the latter category, then he or she may claim that the work was not created in the course of employment under a contract of service, and that therefore the author retains the copyright, possibly with an implied limited licence in favour of the employer. Though there is no single test for determining whether a person has a contract for or of service, several factors are usually weighed together. These factors include the following (Copyright—Employment Situations, 1999, § 76):

1. Direct control by the employer in the manner and method of work;
2. The degree of independence of the worker;
3. The location where the work is created;
4. The obligation on the part of the individual to obey orders;
5. Whether creating the work is an integral part of the business of the employer or merely an accessory to such business;
6. Whether the person was performing the work as a person in business on his or her own account.

Such determinations can be cumbersome. In the case of Web courses, these factors may play differently on different team members in the production of any single course, leading to some perceived inequities in copyright ownership between contributors.

The best means of alleviating at least some of the uncertainty caused by such determination is to take advantage of the provision in the *Copyright Act* that the parties may determine by agreement who will own the copyright (s. 13(3)). No matter if the creators and authors of a Web course are employees or contractors, the rights to copyright may be negotiated and reduced to writing. It is important that a clear determination of ownership be made from the outset of the project.

Universities and colleges may find it expedient to ensure standardized treatment of copyright and moral rights by negotiating faculty collective agreements that clearly state those respective rights. Similarly, standardized contracts should be developed that deal with these same rights for outside contractors (or for faculty acting as freelance contractors, where this relationship is carefully defined), where, by default, copyright would otherwise vest in the creator of the work (Kratz, 1998).

From the Arthur Miller case above, readers will immediately recognize that for both courses created as part of a faculty's employment and for courses created by freelance contractors, more than copyright should be settled. Universities should consider specifically including or excluding the following rights as well:

- All moral rights;
- The right (by either the institution or the course designer) to sell or licence the work to outside parties, and the right of the use of the author's and/or institution's name and logo by the end user; and
- The right to deal separately with identifiable portions of the course, for sale or licence as modules or for incorporation into other courses. In such cases, each discrete such portion should be capable of copyright on its own, and the rights to each such portion should be clear as if such portion was an entire work unto itself.

Models of Ownership

Universities will normally want to own their online courses in order to maximize stability in their course offerings. It would not be appropriate, for instance, to have an author/faculty member leave the institution and take away with him or her a course whose offering was already promised. This argument is similar to that made for any distance education course. This contingency, however, can be controlled through the careful administration of well-drafted contracts. Of course, outright ownership is easier to administer.

The other main argument for course ownership by universities lies in the ability to sell licences to other institutions. Should the faculty member have retained this right, then there is nothing that would prevent the faculty member from selling his or her courseware to "competing" universities. Notably, in the Miller case above, even if Harvard owns the courses Miller teaches at Harvard, it apparently lacks the power to prevent him from creating separate courses that are not specifically offered at Harvard. Perhaps a noncompetition clause in Miller's employment contract would have saved Harvard this difficulty, though it is a matter for interpretation whether such a clause is consistent with academic freedom.

The arguments for ownership of copyright in Web courses by faculty are almost a mirror image of the arguments for ownership by the university. Copyright ownership is not required, however, for faculty/authors to retain moral rights, as mentioned above. Thus the faculty member continues to enjoy recognition for the course's creation even without ownership, unless he or she granted a specific waiver. Also, copyright ownership is not required to enjoy economic benefits such as a share of royalties, provided that a distribution scheme is contracted with the university. Outright ownership of copyright, of course, gives the faculty/author more control and bargaining power at the outset.

Ultimately, this writer believes that there will be several different models developed at different universities for online course management, tailored to the various priorities of the respective institutions. The model suitable to each institution will likely depend on such factors as the importance of Web-based instruction as a core program and the bargaining power of faculty.

A university that puts little value on online education will not likely wish to expend resources on their administration, and may be content to let faculty/authors act as free agents in this respect. In exchange, the success of any online course developed by faculty, whether or not offered through their resident university, would potentially improve the university's reputation.

A university that values online education as a core service (present or future), will likely want to develop a portfolio of copyrighted courses, likely to be managed by a dedicated administration. Such administration might be provided through a converted or expanded distance education department, possibly in conjunction with the technology transfer department if third party sales are anticipated as a core activity. Such universities will likely favour commissioned course development with full intellectual property rights assigned to the university. Course development could be provided in-house or else it could be outsourced.

The Arthur Miller case suggests, however, that no matter what the university's policy might be, individual faculty members' bargaining power might force concessions on the part of the university. Also, universities may lose a competitive edge in retaining its highest-quality faculty if they attempt to contract away too many rights from them. In the end, many faculty will likely retain the ability to sell their privately developed courseware to their resident university or to outside interests, though direct competition with the university might be subject to challenge.

Universities that make online programs a priority might consider hiring dedicated in-house or external courseware developers who control or support the course creation process sufficiently to warrant retaining copyright institutionally. (Faculty might not mind the extra support either.)

Another possibility is that, provided the collective bargaining process is not overly rigid, two alternate streams of faculty might emerge:

1. Those who develop online courses and wish to retain copyright, but who are willing to give something up or will offer some added value in return;
2. Those who wish to pursue traditional-style functions mainly, but who wish to be able to get something in return for contributing to Web courses, to the exclusion of copyright or control.

Parting Words

It is difficult to encapsulate the full effects of online courses to copyright law. The law is still evolving, and will likely surprise a few people as it does so. Meanwhile, universities and faculty must make decisions in order to adapt the technology to their programs in an orderly fashion. While inordinate caution may paralyze development, all parties involved should tread carefully through the morass of issues involved in the transition to education on the Web. In a perfect world, one might expect open dialogue between all stakeholders to help resolve this process. In reality, the Arthur Millers of the world might force the stakeholders to catch up and deal with the issues on the run.

References

Allen v. Toronto Star Newspapers Ltd. 1997. 78 C.P.R. (3d) 115 (Ont. Div. Ct.), rev'g (1995) 63 C.P.R. (3d) 517 (Gen. Div.).

Berne Convention for the Protection of Literary and Artistic Works. 1886, last revised 1971, last amended 1979. (http://www.wipo.org/eng/iplex/wo_ber0_.htm)

Breen v. Hancock House Publishers Ltd. 1985, 6 C.P.R. (3d) 433 (F.C.T.D.).

Canadian Cable Television Assn. v. Canada (Copyright Board). 1993. 46 C.P.R. (3d) 359 (F.C.A.).

Cie Generale des Etablissements Michelin-Michelin and Cie v. C.A.W.-Canada. 1996. 71 C.P.R. (3d) 348 (F.C.T.D.).

Circle Film Enterprises Inc. v. C.B.C. 1959. S.C.R. 602.

Copyright Act. 2000. 17 U.S.C. (U.S.A.) (http://www.loc.gov/copyright/title17/)

Copyright Act, R.S.C. 1985. c. C-42. (Canada).

"Copyright—Employment Situations." 1999. *Canadian Encyclopedic Digest 3rd Edition on CD-ROM.* Scarborough: Carswell.

Johnson, S.M. 1999. "www.lawschool.edu: Legal Education in the Digital Age." (http://merlin.law.mercer.edu/elaw/future.htm)

Komito, E. 1999. "Jurist." (http://jurist.law.pitt.edu/colloq.htm)

Kratz, M.P.J. 1998. *Canada's Intellectual Property Law in a Nutshell.* Scarborough: Thompson Professional Publishing.

Leigh Bureau. 1999. "Arthur Miller: Man in the Middle." Leigh Bureau's Speakers of Substance. (http://www.leighbureau.com/speakers/Miller_Arthur/)

Marcus, A.D. 1999. "Seeing Crimson: Why Harvard Law Wants to Rein in One of Its Star Professors." *Wall Street Journal*, November 22.

North American Free Trade Agreement. 1992. (http://www.sice.oas.org/trade/nafta/naftatce.stm>)

Productions Avanti Ciné-vidéo Inc. v. Favreau. 1997. 79 C.P.R. (3d) 385 (Qué. Sup. Ct.).

Racicot, M., M.S. Hayes, A.R. Szibbo, and P. Trudel. 1997. *The Cyberspace Is Not a "No Law Land"– A Study of the Issues of Liability for Content Circulating on the Internet*, Industry Canada. (http://strategis.ic.gc.ca/SSG/it03117e.html#TOC)

Universal Copyright Convention. 6 September 1952, last revised on July 24, 1971. (http://www.unesco.org/culture/laws/copyright/html_eng/page1.htm)

Wilson, A. 1999. "Harvard Professor Joins Concord School of Law." Kaplan Company, February 17 press release. (http://www1.kaplan.com/view/article/0,1898,3405,00.html)

WIPO Copyright Treaty. 1996. (http://www.wipo.org/eng/diplconf/distrib/94dc.htm)

Zamacois v. Douville and Marchand. 1943. 2 C.P.R. 270 (Ex. Ct).

CHAPTER 9

The Tele-Campus Online Course Directory

Rory McGreal
TeleEducation New Brunswick
Canada

Background

Online course delivery is still in its infancy. The World Wide Web (WWW) has only been in existence since 1992. Sophisticated graphical browsers appeared only in 1994. The first Web-based courses made their appearance in 1995. It will take more years of experimentation before greater sophistication in online courses becomes commonplace. The drive for the creation and distribution of learning objects or modules using commonly accepted standards like IMS and the Dublin core will stimulate the growth of quality in online courses, while helping to reduce the high costs of multimedia course development.

Education and training is a large economic sector in its own right. In fact, some of the industries that the public feels are significant, such as pulp and paper, mining, manufacturing, and fishing, are very small in comparison. Public sector education is a dominant sector of the economy along with health, transportation, and finance. There are few statistics available for private sector training, but we do know that training is like a parasitic growth within all other sectors. Whereas in the construction industry 1 per cent was spent on training twenty years ago, ten years ago it was 4 per cent and now it is closer to 8 per cent. In Canada, the information sector of the economy became larger than the manufacturing sector in 1985. The information sector is growing and the manufacturing sector is falling. As far back as 1983, in the U.S.A., manufacturing represented less than 20 per cent of economic activity. Construction was only 7 per cent and farming was already less than 3.5 per cent.

Education and training in the public and private sectors is growing exponentially. By the year 2020, this learning industry will have overtaken tourism as the world's largest economic sector. The growth of online education is being determined by some general trends in information technology and some more specific trends in education as a whole. The growth of connected computer networks and the exponential growth of the WWW are making the online environment central to economic activity in all sectors. This pervasive network provides anyone connected with access to a wide range of information that was never before possible. In addition, the price of computers is dropping precipitously, in tandem with an even more rapid decline in the cost of telecommunications. Soon the cost of Web access from nearly anywhere in the world will be almost free. Global

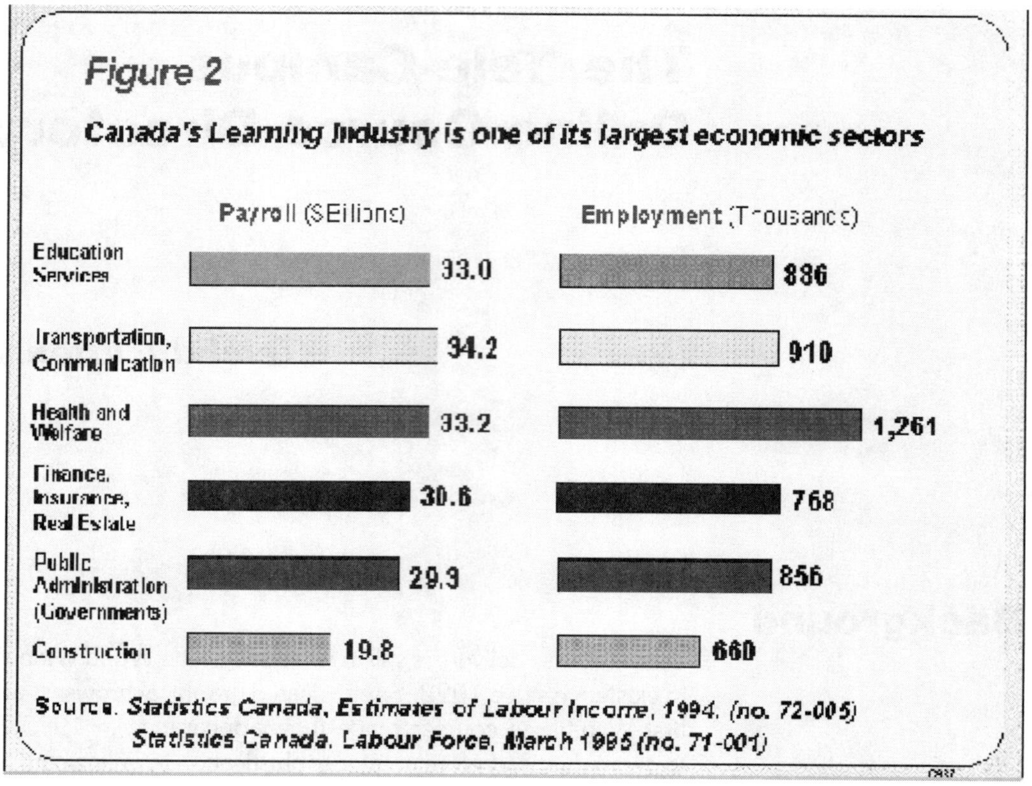

Figure 9.1
Canada's learning industry is growing exponentially

competition within the computer microchip industry and among telephone companies is forcing prices down and service levels up.

In education, following these developments in information and computer technology is an increasing trend toward the integration of online training with traditional face-to-face learning. These developments are growing in step with the increasing demand for knowledge workers, who need lifelong training. In addition, the diminishing shelf life of knowledge is driving up the demand for learning and training. The Web is providing quick access to timely knowledge and skills training that was never possible in the past. At the same time, the growth in popularity of outcomes or competency-based evaluation is making credentials more dependent on what people can do, rather than on the reputation of the institutions that they might have attended. These network and educational trends point to a rapid rise in the importance of education as an economic activity and not just as an enabler.

As part of its economic development strategy, the government of New Brunswick has understood these trends since at least 1993 (Weeks, 1993). Building on the 100 per cent digital fibre optic infrastructure, the province started researching ways to use technology in learning in 1988 by partnering with NBTel, the local telephone company, which was focusing on building the telephone call centre industry. As this industry became established, the government began looking for value-added industries. Based on an understanding of the nature of the knowledge economy, the New Brunswick government focused its efforts on the advanced training technology sector. From less than a dozen people involved in this sector in the province in 1993, this industry grew to more than sixty companies employing nearly 1000 people in 1999 (McGreal, 1998).

Figure 9.2 Education and training will become the predominant economic activity

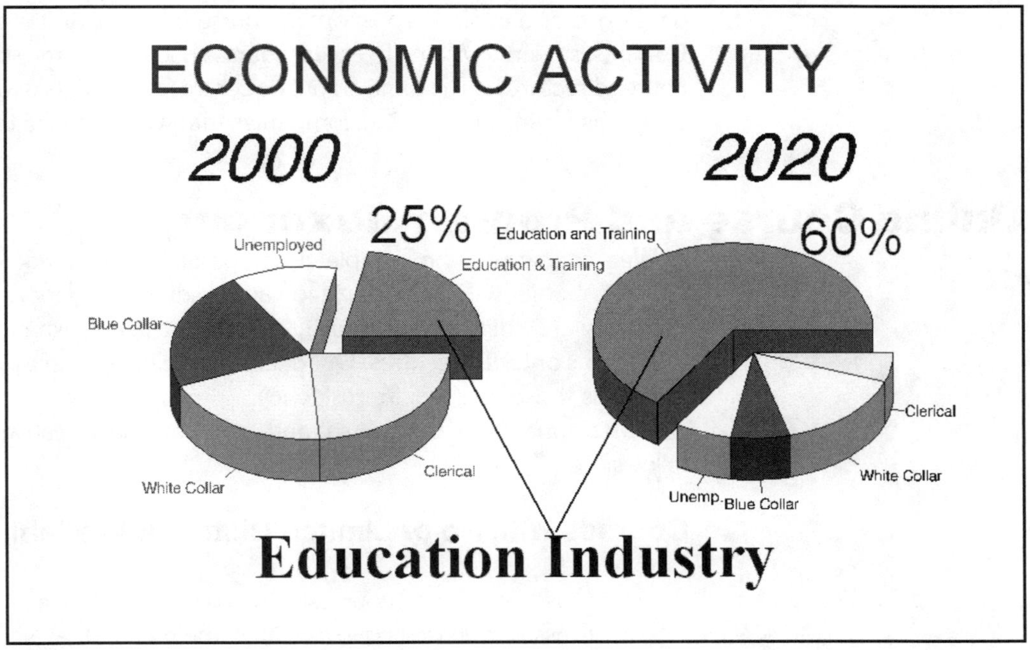

TeleEducation NB, in partnership with the provincial economic development department, played a major role as a catalyst in incubating this new industry. TeleEducation NB stimulated interest in distance education through the establishment of a provincial network of more than seventy distributed learning sites. A program development fund was also established to provide incentive grants to companies and institutions wishing to experiment in the development and delivery of online courses (McGreal, 1998).

TeleEducation NB was the first distance learning organization in the world to open a WWW site. It is a province-wide bilingual distributed learning network that is based on Canadian models developed in Newfoundland, Northern Ontario, and Alberta. It is being supported in the Tele-Campus initiative by the Regional Development Corporation (RDC), the Atlantic Canada Opportunities Agency (ACOA), and the provincial Department of Economic Development and Tourism (TeleEducation NB, 1998).

The Tele-Campus (http://Tele-Campus.edu) grew out of this initiative as an attempt to help New Brunswick companies and institutions build their online course development and delivery skills and provide a marketing site for their course offerings. The Tele-Campus is sponsored by a wide range of organizations. Industry Canada, ACOA, and the province of New Brunswick support the Tele-Campus as a tool for promoting the education industry. The Office of Learning Technologies, the Centre international pour le développement de l'inforoute en français, the Agence de la francophonie, and the Centre international français pour la formation à distance lend support for human and cultural development. The World Bank and the Commonwealth of Learning see the Tele-Campus as an instrument for international development.

Presently, educational institutions and training companies from many different countries are beginning to offer courses and programs online using the WWW. Students can now take these courses from anywhere that has an Internet connection, without being bound to any specific time, place, or institution. The Tele-Campus Online Course Directory has developed as a central repository of course information for students. Prior to the TeleCampus, students wishing to access courses had to do some sophisticated searching. The course directory has become an online centre for students wishing to take online courses as well as for institutions and companies that wish to make their courses accessible.

Online Course and Program Taxonomy

A Web course may be completely or partially presented on the Internet. For some courses, books, CD-ROMs, video- and audiotapes, laboratory materials, and other materials are shipped out directly to students, and examinations are taken at local institutions or testing centres. Our database excludes courses with no online component, as well as those that require residency.

On a continuum, the courses and programs that are advertised online are ranked as follows:

Courses with No or Limited Distance Availability

1. Classroom-based courses with no online features;
2. Classroom-based courses with some materials available online;
3. Classroom-based courses that integrate online materials;
4. On-campus courses that are online but are not available to distant students;
5. On-campus courses that offer limited access to students at a distance (often limited to one region);
6. Teleconferencing courses where students must participate from specified learning centres.

These represent the majority of courses presently advertised. They would not be included in the database because they require residency, either on campus or near an accessible learning centre.

Correspondence Courses (Print, Audio- and Videotapes, Software)

7. Print-based correspondence courses using the postal system with minimal student support;
8. Print-based correspondence courses with continuing access to a tutor by telephone.

These also would not be included, as they are not available online. All of the following categories of courses would be included in the online course database:

9. Print-based correspondence courses also using e-mail for tutor access;
10. Correspondence courses with course content available online in electronic format;
11. Computer-based training (CBT) self-study courses with access online to an instructor;
12. CBT-based self-study courses with no instructor.

The above four categories of courses represent the most primitive form of an online education.

Computer-Mediated Conferencing (CMC)

These courses can include texts and audio/video tapes, and possibly computer-based training courseware. Students may need to download and install client-side software to participate.

13. Courses that use e-mail for submission of assignments and private tutoring and e-mail lists or listservs for discussions and tutoring;
14. Courses that use CMC software for discussions as well as e-mail for submission of assignments and private tutoring;
15. CMC courses with all content, audio/ video, and software available online; students can download and print out content or read it online.

Hypermedia on the World Wide Web

These courses can be followed online on the WWW. They take advantage of the links to other relevant sites using subject trails and other techniques. These courses can be either text-based, thereby available to students with older computers and/or low bandwidth connections, or they can include graphics and animations that require a more powerful computer and higher bandwidth.

16. Courses that use hypertext links and have all necessary course materials online;
17. Courses with hypermedia links with multimedia using Java, Shockwave, QuickTime, or other applications.

Online courses need to be further divided into those in which the course materials can be accessed using a standard Web browser (Netscape or Internet Explorer) and those that require students to download and/or install a client-side application. This can be quite troublesome for students. Some plug-ins like Shockwave and QuickTime are standard and might be considered normally available. Others, however, are nonstandard and can be problematic.

Various permutations of the taxonomy described are possible. For example, a CMC course could contain some hypermedia links and a workbook, or a correspondence course could incorporate multimedia courseware on a CD-ROM with hyperlinks to the WWW. Since the courses are constantly changing, it is very difficult to provide links to real examples of these different course types.

In order to limit the size of our database and make it more useful to online students, this taxonomy limits the online course selection to those courses and programs that are universally available online; that is, those that can be taken from anywhere in the world where there is an Internet connection. If a student is in Johannesburg, Rio de Janeiro, or Kuala Lumpur and has a reliable Web connection (and the price of tuition), he or she should be able to access every course in any user-friendly database. So, the Tele-Campus Online Course Directory only includes courses that can be taken on the Internet from anywhere with no residence requirements or need to attend sessions at a physical location.

Tele-Campus Online Course Directory Description

The Tele-Campus Course Directory provides a full-text search engine for users who can also search using categories or institution. The category list allows users to search by subject, for example, biology, architecture, classics, computer technology. For more detailed information, users are directed to the institutional Web sites. Other search features are being built in, such as searching by program, level, or country/province/state. The aim is to keep the database as simple and useful as possible for users. The database has been built on an open architecture so that additional fields can be added as needed.

The database fields in the Course Directory conform to the Institute of Electrical and Electronics Engineers (IEEE) 1484 Learning Object Metadata standards, which are mapped to the Dublin Core and *ISO Standard 11179*, as developed by Educause's Instructional Management System. The IEEE has formed a Learning Technology Standards Committee (LTSC), which includes the Alliance for Remote Instruction Authoring and Distribution Networks of Europe (ARIADNE). LTSC has joined with the new International Organization for Standardization and International Electrotechnical Commission (ISO/IEC) subcommittee on Learning Technology (called SC36) to further the international development and acceptance of IEEE's Learning Technology (1484) standards. LTSC is working closely with SC36 on the development of common IEEE and ISO/IEC standards for the Internet and other forms of electronic transmission (Farance and McCabe, 1999).

Other Course Indexes

To date, there are only a few online course databases, and they can be difficult to find. Once found, students usually have to sift through courses that are advertised online but not really available, in order to find one that is actually being offered. None are comprehensive. Some directories are not limited to online courses. These are the principal online course directories:

The **CASO Online College Course Site** (http://www.caso.com) includes links to many different U.S. accredited college courses. Many of the courses advertised in the database are not yet available online. Links to institutions are available, but they do not necessarily lead to real online courses that students can enroll in.

A more recent index, developed by International WHERE+HOW in Europe is the **Distance Learning Course Finder** (http://www.dlcoursefinder.com/index.htm). Their list includes correspondence courses and does not provide links to the Web sites of the delivering institutions.

The **Electronic University Network** (http://www.wcc-eun.com/index.html) provides links to courses from only twelve universities and colleges that have joined their consortium.

Founded in 1998, **Ed/X** (http://www.ed-x.com/) aims to be a leading channel for distance education on the Web. They link to nearly 5000 online courses and provide other information about distance education events.

The **Globewide Network Academy** (http://www.gnacademy.org/) includes a database of more than 17 000 courses and programs available at a distance. Many are offered by correspondence, others are based on a mixture of on-site visitations and e-mail. Sometimes no Web site or e-mail contact is available.

Hungry Minds (http://www.hungryminds.com/catalog/index.html) is a relatively new well-marketed knowledge portal that houses more than 13 000 online courses.

The **International Centre for Distance Learning** database (http://www-icdl.open.ac.uk/) provides information about distance education courses available from many different countries. This database contains primarily correspondence courses and is quite useful for institutions that wish to access and purchase self-study course materials, but is of limited use for students who wish to take online courses.

LifelongLearning.com (http://www.lifelonglearning.com/) is a site run by the well-known Peterson's Guides company. They have links to accredited postsecondary distance education courses.

The **World Lecture Hall** (http://wwwhost.cc.utexas.edu/world/lecture/) provides information on different courses available online and off-line. Many available courses do not supply information critical for enrollment (for example, how to enroll, accreditation, cost).

Tele-Campus Online Course Directory Content

The exponential growth in activity of all kinds on the Internet is leading to increased demands for online education and training. The number of courses available online increased from less than 100 in 1996, to close to 1000 in 1998, to more than 8000 in 1999, and over 30 000 in 2000. More than 100 000 courses will be available online in 2002. This represents an increase in the number of students from less than a thousand in 1996, to more than a million by 2002. These worldwide markets are only now emerging. It would be very difficult to estimate the market size, and any attempt at a snapshot of the market at any particular time would be out of date the following day. Students need a user-friendly directory for accessing these course offerings, as well as both specific and general information about courses, institutions, accreditation, distance learning, and studying online.

The Tele-Campus Online Course Directory houses only courses that can be taken on the Internet from anywhere with no residence requirements or need to attend sessions at a physical location. More than 17 000 courses are included in the Directory. These courses are delivered from more than thirty countries in over ten languages.

More than 90 per cent of online courses emanate from North America. The U.S.A. dominates with over 75 per cent of all online courses worldwide. Canada is second with 16 per cent of online courses. Australia, a country with a relatively small population, is third with 5 per cent. Some northern European countries like Finland, Norway, and Sweden deliver many courses online, but these courses all require a residency period on-site, so they are not included in the Tele-Campus Course Directory. The Open University of Catalonia is a European leader in Web-based education, but they too insist on a face-to-face component in each course.

As expected, American states with large populations such as California and New York deliver the most courses. However, if one takes into account the relative populations of these leading countries, Canada enjoys a substantial lead in the number of online

Figure 9.3
Canada provides the second largest number of online courses

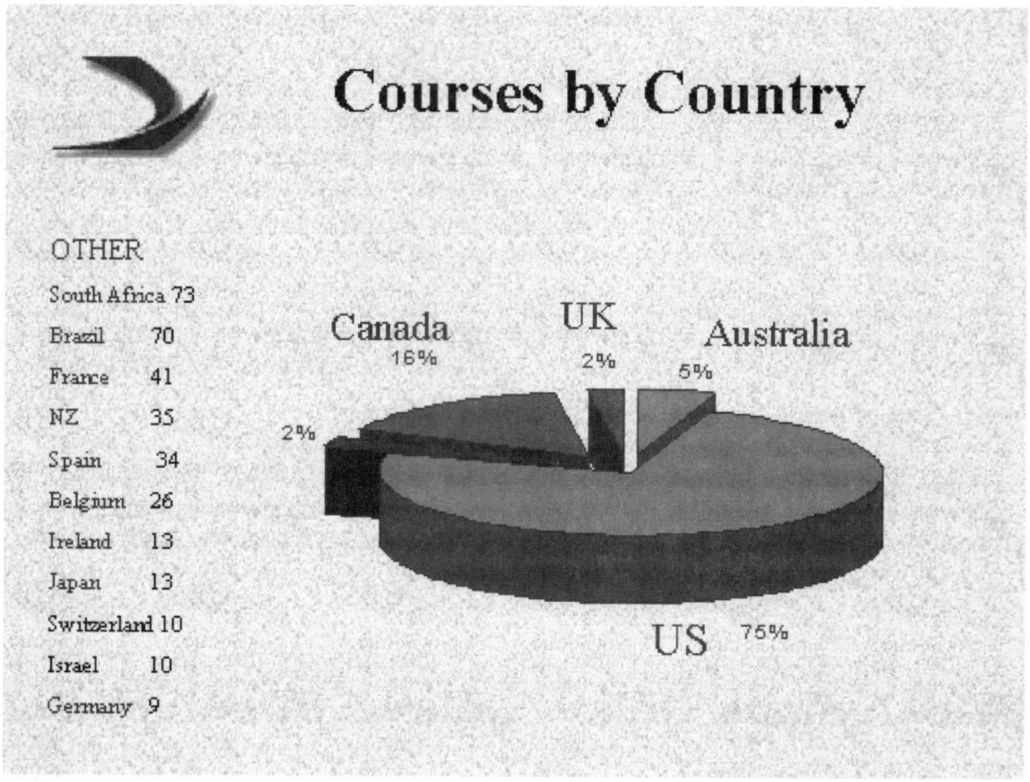

courses offered in relation to its population. Australia is level with the United States, and New Zealand is ahead of the United Kingdom.

Canada profits from the lead of Industry Canada, which understood at an early stage the importance of online learning for the Canadian economy and started up a number of programs to encourage Canadian institutions and companies to participate in the advanced training technology sector. The Office of Learning Technologies has contributed significantly to this growth. Organizations like the Tele-Learning Network of Centres of Excellence have provided leadership on a national basis.

Australia is also a leader in online course export, and they are having significant success in the East Asian market. Their government made explicit policy decisions to support the growth of the online learning industry.

Some smaller provinces and states lead on a per-capita basis. New Brunswick is a small province that is leading all others in online course delivery per capita. The next two leaders, Alberta and British Columbia, are in that position primarily because of the established presence of open universities in their jurisdictions. Alberta is home to Athabasca, "Canada's open university," which began online with their executive MBA program and now offer all their correspondence courses over the Internet. The Open Learning Agency in British Columbia has been a little slower in adjusting to the Internet.

The New Brunswick government has focused its economic development policy on promoting the advanced training technology of the provincial economy, and this focus is bearing fruit. The western states are leading within the U.S.A. No country or region outside of North America is ahead of these leaders. New Brunswick's lead is exaggerated by the presence in Fredericton of Scholars.com, which offers more than fifty courses to

Figure 9.4
Per capita, Canada offers the highest number of online courses

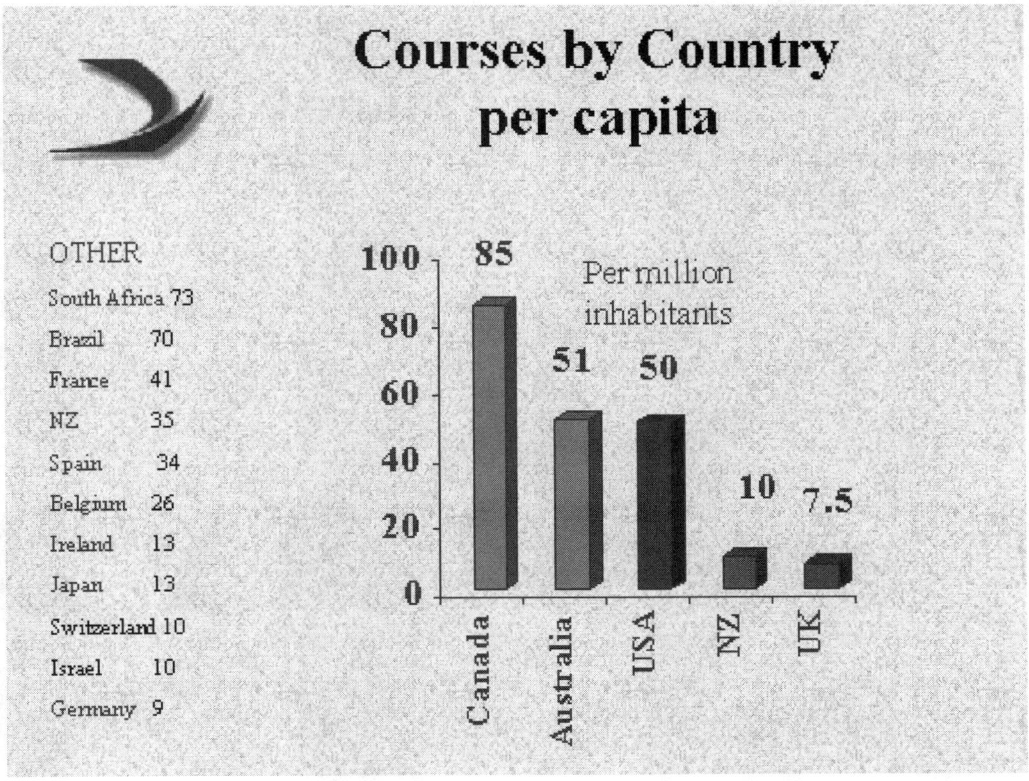

more than 1200 students at any one time. However, the community colleges, universities, and private sector training companies have entered the field early, spurred on by government support and the presence of TeleEducation NB, a province-wide distributed learning network.

English is the dominant language of online courses, comprising more than 95 per cent of all courses offered. French courses are next with only 4 per cent. This is due more to the participation of Québec and the Téléuniversité du Québec than to France. Other languages make up less than 1 per cent of all online courses offered. The rapid growth in Portuguese is an interesting phenomenon, led by Brazilian institutions, which are increasing their online offering very rapidly. Spanish language offerings are being led by Mexico. Europe seems to be trapped in the Middle Ages. Although they are offering more and more learning modules online, most institutions are insisting on a face-to-face component in every course.

Another significant factor is the desire of nationals of many foreign-language countries to study in English, particularly in the high-technology fields. They want to learn the language and jargon of the field in English. This phenomenon can also be found in nontechnology courses as well as international courses, which choose English as a neutral language. For example, the Nordic countries of Finland, Denmark, Sweden, and Norway are sharing courses using English as the common language.

Most online courses are targeted at the postsecondary market. University undergraduate courses are the most numerous, followed closely by community college courses. There is also a disproportionate number of graduate-level courses. This is not surprising, when one considers that online courses are quite often directed at working

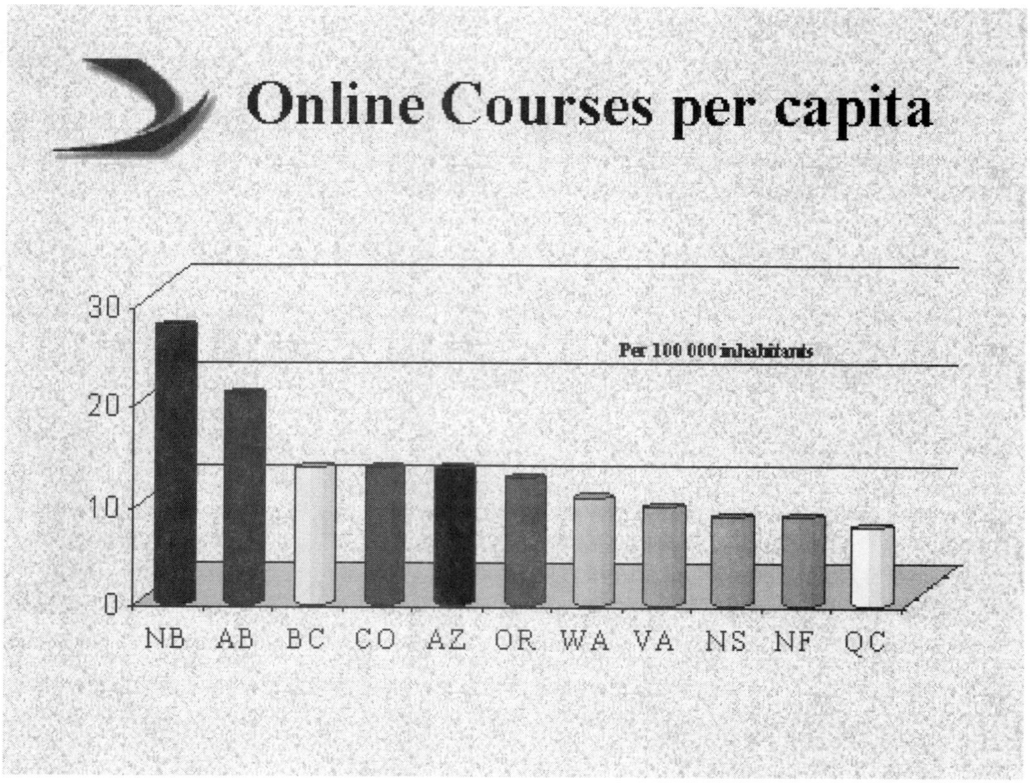

Figure 9.5
By province or state, New Brunswick provides the most courses per capita

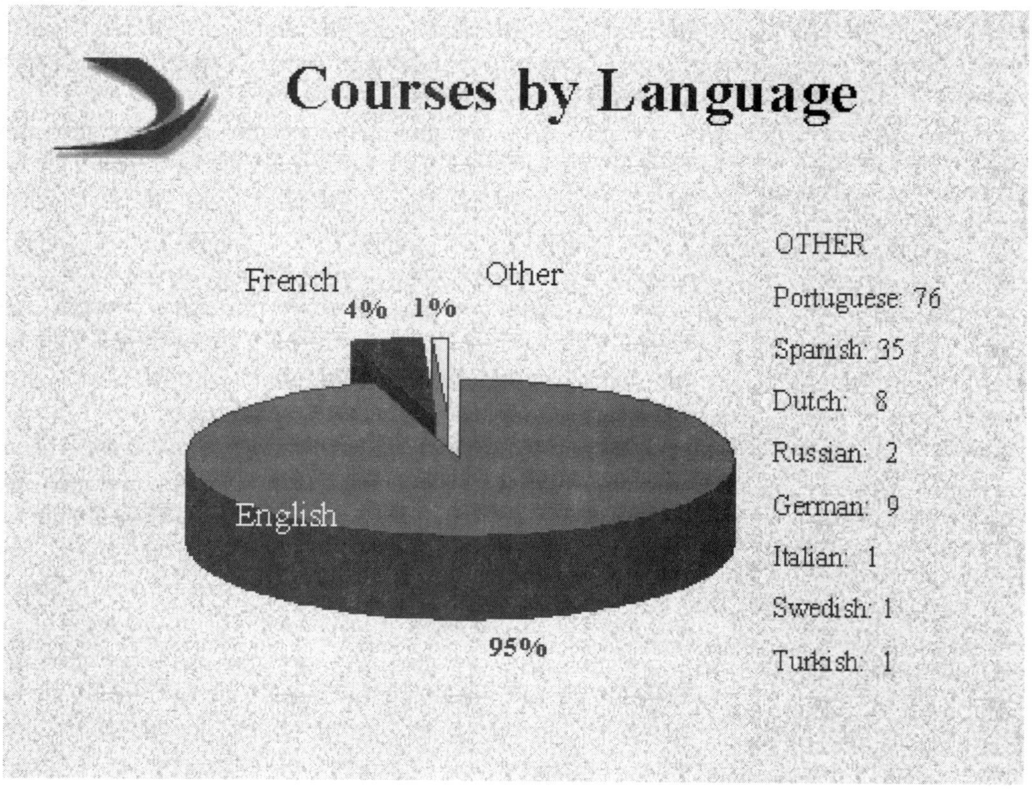

Figure 9.6
English is by far the main language of online courses

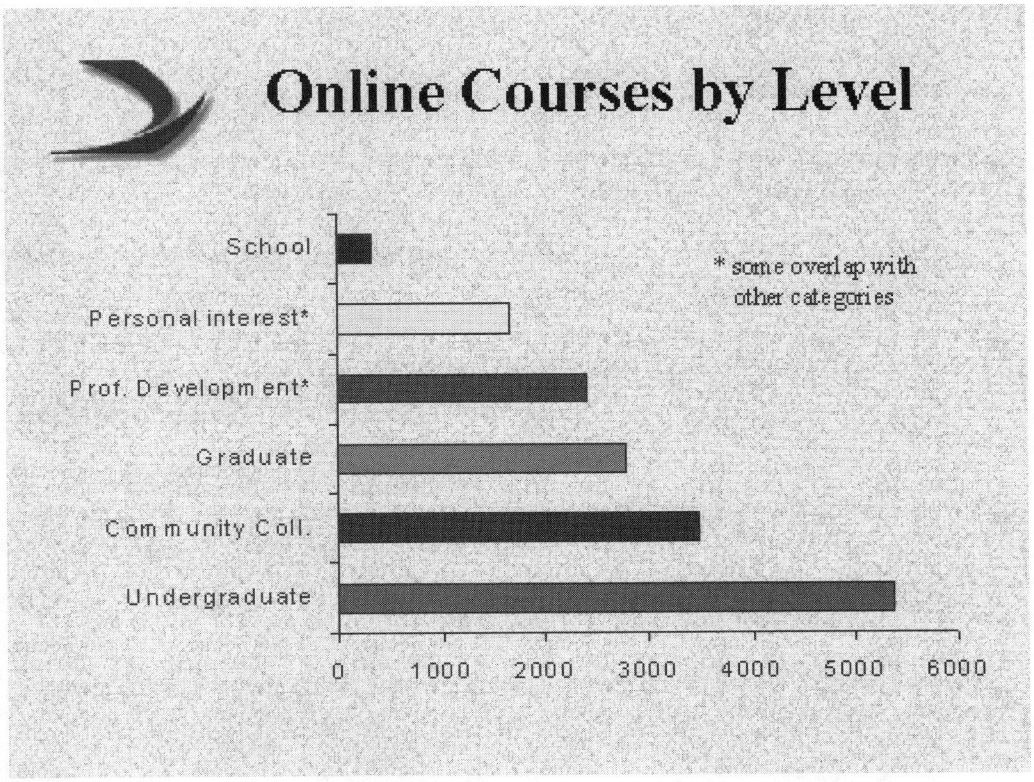

Figure 9.7
Most online courses are at the undergraduate level, but this is likely to change in the future

professionals; this would also explain the number of professional development courses. There are also a large number of non-accredited personal interest courses, which are often available free of charge.

High school–level courses are not as numerous in the Directory because many of them are only offered within a specific jurisdiction. For example, the Florida Virtual High School (http://www.sbac.edu/~fhs/fvhs.htm) offers many courses, but they are not available to students outside the state. Other high school course deliverers limit themselves to sharing courses with other schools in their region. On the other hand, the rapid growth of home schooling is creating a major demand for online courses that presents opportunities for those institutions that are willing to offer their courses globally.

Not surprisingly, computer courses predominate. In any new field, those most familiar with the environment are generally the ones to experiment and make use of the technology in new ways. On the other hand, social science courses are more common than hard science courses. The large number of cash-cow Masters of Business Administration offerings builds up the business subject area. There are also a growing number of personal interest courses like "How to fold a map" or "How to be a gracious house guest" (http://www.learn2.com/browse/tra_2tor.php3).

Universities and, particularly, the open universities are offering the most courses. In North America, nearly every institution is either offering courses online or planning to do so. Still, many of them insist on a face-to-face meeting and therefore are not included in the Directory. Interestingly, a growing number of traditional university students are taking one or two online courses as a matter of convenience. The typical student now holds down a part-time or even full-time job and needs the flexibility that online courses offer.

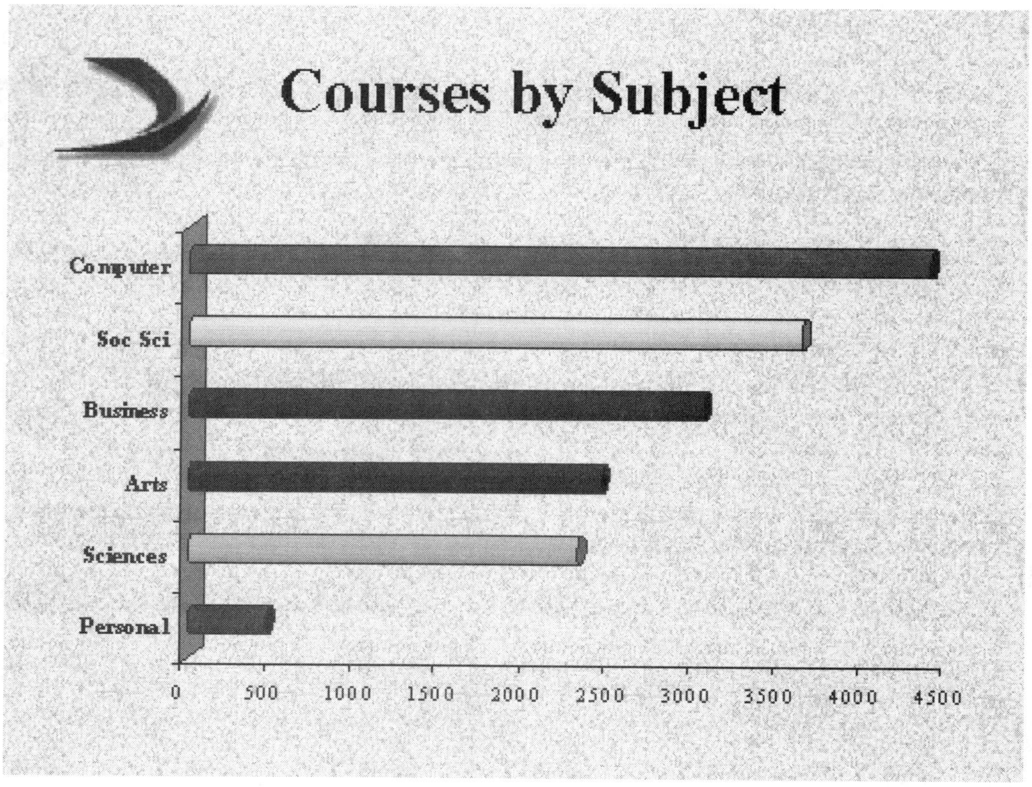

Figure 9.8 Understandably, computer-related courses are the subjects most offered and taken

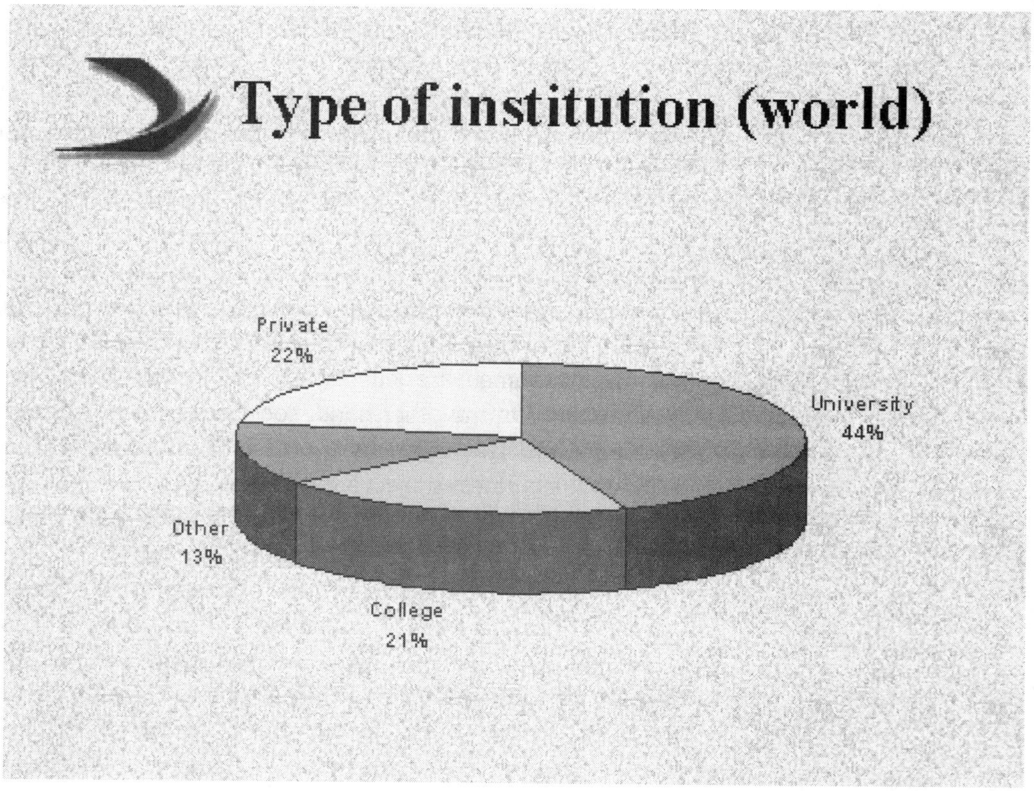

Figure 9.9 Universities still provide the majority of online courses

They can work at home when they have the time. Community colleges and private sector trainers are offering their courses online to working adults. There are many private sector courses online: Large companies are opening online corporate universities to train their employees, and these courses are not normally made available to outsiders.

Conclusion

Historically, small provinces and states such as New Brunswick have been bypassed by the great metropolitan areas in economic development. However, as the new advanced training technology sector of the economy grows, distance from markets is no longer a factor, particularly in the design and delivery of online courses. Small remote areas can participate on an equal footing with the larger centres. The times they are a'changin'. In the past, organizations that were small and out of the way were thought to have liabilities. Today the size and location can be turned into assets. New Brunswick understands this, since it uses its Tele-Campus not only to offer learning opportunities to its own population, but also to promote the economic development of the region. Using its small size, talented people, innovative businesses, and advanced infrastructure, the Tele-Campus has helped to position New Brunswick as an internationally respected leader in the new knowledge economy.

References

Farance, F., and K. McCabe. 1999. "New International Subcommittee Advances IEEE Standards Work on Learning Technology." (http://standards.ieee.org/ announcements/ newintsub.html)

McGreal, R. 1998. *The TeleEducation NB Programme Development Fund Report*. Fredericton, New Brunswick: TeleEducation NB.

Sakaiya, T. 1991. *The Knowledge-Value Revolution or a History of the Future* (2nd edition). New York: Kodansha International.

TeleEducation NB. 1998. "TeleEducation NB Home Page." (http://teleeducation.nb.ca)

Weeks, L. 1993. "Information Technology Marketing Plan." Fredericton, New Brunswick, Department of Economic Development and Tourism, internal departmental presentation. December 24.

Part C

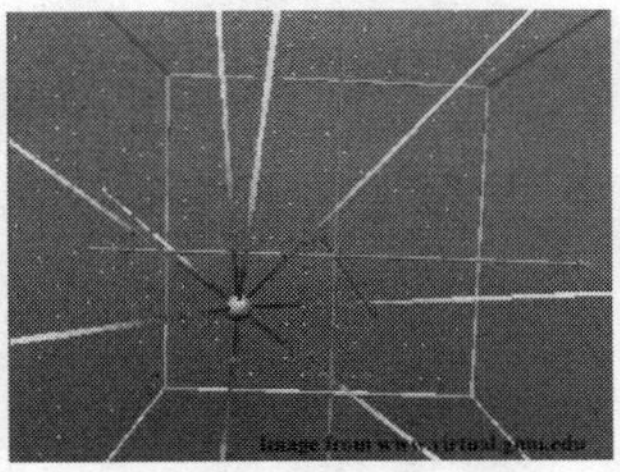

Web Course Tools

CHAPTER 10

Elements of Web Course Design

Rod Heimpel
University of Toronto
Canada

The purpose of this chapter is to provide Web course designers with an overview of some of the fundamental elements of effective Web course design. The approach will be practical and pragmatic. Theoretical principles from education and computer science will be included in the discussion when their relevance can be justified in practical terms. This chapter will focus on the following:

- Tools needed to code a Web page and why the do-it-yourself approach is perhaps superior to using commercial development tools;
- Applications of the principles of effective interface design to Web courses;
- Dynamic and interactive features that have been added to basic HTML coding.

While the first sections of this article are addressed to beginners and users of course development tools, the focus of the paper shifts incrementally toward discussions of more technical concepts.

The Tools of the Trade

In this section, the do-it-yourself option is analyzed as an alternative to commercial course development tools. The advantages of this approach, as well as some of the basic tools required are discussed.

The Task

There is little doubt that educational Web sites are different from noneducational Web sites. One need only sample the staggering differences in design between commercial Web sites and Web courses. Differences in goals clearly translate into different designs and, implicitly, different design principles. Häkkinen (1996) has shown that teachers' and software designers' conceptions of learning and evaluation criteria for educational software are quite distinct. Häkkinen concludes that each group needs to make its theories and assumptions explicit to the other in such a way that greater cooperation and synergy might be achieved. Another equally valid recommendation might have been that teachers should, when possible, create their own computer-aided instruction (CAI) materials.

It is especially important for novice Web course designers to consider the specificity of their task because, with millions of Web users, there will be no shortage of opinions forthcoming. It is often difficult for beginners to evaluate the relevance of Web design principles. For example, usability expert Jakob Nielsen has published several Top Ten Mistakes of Web Design lists (1996, 1999a, 1999b). Some of the principles advanced are quite universal, such as his stance against the gratuitous use of bleeding-edge technology (1996, 1999a). But other principles, such as his invective against frames (1996) reveal a profoundly prescriptive approach to what the Web ought to be and how it ought to function. Usability seems to have superceded the uniqueness and situatedness of users and their goals. Nielsen's texts also imply that all Web sites must be designed for any Web surfer who might just happen upon a site. This assumption is clearly not applicable to Web course site design. One is best to take pronouncements like Nielsen's and those of other Web gurus with a grain of salt.

Do It Yourself Versus Course Development Tools

Considering the range of course development tools available today (and assuming that one is available at your university or college), why would anyone want to spend time learning HTML programming in order to create a course site?

The strongest argument for investing time in the do-it-yourself approach is that the teacher will have much more control over the online learning environment (OLE) than with the use of course development tools. Do-it-yourselfers will be better able to

- Design a Web site tailored to the learning goals, style, and rhythm of their students;
- Design a Web site tailored to the relative power of their students' computers and network connections;
- React and respond to design problems;
- Achieve the greatest level of cross-platform cross-browser compatibility;
- Add new features gradually;
- Incorporate suggestions on an ongoing basis;
- Take preventative actions, such as archiving material or creating a mirror site;
- Adapt to technological innovation.

This final point is crucial. Since do-it-yourselfers use the Hyper Text Markup Language (HTML) as their base markup, or coding, language—a language used by millions of users—they are investing in technological currency that will likely not be devalued anytime soon.

Conversely, users of course development tools tend to learn how to operate only a single piece of software, which could pass out of existence for any number of reasons. Furthermore, as David Jones and Renay Buchanan (1996) point out in light of their desire to create an *integrated* online learning environment, using a tool that is only available from a single vendor introduces problems including dependency on the vendor to keep up with the field and difficulty in integrating tools from other vendors.

Figure 10.1 Interface of NoteTab software

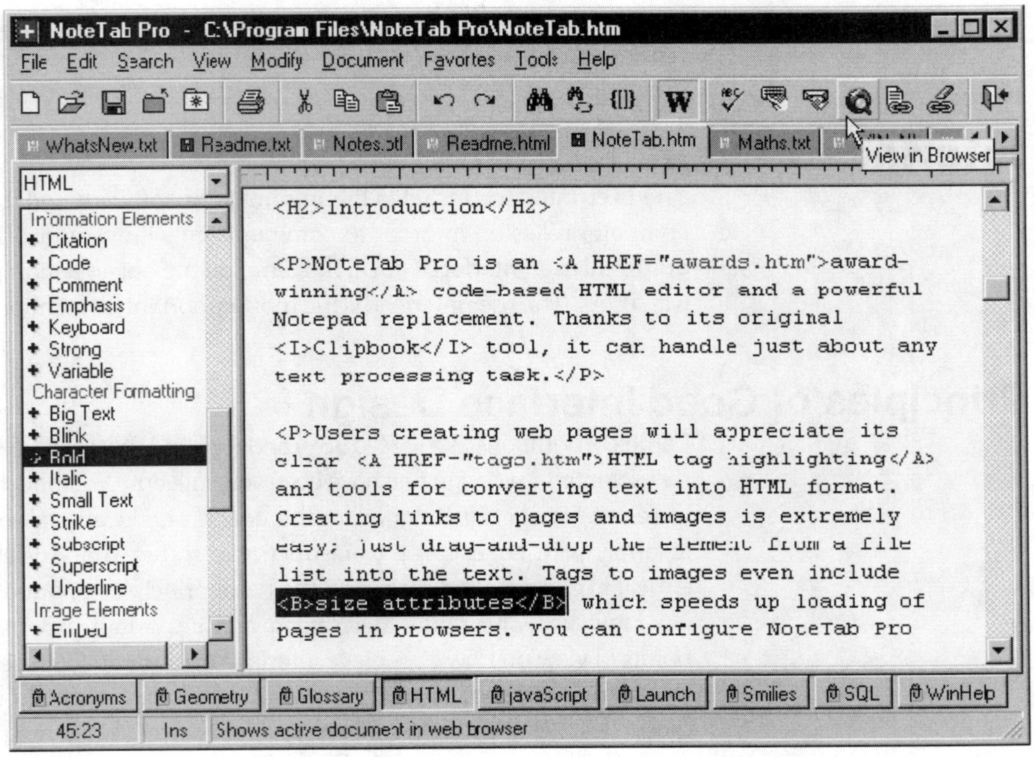

HTML Editors

HTML editors, or HTML publishers as they are sometimes called, are programs used by do-it-yourselfers to code Web pages. HTML is coded in plain text mode. In fact, it is even possible to use a text editor like Notepad (Windows). HTML editors facilitate coding by presenting the editing of HTML code in the familiar *object-action paradigm*. As with modern word processors such as Word and WordPerfect, one simply selects a certain stretch of text (the object) with the mouse or keyboard, to which a certain action can be applied; for example, clicking on the B icon will make the text boldface. The same principle is applied in HTML editors, but instead of the text appearing bold, as with the word processing example, the text is coded as <b>bold</b>. The user's Web browser—Netscape or Internet Explorer in most cases—will decode the encoded text as bold text.[1]

Shareware and freeware archives contain many fine examples of HTML editors for PC, Mac, Linux, Unix, and so on. For example, HTML editors for all levels of users are available as shareware and freeware from Tucows.com, download.com, cnet.com, and other shareware distributors.

One of the best HTML editors for users of Windows 95, 98, and NT4 is called NoteTab. Two shareware versions and a freeware version of this software are currently available at http://www.notetab.com. As in the above example, NoteTab uses the object-action paradigm (see Figure 10.1).

NoteTab is extremely user-friendly and customizable. The sidebar on the left side of the screen contains collections of "clipbooks" that organize the HTML tags (actions) into user-centred categories (for example, information elements, character formatting). Even the freeware version contains an extensive library of clipbooks, and many others are freely available on the NoteTab Web site. The shareware version includes dictionaries in several European languages.

Interface Design

The user interface includes the ensemble of software and/or hardware devices that a computer relies on in order to communicate with its users. Today, most interfaces are graphical user interfaces (GUI) that employ the object-action paradigm to communicate with users. The user interface is the most important element of any computer application.

Principles of Good Interface Design

Large corporations like IBM (1989) and Apple (1987) have developed detailed protocols for user interface design that have been very influential. Although these and other principles were not specifically designed for the WWW or educational software, most of them tend to apply with equal force to instructional software and Web pages. Researchers are largely in agreement concerning the basic principles of good interface design.[2]

However, one rather perplexing and important exception concerns two distinct points of view on how to achieve interface transparency. Researchers agree on the need for interface transparency, but cannot agree on how it should be achieved. The first group believes that "less is more" and that through planning and good design practice they will achieve their goals. As David Gilmore puts it, "users need a 'sense of engagement' with the learning materials, not the interface" (Gilmore, 1996, p. 119).

Other designers, influenced by a more recent movement toward metaphorical scenarios, advise designers to make the user interface captivating in such a way that it draws the user into the mental world of the application (Davies and Brailsford, 1994; Pincas, 1998; Ohl and Cates, 1997). Stoney and Wild contend that "[i]nterfaces that motivate learners are realistic, easy to use, challenging and engaging" (1998, p. 40). Houser and DeLouch (1998) go further by demonstrating that computer games are, according to their criteria, ideal models of metaphorical scenarios. They suggest that games create a transparent interface by emphasizing the story and metaphor, and by de-emphasizing game options.

Unfortunately, whether it is because metaphors are most often inappropriate or prosaic, or because the relentless pursuit of "engaging" interface designs makes victims of function and usability, metaphorical approaches often fall short of their stated goals.

New Frontiers of Learning: Guidelines for Multimedia Courseware Developers in Higher Education by Davies and Brailsford (1994) presents a particularly compelling set of user interface principles. They are compelling because of their high level of generality and thus, by extension, also their high level of applicability. While the principles developed were not necessarily developed with Web courses in mind, they were designed for a closely related field: multimedia educational applications. The authors advance eight principles:

1. Corporate conventions: such as those elaborated at IBM and Apple;
2. Balance: the need for visual symmetry;
3. Proportion: relative size of visual elements;

4. Sequence: our senses crave symmetry, consistency, and stablility. Visual attention tends to move from a large image to a smaller one, from a nonsymmetrical image to a symmetrical image, from a saturated texture to a de-saturated texture;
5. Unity: various screens of software must appear as though they belong to the same application;
6. Emphasis: disrupt sequences, vary size and symmetry to attract user's attention;
7. Similarity: similar elements are assumed to have similar functions;
8. Foreground/ background symbol stability: that is, make sure there is enough contrast between image colours and the design so that the elements can be clearly viewed on the background.

Like many other experts in the field, Davies and Brailsford emphasize the complementary relationship among principles of interface design, usability engineering, and human-computer interaction (HCI) (see also Gilmore, 1996; Head, 1999; Starr, 1997).

Simplicity and straightforwardness are recurring themes in the literature (Denning, Shuttleworth, and Smith, 1998; Nielsen, 1996, 1999a, 1999b; Pincas, 1998; Stoney and Wild; Wright et al., 1997). Simplicity is strongly correlated with usability and effectiveness of design.

There is a notable difference between the principles advanced by designers and those put forward by teachers: flexibility and extensibility of design is emphasized to a greater degree by designers, but should, of course, be an important consideration for both parties.

With the exception of flexibility, all of the preceding principles can be reformulated as two simple metaprinciples of interface design: clarity and consistency. This reformulation is possible because notions of clarity, consistency, and simplicity are all *literacy concepts*. The application of these metaprinciples to specific elements of Web design will therefore motivate a much-needed concept of *Web design literacy*.

Applications of User Interface Design Principles to Web Course Design

In this section, the principles of clarity and consistency will be applied to specific elements of Web course design (which is not to say that these principles do not also apply elsewhere).

Overall Design

Like HTML itself, Web pages used for online learning should be robustly structured. Human perception is quick to identify consistency and clarity problems, so a reliable and simple procedure for creating Web pages for a course site is to create a sample page that will serve as the model or template for all other pages.

A sound approach to designing this template is to think of which objects will need to appear on every page. For example, in a course I have designed, the essential objects are the navigation bar, course title graphic, title of page, subtitle of page, body text, navigation bar (repeated), and copyright notice. Create a file called template.htm, and do not vary from it, unless you decide to modify all the pages on the site.

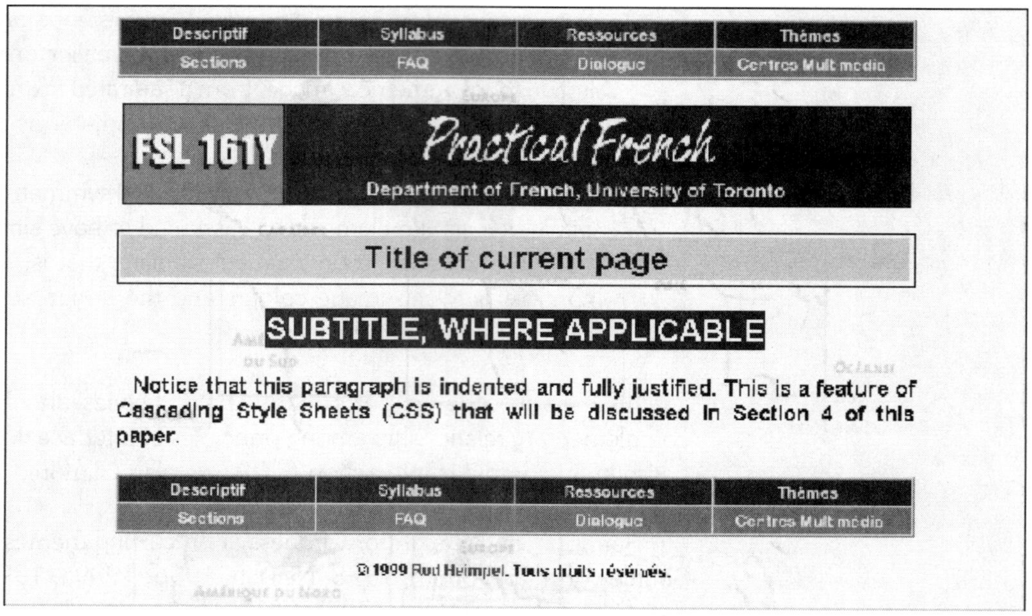

Figure 10.2 Netscape 4.7 view of the essential "objects" on a sample course page

When creating a template, do not forget to leave white space on the page. Since the viewing area on monitors is growing exponentially today, another good technique is to centre the contents of the page.[3] By spacing these objects and writing clear, effective text, you will reduce the risk of your students experiencing cognitive overload.[4]

Navigation

Navigation must be clear, consistent, and intuitive. A reliable and well-tested approach consists of inserting a navigation bar on every page, in exactly the same position on the page, preferably on both the top and bottom. Users quickly come to rely on the navigation bar on every page. Also, the navigation bar, as part of the overall design, creates a sense of unity; that is, it corresponds to a user's assumption that all pages that belong to a course look the same.

The navigation bar in Figure 10.2 above combines true navigational features with actions such as Dialogue. This action has been included with the other navigational buttons since it would have been odd to have had another menu for a single action. If there were a search feature on this course site, then it would have been a good idea to create another menu.

There are essentially three ways of presenting buttons: (1) text only, as in the above example; (2) image only; and (3) image and text. Text with a single-coloured background is the best choice because colour is generally a stronger signifier than icons. Icons are often far less intuitive than Web site designers imagine. For example, the following experience is common:

> ...our experience has been that the images are not as intuitive as the designers expected them to be. For example, the image to cast a ballot has been described as a "Kleenex box," a "guy with his tongue sticking out," and by various other colorful metaphors. (Romano et al., 1998, p. 662)

Words and colour(s) require no particular artistic talent and are still most likely more effective communicators.

Use of Colour

The appropriate use of the colour is an important part of Web course design and Web literacy in general. One of the worst mistakes a novice Web designer can make is to use a dark background. The general rule of the screen is to use dark colours on light backgrounds. Never use a black background because your students will be unable to print out pages from the course site. The following suggestions for effective use of colour are adapted from Wright et al. (1997):

- Limit the number of colours used.
- Use bright colours for danger or for getting the user's attention.
- Avoid the simultaneous display of highly saturated, spectrally extreme colours.
- For colour-deficient observers, avoid single-colour distinctions.
- Opposite colours go well together.

New and Improved HTML

In this section, two advanced scripting languages are introduced: Cascading Style Sheets (CSS) and JavaScript (JS). The usefulness of these additions to basic HTML will be examined in conjunction with the applications of good user interface design principles discussed above. These features will help teachers become better designers of course interfaces.

Overview of HTML Specifications and Orientations

In order to understand the significance of the developments and additions to HTML, one must also know something of the history of HTML.

The original HTML specification, HTML 1.0, was intended to structure a document for Web transport in terms of a few tags: headings tags <H1> to <H6>; paragraph tag <P>; lists <OL> and <UL>; horizontal rule <HR>; <BODY>; and a few others. It was not intended as a presentation language, so there was no provision made for fonts, indenting, or extensive use of colour. As the Web matured, the need for more aesthetically pleasing and sophisticated pages emerged, perhaps spurred on by the "browser wars."[5] By the time HTML 3.2 (January 14, 1997) was recommended by the W3 Consortium, a whole new series of tags had been added. Specifically, the <FONT> tag was introduced, along with attributes for size and colour: for example, <FONT FACE="arial" SIZE="+1" COLOR= "green">Text</FONT>.

The browser companies introduced the FACE attribute. The <FONT> tag was quite clumsy and long and, furthermore, it completely compromised the elegance of the original structure of HTML, not to mention cluttering and bulking up HTML files.

HTML 4.0, through the introduction of cascading style sheets (CSS), put a stop to the proliferation of formatting codes. Several tags, including the <FONT> tag (and all of its associated attributes), have been deprecated in HTML 4. A deprecated element or attribute is one that has been outdated by newer constructs. Deprecated elements are defined in the reference manual in appropriate locations, but are clearly marked as deprecated. Deprecated elements may become obsolete in future versions of HTML.[6]

In short, by separating structure and presentation in HTML 4—or at least moving in this direction—the W3 Consortium has restored flexibility, elegance, and universality to this strategically important language.

Cascading Style Sheets (CSSs)

CSSs allow basic HTML tags to be assigned certain rules of presentation. Instead of coding every attribute of a tag every time it is used (as with <FONT>), the savvy designer can assign specific attributes to basic HTML tags using a style sheet. Dynamic and dramatic change can be effected across a Web site by changing the screen presentation attributes of a tag from one central location. For example, the <P> tag (paragraph) can be programmed to function with an indent, and the font can be set at the same time. In fact, this is exactly what has been done in the example page in Figure 10.2 above.

The attributes of the <P> tag have been defined in a separate file. The code of a style sheet for <P> would look like this:

```
P, UL, OL {        font-size: 14pt;
                   font-family: "Arial", "Helvetica";
                   font-weight: bold;
                   text-align: justify;
                   text-indent: 10pt }
```

In the above example, the <UL> and <OL> list tags were grouped and set at the same time. The basic syntax in CSS is as follows:

```
                              Tag  {attribute}

Or for multiple attributes:   Tag  {attribute 1;
                                    attribute2 }
```

These tag definitions can be nested in the HTML document in the <STYLE> tag, but this would only apply the style locally, that is, to the document into which it was inserted. To capitalize on the dynamic changes made possible by CSS, it is better to create an external file [*filename.css*] with a list of tags and attributes, as indicated above. This document is then called from within the HTML document by nesting a <LINK REL> in the <HEAD> tag:

```
<HTML>
<HEAD>
<TITLE>My Web Course</TITLE>
<LINK REL=stylesheet TYPE="text/css" HREF="style.css">
</HEAD>
<BODY>

<<--The rest of the document would appear here — N.B. the marks
enclosing this comment ensure that it is not confused with HTML tag-->

<BODY>
</HTML>
```

This style sheet (or several of them) must be called from within every separate Web page on the course site. This is a small price to pay for the convenience and power of being able to change fonts, colours, and page layouts without actually editing individual HTML documents.

Furthermore, it is quite possible that CSS will make teachers better designers in that this structured language of presentation will ensure that the principle of consistency is rigorously respected on entire course sites (provided that the coding has been carefully and consistently applied). For example, in Figure 10.2 above, both the title ("Title of current page") and subtitle ("SUBTITLE, WHERE APPLICABLE") have been defined by an external style sheet.

```
div.subtitle    { background: gold;
                padding: 1;
                border-width: thin;
                width: 610pix;
                font-size: 18pt;
                font-weight: bold;
                font-family: "Verdana", "Arial", Helvetica;
                text-align: center }

H2  { text-transform: uppercase;
    font-size: 18pt;
    font-family: "Verdana", "Arial", Helvetica;
    background: blue;
    text-align: center;
    color: white }
```

The colours and proportions have been chosen very carefully. After the title graphic (FSL 161Y) and the navigation bar (the largest images on the page), the eye is most likely to focus on the title because of (1) the intensity of the gold background; (2) the relative largeness of the font; and (3) its size (same width as the "navbar").

Next, the eye will naturally be attracted to the subtitle, because of the intensity of the blue background and the size of the font, and also because of the use of block caps. The inversion of the title scheme (dark colour on lighter background) will also attract a user's gaze.

Once these colour strategies have been tested for clarity and usability, CSS will ensure the consistent application of the style attributes. The title uses the <DIV> tag whereas the subtitle style is mapped on to <H2>. Represented below are the lines of code inserted into the style sheet:

The <DIV> tag is very useful for creating different presentation effects. Like all HTML tags, <DIV> can also have classes appended to it. In the above example, the class "subtitle" was added to the ordinary <DIV> tag. The text for the subtitle was auto-transformed into block caps. Here is the HTML code behind the title and subtitle in Figure 10.2:

```
<DIV CLASS="subtitle"><H1 ALIGN="center">Title of current page</
DIV></H1>

<H2 ALIGN="center">Subtitle, where applicable</H2>
```

Many of the attributes available in CSS (such as background, text-transform, border, padding) are simply not available in ordinary HTML. of course, the above are only very rudimentary examples of what CSS can do.[7]

CSS Implementation in Netscape and Internet Explorer

Although CSS is a powerful tool, it also has several limitations and serious problems. First of all, CSSs work only in Netscape and IE version 4 and after. As a result, designers most often have to make provisions for backwards compatibility. This is why there are redundant tagging attributes in the last example (for example, <H2 ALIGN="center"> when the style sheet centres it as well). If the <P> tag is justified via an external style sheet, the text will be read as centred in Netscape 3.x. As a result, and against all good logic, <P ALIGN="left"> must be used to make paragraphs behave normally in Netscape 3. Figure 10.3 below shows the same page from Figure 10.2 as it appears in Netscape 3.

Moreover, the implementation is asymmetrical in Netscape and Internet Explorer. In fact, there are only a limited number of tags that work consistently well.[8] Yet despite these problems, CSS remains an excellent tool for ensuring the clarity and consistency of Web sites.

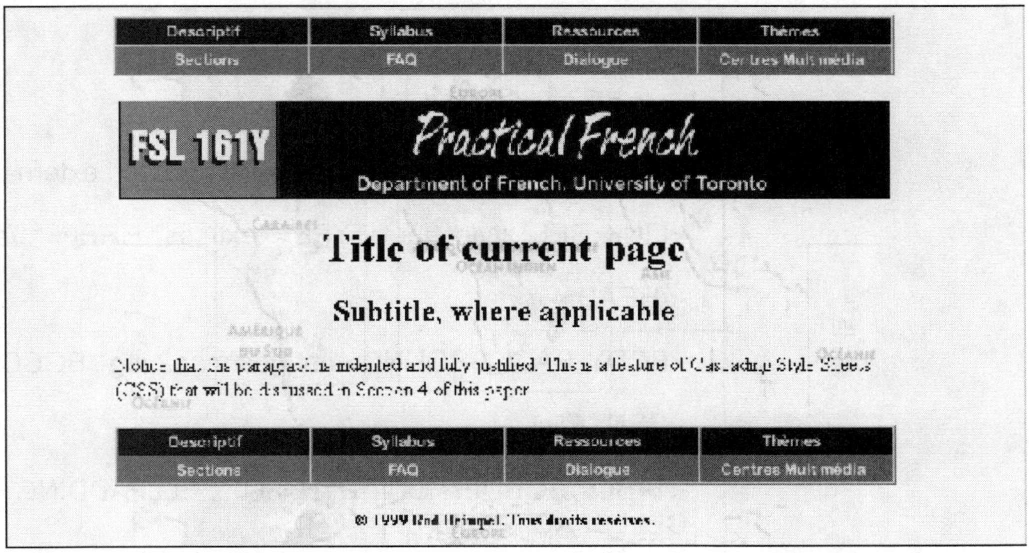

Figure 10.3
View of sample page in Netscape 3 (not CSS-compatible)

JavaScript (JS)

JavaScript is a programming language that adds many interactive functions to basic HTML pages. For example, if you have ever seen an image change when the mouse passed over it, then you have seen JavaScript in action. This is called a *rollover*, and it is only one of many possible applications of JavaScript. Other uses of JavaScript include (but are not limited to) the following:

- Sniffers: scripts that determine your browser type, for example, and then automatically load the appropriate page;
- Date-time functions;
- Calculators;
- Form validators: scripts that check to make sure certain information has been typed correctly;
- Online quizzes.

While JS requires some programming know-how, scripts can be downloaded for free from JavaScript archives on the WWW and pasted directly into HTML documents.[9] NoteTab.com offers several clipbook libraries containing JavaScripts.

JavaScript is also extremely useful for inserting dynamic content into HTML pages. In Figure 10.2, the navbar and title graphic are written in an external JavaScript file called *header.js*. The navbar and copyright notice are also appended to the HTML file in the same way via *footer.js*.[10] These files are named in the same way as the external style sheet is named. The following lines of code are responsible for the Web page seen in Figure 10.2 (in Netscape 4.7) and Figure 10.3 (in Netscape 3.01). Notice that the code for the navbars and title graphic in the header, and the navbar and copyright notice in the footer are nowhere to be seen (because they have been placed in external .js files).

The code in the *header.js* file is very straightforward. To write text to the screen in JavaScript, use the document.write command as follows: *document.write('Content')*. Below is an example of how a line of HTML would be coded in JavaScript.

```
<HTML>

<HEAD>

<TITLE>Web course example with CSS and external .js</TITLE>

<LINK REL=stylesheet TYPE="text/css" HREF="../style.css">

</HEAD>

<BODY BACKGROUND="images/map2.jpg" BGCOLOR="white">

<CENTER>

<TABLE BORDER=0 WIDTH=600 CELLPADDING=0
CELLSPACING=0><TR><TD>

<script language="JavaScript" scr="header.js"></script>

<DIV CLASS="subtitle"><H1 ALIGN="center">Title of current page</
DIV></H1>

<H2 ALIGN="center">Subtitle, where applicable</H2>

<P ALIGN="left">Notice that this paragraph is indented and fully justified.
This is a feature of Cascading Style Sheets (CSS) that will be discussed
later in this paper.</P>

<script language="JavaScript" src="footer.js"></script>

</TD></TR>
</TABLE>
</CENTER>

</BODY>

</HTML>
```

In HTML file	In header.jc file

`<H1>Title of course</H1>`	`<!-- begin`
	`document.write('<H1>Title of course</H1>');`
	`//end -->`

The purpose of the "<!-- begin" and "// end -->" nested in the comment tag is a convention of JavaScript writing that prevents pre–second generation browsers, which are not JS-compatible, from printing to screen codes that they do not recognize.

By using external .js files, which function in Netscape 3 and after, not only is it possible to dynamically modify important aspects of pages, but it also avoids the frames controversy.[11]

The Future and Recommendations

The trend toward building greater interactivity and dynamic features into the Web appears to be gaining momentum. New markup languages and important extensions of HTML are already in use. Dynamic HTML is being used by some adventurous Web designers. DHTML is a hybrid language, consisting of HTML 4.0+, CSS, and JavaScript. Used in the correct combination, these languages allow Web pages to be modified, restructured, and updated, even after they have finished loading. This will pave the way for even more dynamic elements, such as interactive menu bars, movable text, instant onscreen feedback, and quizzes.[12]

XML (Extensible Markup Language) goes even further by creating a language based on SGML (of which HTML is merely a static series of elements) that will be expandable, customizable, and rich in structure and commands.[13]

Much of the future of these markup languages will be determined by the quality and completeness of the implementation of these new specifications in the fifth generation browsers. Whatever happens, teachers will continue to deliver Web-based courses, and there will be increasing pressure to do so. Accordingly, I will conclude this short and practical overview of do-it-yourself Web course design with the following recommendations:

1. Code your own course Web pages—if you can learn to use a word processor, you can learn and reap the benefits of the do-it-yourself approach.
2. Respect the well-tested guidelines for interface design—let simplicity, clarity, and consistency be your guiding principles.
3. Utilize dynamic features such as CSS and JavaScript in order to ensure consistency of pages and to save time.
4. Use colour to guide and cue users.
5. Use white space and limit text/hyperlink density to avoid cognitive overload (see endnote 4).
6. Design with an eye to the future, but don't make gratuitous use of emerging technologies.
7. Ignore know-it-alls, would-be gurus, and definitive claims about what the ideology of the Web is or should be.
8. Design for your students, their needs and learning styles, the browsers they use, and for their own computer equipment or the facility where they will work.
9. Poll your students often and (re)design on an ongoing basis.
10. Work collaboratively with other faculty and staff Web course designers to avoid duplication and overlap.

Notes

1 The HTML language is developed, coordinated, and assessed for wide public use by the World Wide Web Consortium (http://www.w3.org). The latest version of HTML is 4.0, which was recommended by the W3 Consortium in 1997 (revised April 24, 1998). The HTML 4.0 specification will be discussed later in this chapter.

2 This survey is not intended to be exhaustive or conclusive, only suggestive of general tendencies. The interface researchers considered were Davies and Brailsford; Houser and DeLoach; Denning et al.; El-Tigi et al.; Gilmore; Häkkinen; Head; Jones and Buchanan; Nielsen; Ohl and Cates; Pincas; Romano et al.; Rowley; Starr; Stoney and Wild; and Wright et al. Only six of the above were not specifically concerned with educational application interface design. Houser and DeLoach were interested in why people do not approach business applications with the same zeal they have for games. Denning et al. studied a Web information retrieval system (database). Head, Nielsen, Rowley, and Wright et al. make claims about all computer interfaces. Their assumption is that guidelines are to some degree independent of context and disciplinary borders. Most of the researchers mentioned seek to define guidelines for broad-based areas of application development. For example, Davies and Brailsford; and Stoney and Wild concentrated on instructional multimedia development while Nielsen and Star were specifically concerned with Web interface design. Gilmore and Häkkinen discussed educational applications in general. The principles articulated by Head and Wright et al. were intended for any computerized application. Conversely, Denning et al. studied productivity/database applications. Jones and Buchanan studied a specific OLE they had authored. Ohl and Cates discussed a specific Web site. Pincas examined certain aspects of FirstClass, and Romano et al. studied a specific educational conferencing system. Despite the multiplicity of their particular orientations, most of their claims and concerns were the same or similar. For further reading on interface design, see the "User Interface Design Bibliography" (Kotlas, 1996).

3 In the example in Figure 10.2, all of the screen data is enclosed in a 600 pixel wide table (all of the text on the page) with the border set to 0; that is, invisible. All of the text is placed within the table, and the table is centred. The 600 pixel width is approximately the width of the screen on 14" monitors. With larger monitors, there is more white space in the left and right margins, and the pages remain pleasing to the eye. If text were not enclosed in this fashion, whole paragraphs could be presented on a single line. Even with a relative attribute (width = 80%), readability suffers because text is too dense on the 14" monitor and lines are still too long on larger monitors. The full HTML code for Figure 10.2, including the table definition, appears later in this chapter.

4 Stoney and Wild (1998) cite a series of user guidelines for avoiding cognitive overload, recommended in Oren (1990). Cognitive overload can be reduced in the following ways:

- Reduce the number of options at any one point in the program.
- Encourage users to externalize their thinking, for example, by the use of text annotations and place markings.
- "Hide" program options not likely to be needed by most users.
- Provide strong visual clues to aid navigation.
- Reduce the number of hypermedia links between information nodes.

5 The term *browser wars* refers to the rivalry between Netscape and Microsoft. Reminiscent of the "space race," the term browser wars first began appearing on the Web in 1996 (according to an AltaVista date-delimited search). Despite Netscape's acquisition by America Online (AOL) in 1999, the browser wars rage on. For up-to-date coverage, see http://browserwatch.internet.com/.

6 See the W3 Consortium Web site at http://www.w3.org/TR/REC-html40/conform.html#deprecated. The W3C also provides a complete list of tags and their current status at http://www.w3.org/TR/REC-html40/index/elements.html. Another useful site for information and tutorials pertaining to HTML 4 is available at http://www.htmlhelp/com/reference/html4.

7 For further reading, visit the following sites: CSS Reference (http://www.htmlhelp.com/reference/css/); W3 Consortium (http://www.w3.org/Style); Known CSS bugs in Netscape 4 (http://developer.netscape.com/support/bugs/known/css.html).

8 For detailed information on the implementation of CSS in Netscape and Internet Explorer, visit http://style.webreview.com/.

9 A useful introductory tutorial is online at http://www.htmlhelp.com/reference/html40/special/script.html. A more technical reference (Netscape) is located at http://developer.netscape.com/docs/manuals/communicator/jsref/index.htm. The following are useful JavaScript archive sites (they include scripts for quizzes):

- The JavaScript Source: http://javascript.internet.com/
- Cut-N-Paste JavaScript: http://www.infohiway.com/javascript/

10 Note that the .js extension must be configured on the server in order for this file type to function.

11 Many designers disavow frames for the following reasons:

- Toolbars on separate frames can sometimes get lost if users enter sites through "back door" Internet addresses.
- The URLs of individual pages are not displayed.
- It is difficult to link to secondary pages on sites with frames since frames are usually set on the main, or launch, page.
- Frames can cause confusion when it comes time to print pages (you must click on the individual frame you wish to print).

On the other hand, education researchers El-Tigi et al. (1997) present a favourable view of frames use in general and in terms of cognitive implications.

12 On the use of DHTML for simple quizzes, see Bull et al., 1998. Also, a DHTML clipbook is freely available from NoteTab.com to help get you started.

13 For an overview of some of the possibilities of XML, see Bosak, 1997.

REFERENCES

Apple Computer Inc. 1987. *Human Interface Guidelines: The Apple Desktop Interface*. Reading, Massachusetts : Addison-Wesley Publishing Co.

Bosak, J. 1997. "XML, Java, and the Future of the Web." (http://metalab.unc.edu/pub/sun-info/standards/xml/why/xmlapps.htm)

Bull, Glen., Gina Bull, and D. Lewis. 1998. "Introducing Dynamic HTML." *Learning and Leading with Technology* 26(2), 43–45.

Davies, P., and T. Brailsford. 1994. *New Frontiers of Learning: Guidelines for Multimedia Courseware Developers in Higher Education*. University of Nottingham. (http://vsb.life.nottingham.ac.uk/guidelines/title.html)

Denning, R., M. Shuttleworth, and P. Smith. 1998. "Interface Design Concepts in the Development of a Web-Based Information Retrieval System." *Bulletin of the American Society for Information Science* 24(4), 17–20.

El-Tigi, M., and M.B. Branch. 1997. "Designing for Interaction, Learner Control, and Feedback During Web-Based Learning." *Educational Technology* 37(3), 23–29.

Gilmore, D.J. 1996. "The Relevance of HCI Guidelines for Educational Interfaces." *Machine-Mediated Learning* 5(2), 119–133.

Häkkinen, P. 1996. "Software Designers and Teachers as Evaluators of Computer-Based Learning Environments." *Machine-Mediated Learning* 5(2), 135–148.

Head, Alison J. 1999. *Design Wise: A Guide to Evaluating the Interface Design of Information Resources*. Medford, New Jersey: Information Today.

Houser, R, and S. DeLoach. 1998. "Learning from Games: Seven Principles of Effective Design, Technical Communication." *Journal of the Society for Technical Communication* 45(3), 319–329.

International Business Machines System Application Architecture. 1989. *Common User Access, Advanced Interface Design Guide*. IBM Corporation.

Jones, D., and R. Buchanan. 1996. "The Design of an Integrated Online Learning Environment, Making New Connections." Pp. 331–345 in *Proceedings of ASCILITE'96 Adelaide*, eds. A. Christie, P. James, and B. Vaughan. (http://cq-pan.cqu.edu.au/davidjones/Publications/Papers_and_Books/96ascilite/index.html)

Kotlas, C. 1996. *User Interface Design Bibliography*. Chapel Hill, North Carolina: University of North Carolina, Center for Instructional Technology (http://www.unc.edu/cit/guides/irg-05.html)

Nielsen, Jakob. 1996. "Top Ten Mistakes in Web Design." (http://www.useit.com/alertbox/9605.html)

Nielsen, Jakob. 1999a. "Top Ten Mistakes Revisited Three Years Later." (http://www.useit.com/alertbox/990502.html)

Nielsen, Jakob. 1999b. "The Top Ten 'New' Mistakes of Web Design." (http://www.useit.com/alertbox/990530.html)

Ohl, T.M., and W.M. Cates. 1997. "Applying Metaphorical Interface Design Principles to the World Wide Web." *Educational Technology* 37(6), 25–38.

Oren, T. 1990. "Cognitive Load in Hypermedia: Designing for the Exploratory Learner." Pp. 126–136 in *Learning with Interactive Multimedia*, eds. S. Ambron and K. Hooper. Washington: Microsoft Press.

Pincas, Anita. 1998."Management Issues for Online Courses." *Active Learning* 9, 41–45.

Romano, N.C., Jr., J.F. Nunamaker, Jr., R.O. Briggs, and D.R. Vogel. 1998. "Architecture, Design, and Development of an HTML/JavaScript Web-Based Group Support System." *Journal of the American Society for Information Science* 49(7), 649–667.

Rowley, J. 1998. "Towards a Methodology for the Design of Multimedia Public Access Interfaces." *Journal of Information Science* 24(3), 155–166.

Starr, Robin M. 1997. "Delivering Instruction on the World Wide Web: Overview and Basic Design Principles." *Educational Technology* 37(3), 7–15.

Stoney, S., and M. Wild. 1998. "Motivation and Interface Design: Maximising Learning Opportunities." *Journal of Computer Assisted Learning* 14(1), 40–50.

Wright, P, D. Mosser-Wooley, and Bruce Wooley. 1997. "Techniques and Tools for Using Color in Computer Interface Design." *Crossroads (Association for Computing Machinery)* 3(3). (http://www.acm.org/crossroads/xrds3-3/xrds3-3.html)

CHAPTER 11

Adding Digitized Speech to Web Courses

Bruce Mann
Memorial University of Newfoundland
Canada

The procedure for adding digitized speech to a Web course is inextricably linked to empirical research and theory on human attention and educational technology.

Human Attention

Attention is critical to learning; without it there can be no learning. Educators typically seek to obtain and maintain our attention (Fleming, 1987). Attention sustains our vigilance with sensations, regulating the search and enhancing our sensory acuity that makes us aware of any new cues. Current theories of attention in the cognitive disciplines state that there are different kinds of attention relative to the difficulty of the assigned tasks and the familiarity of the content under study (Gagne, Yekovitch, and Yekovitch, 1993). Figure 11.1 shows a representation of human verbal and spatial memories during difficult and unfamiliar tasks.

For easy tasks with familiar items, the student will implement automatic (Schneider and Shiffrin, 1977) or pre-attentive (Treisman, 1986) mental processing. Pre-attentive processing can occur in parallel; that is, the student mentally processes two or more different inputs simultaneously. For difficult, divided-attention tasks with unfamiliar items, however, the student must consciously control their mental processing (Schneider and Shiffrin, 1977) to focus their attention (Treisman, 1986). Under these conditions, attention focusing becomes serial; only one task is processed at a time. To engage the appropriate attentive state in the Web course, the student must self-initiate the appropriate system of information processing (Borich and Tombari, 1995).

However, research (Mousavi, Low, and Sweller, 1995; Ragsdale, 1988) and expert opinion (Heinich, Molenda, and Russell, 1992; Jaspers, 1991) suggest that students using educational multimedia usually ignore or forget to read important instructions and feedback presented in text or other visual displays. "Many students will not notice the option to read directions or will try to save time by skipping them" (Alessi and Trollip, 1991, p. 22).

In a recent study, Mann, Newhouse, Pagram, and Campbell (2000) found that adding digitized speech on tasks that were too easy and familiar did not enhance student

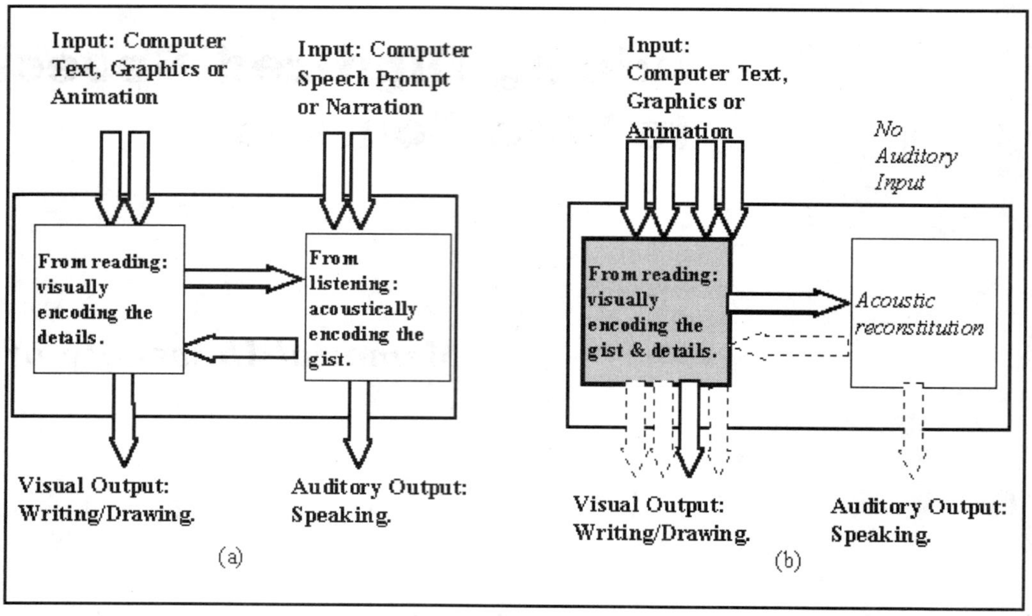

Figure 11.1
Human verbal and spatial memories

(a) Normal mental effort with normal cognitive load from a balanced input across both channels, and (b) high mental effort associated with high cognitive load from an unbalanced input.

Mann, Newhouse, Pagram, and Campbell, 2000

learning. The significance of this finding resides in the discovery that adding digitized speech to a Web course is unlikely to enhance student learning on tasks that are too easy or familiar. The implications suggest that adding digitized speech to a Web course need only be employed on difficult, divided-attention tasks.

Educational Technology

Since the late 1950s, educational technology researchers believed that converting some information into digitized speech could offer students a more effective alternative to reading instructions and feedback from a computer screen (Blyth, 1960; Skinner, 1960). Students were required to control their own processing of these separate sensations. At that time, however, little was known of the effects of auditory manipulations on language learning (Porter, 1960). So human interactions with technology were often explained as a function of playback system performance instead of describing how students divided their attention on difficult and unfamiliar tasks (see Skinner, 1960). Those who did write about attention (Broadbent, 1958) emphasized that people are extremely limited in the amount of information they can process at any given time. A common metaphor was the bottleneck concept that proposed that there is a narrow passageway in our working memory that limits the quantity of information to which we attend at any one time. Furthermore, the research preoccupation with visual information at that time was based on the assumption that the sound would take care of itself. However, experimentation showed that sound did not take care of itself (Hartman, 1961). Consequently, early approaches to learning from auditory-visual delivery technology were found to be ad hoc and unproven, and required frequent re-examination and clarification (Conway, 1968).

In the 1970s and 1980s, researchers disputed the bottleneck metaphor and the limit to our capacity for information. Neisser (1976) established that our efficiency can be increased with practice. In 1982, Hildyard and Olson determined that readers and listeners tend to extract different kinds of information from oral and written presentations: said another way, verbal information presented visually is processed differently than verbal information presented acoustically. Readers tend to process information largely at word level (the detail), and to recall more of the surface or verbatim features of the information. Listeners tend to process information largely at the level of meaning (the highlights), and to recall more of the gist of the information. And Fleming (1987) and Gagne, Briggs, and Wager (1988) found that learning could be improved for some students by designing the external conditions of the learning environment. In 1989, Penney detected superior performance on concurrent tasks using verbal information when the stimuli were presented in two modalities rather than one, and higher recall when two presentation modalities were used instead of one.

In the 1990s, Mayer and Moreno (1998) reported that students learning from animation with narration produced 50 per cent more creative solutions on problem-solving questions than students in an animation-with-text group. And Mann (1995a) conducted a protocol analysis of student verbal reports, and found that temporal speech cueing helped students to attend to screen information by affecting their constructive ability. In a study involving static diagrams for geometry problems, Mousavi, Low, and Sweller (1995) stated that students learned better when auditory narration was presented simultaneously with corresponding diagrams. Mann (1997a) compared the relative effectiveness of three versions of a hypermedia system (text, sound/text, sound) and found that students working with sound could focus their attention on the critical information needed to make successful interpretations.

These reports have become the basis of current models and theories, including Penney's (1989) separate streams hypothesis; Baddaley's (1992) model of working memory; Paivio's (1986) dual coding theory; Mayer and Moreno's (1998) dual processing theory of working memory; Mayer's (1997) theory of multimedia learning; and Mann's structured sound functions model (1992, 1995a, 1997a). With knowledge of the empirical research and pedagogical theory concerning their application in a Web course management setting, we can now apply the procedure for adding digitized speech to a Web course.

Procedure for Adding Digitized Speech to Web Courses

In this section, the procedure will be discussed for combining sound with static or moving visuals for a Web course. There are several possible functions for digitized speech in a learning environment (Mann, 1995a; 1992). Decisions about how much information to convert into digitized speech, and the function the digitized speech should have in your Web course (for example, instruction, feedback, directions for using a tool), can either precede or occur during the speech digitizing process. The HTML coding can precede or follow speech digitizing; the sequence of the procedure is unimportant. Your particular situation will determine the eventual sequence in the procedure. The five steps, explained in detail below, are as follows.

1. Determine the gist.
2. Prepare your Web course for digitized speech.
3. Digitize the speech prompts.

4. Check your speech prompts.
5. Play your speech prompts on a browser.

Step 1: Determine the Gist

The first step is to determine the gist for conversion into digitized speech, and what function the digitized speech should have (for example, instruction, feedback, directions for using a tool) in your Web course. You'll recall, we determined that listening tends to favour recall of gist: students processing the meaning of the information. So only the gist should be presented in sound, and the details left in text. Sometimes the Web course manager already knows the situation in which to add audio before knowing its exact function or purpose. Other times contriving an audio situation is the most realistic approach. In either case, it is important to ensure that the meaning contained in the sound prompt is related to but not redundant with the meaning presented in the text and graphics on the target screen; this gives the sound a function in the program.

The structured sound functions (SSF) model is useful for combining speech with text, graphics, and video clips. See Mann (1995b, 1997b) for empirical research on the SSF model in the higher education context. The model is both structured and flexible enough to accommodate most logistical constraints, particularly when rapid changes must be made without physically including them in a storyboard. A full description of the elements, origin, and detailed applications of the SSF model can be found in Mann (1992, 1995a, 1997a). Two of the more well-researched functions from the model (temporal sound and point-of-view sound) are described below.

Temporal Speech Prompts

In general, the use of temporal speech prompts should be considered for a Web course when the primary intent of audio is to orient learners in a Web course about a future event (on a target screen), or to give feedback about a past event (on a previous screen) (Mann, 1995b). The rationale is that once students discern that they can "click back to the information whenever they want" they tend to ignore or forget to read instructions and feedback presented in text or other visual displays (DeHaemer and Wallace, 1992; Jaspers, 1991). Future and past event prompts focus students' attention by requiring them to control their mental processing of the visual and audio stimuli long enough for them to connect the inferences made between nodes (that is, between Web pages and tools in a Web course). Temporal speech prompts are especially recommended when students are clicking forward and back between pages and tools in a Web course. Figure 11.2 shows the text of a Web page that automatically plays temporal speech prompts with the following audio script.

> The Lieutenant Governor assigns powers and duties to an Education Improvement Commission (Mann and Skanes, 1997).

As suggested in the research (above), the gist of the information is presented in sound, and the details are left in text. In this way, temporal sound is used when the students' objectives require them to make associations between nodes in a knowledge network, as in a Web course.

Figure 11.2
Temporal speech prompt plays automatically

Mann and Skanes, 1997

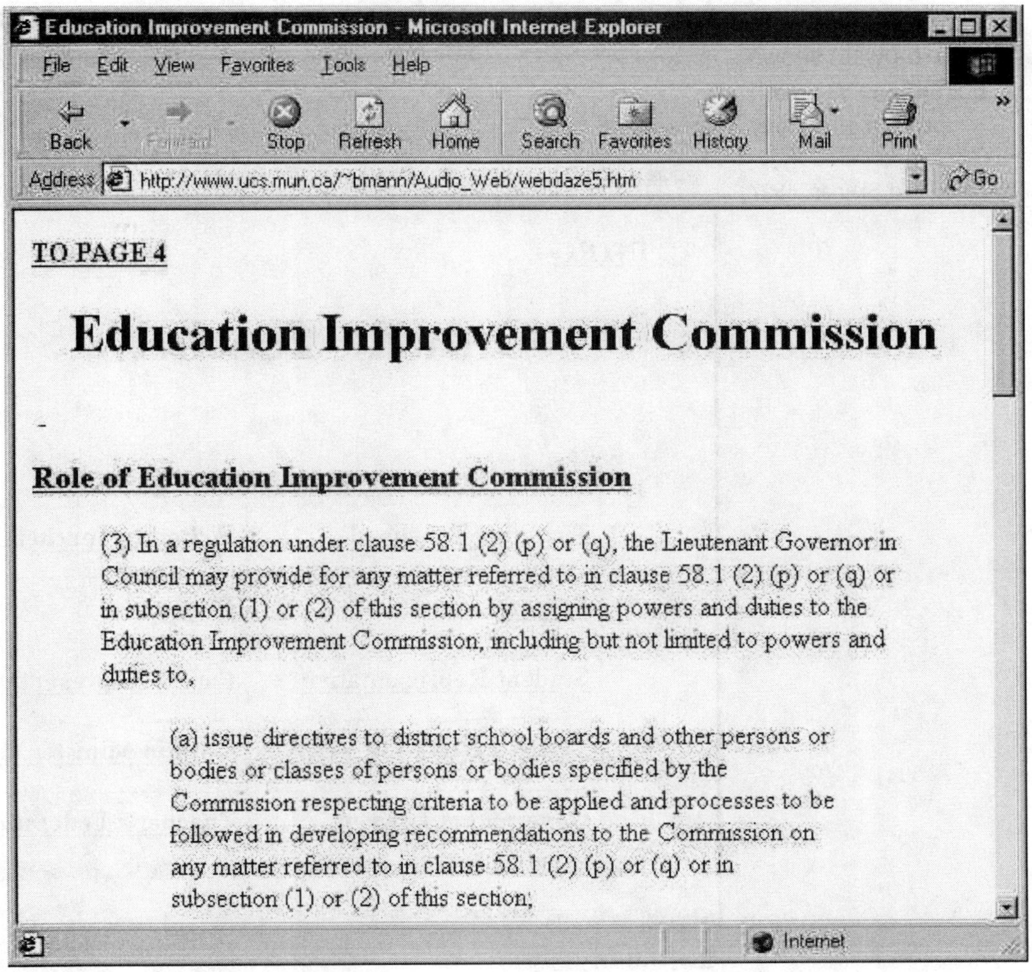

Point-of-View Sound

Another method of reducing the need for students to click forward and back (described earlier) is to add point-of-view sound. POV sound can stand alone, as shown below in a lengthy text version, to conserve screen real estate, or can augment text or static or moving visuals. Unlike the lengthy text version, Figure 11.3 shows how ten subjective points of view are represented as POV. Students can click on any tag with only the labels showing, to hear an original point of view on a topic of contention.

> We've been right all along. And now the people of Ontario are finally listening to us... and the judge obviously agreed with us. (Picketing Teacher 1)
>
> I'm happy. I think that if he had ordered us back to work that nothing would have gotten solved. (Picketing Teacher 2)
>
> It's kind of annoying when you have to be in this when you really didn't do anything. (Student 1)

Figure 11.3
Web browser shows point-of-view speech prompt capability

Mann and Skanes, 1997

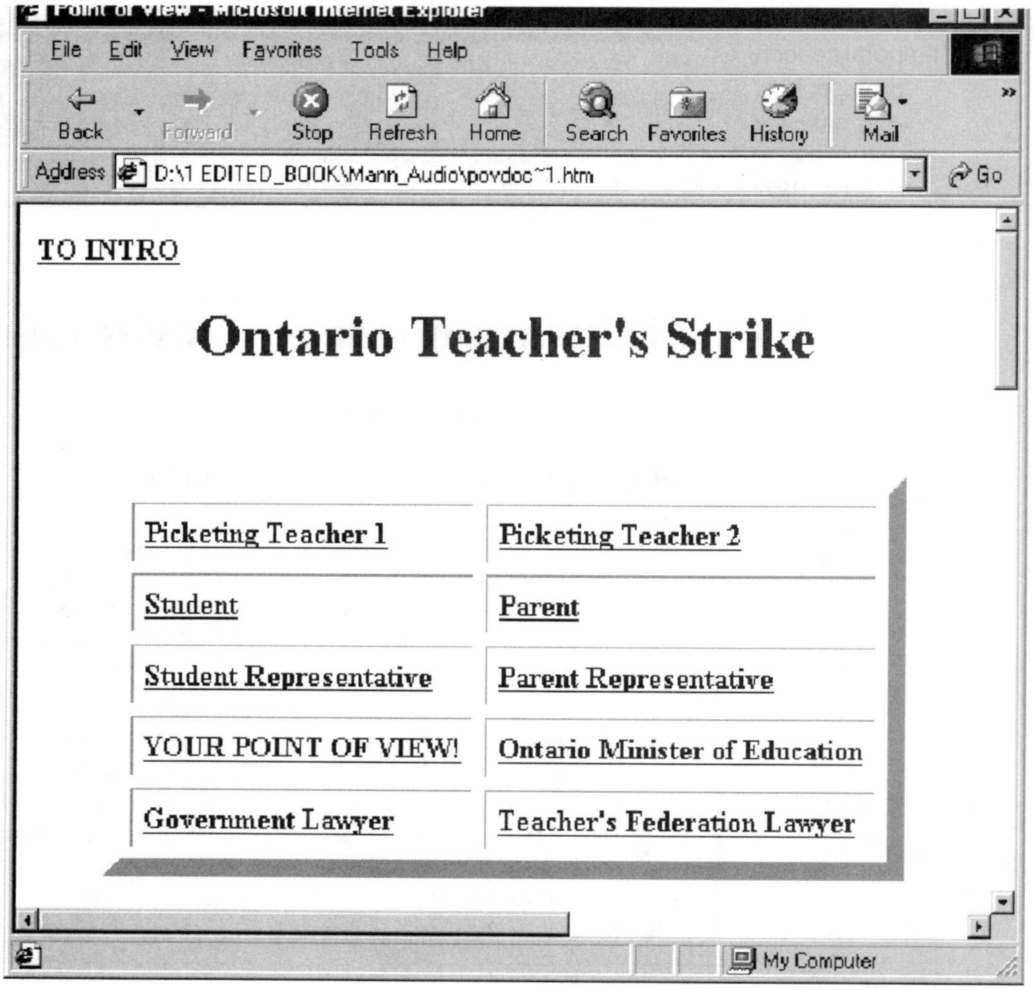

> It's time to [go] back 'cause I think if you don't go back right now, then we'll lose more…and its going to affect us greatly…. (Student 2)

> The matter will be discussed with our clients, and uh other than to say that with thought it was a very thoughtful, well-reasoned judgement. (Lawyer for the Teacher's Federation)

> I think the message is, is that you can't bully your way through a public process. (Lawyer for the Ontario Government)

Similarly, objective, subjective, or performer POV sound can be prescribed as a function of character. A whispered voice-over, for example, may indicate a subjective POV sound function. A formal narrator voice-over can provide an objective POV sound function. Cocktail party sound using some combination of subjective and objective voices would be one example of a performer POV sound function.

In this way, digitized speech can be fully integrated into the management of the Web course and not remain just another feature of it. The great benefit of the model to the

Web course manager is that it can be used either to examine the educational message design in a Web course, or for prescribing sound with static or moving visuals for a Web course. Once the gist is determined, it's time to prepare your Web course to receive digitized speech.

Step 2: Prepare Your Web Course for Digitized Speech

Preparing the relevant Web pages in your Web course to receive digitized speech requires launching a text editor or HTML editor, and typing commands to play the speech files, saving the new HTML document, and giving it a file name. HTML authoring is relatively easy to learn, produces aesthetically pleasing screen and sound designs, and permits fast prototyping of new design ideas. Figure 11.4 shows the source code in a Web page that will automatically play a temporal speech prompt with the filename *Fran_1a.wav* with the audio script.

> < EMBED SRC="fran_1a.wav" HIDDEN=TRUE AUTOSTART=TRUE VOLUME=50% >
>
> The Lieutenant Governor assigns powers and duties to an Education Improvement Commission. (Mann and Skanes, 1997)

Figure 11.4 also shows the code for a speech prompt with the filename *Fran_3a.wav* to play in a Windows Media Player pop-up window with the following audio script.

> < a HREF="fran_3a.wav" AUTOSTART=TRUE VOLUME=50% >
>
> On your own paper, list the powers and duties as outlined in number three; the boards, classes, determinations, orders, and deadlines. (Mann and Skanes, 1997)

In both cases, the code for a temporal speech prompt is embedded in the source page. The net effect is that the prompt plays as the Web page loads, or shortly thereafter, orienting the students about a future event (for example, something they should start thinking about now), or giving them feedback about a past event. The next stage is to digitize those speech prompts.

Step 3: Digitize the Speech Prompts

Once the Web browser has been programmed to read digitized speech files, it is time to digitize the speech files. Under certain conditions, vocal gender and expressiveness appear to contribute to learning from visuals. Highly expressive female instructions and program directions have had a positive effect on student learning (Mann, 1995a; Meyrow, 1991). However, the sampling rate for digitizing speech does not appear to be a significant factor in learning from visuals with sound (Carroll, 1992). Decisions about the sampling rate for digitizing speech should be made as a trade-off between the quality and quantity of speech you want to digitize, and the limitations on the server.

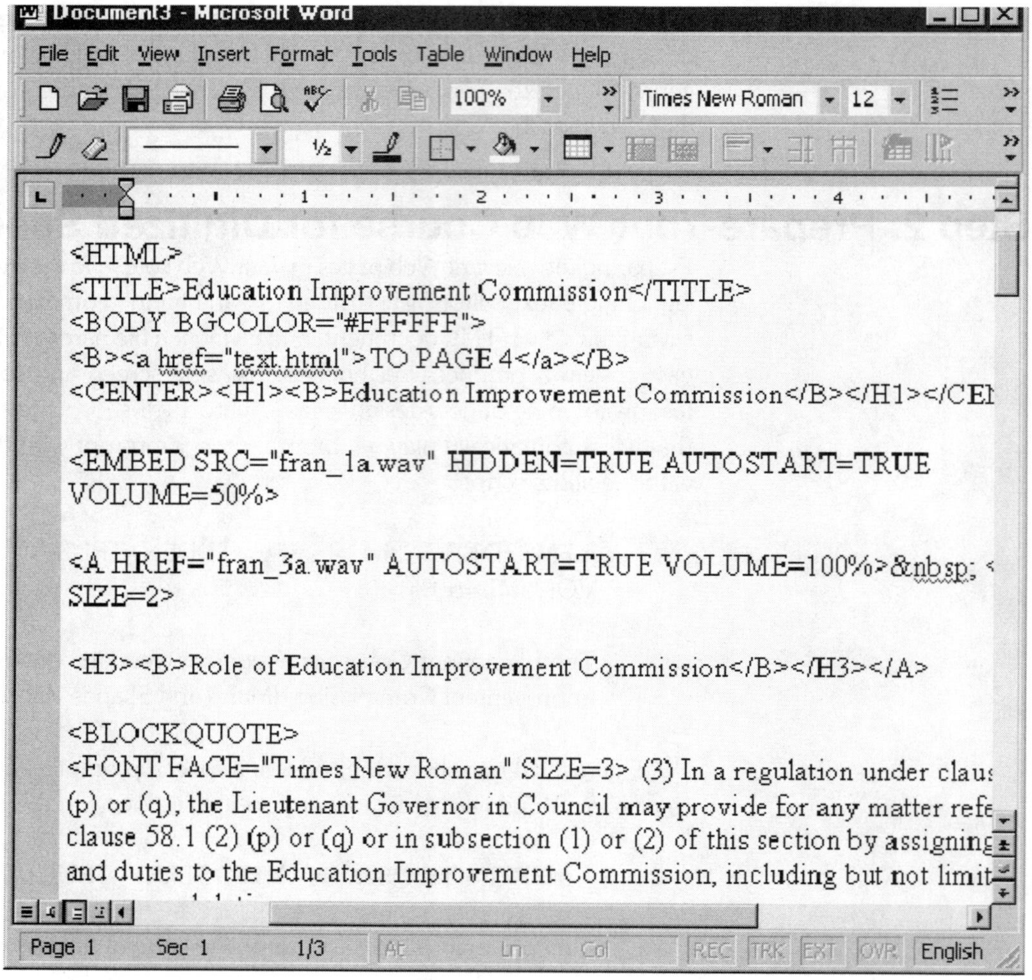

Figure 11.4 HTML source for a speech prompt that plays automatically, and one that plays from a pop-up media player

Mann and Skanes, 1997

To digitize a speech file, ensure you have an audio input device connected to your computer. An audio input device usually records voice or music input. Examples of audio input devices include microphones and CD-ROM players. On the File menu, launch the Microsoft Sound Recorder, go to File and select New. Sounds can be easily recorded and mixed using the media recorder provided with the Microsoft Windows operating system. Figure 11.5 shows a graphical representation of the Microsoft Sound Recorder.

Microsoft Sound Recorder, like other programs of its kind, makes it possible for Web course managers with a personal computer and a sound card to record, play, and edit their own speech prompts, as follows:

1. To begin recording, click ● .
2. To stop recording, click ■ .
3. From the File menu, click Save As to save and close the file in the same directory/folder as the HTML file.

Figure 11.5
Microsoft Sound Recorder

Microsoft Corporation, 1995

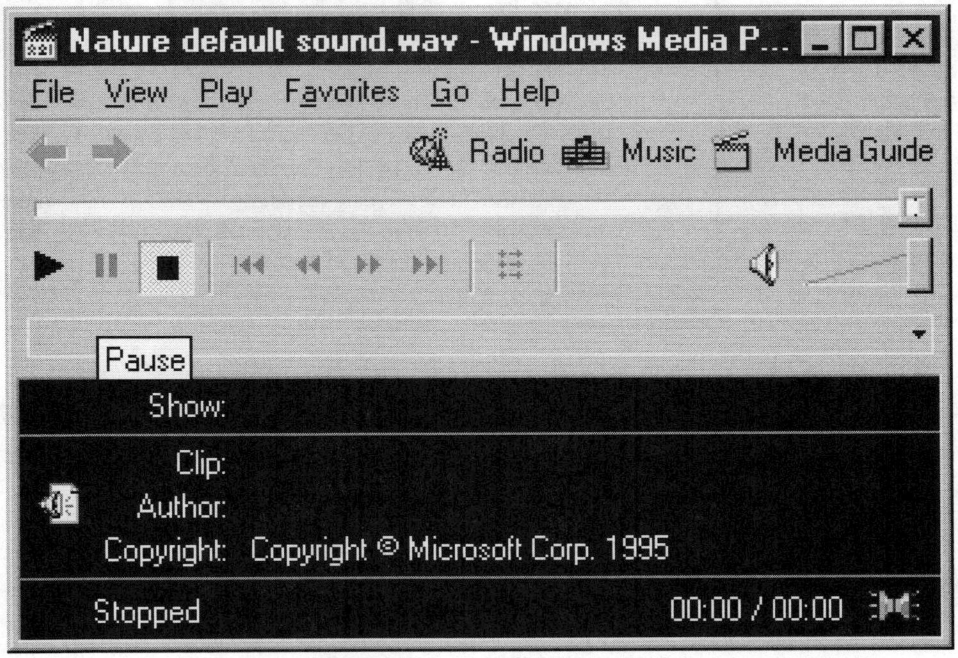

Figure 11.6
Microsoft Media Player

Microsoft Corporation, 1995

Step 4: Check your Speech Prompts

You can play back your recording in Sound Recorder or in Media Player. Figure 11.6 shows a graphical representation of the Microsoft Media Player.

1. Go to the File menu, and click Open.
2. Open the folder containing the file you want to play, and click Open.

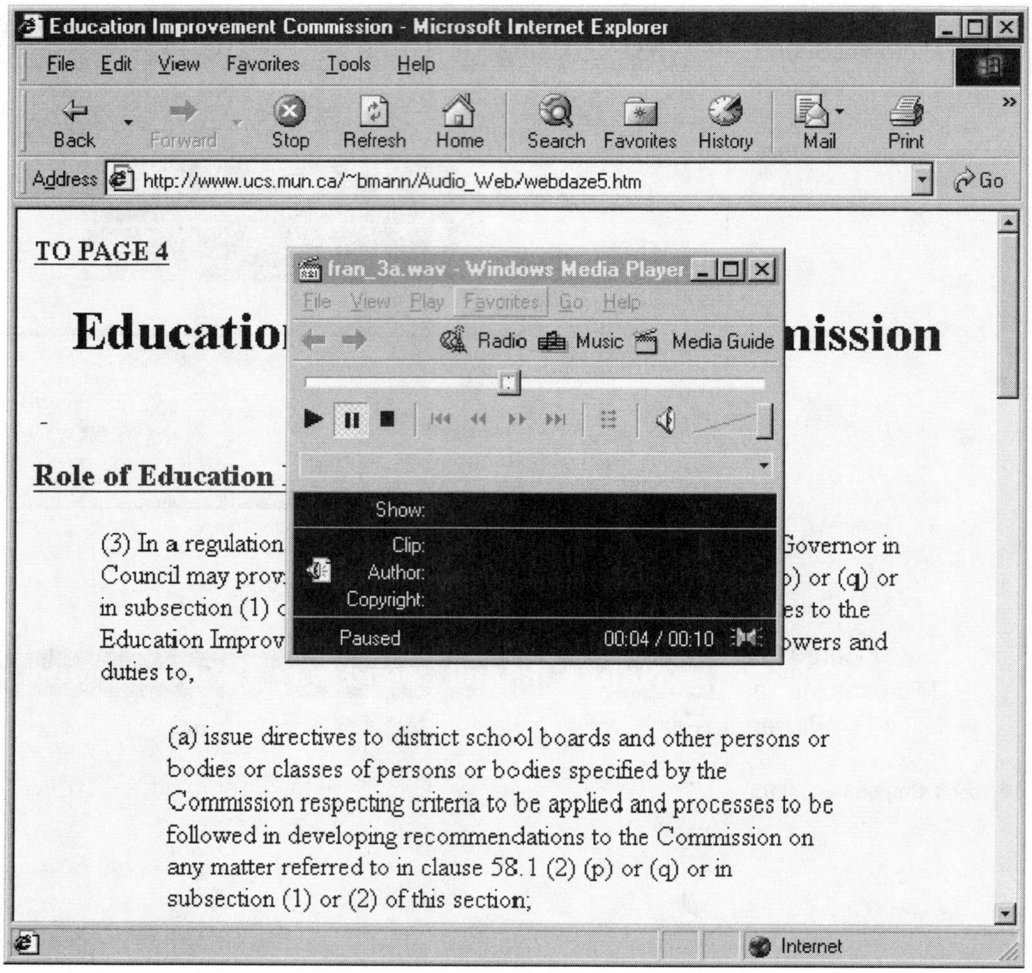

Figure 11.7 Media Player runs from a hypertext link

Mann and Skanes, 1997

3. Click [play] to start playing the sound, and [stop] to stop it playing. You can move to the beginning of a sound file by clicking [rewind] and to the end by clicking [fast forward].

Step 5: Play Your Speech Prompts on a Browser

In the Web browser, view the prototype document. If the "A HREF" code is programmed properly, this speech prompt should play automatically. If the "EMBED SRC" code is programmed properly, clicking on the appropriate link on the Web page should invoke the Windows Media Player to play the other speech prompt. Figure 11.7 shows that clicking on the hypertext link on a Web course activity called the Role of the Education Commission invokes a Microsoft Media Player that pops up over the screen and plays as a hypertext reference.

Figure 11.8 shows that clicking on the hypertext link on a Web course activity about the Hubble Space Telescope invokes a reduced instance of the Microsoft Media Player.

This concludes the process of adding digitized speech to a Web course. For best results, the procedure should reflect current research and theory on human attention and educational technology.

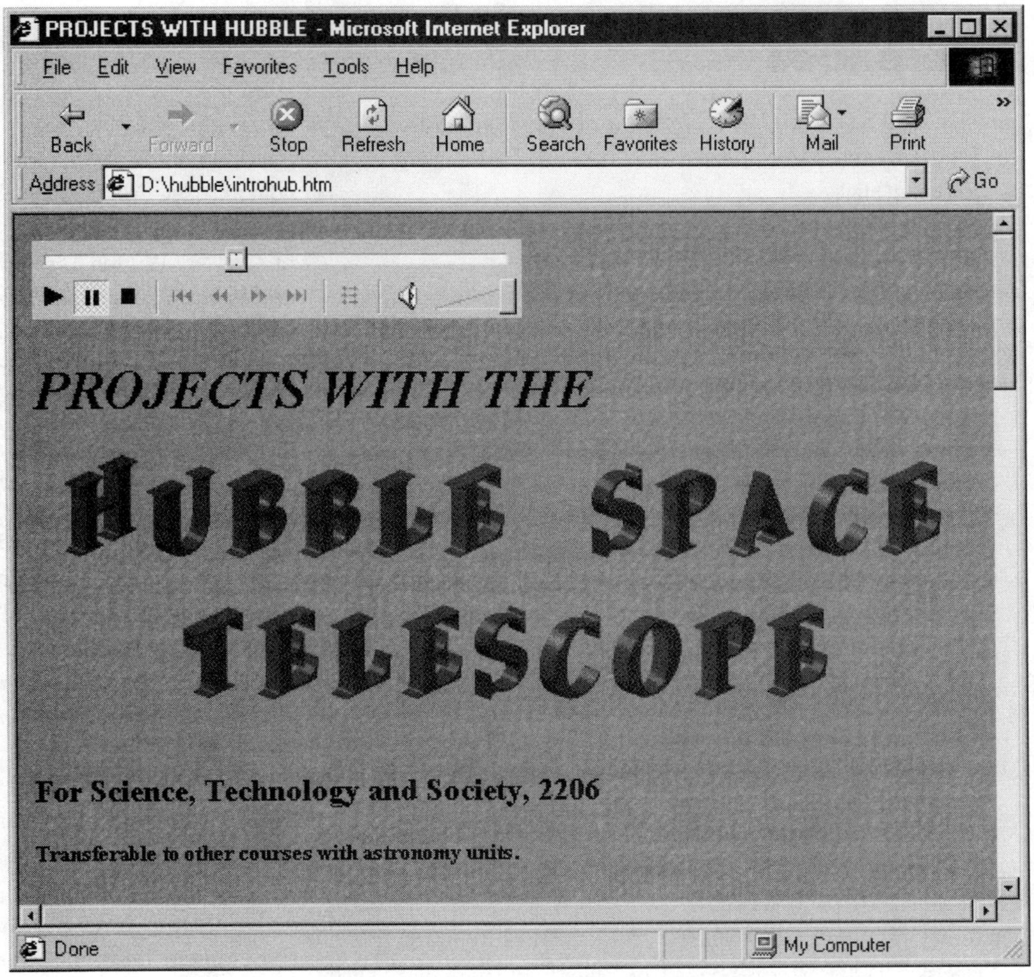

Figure 11.8
Condensed image of the Microsoft Media Player runs when linking to an activity about the Hubble space telescope

Mann and MacDuff, 1996

Summary

This chapter addressed the problem of student inattention to important text, static or moving graphics, or videos presented in a Web course, and promising psychological solutions using digitized speech prompting. Although there are other methods of focusing attention on critical information, this paper was only concerned with psychological solutions using digitized speech prompting. A description of the limits of human attention were examined; a procedure was presented for digitizing and uploading speech prompts into a Web course; and a message design model was proffered for adding digitized speech to visuals presented on a Web site. Also, the current view about how sound enhances learning was presented; namely, under certain conditions, students will acoustically encode the gist or verbatim data from a computer presentation from which to generate creative solutions to problem-solving questions.

References

Alessi, S., and S. Trollip. 1991. *Computer-Based Instruction: Methods and Development* (4th edition). New Jersey: Prentice Hall.

Baddaley, A. 1992. "Working Memory." *Science* 255, 556–559, January.

Borich, D., and M. Tombari. 1995. *Educational Psychology: A Contemporary Approach*. New York: Harper Collins Publishers.

Blyth, J. 1960. "Teaching Machines and Human Beings." Pp. 401–415 in *Teaching Machines and Programmed Learning: A Sourcebook,* eds. A. Lumsdaine and R. Glaser. Washington: Department of Audiovisual Education, National Education Association.

Broadbent, D. 1958. *Perception and Communication*. Oxford: Pergamon Press.

Carroll, D. 1992. "The Effect of Sampling Rate of Digitally Recorded Sound on Recognition Memory in a Computerized Audio Production Tutorial." *Dissertations Abstracts International* 53(05), SECA, PP1380. University Microfilms No. ADG92-26413.

Conway, J. 1968. "Information Presentation, Information Processing and The Sign Vehicle." *AV Communication Review* 16(4), 403–414.

Dehaemer, M., and W. Wallace. 1992. "The Effects on Decision Task Performance of Computer Synthetic Voice Output." *International Journal of Man-Machine Studies* 36, 65–80.

Fleming, M. 1987. "Displays and Communicaton." Pp. 233–260 in *Instructional Technology: A History*, ed. R.M. Gagne. Hillsdale, New Jersey: Lawrence Erlbaum Associates.

Gagne, E., C. Yekovitch, and F. Yekovitch. 1993. *The Cognitive Psychology of School Learning* (2nd edition). New York: Harper Collins.

Gagne, R., L. Briggs, and W. Wager. 1988. *Principles of Instructional Design* (3rd edition). New York: Holt, Rinehart and Winston.

Jaspers, F. 1991. "The Relationship: Sound-Image." *International Journal of Instructional Media* 18(2), 161–174.

Hartman, F. 1961. "Single and Multiple Channel Communication: A Review of Research and A Proposed Model." *AV Communication Review* 9, 245–267.

Heinich, R., M. Molenda, and J. Russell. 1992. *Instructional Media and the New Technologies of Instruction* (4th edition). New York: Macmillan Publishing Company.

Hildyard, A., and D.R. Olson. 1982. "On the Comprehension of Oral vs. Written Discourse." Pp. 19–24 in *Spoken and Written Language: Exploring Orality and Literacy*, ed. D. Tannen. Norwood, New Jersey: Ablex Publishing.

Mann, B. 1988. "Guidelines for the Instructional Design of Motion Picture Sound." Master's thesis. Concordia University, Montréal, Canada.

Mann, B. 1992. "The SSF Model: Structuring the Functions of the Sound Attribute." *Canadian Journal of Educational Communication* 21(1), 45–65.

Mann, B. 1993. "Effects of Temporal Sound on Computer-Based Learning." Doctoral dissertation. University of Toronto, Canada.

Mann, B. 1995a. "Focusing Attention with Temporal Sound." *Journal of Research on Computing in Education* 27(4), 402–424.

Mann, B. 1995b. "Enhancing Educational Software with Audio: Assigning Structural and Functional Attributes from the SSF Model." *British Journal of Educational Technology* 26(1), 16–29.

Mann, B. 1996. "Catching the .wav: Adding Sound to Hypermedia Learning Environments." *Hypernexus: Journal of Hypermedia and Multimedia Studies* 6(3/4), 18–21.

Mann, B. 1997a. "Evaluation of Three Variations of a Hypermedia System." *Computers and Education: An International Journal* 28(2) 133–147.

Mann, B. 1997b. "Shifting Attention in Multimedia: Stochastic Roles, Design Principles and the SSF Model." *Innovations In Education and Training International* 34(3), 174–187.

Mann, B., and G. Macduff. 1996. "Digitized Speech Prompting of the Hubble Space Telescope." Unpublished manuscript. St. John's, Newfoundland, Memorial University.

Mann, B., P. Newhouse, J. Pagram, and A. Campbell. 2000. "Divided Attention in Multimedia Learning." ED-Media 2000: World Conference on Educational Multimedia, Hypermedia and Telecommunications, June 26–July 1, Montréal, Canada.

Mann, B., and J. Skanes. 1997. "Auditory Communication from Web Browsers: Point-of-View and Temporal Digitized

Speech Prompting on the Ontario Teachers' Strike." A presentation to faculty and staff. St. John's, Newfoundland, Memorial University.

Mayer, R. 1997. "Multimedia Learning: Are We Asking the Right Questions?" *Educational Psychologist* 32(1), 1–19.

Mayer, R., and R. Moreno. 1998. "A Split Attention Effect in Multimedia Learning: Evidence for Dual Processing Systems in Working Memory." *Journal of Educational Psychology* 90(2), 312–320.

Meyrow, A. 1991. "Effect of On-Screen Instructor Gender and Expressivity Upon Adult Learning of Computer Skills from an Instructional Videotape." *Dissertation Abstracts International* 52(12), SECA, PP4188. University Microfilms No. ADG92-14588.

Mousavi, S., R. Low, and J. Sweller. 1995. "Reducing Cognitive Load by Mixing Auditory and Visual Presentations Modes." *Journal of Educational Psychology* 87 319–334.

Neisser, U. 1976. *Cognition and Reality*. San Francisco: Freeman.

Paivio, A. 1986. *Mental Representations: A Dual Coding Approach*. New York: Oxford University Press.

Penney, C. 1989. "Modality Effects and the Structure of Short Term Verbal Memory." *Memory and Cognition* 17(4), 398–422.

Porter, D. 1960. "A Report on Instructional Devices in Foreign Language Teaching." Pp. 186–205 in *Teaching Machines and Programmed Learning: A Sourcebook*, eds. I. Lumsdaine and R. Glaser. Washington: Department of Audiovisual Education, National Education Association.

Ragsdale, R. 1988. *Permissible Computing in Education: Values, Assumptions and Needs*. New York: Praeger Books.

Schneider, W., and R. Shiffrin. 1977. "Controlled and Automatic Human Information Processing: Detection, Search and Attention." *Psychological Review* 84, 1–66.

Skinner, B.F. 1960. "Teaching Machines." Pp. 137–158 in *Teaching Machines and Programmed Learning: A Sourcebook*, eds. I. Lumsdaine and R. Glaser. Washington: Department of Audiovisual Education, National Education Association.

Treisman, A. 1986. "Features and Objects in Visual Processing." *Scientific American* 255(5), 114B–125.

CHAPTER 12

Managing Large Classes in WebCT

Joe Luca
Edith Cowan University
Australia

This chapter outlines and discusses the process of designing, implementing, and evaluating an online course at Edith Cowan University to teach final year multimedia tertiary students how to manage the development of a multimedia product. The course was offered to eighty final-year students who worked in collaborative teams to create a Web-based product.

The online method was used to promote communication and collaboration among team members as a means of exchanging ideas and information related to managing the development of a multimedia product. The use of the WebCT courseware environment was meant to promote understanding among students through dialogue and reflection with peers and tutors. This is reflected in the design of the WebCT environment and forms of assessment. The chapter provides an analysis of the following issues involved in building this online course, which relied heavily on collaborative and team aspects:

- Background
- Justification and pedagogical approach
- Designing the home page: which icons to use
- Assessment criteria
- WebCT student database and maintenance issues
- Server maintenance, backup, and reliability
- Tutor and coordinator issues
- Student feedback
- Future refinements

Background

Students completing the final year of the interactive multimedia course at Edith Cowan University are required to develop skills and expertise in project management methodology. These include developing quality assurance procedures for analysis, design, development, and evaluation, and other project management aspects such as contract development, copyright, costing, scheduling, and communication.

Before putting this unit online, it was run as fourteen, 3-hour class sessions, which were a combination of traditional lectures and team-based activities aimed at developing a Web site. This unit was intended to consolidate multimedia skills learned in other units. The unit promoted teamwork and collaborative skills between team members and the client in order to assist in the smooth development of a Web site. Therefore, it was important to provide a virtual environment that promoted collaboration for discussing project management methodology, and teamwork issues needed for building a Web site. Each student team consisted of about four students who were responsible for different aspects of development within a project.

There were three major assignments, based on the analysis phase, design phase, and the final product, all of which contained the following assessment aspects:

- The project team mark, based on the written assignments and final Web product;
- The task team mark, based on the delivery of an online lesson;
- The individual reports to encourage reflection on different aspects and how they would improve on the process the next time;
- The client mark;
- The peer assessment mark, negotiated with the team to encourage students to carefully consider their role and contribution.

Justification and Pedagogical Approach

Employers are becoming increasingly vocal about the lack of generic skills shown by higher education graduates. They are clearly dissatisfied with the quality of graduates, even though their academic scores may be high. A study by Marginson (1993), revealed that the three most desired characteristics of university graduates by business and industry in Australia were communication skills, capacity to learn new skills and procedures, and capacity for cooperation and teamwork. Employers' views are consistent with many research findings that indicate high school teachers and tertiary lecturers teach too much content and do not promote the development of generic skills (Bennett, Dunne, and Carre 1999; Oliver and McLoughlin, 1999; Candy, 1994).

A project-based learning approach was used in this unit in an attempt to promote the development of these generic skills such as collaborative learning, problem solving, critical thinking, and social skills (Collis, 1997). All students were required to participate in two different teams:

1. A **project team** to develop a Web site, the content of which was related to some aspect of multimedia project management such as interface design, rapid prototyping, storyboarding, or legal issues;
2. A **task team** to coordinate an online presentation over one week, which involved developing an overview posting on the weekly topic, moderating the discussion on a bulletin board, and, at the end of the week, developing a summary posting of the comments and attitudes portrayed during the week. This summary posting was used the following week to review the material and discuss the different attitudes portrayed by the students (Ramsden, 1992).

Lecturer modelling was used to demonstrate how to submit and organise online presentations (Brown, Collins et al., 1989; Collins, Brown et al., 1989) and showed the students what standard of work and amount of effort was required. Also, tutors were always available for advice and support, especially when the task teams presented their work on the bulletin boards.

In reviewing literature relevant to communities of online learners, a socio-constructivist perspective seemed most appropriate for the online forum. The aim of the forum was to provide a learning environment where participants could share knowledge, discuss ideas, and contribute to each other's understandings of important issues in the management of multimedia development.

Designing the Home Page: Which Icons to Use

WebCT offers many icons to choose from when considering how to design the home page for a new course. The choice of icons was driven by the type of learning outcomes required, which in turn determined the instructional strategies relevant for the course.

Before starting any work on WebCT, a syllabus and thirty-page course content booklet (the Guide) was created, which summarised key issues related to the weekly topics. Also, two readers and a textbook (Luca, 1997) were developed for the course. Therefore, careful consideration was given to all the instructional and assessment activities needed for the course. A summary of each week's topic was given along with individual and team exercises. A sample of the syllabus is shown in Table 12.1.

After the content and instructional strategies for the course were completely developed, the next stage included consideration of which WebCT icons would be used for the design of a home page. Much reading, advice, and experimentation with WebCT icons were required before settling on a home page that appeared to satisfy all the course requirements. It became obvious that there were many ways of designing the home page. Using different combinations of icons in WebCT could change the instructional focus of the course, or change the way that students accessed the content. Also, careful consideration for interface design issues was needed, since too many or inappropriately designed icons would be confusing to new users and add an unnecessary cognitive load.

After much consultation and experimentation, the icons shown in Figure 12.1 were used on the WebCT home page. Table 12.2 shows the order of importance of each of the icons for the instructional strategy used in this case.

The *bulletin boards* were the most heavily used part of the WebCT environment. As shown in Figure 12.2, a bulletin board was created for each of the ten weeks that content was delivered. From week 3 onwards, a student task team was responsible for the delivery of this content. The main bulletin board, which included over one-third of the total messages, was set up to allow students to ask questions or raise issues about anything other than the weekly discussion topic.

There was little intervention by the tutors on the bulletin boards, except to assist when it was obvious after a few days that the students would not resolve an issue or question by themselves. It was important that tutors gave students the opportunity to answer the question, since marks were given for bulletin board contributions, which accounted for 30 per cent of a student's total mark. Students were encouraged to develop discussion threads that were relevant to a weekly topic, or other issues related to multimedia project management, making the environment truly student-centred.

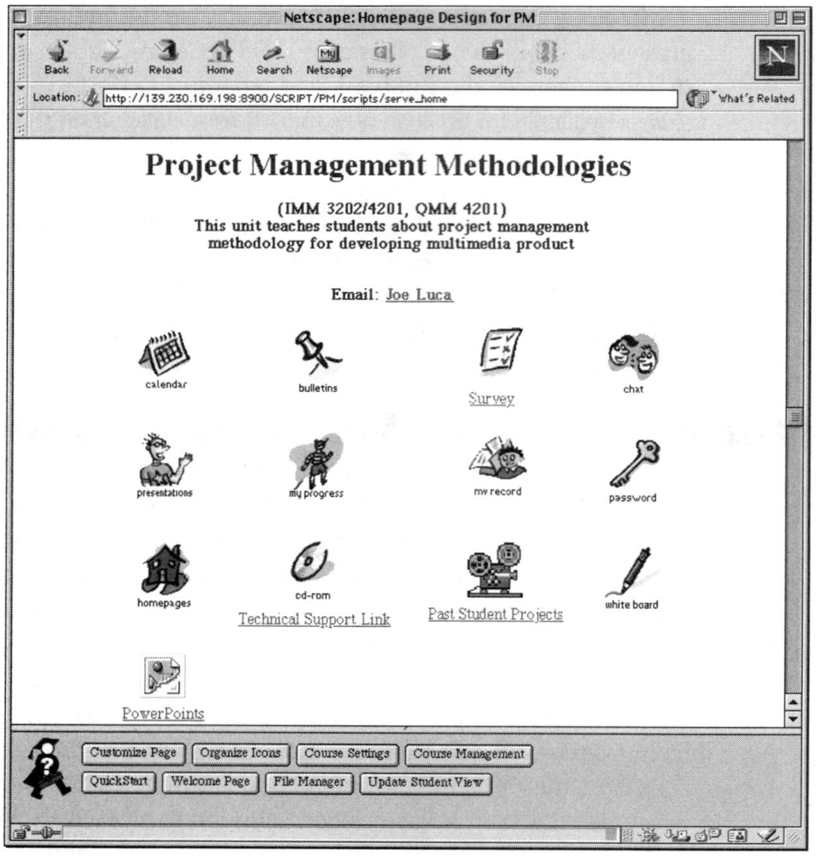

Figure 12.1 The Project Management Methodologies course home page shows the many capabilities provided in WebCT

Students were also given the opportunity to set up private bulletin boards for their own teams where they could discuss issues privately. However, not many teams took up this option, and even the ones that did, did not use it heavily. Students preferred using e-mail (external to WebCT) for the team communication aspects.

The *password* option was essential. All students knew that their surname was the initial username and password (with a few exceptions where some students had the same surname). On their first login they had to access this icon and change their password. Also, a security issue was related to proper use of the password: Students had to QUIT the browser in order to securely logout from the WebCT environment. If students remained logged on to WebCT by not quitting the browser, other students could access their private account by simply pressing the Back arrow in the browser!

The *home pages* option was useful in building a sense of community among the whole student group. By allocating a mark (out of 3) for the best personal home page, students became creative in their endeavours to develop a light-hearted page about themselves. WebCT provided simple and easy-to-use tools for this function. The criteria for this exercise are given below, with sample responses shown in italics:

> Introduce yourself to your fellow students by publishing a personal home page in the WebCT home page area. Feel free to include as much

Table 12.1 Sample of syllabus for project management unit delivered via WebCT

Week	Topic	Activities	Act.	Day	Who
1	Introduction to project management course and WebCT	WebCT tutorial	1.1	M	All
		IMM 4201 Web site access, and post message to week 1 forum	1.2	M	All
		Publish personal Web page	1.3	M	All
		Fill out online questionnaire on student skills	1.4	M	All
		Task group allocations		M	Tutor
2	What is project management?	Assign project teams and project topics	2.1	M	Tutor
		Post message to week 2 forum: "What is project management?"	2.2	M	Tutor
		Submit URL on project management	2.1	M–F	All
		Online discussions on posted topic	2.1	T–Th	All
		Post synopsis			Tutor
3	Team issues, timesheet categories, project diary, and basic quality assurance	Summary paper post to week 3 forum	3.4	M	Group 1
		Post messages to week 3 forum: "What is a script?"	3.1	M	All
		Fill in team style questionnaire	3.2	M	All
		Produce team communication standards	3.3	M-F	All
		E-mail team procedures to lecturer	3.3	F	All
		Online discussions on posted topic	3.4	T-Th	
		Post synopsis	3.4	F	Group 1

information about yourself as you want, including graphics or links to your personal home page, if you have one.

Please include the following information on your page (take a light-hearted approach):

- Your nickname: *Goose*

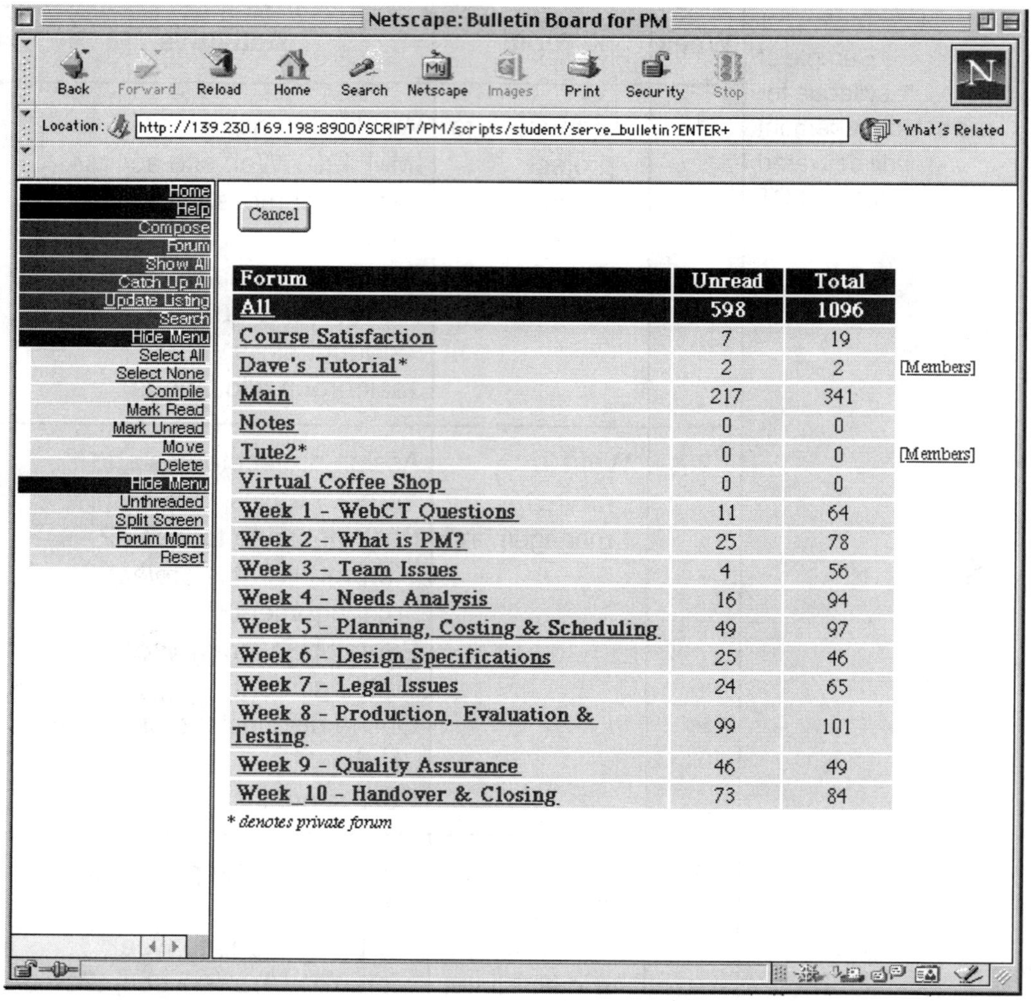

Figure 12.2 WebCT bulletin board summary of messages posted

- Dreariest place ever lived: *Schenectady, NY, in Winter*
- Best place ever lived: *Fremantle, WA, in Summer*
- Most interesting event: *a mustering season in the Pilbarra*
- Most embarrassing event: *not knowing a he-calf from a she-calf while masquerading as a stockman*
- Person I'd like to be reincarnated as: *Gina Lollabrigida*
- Person I'd hate to be reincarnated as: *Paul Keating*
- Favourite TV show: *Mr. Bean*
- Toughest management task ever experienced: *telling a team member that no one wanted to work with him because he smelt so bad!*
- Favourite pastime: *flying off somewhere with no set return date*
- Ambition/motto: *keep learning, keep moving, carpe diem*

The *presentation* icon allowed students to show ongoing progress on the development of their Web sites. Student teams would place samples of their work and prototypes in this area and then ask other students (via the bulletin boards) for feedback. This

Table 12.2 WebCT home page icon ranking

Rank*	WebCT Icon Used	Description
1	Bulletin board	Discussing weekly topics and any general questions
2	Password	Changing student passwords
3	Home page	Each student presents their background and interests
4	Presentation	Server space for students to put samples of work for comment and final Web sites
4	Technical support	Help for students in down-loading and using hotline to transfer files into the presentation area
4	Past student projects	Completed Web sites from previous semester's students
5	My progress	Used mainly by the tutors to assess the number of messages posted and read by each student
5	Survey	Survey form to evaluate the course
7	PowerPoint presentations	Lecture slides made available
7	My record	Shows students' marks for different assessment points
7	Calendar	A day-by-day breakdown of student activities and assessment points
10	Chat	Chat tool
10	Whiteboard	Interactive whiteboard tool

*Ranking Code: 1 = most important, 10 = least important

presentation area was set up externally to the WebCT environment for the following reasons:

- The completed Web site would be located at this external site, and students could easily use this URL as part of their electronic CV (as a sample of completed multimedia work);
- It was easier for students to upload and edit Web pages on an external server space;
- It was easier to show samples of the past student projects in an external area.

The *technical support* icon gave the students information about the required software ("Hotline") that allowed transfer of project files from desktop computers to the server. It also provided information about the required IP address and other information needed to transfer files to the server being used for student presentations.

Past student projects provided a valuable source of past students' work, which illustrated the standard of work expected. Students would often criticise past students' work, commenting on the lack of design and technical aspects of the Web sites. Students make great critics when discussing other students' projects!

The *my progress* icon was useful for both tutors and students to see how many times they had accessed the bulletin boards. As shown in Figure 12.3, tutors could sort messages Posted, Read, or Hits to receive the totals by student name. Even though this only gave a quantitative measure of student activity, it still provided a reasonable means of tracking student contributions and activity. Only the tutors were able to see all of the student details. Students could only see their own record.

The *survey* icon provided a convenient means of evaluating the course. This icon was not shown on the home page at the beginning of the semester. Toward the end of the semester, it was placed on the page and students were asked to complete the survey form. Discussion was then encouraged through the main bulletin board and by private e-mail if necessary. By using the functionality of the survey icon, WebCT collated the students' responses in a compact fashion for easy analysis.

During the semester, traditional lectures were also given in this unit for the students who were on campus. The slides used in these lectures were converted to HTML for students to access through the *PowerPoint presentations* icon. Even though students did access these slides, it was not a valid representation of the lecture, as the slides contained mainly bullet points that were elaborated on in the lecture.

The *my record* icon provided a means for tutors to enter student marks and grades at any point. With password access, students could view their own progress. This icon is useful for getting scores and grades out to remote students quickly. However, tutors must maintain this area by entering and updating marks on a regular basis.

The *calendar* icon was not heavily used in this course. This could be because early in the semester before students became familiar with WebCT, they were given a paper-based syllabus that outlined weekly responsibilities. It seemed that this was an easier option for students to use than accessing the calendar icon in WebCT. To become more relevant to the students, the calendar icon would need to be carefully maintained and contain some information that was not in print format.

The *chat* and the *whiteboard* tools were rarely used over the semester. This was due to early technical problems with these two tools. At the beginning of the semester

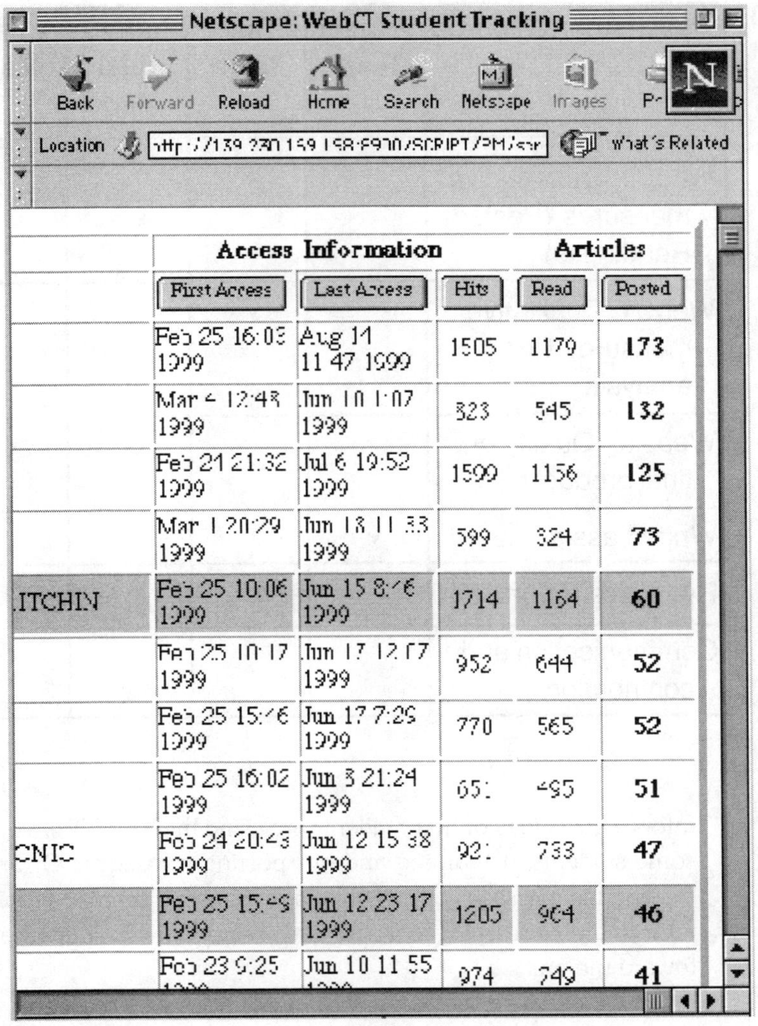

Figure 12.3 The My Progress area shows a record of each student's access, articles they've read, and postings they've made

the tools did not work properly and students lost confidence in using them. Students used external e-mail (rather than WebCT e-mail) as the main form of communication with team members.

Assessment Criteria

The five elements used for assessing the students' progress in the project management unit are shown in Table 12.3. Their final mark was a combination of project team, task team, individual, client, and peer assessment marks. This provided a rich form of assessment for the students, but was found to be time consuming by all the tutors.

Quantitative Measures

WebCT provides comprehensive quantitative measures for the number of messages Posted and Read, and for the Hits made by students, as shown in Figure 12.3. This gives

Table 12.3 Assessment methods

Assessment Method	Project Team	Task Team	Individual Mark	Client Mark	Task Peer Mark	Peer Mark
WebCT: Quantitative measures (Posted, Read, Hits)		✓	✓			
WebCT: Qualitative measures text analysis		✓	✓			
Website: Quality of final product	✓			✓		
Written assignment	✓			✓		
Reflective report			✓			
Communication and contribution				✓	✓	✓

tutors a quick idea of how students are using the WebCT environment. For example, are some students just lurking and not posting messages? Or are most students who are reading the messages also posting a response? This may provide some valuable data for tutors if there are trying to assess the amount of effort individual students are contributing toward the unit.

Qualitative Measures for Analysing Online Talk

To encourage student collaboration and communication on the WebCT bulletin boards, it was decided to allocate 30 per cent of the overall mark to individual contributions made to the bulletin boards for task and project team contributions. This, however, raised the difficult and time-consuming issue of how to assess quality cybertalk through examination of transcripts of the text-based discussions.

Henri (1992) developed a content analysis model based on five categories, which relates the educational quality of messages along participative, social, interactive, cognitive, and metacognitive dimensions. Alternatively, Gunawardena, Lowe, and Anderson (1997) had a social constructivist approach to knowledge-building in online environments. Their five-phase analytic model proposes that knowledge construction moves through five levels, from knowledge sharing to knowledge building as follows:

Phase 1. Sharing and comparing of information. Verbal transactions take the form of statements and observations.

Phase 2. Discovery and exploration. Participants become aware of differences in views and interpretations. Typical utterances at this stage would be questions, clarifications, and elaboration of concepts.

Phase 3. Negotiation of meaning and co-construction of knowledge. Here there is evidence of negotiation of outcomes and areas of agreement and disagreement, with proposals for mutual understanding.

Phase 4. Testing and revision of ideas. Interactions include statements of evidence against criteria, use of examples, and investigation of alternative viewpoints.

Phase 5. Awareness of newly constructed knowledge. Would entail metacognitive statements demonstrating new knowledge construction and reflection on areas of agreement or disagreement.

The Gunawardena model of knowledge-building reflecting the collaborative and social processes of learning in online forums was adapted to create the following assessment strategy of bulletin board contributions made by students. The following categories where defined in an attempt to classify students' online comments:

E—Irrelevant comments

D—Monitors discussion by agreeing with comments

C—Attempts involvement, but not fully grasping ideas

B—Good effort, shows comprehension and progresses the debate

A—Excellent comments, strong comprehension and synthesis

Marks were then allocated to students by considering how many quality comments were made, as follows:

5 marks = 2 x A or 1 x A and 4 x B

4 marks = 1 x A and 3 x B

3 marks = 1 x B and at least 3 x C

2 marks > 3 x C

1 mark = any number of D's

This assessment procedure was time consuming and difficult, since often it was hard to easily categorise comments into one of the categories. However, this system did provide a relatively simple means of grading students' contributions on the bulletin boards. The students were given this assessment criteria, so they knew how the marks were being allocated. Students were continually reminded that it was quality and not quantity of messages that counted.

WebCT provided useful tools to enable the printing of students' individual contributions to the bulletin boards. Within the bulletin board area, the tutor could use the Search button and type a student's name; WebCT would find all the contributions made by that student. Then, using the Compile button, all the messages were provided in a print-ready format so that a complete record of the student's contributions could be obtained.

Peer and Client Assessment

Peer assessment was part of each assessment item. Students negotiated marks with their team to decide whether each team member had made a sufficient contribution. This encouraged students to carefully consider their role and contribution in relation to the others while working in a team.

This peer assessment used a "passive" strategy. If students made no submission for peer assessment, then all the team marks would remain constant. However, if the team negotiated among themselves that some team members deserved more marks than others, then marks would be subtracted from team members who were not performing and added to the score of other team members. Therefore, the total marks awarded for the peer assessment would equal zero.

Client assessment was included in order to simulate a real world project; therefore, clients had to be carefully considered and communicated with. For each assessment, pseudo-clients (usually other lecturers) would assign a mark (out of 3) for the student teams' negotiation skills and conduct. Criteria included being efficient with communication strategies, listening to feedback, and demonstrating organisational skills.

WebCT Student Database and Maintenance Issues

With this implementation of WebCT, there was no access of student records from a central university database, so it was up to the unit coordinator to enter all of the student records into the WebCT database to enable student logins. Much time and effort could have been saved if the university's central student database was connected to WebCT, or if student files could have somehow been easily transferred into the WebCT database.

None of these options were available for this implementation, so the following manual process was used to create the initial database in WebCT:

- Student names were copied and pasted into Microsoft Word from the central university student database, which included the fields First Name, Last Name, Student No., and Phone.
- These fields were then converted into a Word table.
- All of the spaces were stripped out.
- Extra columns were included for Login ID, Group, and E-mail.
- The Last Name column was copied to the Login ID column.
- The Word table was then converted into text with comma delimiters.
- A new first line of text was included to define each field needed by WebCT: First Name, Last Name, Login ID, Student No., Group, Phone, and E-mail. The order of these fields need not correspond with the order of the columns.

- The Word file was saved as text format.
- Duplicate surnames and logins could not have duplicate (same as logins).
- The fields defined here had to correspond with the fields defined in the course management section of WebCT.
- The file manager was used to upload the text file into WebCT.
- From WebCT, the tools Course Management, Student Management, Students, and Update from File were used to load the file and answer the questions.
- When this process was complete, students were able to login with a password (which was the same as their login), and then use the password icon to change their passwords into something more secure and private. They then had secure access to their WebCT account.

With this implementation of WebCT, there were eighty students using the WebCT server. Since assessment was tied to the students using the WebCT environment, the reliability of the system became an important issue. In this case, a Linux server was maintained by a technician within the department. He regularly backed up the system and managed to keep it running without any major problems throughout the semester. However, it would have been preferable to maintain the server as a centralised university responsibility with full after-hours technical support and backup.

Tutor and Coordinator Issues

Two 3-hour sessions were devoted to training the tutors how to access and use the WebCT environment. This included learning to access the student database to add/delete students, to include students' details, and to assist students with gaining entry into the WebCT environment if their passwords didn't work.

Each of the four tutors involved with the program was given the main designer's password. This saved the coordinator valuable time, since for large classes, it would have been very difficult for one person to check all the passwords and add/delete new students.

All of the tutors in the program were highly motivated and didn't mind putting in extra effort to get the job done. However, from the experience of setting up and running this type of collaborative course on WebCT, there is no doubt that a lot more effort is required than for a traditional lecturing format. With centralised university technical and database support, the amount of effort needed would definitely be more manageable.

Student Feedback

Student feedback included the following comments:

> Even though I liked the forum and found it valuable, it was very time consuming. Some people were contributing just to get their hit rate up!

> I found the forum discussions a good learning tool. It helps reinforce the relevant points just by going through the views other people throw in the forum. However, I find the course very time consuming.

The WebCT student homepages are quite humorous, while the forums are to some extent information overload, especially if you do not have a computer at home.

I think that WebCT is a fantastic tool and the homepages are a great way to get to know the other students.

As I didn't have a computer at home, I found I was disadvantaged by the course, as other students could go home, and while watching TV answer queries made on the bulletin boards.... Not having a car to get into university made it even more difficult.

I think the bulletin boards in WebCT are a great way of communicating, sharing ideas, and helping other students. However, I am not comfortable that it is assessed.

Future Refinements

Three aspects of this course would be changed were I to conduct this course again using WebCT.

First, an instructional approach should be implemented that demands fewer postings to be read and assessed by the tutors. This would probably involve a problem-based approach with inter-group peer assessment of the solutions. Students would communicate and collaborate within their own teams and then post only solutions to problems on the bulletin boards.

Second, a more centralised university server and maintenance solution should be used with WebCT.

Finally, greater equity of access should be ensured for all students who do not have a computer at home, possibly by using a computer leasing program, fully integrated with all the required academic software.

References

Bennett, N., E. Dunne, and C. Carre. 1999. "Patterns of Core and Generic Skill Provision in Higher Education." *Higher Education* 37(1)

Brown, J.S., A. Collins et al. 1989. "Situated Cognition and the Art of Learning." *Educational Researcher* 18(1), 10–12.

Candy, P., G. Crebert, and J. O'Leary. 1994. "Developing Lifelong Learners Through Undergraduate Education." Canberra: National Board of Employment, Education and Training.

Collins, A., J.S. Brown et al. 1989. "Cognitive Apprenticeship: Teaching the Crafts of Reading, Writing, and Mathematics." Pp. 453–494 in *Knowing, Learning, and Instruction: Essays in Honour of Robert Glaser*, ed. L.B. Resnick. Hillside, New Jersey: Lawrence Erlbaum Associates.

Collis, B. 1997. "Supporting Project-Based Collaborative Learning Via a World Wide Web Environment." P. 463 in *Web-Based Instruction*, ed. B.H. Khan. Englewood Cliffs, New Jersey: Prentice Hall.

Gunawardena, C., C. Lowe, and T.Anderson. 1997. "Analysis of a Global Online Debate and the Development of an Interaction Analysis Model for Examining the Social Construction of Knowledge in Computer Conferencing."

Journal of Educational Computing Research 17(4), 397–431.

Henri, F. 1992. "Computer Conferencing and Content Analysis." Pp. 117–136 in *Collaborative Learning Through Computer Conferencing*, ed. A.R. Kaye. Berlin: Springer-Verlag.

Luca, J. 1997. *Project Management for New Media*. Perth: New Media Management.

Marginson, S. 1993. *Arts, Science and Work*. Canberra: Department of Employment Education and Training, Evaluations and Investigations Programme.

Oliver, R., and C. McLoughlin. 1999. *Using Web and Problem-Based Learning Environments to Support the Development of Key Skills*. Brisbane: ASCILITE.

Ramsden, P. 1992. *Learning to Teach in Higher Education*. London and New York: Routledge.

Part D

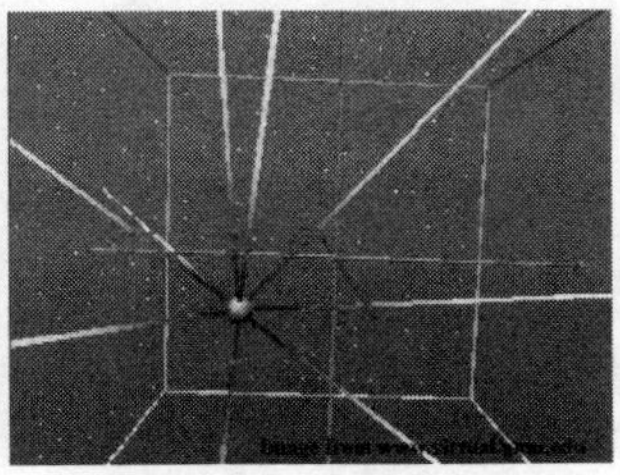

Web Course Assessment

CHAPTER 13

Evaluation Methods for In-Context, Consistent Comments and Hierarchical Marking

Denise Woit and Dave Mason
Ryerson Polytechnic University
Canada

We focus on the issue of student evaluation in Web-based course management systems. In particular, we describe evaluations for two common situations: first, when a hierarchy of markers is assigned to a course (instructor, graduate students, T.A.s, graders); and second, when consistent, in-context comments are desired as part of student feedback. These two special conditions occur, for example, in our first-year core courses. These courses tend to be very large (sometimes requiring up to fifteen markers per course), and the students benefit tremendously from in-context, consistent feedback on their assignments and tests. Both of these special requirements are handled by WebCoDe, a Web-based course management system that supports a broad spectrum of evaluations, such as short-answer, multiple-choice, true-false, fill-in-the-blanks, essay, and computer programming questions. WebCoDe supports the online specification and automated evaluation of these various types of questions. It allows for in-context, consistent, detailed feedback and hierarchical interaction among students, instructors, and various markers.

In-Context Requirements

The subject matter in each of our first-year core courses is cumulative; students cannot master new material until they have a firm grasp of previous material. In previous regular classes (non–Web-based), we assigned weekly marked evaluations to encourage students to explore the topics as they were covered in class. We provided prompt, consistent, and detailed feedback so that students learned from their errors before continuing. The feedback was placed in context; that is, attached directly to that part of the work on which we wished to comment. Both students and instructors found that weekly evaluations, along with prompt, detailed, in-context feedback, increased the students' overall comprehension of course material (Woit and Mason, 2000). When we switched to Web-based course management and evaluation, we found that prompt, consistent, detailed, in-context feedback was still required.

Hierarchical Evaluation Requirements

Because of the large class sizes, in the original, non–Web-based courses we organized the markers into a hierarchy with an instructor at the top. Under this instructor was a course leader, who was a graduate student or an undergraduate lead T.A. Under this leader were graders. This system is typical of course organization at some universities. It worked well as long as we maintained a high level of marking consistency, and provided detailed feedback. The necessity for detailed feedback was discussed above. Maintaining consistency was important because different students had the same assignment marked by different graders at the lowest level. A leader reviewed the overall work of a group of graders, then re-marked the work, added comments, or adjusted grades to improve marking consistency. The instructor then repeated this process at a higher level. Thus, marking proceeded bottom-up through the evaluator hierarchy. We wanted to preserve this grading system (and if possible improve upon it) in the Web-based versions of the courses.

Consistency Requirements

In the original, non–Web-based courses, we supplied detailed marking schemes, and the graders included their own comments when they deducted marks. When graders commented on a given issue, it was imperative that they phrased their comments in the same way to ensure consistency of remarks given to students. It was also imperative that they deduct the same number of marks for the same problems. We had difficulty maintaining consistency in the non–Web-based courses because there were so many markers. We wanted to improve the level of consistency when we moved to Web-based course management systems. We envisioned accomplishing this by having the graders mark in an online environment in which only specific, instructor-defined comments were available. We expected the system to attach grade deductions to the comments automatically.

Requirements in Web Courses

Now that our courses are Web-based, we still require large numbers of graders because the class sizes remain large. We have the same requirements for detailed feedback and hierarchical evaluation. However, we have more stringent consistency requirements because this is now possible in the Web-based environment.

Evaluation-Based Selection of a Course Management System

Several Web-based course management systems incorporate evaluation and marking facilities, including WebCT (Goldberg, 1997), Web Course in a Box (MadDuck Technologies, 1999), TopClass (WBT Systems, 1995), CourseInfo (Blackboard, 1997), LearningSpace (Lotus Corporation, 1998), IntraLearn (IntraLearn Software Corporation, 1994), ToolBook II (Asymetrix Learning Systems, 1999), and Generation21 (Generation21 Learning Systems, 1997). A comprehensive comparison of these and many more Web-based course management systems is available from Industry Canada (1999). Most of these systems contain facilities to create evaluations, to mark evaluations, to report and record marks, and to calculate statistics. For example, WebCT and Web Course in a Box each allow the instructor to create evaluations that are multiple-choice, true-false, fill-in-the-blank, essay, an so on. For automatically markable evaluations, such as multiple-choice, the instructor can supply answers, and the evaluations are automatically graded; the grades are then automatically entered into a database (such as an electronic gradebook.)

Typically, course management systems capture marker feedback for each evaluation in a separate area that the student and markers can access. We find this ability to comment useful for essay-type questions, for which one large comment at the end of the evaluation is appropriate. However, for our courses that require extensive in-context comments, this approach is inadequate. The graders are also less happy with this kind of evaluation because they find themselves cutting-and-pasting the same comments over and over, in order to comply with our consistency requirements. Some course management systems allow several markers to supply comments and grades for evaluations; for example, in WebCT, evaluations can be commented on by instructors, guest instructors, or markers. While such systems are appropriate in many cases, they do not support our requirements for hierarchical evaluation.

In-Context, Hierarchical Evaluation with WebCoDe

WebCoDe is a Web course management system that incorporates many of the typical evaluation features, such as online specification of evaluations, online submission of evaluations, online marking, automatic marking, grade recording, and statistics calculations. It also allows structured, detailed, consistent, in-context feedback and facilitates hierarchically based grading of work.

When both the class size and the number of graders are large, it is imperative that all efforts be made to provide consistent comments and grades on student evaluations. In WebCoDe, this is accomplished by providing options to graders with pop-up menus. When a menu item is selected, the appropriate comment will be inserted in context, and the grade deduction associated with this comment will be recorded automatically. To make the grading task more efficient, the order of items in the pop-up menu is constantly updated, with the most frequently used items displayed near the top of the list. The instructor or lead grader may insert, delete, and modify items on the pop-up menu at any time. Other graders may use, but not modify, the menus.

User Levels in the Hierarchy

WebCoDe allows several levels of users for a course—students, graders, lead graders, and instructors—with each type of user obtaining an appropriate, customized view of the course information, marks, and analysis. Because WebCoDe can administer more than one course at a time, users may be assigned multiple levels within the WebCoDe environment. For example, a user may be a grader for more than one course. A user may also have different roles within different courses. This occurs typically when a user is a grader for one course and a student in another. A course may be maintained in the WebCoDe environment over several terms/years, and a user will have different (or the same) status among different offerings. For example, a person may be a student for a course one year and a grader for the same course the next year; or a student may enroll in the same course in different offerings in order to upgrade a mark. Each WebCoDe course may be assigned any number of instructors, lead graders, graders, and students, in a hierarchical fashion.

WebCoDe maintains an internal database of course information and uses this information to determine user roles within particular courses. For example, if the user is a student in CPS400 and a grader in CPS225, then WebCoDe will assign student status when the user accesses the WebCoDe site for CPS400, but grader status when accessing the site for CPS225.

Instructors may access WebCoDe's full range of course management functions, evaluation functions, and statistics. Graders may access only evaluation functions for the students assigned to them. Students may view only their own submissions, feedback, and marks. All users may view overall comparative statistics.

Instructor-Only Views and Functions

WebCoDe functions that are available only to instructors are listed on the main instructor WebCoDe page. Listed below are some of the functions:

Change course info. Allows the instructor to create and subsequently modify information about the course, such as its code, its term, the graders, and its submit folder. The instructor enters the submit folder to be used as a repository for work submitted online by the students. Typically, this is a folder (directory) in the instructor's file space so that it cannot be accessed by students and graders except through WebCoDe. If desired, the instructor could access submitted files directly through this folder; however, this is not necessary, since all submitted files are viewable from the WebCoDe environment.

Change password. Allows instructors to change their own passwords. The instructor can use Reset User Password to change the password of any grader, lead grader, or student. Typical password-type error checking is also performed. For example, when an instructor tries to change a password for a grader, the system verifies that the person is a valid grader for this course. Passwords are used for security purposes so that users can access WebCoDe from any Internet service provider. This is especially important to graders because it allows them to mark off-campus.

Grader records. Used to define a template for information that the instructor wishes to maintain about graders, and to add and modify records for each grader.

Evaluations. An evaluation is created, modified, and marked via this link. When creating an evaluation, the instructor must fill in the evaluation name and the number of questions. Other fields (such as "question is marked out of") are assigned default values if they are not filled in by the instructor.

Assign graders to sections/groups. Used to equate a particular grader with a group of students for marking purposes. If a course has many students, we allow "groups" to refer to parts of sections. The instructor assigns graders to sections/groups via pop-up menus containing group numbers and grader names.

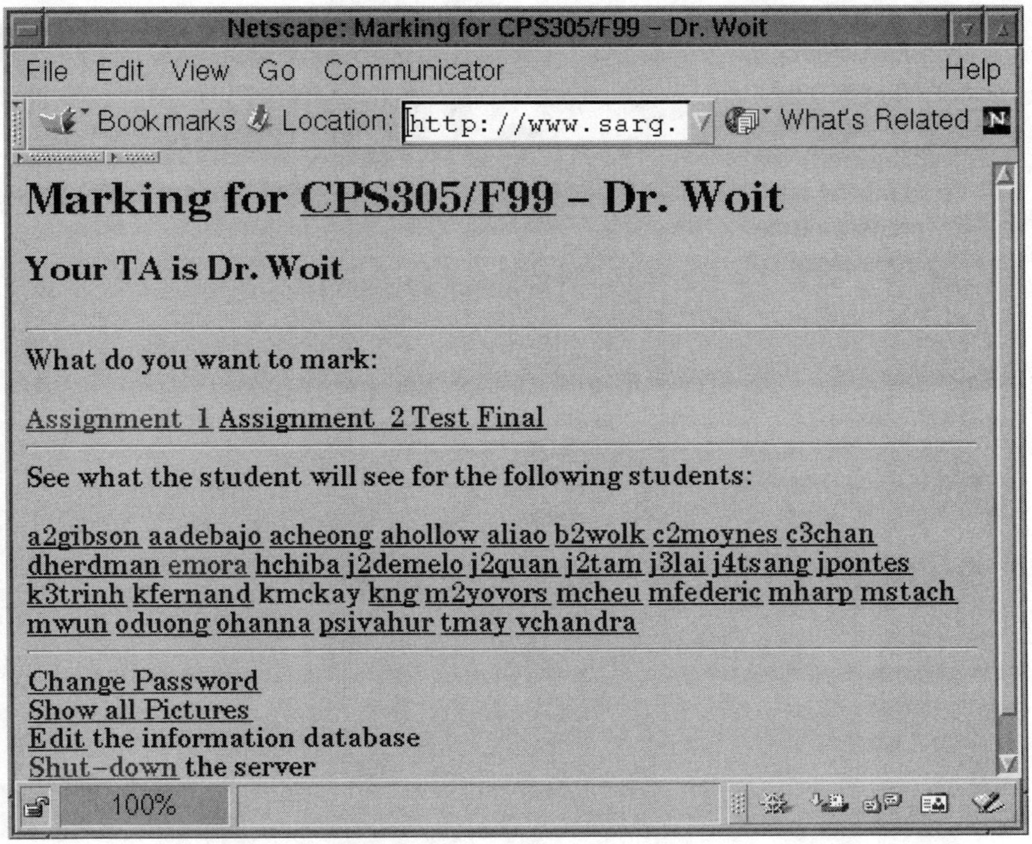

Figure 13.1 Evaluation page, instructor view

Evaluation Functions

Consider the instructor's view of evaluations shown in Figure 13.1. This page indicates that the instructor has assigned four evaluations so far: two assignments, a test, and a final. Student login names appear below evaluations. The student name *kmckay* is not underlined because this student has not submitted any work.

In order to see more information about a particular evaluation, the instructor simply selects the appropriate link. For example, if the instructor selects the Assignment 1 link on this page, the page shown in Figure 13.2 appears, which is a synopsis of information for Assignment 1. Here, the instructor sees a list of the graders: Rhol Kisti (g1), Lise Benham (g2), and Jack Yom (g3). Under the name of each grader is a list of students for whom the grader is responsible. Notice that student names may be formatted differently. If the name is not underlined, as in *aceong*, *bwok*, and *jtang*, then the student did not submit the evaluation. If the name is underlined and in boldface type, as in *aadajo* and *myoors*, the evaluation has been submitted but not yet marked. Marked evaluations appear underlined, with a mark synopsis following in parentheses. For example, Assignment 1 had three parts, and *agison* received marks of 10, 20, and 3 on these parts, respectively. From this page the instructor can quickly ascertain the progress of the graders and students.

If the instructor selects a particular student, say *ccan*, from the list in Figure 13.2, the information about Assignment 1 for student Chi Can appears (see Figure 13.3).

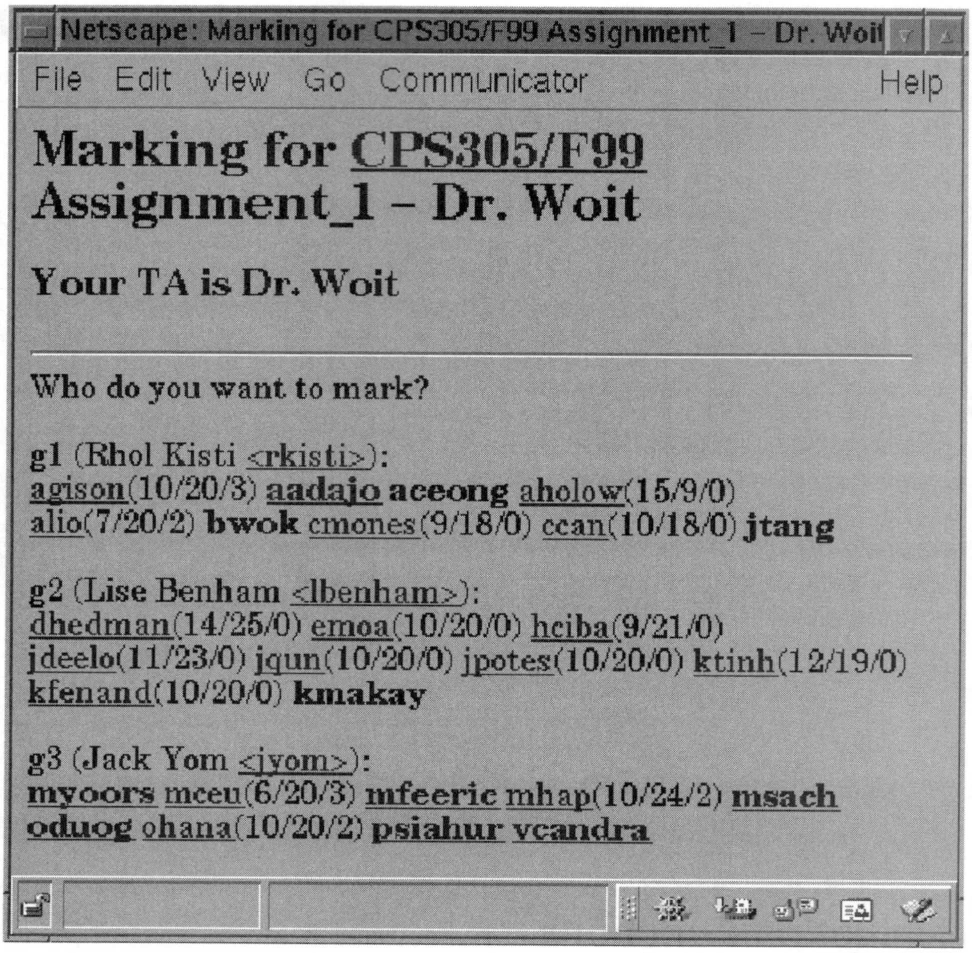

Figure 13.2
The instructor-only view of an assignment shows three graders (g1, g2, g3), the students for each grader, and the grades assigned

This student has been graded by the instructor, Dr. Woit, and has been graded 10 for Documentation, 18 for Code, and 0 for Execution. These values appear just under the Remark This Work button. The three buttons labelled Documentation, Code, and Execution are used by a marker to select a mark for each of these items. The number that appears on each of the buttons is the maximum mark for that item (although bonus marks are possible.) The actual marks, however, appear just under the Remark This Work button. Just under the marks, the Comment section is empty in this example; if an overall comment were appropriate, it would be displayed here. Such a comment is similar to the type of comments the typical Web-based course management systems allow for evaluations. If the instructor wishes to re-mark the evaluation, the comment box is modified, and/or the marks are changed using the pop-up menus. When the Remark This Work button is selected, the new marks are recorded.

Notice that certain parts of the evaluation are underlined. This indicates that a further, specific, comment is associated with this area. If the instructor selects one of these areas, the specific in-context comment and mark deduction, if any, are displayed along with the part of the evaluation it references. Comments and mark deductions are available here because this student's Assignment 1 has already been graded. The instructor can change the comments and grade deductions using the pop-up menus, if desired. When an in-context mark deduction is modified, WebCoDe automatically adjusts

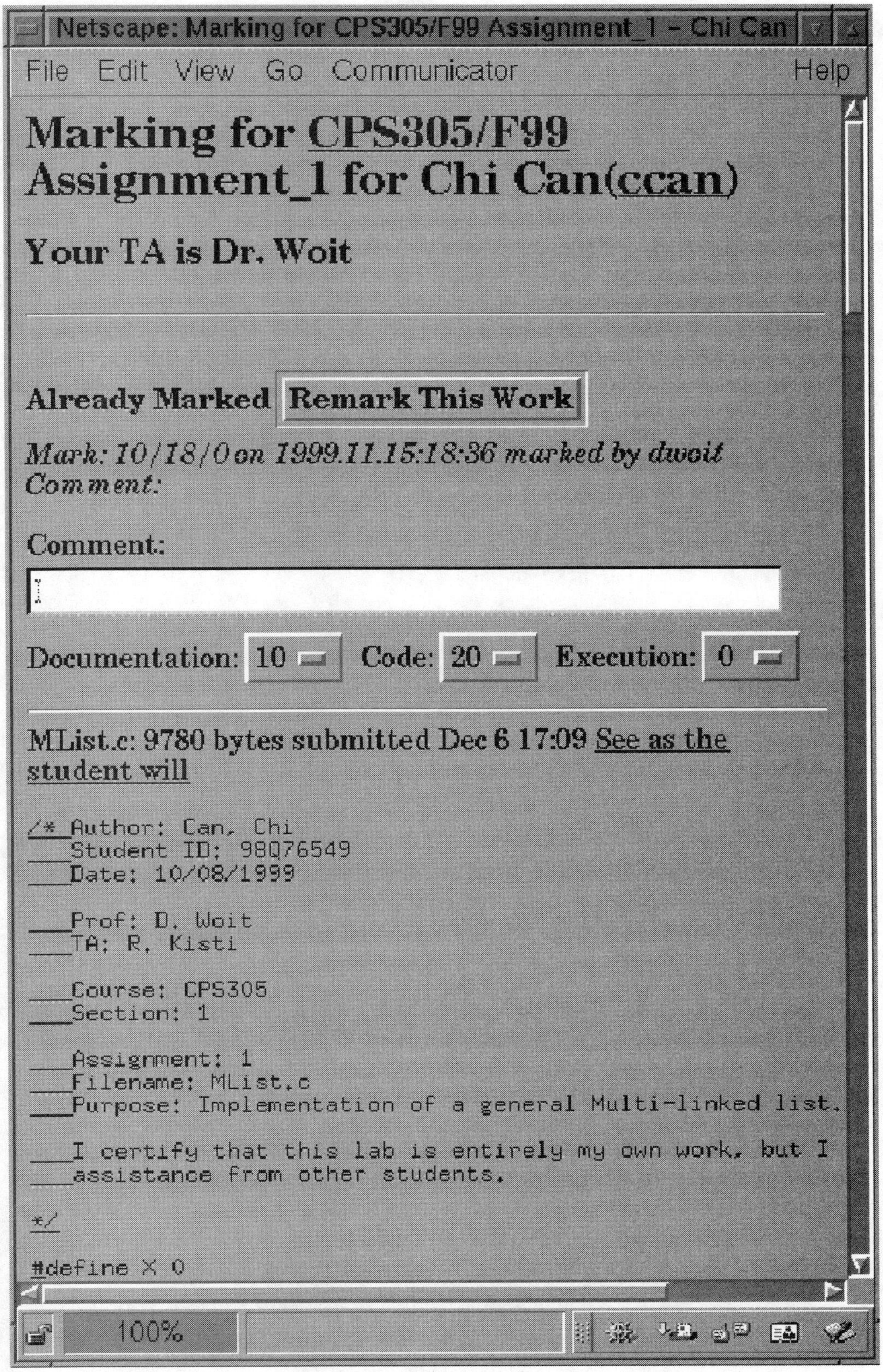

Figure 13.3 Assignment 1, instructor view for student Chi Can

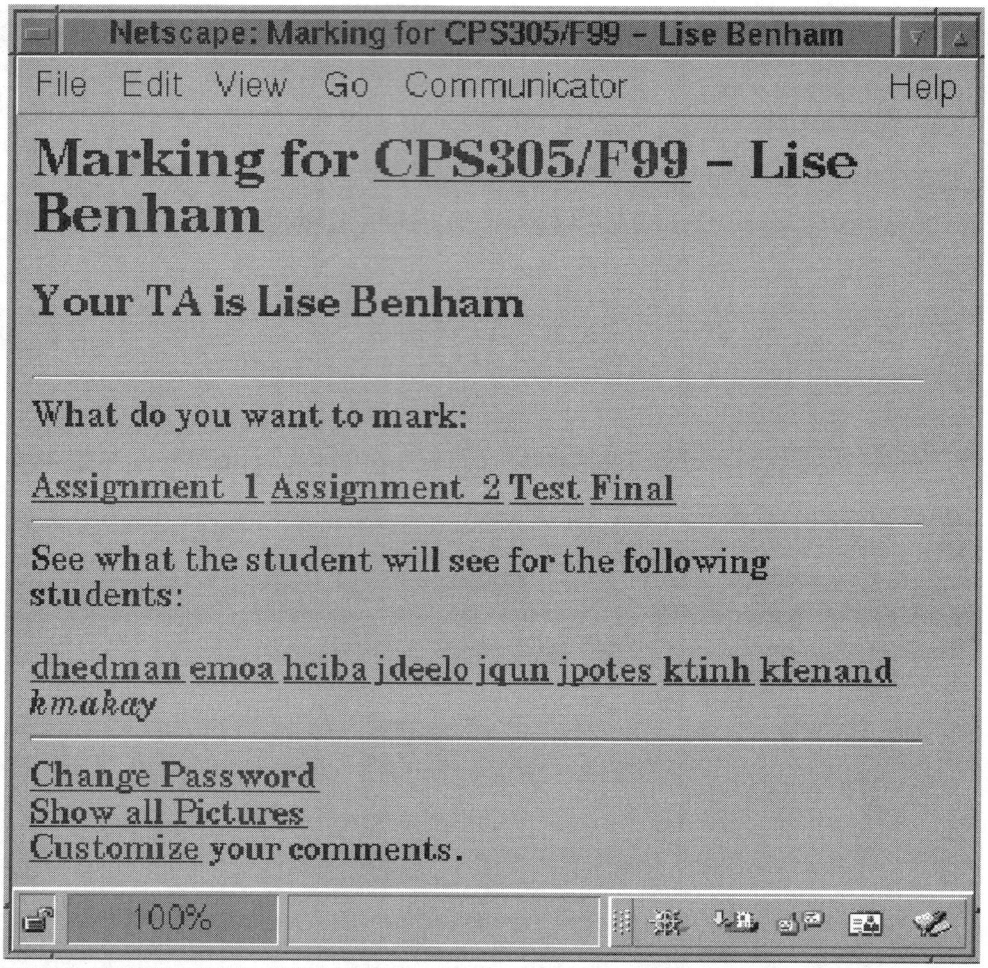

Figure 13.4 Grader view, general

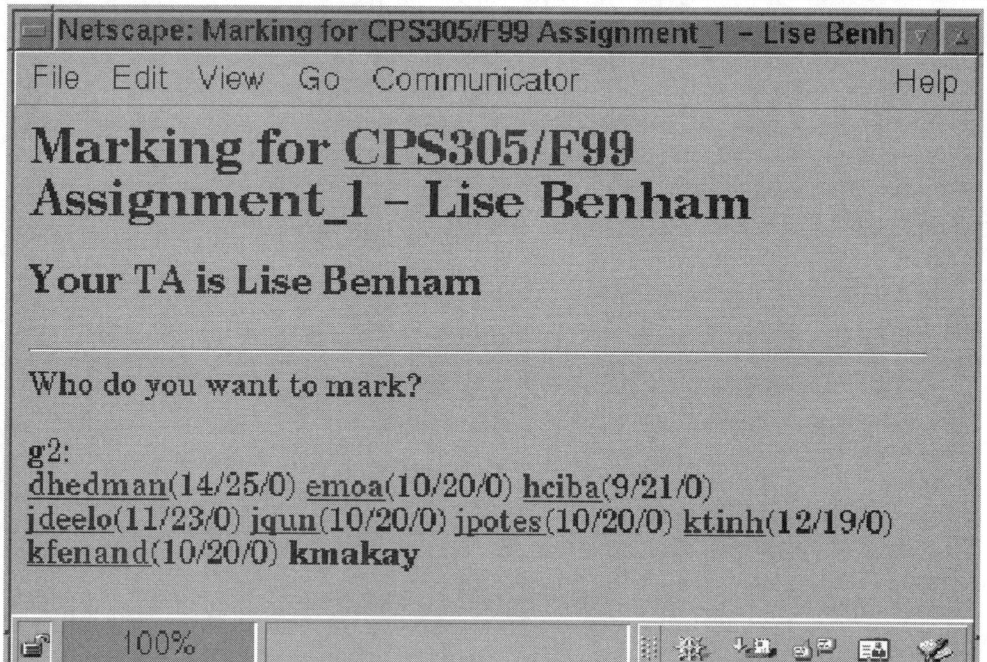

Figure 13.5 Grader view, Assignment 1

Figure 13.6 Grader view, for a student

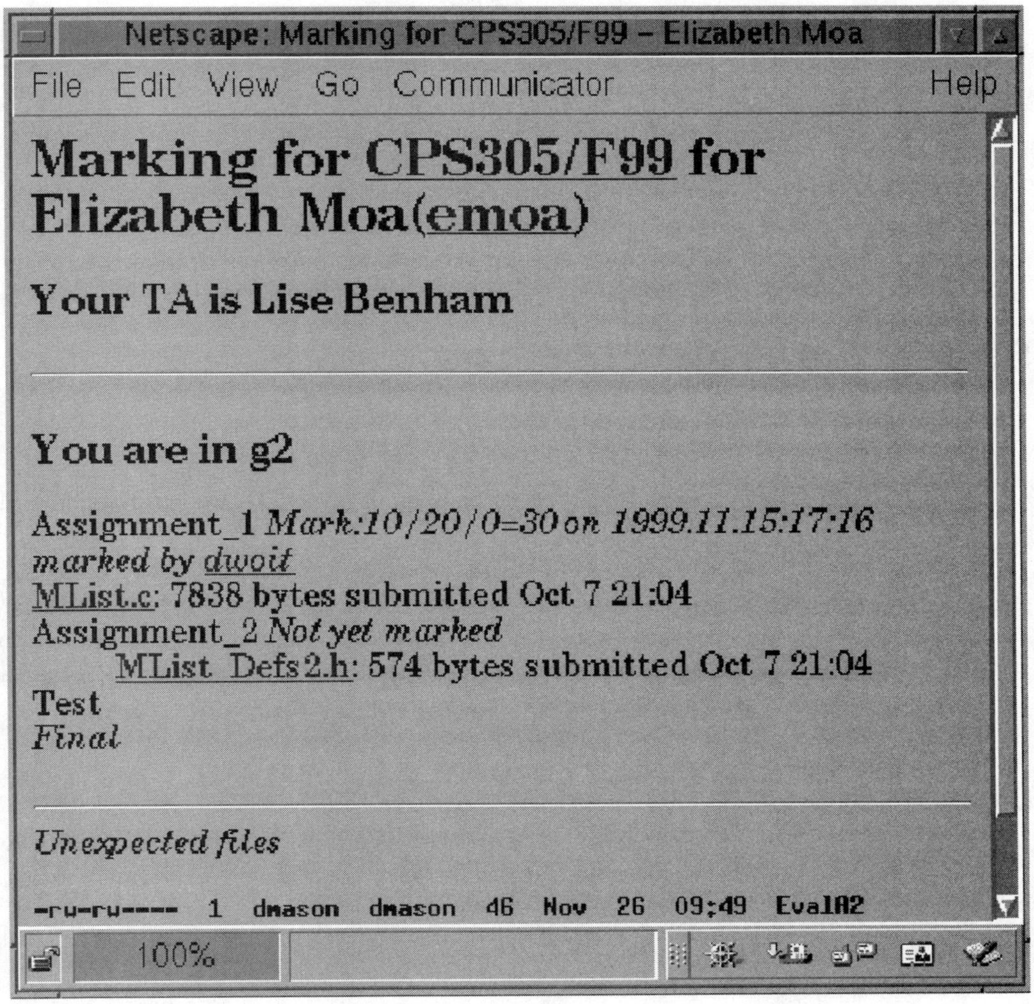

the overall mark appropriately. For example, if the instructor adds a mark deduction of –2 for the line "#define X 0" then the mark for the Code section changes from 18 to 16 automatically (remember that the actual mark appears just under the Remark This Work button.) The instructor assigns the –2 by selecting it from the pop-up menu for Code.

Grader Views and Functions

When a grader accesses the WebCoDe system, a page such as that presented in Figure 13.4 is displayed, and it provides a link to each assignment and student for which this grader is responsible.

If the grader selects a particular assignment, the page shows a synopsis of student progress for the given evaluation (see Figure 13.5). On this page, each student, except *kmckay*, has already been assigned a mark, as indicated by the parentheses after each name, which shows the mark for documentation/code/execution, in this case.

If the grader selects a particular student from the assignment page, a synopsis page is given for that student. For example, Figure 13.6 shows the page displayed if the grader selects student *emoa*.

The student synopsis in the example shows submission dates and marking dates (if applicable) for each evaluation. It shows that the Assignment 1 mark totals 30, and that it was marked by Dr. Woit. It shows that Assignment 2 is not yet marked (although the student has submitted two required files, MList and Defs2.h), and that nothing has been submitted yet for the test or final evaluations. Near the bottom of the page, it indicates that the student submitted a file named EvalA2, but that this is not a submission expected by the instructor for any evaluation. The grader marks an evaluation by selecting it from this page; marking proceeds in the same manner as for instructors.

Student Views and Functions

When a student accesses WebCoDe, an evaluation synopsis page is presented, as in Figure 13.7. Much of this information is the same as the information on the grader synopsis above. In addition, it shows who the student's grader is, and to which class group the student belongs. It allows the student to submit files for evaluations and to change the password.

The student can select any underlined link to see a submitted evaluation. If this evaluation is already marked, then parts of it are displayed with underlines, similar to the page shown in Figure 13.3, indicating that an in-context comment is attached to that part of the evaluation. The student can select a link to see a particular comment and grade deduction, if applicable.

Conclusions

There are several aspects of WebCoDe that contribute to consistent, detailed, in-context marking and feedback in large courses with numerous graders organized into a hierarchy:

- WebCoDe automates the submission of student evaluations, the recording of marks, and the creation of overall statistics.
- The system maintains a hierarchy of evaluators, providing different views and functions for instructors, for graders, and for students. Instructors can view all grader marking. On synopsis pages, the instructor can view the hierarchical structure of graders, students, and evaluations. Those evaluations that are not yet marked, or are not yet submitted, are identified for the instructor. Graders are presented a similar view of their students and evaluations, with ungraded submissions identified.
- The student submissions are annotated with detailed, consistent, in-context comments. This feedback allows a student to quickly and easily see where a submission is deficient or exemplary.
- Grading consistency is maintained by the use of instructor-supplied marking schemes and pop-up grading menus. The items on the menus are constantly re-ordered by frequency of use.
- Graders find the pop-up menus greatly increase the speed and consistency with which they can mark, compared with evaluation methods in traditional Web-based course management systems.

Our Web-based course management system, WebCoDe, incorporates the instructor, lead graders, and graders in a hierarchical fashion. With WebCoDe, graders find it easy

Figure 13.7
Student view

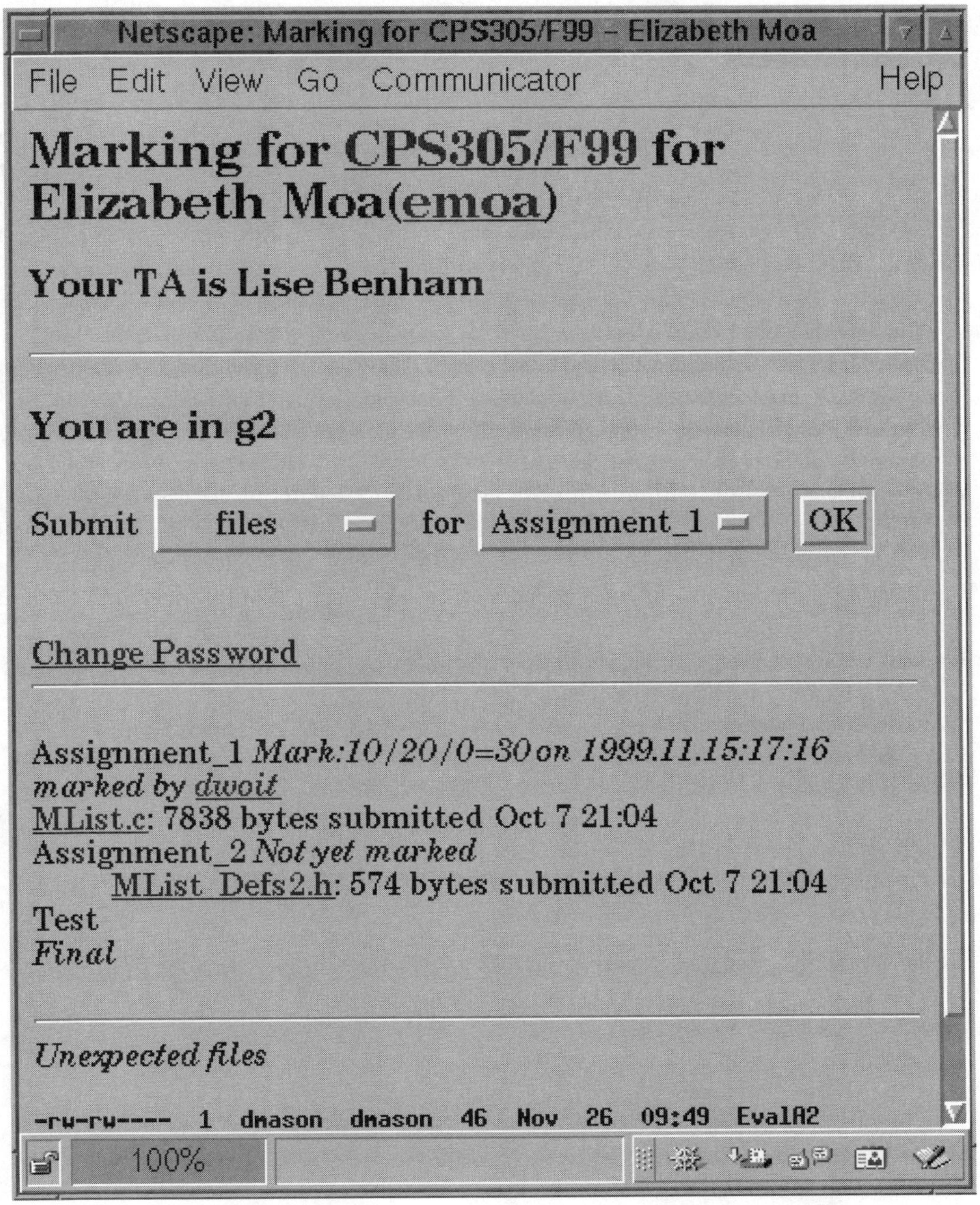

to provide detailed, in-context, and consistent student feedback. We have received much positive feedback from all users of WebCoDe—instructors, graders, lead graders, and students. We are continuing to improve the system based on the feedback we have received. We are also producing more effective user documentation so that WebCoDe may be more easily utilized by a variety of instructors in a variety of environments. Reports about using WebCoDe's predecessors for course management and for online testing of students may be found at www.sarg.ryerson.ca/sarg/papers. To discuss access to WebCoDe itself, please write to the authors.

References

Asymetrix Learning Systems. 1999. *Toolbook II*. Bellevue, Washington: Asymetrix Learning Systems Inc. (http://www.asymetrix.com)

Blackboard. 1997. *CourseInfo*. Washington: Blackboard Inc. (http://www.company.blackboard.com/courseinfo)

Generation21 Learning Systems. 1997. *Generation 21*. Golden, Colorado: Generation21 Learning Systems, Inc. (http://www.gen21.com)

Goldberg, M. 1997. "Communication and Collaboration Tools in WebCT." In proceedings of the Conference Enabling Network-Based Learning, Espoo, Finland, May 28–30. (http://homebrew.cs.ubc.ca/Webct/docs)

Industry Canada. 1999. *Online Educational Delivery Applications: A Web Tool for Comparative Analysis*. Office of Learning Technologies Bureau, Centre for Curriculum Transfer and Technology, Industry Canada. (http://www.ctt.bc.ca/landonline)

IntraLearn Software Corp. 1994. *IntraLearn*. Northboro, Massachusetts: IntraLearn Software Corp. (http://www.intralearn.com)

Lotus Corporation 1998. *LearningSpace*. Cambridge, Massachusetts: The Lotus Corporation. (http://www.lotus.com/home.nsf/tabs/learnspace)

MadDuck Technologies. 1999. *Web Course in a Box*. Richmond, Virginia: MadDuck Technologies. (http://www.madduck.com/index.html)

Mason, D., and D. Woit. 1999. "Providing Markup and Feedback to Students with Online Marking." In proceedings of 1999 ACM Conference on Computer Science Education (SIGCSE'99), New Orleans, Louisiana, March. (http://www.sarg.ryerson.ca/sarg/papers)

WBT Systems. 1995. *TopClass*. Dublin: WBT Systems Inc. (http://www.west.ie/company/index.html)

Woit, D., and D. Mason. 2000. "Enhancing Student Learning Through Online Quizzes." In proceedings of 2000 ACM Conference on Computer Science Education (SIGCSE'00), Austin, Texas, March. (http://www.sarg.ryerson.ca/sarg/papers)

CHAPTER 14

Multiple Assessment in an Online Graduate Course: An Effectiveness Evaluation

Nada Dabbagh
George Mason University
U.S.A.

This chapter will describe the process of designing, developing, and implementing a graduate-level course aimed at teaching the concepts and principles underlying Web-based instruction (WBI). The effectiveness evaluation was conducted using a variety of qualitative and quantitative measures. The data analysis techniques included content analysis of nine student reflection statements, a standard end-of-semester course evaluation survey, and student comments and anecdotes recorded by a peer observer. The data were also analyzed by an independent researcher. In conducting a process analysis, the authors were able to determine *what worked and why*. More specifically, the analysis revealed several important results leading to the identification of successful and unsuccessful instructional activities and the level of technological scaffolding required to support students when implementing these activities. The findings also revealed key features in designing courses aimed at teaching WBI and how to effectively design a WBI prototype. These findings and their implications on the design of similar courses are discussed below.

Theoretical Framework

According to Khan (1997) "WBI is a hypermedia-based instructional program which utilizes the attributes and resources of the World Wide Web to create a meaningful learning environment where learning is fostered and supported" (p. 6). Depending on how those attributes and resources are used in a course by the instructor and the learners, the pedagogical philosophy underlying the teaching and learning process can range from a strict instructivist approach to a radical constructivist approach (Reeves and Reeves, 1997). A strict instructivist approach typically results in a Web-based course that has a tutorial structure in which the content is organized by the instructor and *delivered* or imparted to the students; and a radical constructivist approach typically results in a more learner-centered pedagogy where students use Web features as tools to construct their own knowledge representations by restructuring content information and creating and contributing their own resources to the course structure (Bannan and Milheim, 1997; Reeves and Reeves, 1997).

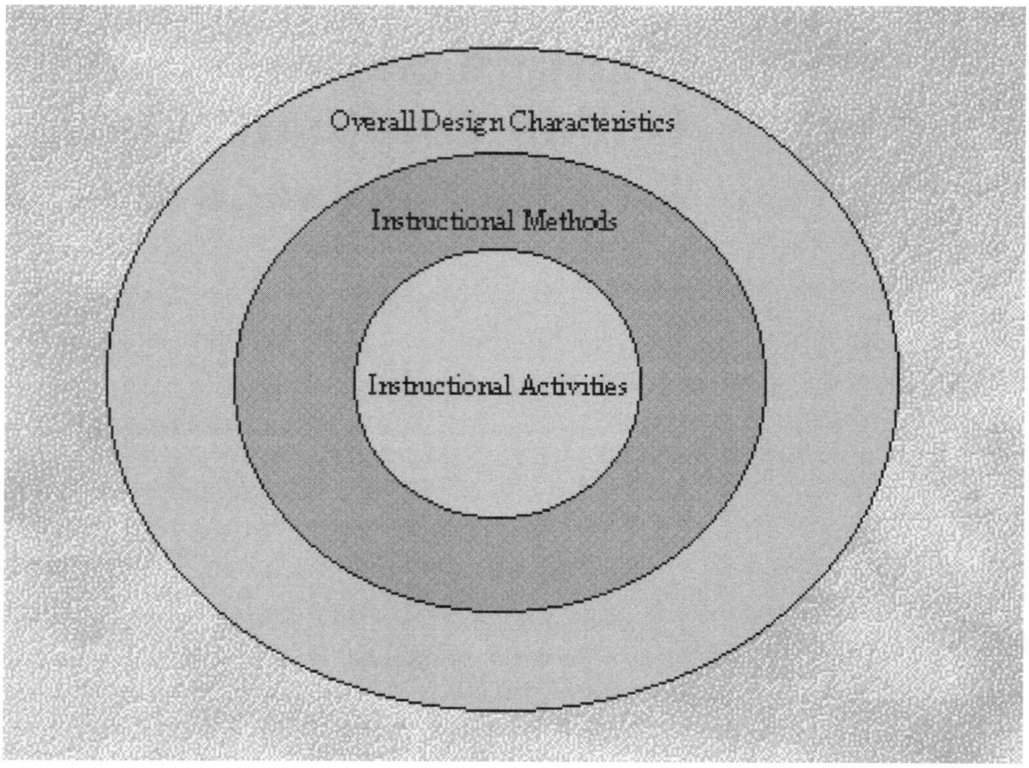

Figure 14.1
A three-dimensional framework for describing Web-based courses

Bannan-Ritland, Harvey, and Milhelm, 1998

Several frameworks have been suggested to guide the design, management, and evaluation of courses that utilize online technologies. One such approach, which can be used to analyze and describe educational Web-based materials, is a three-dimensional framework proposed by Bannan and Milheim (1997). The first dimension of this framework describes the overall design characteristics of a Web-based course in terms of its instructional model (for example, self-contained course or adjunct to classroom instruction) and its pedagogical philosophy (for example, instructivist or constructivist). The second dimension describes the instructional methods and strategies used to facilitate learning and to deliver the course content via the Web. The third dimension describes the instructional activities that are mediated through the components (technological tools) of the medium, such as electronic mail, Web page creation, posting projects to the Web, and computer conferencing. Figure 14.1 illustrates the three-dimensional framework.

Another framework is the Web-based learning (WBL) model proposed by Khan (1998). It consists of eight dimensions: pedagogical, technological, institutional, ethical, interface design, resource support, online support, and course management. Each dimension has various items addressing its constituents in relation to Web-based learning environments.

The **pedagogical** dimension addresses issues such as instructional goals and objectives, the overall design approach of the course, content sequencing and organization, instructional methods and strategies, the instructional medium (the Web in this case), and the extent to which the course uses its attributes, accuracy of subject matter, and learner assessment.

The **technological** dimension addresses issues related to hardware, software, and course infrastructure.

The **institutional** dimension addresses issues related to institutional policy in delivering WBI.

The **ethical** dimension addresses issues such as course sensitivity to diverse populations, copyright issues, netiquette, and provision for representation of concepts for a worldwide audience.

The **interface design** dimension addresses issues pertaining to the "creation of a seamless integration of content and control" through the physical layout of the information and the conceptualization and implementation of the navigation of the instructional program. (Jones and Farquhar, 1997, p. 241)

The **resource support** dimension addresses issues related to various online and off-line learning resources, which include archives, bibliographies of related books/ journals, searchable glossaries, class distribution lists, and other resources related to WBI.

The **online support** dimension addresses issues related to the provision of online resources that aid the learner in instruction or serve as information facilitators if students encounter unanticipated technical problems or questions on the course content.

The **management** dimension refers to the administration, maintenance, and operation of Web-based courses, which includes security issues, updating of course information, provision of course evaluation, tracking of student progress, and feedback on student progress.

A third Web-based instructional framework, developed by Bannan-Ritland, Harvey, and Milheim (1998), provides a six-level hierarchy based on increasing levels of interactivity of instructional elements (see Figure 14.3). The higher levels of the framework "encourage learners to reorganize, manipulate and personally synthesize course content" (p. 78), resulting in a more constructivist approach to the utilization of Web-based features and components.

Conceptualizing this course was based on the above theoretical underpinnings in an effort to expose students to current frameworks utilized in guiding the design, development, implementation, and evaluation of WBI, and to instructional methods, strategies, and activities that could influence the pedagogical philosophy of the resulting learning environment in the process of applying such frameworks.

Course Description

The emerging theoretical knowledge base of Web-based instructional frameworks combined with the move to online technologies in supporting the teaching and learning process and the job market demand for related skills was instrumental in steering the IT

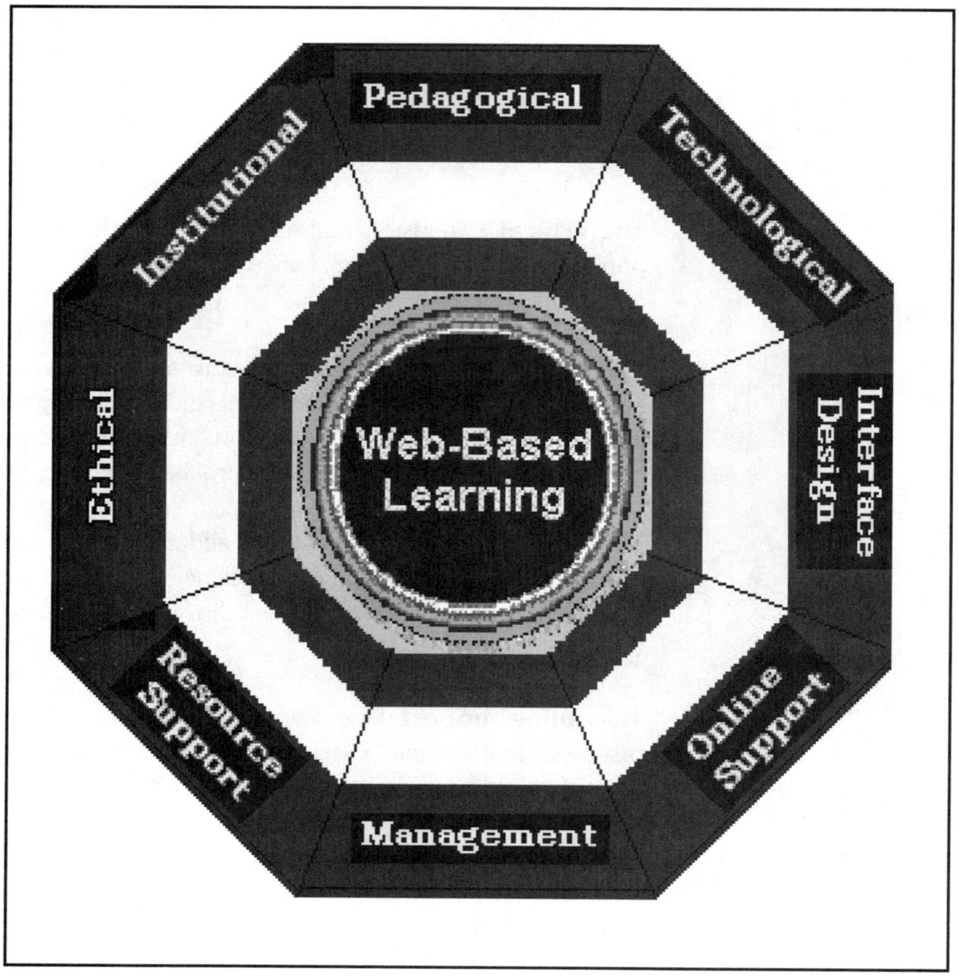

Figure 14.2
A Web-based learning framework; uses eight dimensions

Khan, 1998

faculty at Towson University to begin designing a course that would address these issues. Moreover, faculty (at TU and elsewhere) were increasingly using the Web to support teaching and learning, and most higher education institutions were either developing or offering courses designed to teach the skills and competencies of designing, delivering, and implementing WBI.

With the need defined, two faculty members were designated to the task of developing a course about Web-based instruction. The design process began with a search for similar efforts at other institutions, an informal task analysis on the emerging content on WBI, and a literature review of relevant information. As a result, the following course objectives emerged. Upon the completion of this course, students will be able to

- Identify criteria for evaluating the validity and accuracy of Internet resources and apply those criteria to the evaluation of educational resources in particular;
- Identify parameters of acceptable use policies of the Internet/Web in educational environments;

Figure 14.3
A six-level Web-based instructional framework

Bannan-Ritland, Harvey, and Milhelm, 1998

Web-based Instructional Framework

- Level 1 - Information Delivery;
- Level 2 - Information Delivery with Pre-Defined Resources;
- Level 3 - Information Delivery with Online Interaction;
- Level 4 - Pre-Designed Instructional Delivery;
- Level 5 - Information Synthesis and Creation of Resources;
- Level 6 - Immersive Collaborative Environments

- Discriminate between educational and noneducational uses of the Web;
- Discriminate between WBI and other educational uses of the Web;
- Utilize the Web to locate educational and instructional resources;
- Demonstrate an understanding of the fundamental principles of the Internet and the Web and their implications on teaching and learning;
- Demonstrate an understanding of the principles of linear and nonlinear multimedia design and the implications of each on teaching and learning;
- Demonstrate an understanding of the levels of interactivity of WBI and their implications on the design and development of instructional modules;
- Demonstrate the use and application of appropriate instructional strategies for developing WBI;
- Demonstrate the use and application of Internet/Web-related technologies;
- Demonstrate an understanding of Web-based management tools and their application to the development of WBI;
- Design and evaluate a Web-based instructional module using the principles above.

The overall course goal was to provide an introduction to the principles of WBI and its role in creating learning environments that utilize the attributes and resources of the Internet and the World Wide Web. Particular emphasis was placed on pedagogical, technological, organizational, institutional, and ethical issues related to the design, development, and delivery of WBI.

The Learning Environment

Next, it was important to determine how this course would be offered. Should it be an online course, considering its topic? Would it be offered partially online with some face-to-face classes? Or would it be offered in a face-to-face format with some online activities and Web-supported material?

It was decided that while this course could be *about* WBI, the use of the Web in delivering the content and implementing learning activities would be supplementary to in-class instruction. Several factors influenced the decision, including the ability of the technological infrastructure at the university to support a fully online course, students' accessibility to the Web from off-campus locations, provision of online support to students and faculty, and finally, the acceptance or comfort level of students working in an online versus a traditional learning environment.

Towson University had adopted the WebCT (Goldberg, 1997) Web course management system, and offered workshops to familiarize faculty with its application for teaching online. However, the online support dimension for WebCT, as for other systems of this type, were either "under construction" or unavailable at the time. And there were no guarantees that student support would be available in time for delivering this course in an online format. Furthermore, the departmental chair felt strongly that our graduate students were not ready to enroll in an online course, and that most would prefer face-to-face instruction and interaction. The anticipated class size was between eight and twelve students.

The class met on a weekly basis for the duration of the semester, and all Web-related and online activities were adjunct to this traditional classroom format. This is known as Web-supported or Web-enhanced instruction. However, the classroom was equipped with state-of-the-art computers with Internet connections and Web development software to support the course objectives. Each class session usually began with a brief discussion of the readings for the week followed by an online quiz and a presentation by the instructor on a concept in WBI. The second half of the class was devoted to teamwork on a group project and other related assignments whose details are discussed below.

The Participants

A total of nine students enrolled in the class. The students were teachers, multimedia developers, instructional designers, and technology coordinators, employed full time and attending the IT program at Towson University on a part-time basis. The course was intended to be an elective course, taken towards the end of their coursework to insure entry skills in instructional design and development (IDD) or a working knowledge of integrating technology into instruction. Knowledge in basic desktop computing applications and Internet applications was assumed.

Instructional Activities

Several instructional activities were developed to support the course objectives stated above. Weekly online discussions aimed at facilitating students' articulation of their understanding of issues discussed in the readings were conducted through a class listserv. Each student was required to post two questions to the listserv related to the topic of the week, respond to another student's questions, and provide feedback on responses to their questions by others. The questions and validated responses were used to construct weekly online quizzes administered during class time. A brief discussion guided by the instructor preceded the administration of the online quiz each week, allowing students to further elaborate on issues that needed clarification. Presentations by the instructor and guest speakers on related topics also supported this process. At the end of the semester, a final exam, with questions from the quizzes, was administered. Students were also required to submit a two-page reflective statement discussing their viewpoint on the effectiveness of the online discussions, online quizzes, and online resources in enhancing their learning of the concepts articulated in the readings.

The main percentage of the course grade, however, was assessed through the design and development of a WBI prototype on an instructional topic of their choice. This was a group effort. Prior to commencing this project, students were asked to evaluate existing online courses using the Web-based learning (WBL) framework mentioned above. Having completed this activity, the students were a step closer to understanding the issues involved in designing an online course, and discussed these issues within their groups. The group assignments were based on mutual interests in content domains that students had communicated to the instructor via a class survey administered at the beginning of the course. One of the questions on the survey specifically asked each student to select an area of interest for which they would like to develop a WBI prototype. After the groups were identified, subject matter experts in the designated content areas were assigned to each of the groups. The role of the subject matter expert was to support students in content design and to provide a review of the prototype as formative evaluation. The prototype was evaluated on its interface design, usability, and instructional design and delivery components. (This chapter does not address the evaluation of the WBI prototype as a product, but instead analyzes the process.)

Process Analysis Evaluation Method

The process of designing, developing, and implementing this course was evaluated on the effectiveness of the course organization and structure in supporting the students toward achieving the course objectives. The reflection statement, student comments and anecdotes recorded by a peer observer, and a standard end-of-semester course evaluation survey served as instruments for this evaluation. In the following sections I will discuss these methods, the data collected using these methods, and finally the findings, recommendations, and conclusions.

Student Reflection Statements

The reflection statement required each student to describe his/her experiences with the online components used in the course; mainly the quizzes, listserv, and online resources. Students were asked to discuss the effectiveness of these course components in enhancing their learning. Students were also required to reflect on the WBI models and frameworks that they learned about in the readings and to select a *preferred* model, and provide adequate reasoning for selecting such a model, or suggest their own model if they found fault with other models. Below are the two questions of the reflection statement:

1. This course had three online components:
    - Listserv discussions;
    - Online quizzes;
    - Online resources (through course home page, syllabus, and instructional resources page).

Describe your experiences with these components, both positive and negative, in terms of their effectiveness in enhancing your learning.

2. The readings offered several models/frameworks for the design of WBI (Khan's WBL framework, Keller's model, the instructional framework, Reeves and Reeves' dimensions, event-oriented design model, active learning principles, etc.). Pick your favorite model/framework and tell why it might be more effective than the others; or better yet, come up with your own model for designing effective WBI and explain its basic principles.

Student responses to question 2 of the reflection statement will be discussed to the extent that they bear relevance to the evaluation of the course organization and structure. To this effect, these responses will be used to demonstrate how much students learned, which the students were required to address in the end-semester course evaluation. It is also important to mention here that after a couple of class sessions a new activity emerged to complement the listserv discussions. Students expressed the need to engage in an in-class discussion prior to taking the online quiz. They felt that posting, responding, and validating questions using the listserv was not sufficient in preparing them for the online quiz. As a consequence, an in-class discussion was facilitated by the instructor at the beginning of every class. Students also reflected on this instructional activity in their statements. Below are excerpts from these statements on each of the online activities as well as the in-class discussion.

Listserv Discussions

> I liked the idea of generating our own questions about the topics we read and having our classmates answer them. In this way we could bring ideas that we felt were interesting or important about the subject to the group and we could see what others had to say through their answers.
>
> I did not feel that these question and answer sessions could be considered a true discussion. I don't recall there being any third party involvement in any of the questions/answers posted.
>
> The idea of selecting and posting two questions which typify the content of the article(s) was also helpful. Selecting important questions is a type of synthesis-thinking. A reader who doesn't think synthetically is not reading actively and will not retain much of what is read.
>
> One thing that I find unusual is its very nature of being asynchronous. Often students misunderstand each other because they have long forgotten what other students' arguments were before they hit on the next topic. I would rather see this discussion carried out synchronously on a chat line as the class size is quite small. This will certainly bring about other problems in practice as most students are studying part time while engaged in their professional jobs full time however it might be a more effective learning experience.

I found the listserv discussion to be the most enriching.... It was very interesting to see the different questions that each of us developed. I also enjoyed the variety of topics each of us covered. It was an interesting way to get a more in-depth look into a point of the chapter that I may not have been drawn to.

Early in the semester it was very demanding to keep up with the reading and post questions, answers, and verifications. It was a constant pressure on the mind that you needed to check the listserv to see who posted what so you can respond and who answered your question so you can verify it.

A lot of the questions were rather simple and did not require higher-order thinking skills. People were intentionally looking for easy questions because they knew the questions would be on the quizzes and then on the final exam. It is also very easy to compose and answer a question without actually reading the whole chapter.

I think I would like to have more discussion on the listserv. Just posting questions did not seem to really use the best part of the listserv to its best ability.

In-Class Discussions

The in-class discussions which evolved after several weeks of readings was a positive thing. Giving the class an opportunity to voice opinions regarding aspects of the readings promotes active learning. Voicing one's thoughts helps to codify and structure them. Also, hearing others' viewpoints causes re-examination of one's own ideas—always a healthy activity.

Eventually we began discussing the questions and ideas before each quiz in class. I felt these discussions enhanced what we did throughout the week, while the quizzes did not offer the same enrichment.

I found the in-class discussion to be very helpful and enlightening. It should be moved partially to an online discussion form.

Online Quizzes

Rather than online quizzes, I would have preferred to have been graded on the quality of my contributions to the in-class discussion which happened prior to taking the online quiz. I think that such an approach would have caused all the students to examine and review the articles more thoroughly—and learn more from them.

I found the multiple-choice questions easier to answer online than the essay type. There is so much typing to do and as a student, I would rather write on paper when under the pressure of taking a quiz.

The quizzes, although certainly an evaluation tool, I do not believe enhanced my learning. Since they were the exact questions we developed during the week through our listserv, I did not feel that the quizzes tested our learning and comprehension of the information.

It became difficult after a while to keep the facts straight with all the different frameworks and models that we were reading about therefore the quizzes were not very effective in helping us discriminate between the many concepts underlying these frameworks.

Online Resources

I made very little use of these resources, accessing them only two or three times during the term. Whenever I needed the syllabus, I was able to reference the paper copy to obtain the information that I needed. The instructional resources available from the course homepage were of minimal use. I saw no compelling reason to view, for example, the PowerPoint presentation on the Instructional Framework.

The online resources page had a few items for us to investigate. One of the resources offered our WBL dimension reviews. I thought this was a great idea if others posted as well.

Other than at the very beginning, I seldom accessed the pages except to link to Khan's framework or the Levels of Interactivity.

An idea for this page is to include a bulletin board posting section where we as students could post site findings and other resources. Going back to our diverse experiences, I know we have discovered a great variety of resources and this would be a wonderful common area to share them.

Overall, I learned a lot by browsing through the instructional resource pages to utilize and locate educational resources and discriminate between educational and non-educational sites.

It is very good to have both options, online information and hardcopy by printing online information.

Participant Observations

The faculty member who attended every class and was a full participant in all class activities recorded her observations on specific instructional strategies as outlined below.

Her observations encompassed all class activities and therefore were not limited to the online components of the course.

Presentations on Special Topics

Instructor presentations frequently included examples to illustrate the concepts under study. On several occasions, outside experts were brought in to facilitate discussion and answer students' questions. One session that was particularly interesting and helpful was when the instructor arranged for the author of the course text to come and meet with the class. The author's explanations made his framework more meaningful. We had used his framework to evaluate existing online courses prior to starting our own WBI prototype.

Another session that was particularly helpful was when a professor who was an expert on WebCT explained how he had used this tool in an introductory Computers and Creativity class to conduct online activities and present the course content. He shared some insightful findings about the features of this tool that were very helpful in the development of our prototype.

Evaluating Existing Online Courses

An excellent learning experience was looking at various online courses on the Web to see examples of the types of courses that were available online and actually being used. Students were given lists of several existing online classes and were asked to review these courses based on a Web-based learning (WBL) framework developed by Khan (1998). Aspects of this framework were presented and discussed and students were required to compare and contrast the features of the online courses in relation to the dimensions of this framework. This was an interesting and informative assignment, which took several weeks to complete. It allowed students to look more critically at specific elements of the online courses, such as interface design, perceived interactivity, instructional strategy, online support, institutional support, management support, and technological issues.

Teamwork

Teamwork was a major part of the course. The group experience was interesting and challenging. The instructor surveyed students in the class about their background and interests and suggested the group makeup. My group was composed of three students. Like many adult learners taking college courses, time available for group meetings outside the class was limited since all members had the equivalent of full time jobs in addition to taking the course. The only time that our schedules permitted out of class meetings was a half-hour before the scheduled class time.

At our first meeting we briefly brainstormed ideas to determine an instructional topic for the WBI prototype. One member was interested in developing a Web site to support people who are in grief due to a crisis situation since she had reviewed a similar Website and had some experience in that area. The other, an elementary school teacher was interested in a site that teaches young children how to discriminate [among] animal sounds, and I suggested something related to computer or Internet basics since there was a definite need for online education in that area as well as it being a topic in which we all had a basic knowledge. After two more meetings that included much discussion of these as well as other ideas and investigation of other instructional Websites, we chose computer basics as the topic for our instructional Website.

In subsequent meetings we determined how to go about organizing this Website. Each group member had ideas that were usually compatible with what others were thinking. These ideas were largely based on what we gleaned from the online courses that were evaluated earlier in the semester. When our ideas differed, we discussed and negotiated until we came to a consensus or agreeable solution.

At times, group members disagreed on interface design issues but were able to resolve these issues based on suggestions from our subject matter expert and the readings. As group work evolved, email became more frequent and was important in determining each group member's tasks. At times, group members were frustrated by the slow response of other members that was usually due to limited access, technical problems, lack of time, or members just not regularly checking email.

Throughout the group experience, the instructor met periodically with groups. The instructor gave very detailed feedback in the later development stages of the prototype which was extremely helpful.

Online Listserv

The instructor had set up the listserv before the course began and during the first class session the online expectations and protocols were explained. Overall, the established listserv protocols worked well even though it did take a few weeks for all to become accustomed to them. The instructor assisted by reminding students either via email or in class of the protocols when she observed that students were not following them.

This experience required going online three or four times a week. This would not be a problem for full-time graduate students who are often on campus, but since most students in the class had full time jobs or worked part time and took several classes; finding the time to get online at the appropriate times took some planning on the student's part. Calling in from remote locations to the campus computer often took longer than necessary. However, even with these circumstances, most students met the course requirements. If requirements were not met, the instructor checked with students either before the class sessions or in the next class session as to what had occurred. On several occasions, students thought they had posted to the listserv, but for some reason, their questions had not gone through.

Overall posting to the listserv was very helpful as a learning tool as it forced me to look at assigned material early in the week even though at times I was less enthused about participating than at others. However, it just became one of the things that I knew I was to do early in the week. Although this activity did encourage students to at least look at the assigned chapters early in the week, I frequently found myself just perusing the chapters to search for good question material instead of studying the concepts. Some chapters seemed not to have material that was worthy of asking intelligent or higher level questions, but most contained significant concepts.

Answering Others' Questions

I found that trying to find the answers did help me learn the material for in looking for the answers I frequently reviewed material I had looked at before when I was attempting to compose a question. Additionally, I often encountered material that I found interesting and would get sidetracked reading that material. Sometimes, I would have to go online several times to find an unanswered question. In answering questions, when several were available, I often found myself choosing easier questions, or ones I already knew the answer to rather than ones I had to spend more time seeking the answer. However, on several occasions I enjoyed engaging in discussions centering around the question and posting my opinions in reaction to or about questions.

For the most part, students composed questions that were significant in learning major frameworks or concepts in WBI. I was impressed that most questions were well designed and indicated that the student had reflected on the content and put thought into the development of the question.

Validating Answers to Questions

Validating others' questions was usually fairly simple. It was just a matter of reading the answer and usually sending a comment to the person answering the question such as "This is exactly what [I] wanted!" or

"Your answers are correct. Great job!" Occasionally a question would be answered either partially or totally incorrect and the correct answer with explanation needed to be given.

Reviewing Others' Questions

Reviewing and studying other students' questions gave me a perspective of what other students in the class perceived to be significant content. I found reading the questions to be helpful in learning the material and sometimes they would motivate me to go to the chapters to find other related material. For example, if a student asked a question that requested naming and describing four of the six factors of a concept or framework, after reading the answer given, I would go to the chapter to find the factors that were not named in the answers.

Quizzes from Online Questions

During the first several weeks of class I felt that the online quiz was anxiety producing and did not create a positive learning experience especially the first 20 minutes of class time. In other words, instead of going to the class looking forward to an enjoyable learning experience, I went in just hoping that I could remember all the information I had reviewed from the listserv questions.

At times I felt that the quizzes took more class time than the learning that resulted from the overall experience. Even though the quizzes were short, they seemed to take about twenty minutes of class time each week. A possible alternative would be a short discussion on the material each week and quizzes given less often such as every two or three weeks.

Sometimes I felt that the rewards of the online learning experience were not worthy of the time required for the activity. However, in my above analysis I probably am not taking into consideration the rewards that the experience provided in learning about the value of online communication in the learning process.

End-of-Semester Course Evaluation

This was a standard quantitative assessment based on a scale of 1–5 that rates the instructor as well as the course on several criteria. Since this case study is about evaluating the course organization and structure, only items related to the course will be discussed. Students were required to rate the course in terms of the following:

1. Its relevance and importance;
2. Relationship to the syllabus;
3. Consistency of assignments with course objectives;

4. Text and/or class materials;
5. How much they learned;
6. Overall rating.

All nine students completed this assessment during the last class session. The results were not as anticipated by the instructor. This was a new course in its experimental stages, which required the use of online technologies for the completion of learning activities, and students had no benchmark for comparing expectations. The course was rated high in terms of its relevance and importance to the field; however, the other items received a range from satisfactory to unsatisfactory ratings. Item 5 received a satisfactory rating, and the following excerpts from students' reflection statements (in response to question 2 of the statement) demonstrate their learning about the pedagogical aspect of WBI, which was an important goal for this course. The students were asked to reflect upon the many frameworks and models that were presented in the readings and to select a favorite framework for the development of WBI or to design their own.

> The event-oriented design (EOD) model proposed by Thomas M. Welsh in chapter 19 of Khan's WBI book (1997) attracted me more than the other formal models and frameworks mentioned in the readings. The EOD model was down-to-earth and prescriptive, rather than an abstract statement of certain theoretical notions. There were actual steps described for implementing the model. By far, though, the most attractive aspect of Welsh's ideas was that his model made it "a relatively simple matter to enable the same events in a more traditional campus environment" (page 164). In my current community college situation, the development of online courses is proceeding in fits and starts. I think that Welsh's model will fit that environment well, allowing even for a partial online implementation in the context of a regular classroom-based offering. Also, as Welsh points out in his conclusion, I may be required to teach a classroom-based offering of a given course (such as statistics) while developing and making available an online version of the same course. The EOD model allows for the flexibility demanded in that situation.

> Schrum's framework is cohesive and easy to comprehend. It includes four major areas for consideration in the design and development of WBI: pedagogical, technological, organizational, and institutional. However aspects like online support, interface design, and resource support should be incorporated or addressed under the technological dimension and aspects concerning management of online instruction should be incorporated under the organizational dimension.

> The two frameworks that made the biggest impressions on me were Khan's WBL framework and Reeves and Reeves interactive learning dimensions. I think Khan's framework is useful as a checklist for helping authors determine what components and features they may need in their particular WBI program, and reminding them about the necessary,

> but less important details of information that aid the learners who are taking the course online such as navigational tools. Reeves and Reeves model however came across as being the most down to earth, comprehensible explanation of ways to approach the design and evaluation of WBL. The model does not offer cut and dry solutions as to how to design the *best* course or module, rather how to determine what type of instructional strategy, what components of the Web, etc., an author could use to design the most appropriate instruction for his/her purposes.
>
> In designing my own model I would include three categories: content or pedagogical, technical, and Web components. In the content or pedagogical category I would include accurate content, course requirements, objectives, and assignments. I would also include ethical issues associated with creating an online course making sure that the information is presented in a clear and unbiased way so as not to offend anyone. Instructors should make sure that proper netiquette is used and that their design approach is clear. This includes varying the material to meet the needs of different learning styles. Students should also be allowed to give anonymous feedback about the site. The technical category would include student support and instructor/facilitator support. The Web components category would include usability issues, interface design, navigation structure, and hyperlink structure and accuracy.

As demonstrated in the above excerpts, students were able to synthesize their knowledge on WBI and go beyond the information given to provide their own rationale for selecting their most-preferred framework or design their own framework for guiding the development of WBI. Although transfer of learning was evident, the overall rating of the course (item 6 on this evaluation form) was unsatisfactory. A positive correlation of this rating with the ratings on items 2 (relationship to the syllabus), 3 (consistency of assignments with course objectives), and 4 (text and/or class materials) was apparent. The rationale for this correlation is evident in the discussion of our findings and conclusions below.

What Worked and Why

This analysis revealed several important findings that formed the basis of a set of guidelines for designing, developing, and implementing a course on WBI. The framework used to present these guidelines was the instructional activities themselves. The evaluation results and the ensuing recommendations for each activity will be discussed below, beginning with the least effective and progressing to the most effective instructional activity. Figure 14.4 presents a visual of this progression.

Online Quizzes

Generally the comments on the online quizzes were negative. This activity was perceived as anxiety producing and cumbersome in terms of online requirements. The participant observer noted that quizzes should be given less frequently and at the end of the class

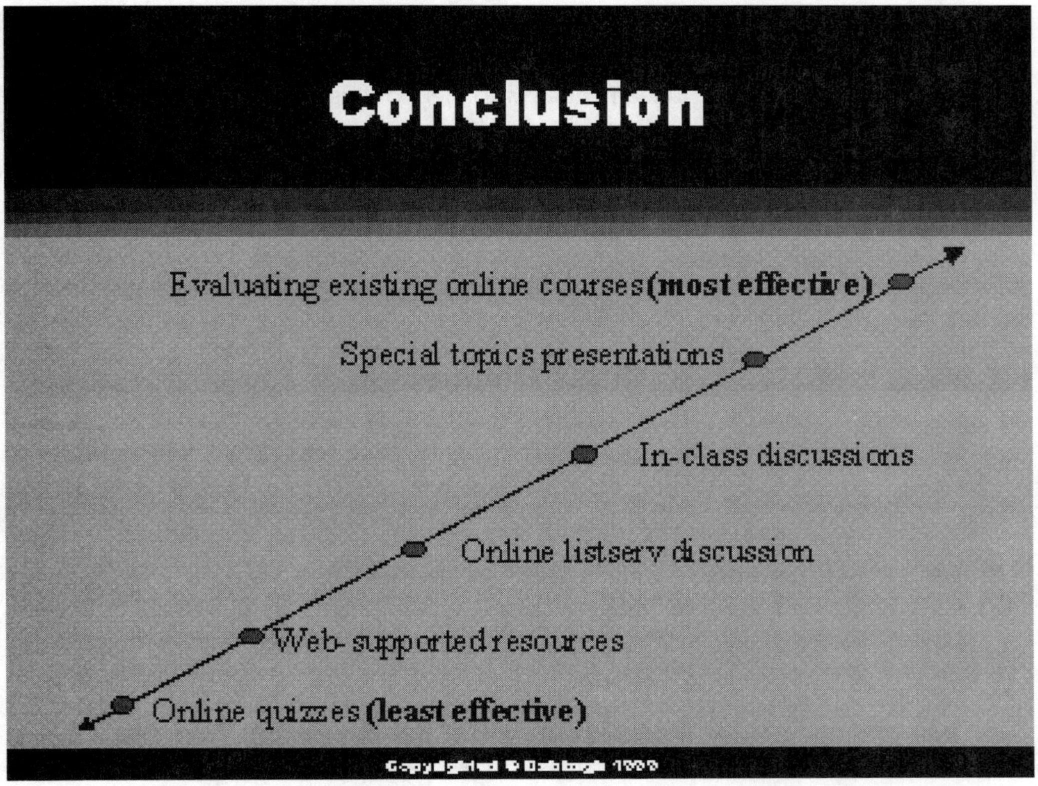

Figure 14.4 Evaluation of the effectiveness of instructional activities

after students had been given the opportunity to discuss the material. Students echoed these comments in their reflection statements and added that the online format was limiting due to time constraints and the types of questions asked. Most of the students resorted to multiple-choice type questions, which were easier to generate for the online listserv but difficult to answer due to their inflexible nature, especially when the material became increasingly complex with the many frameworks and concepts. The few open-ended questions that were included in the quizzes also presented some difficulties for the students in terms of typing and space limitations. Students did not think that the online quizzes enhanced their learning experience. It is therefore not recommended that this activity be used in a course on WBI.

Web-Supported Resources

Mixed results were expressed regarding the usefulness of online resources to support the instructional process. It is important to keep in mind that this course was conducted in a traditional format where students met face-to-face on a weekly basis. Had the course been conducted partially or fully online, the authors feel that the usefulness of the online resources would have been more prevalent. Some students did not feel the need to visit these resources unless they were instructed to do so as part of a specific activity. Others enjoyed browsing the many sites provided and most liked the convenience of having access to the syllabus and other course material as needed. Some of the Web resources may have been regarded by the students as redundant since the instructor also provided print-based copies for most of the class assignments and activities.

Listserv

Posting, responding to, and validating questions through an online listserv was also a fundamental component of this course. The instructional goal was to provide students with a means of interacting with the reading material and enhancing group communication. This goal and the students' reflective statements were evaluated by the participant observer. Although most students agreed that generating questions was a reflective activity that engaged students in higher level processing of the material and provided multiple perspectives of the content, the results were a mix of positive and negative comments.

In-Class Discussion

Although this was not a planned but rather an emerging activity, the consensus was that it was a very positive learning experience, which further enhanced the knowledge of concepts articulated in the readings and helped reduce the anxiety that preceded taking the online quiz. Students were able to ask questions about the readings and explain to others how they generated their quiz questions and what they were looking for as responses. This provided the comfort zone that was lacking on the online listserv. The absence of a third-party intervention on the listserv, as one student put it, created an anxiety level that negatively impacted the learning process.

Presentations on Special Topics

This was described as a positive learning experience from the standpoint of the participant observer. Bringing in experts to present on special topics helped contextualize learning and allowed students to interact with the experts meaningfully.

Evaluating Existing Online Courses

This activity was described as an excellent learning experience by the participant observer and was also discussed by students in their reflection statements as being instrumental in guiding the design and development of their WBI prototypes. The students used the WBL framework to evaluate existing online courses and synthesize their findings in a report that was posted on the Web. In doing so, students engaged in critical thinking skills. Posting the reports on the Web also provided examples that could be shared among students. These examples could be used for modeling, discussion, or review.

Teamwork

Teamwork was a fundamental component of this course and was evaluated only by the participant observer and therefore was not included in Figure 14.4. It was noted that graduate students frequently have many time-consuming obligations such as work and family, which made it very difficult to schedule class group meeting times for assigned group projects. Students therefore should be encouraged to use electronic communications for group meetings as much as possible. It was also suggested that the instructor should be copied on group communications and should take a larger role in facilitating and monitoring group activities. It was noted that graduate students often have differing backgrounds and areas of interests and that getting group members to agree on project topics is difficult. Offering a list of pre-selected topics for students to choose from may expedite this process.

Conclusion and Recommendations

Courses in WBI are at the forefront of every higher education institution, and the need for guidelines on how to design, develop, and implement such courses is imminent. This case study demonstrated that certain instructional activities are more effective than others in facilitating learning about WBI. It also demonstrated that some activities could be improved to increase the comfort zone of novices in this emerging and evolving field of WBI. This analysis of *what worked and why*, coupled with specific recommendations, may be used as a guideline to increase the effectiveness of instructional activities when designing courses aimed at teaching about WBI.

1. Elicit student-generated questions on the readings, and follow this up with a discussion (online or in-class) that is facilitated by the instructor. In addition to simply posting, answering, and validating questions, students should be encouraged to discuss material and offer opinions about topics or other posted questions on the listserv.
2. Encourage students to contribute to course content by posting resources to a designated Web area. This is an important learning activity in a course designed to teach the principles of WBI. In addition, allow students to post their work on course assignments. This provides a shared resource for the class and an opportunity for students to learn from other students.
3. If content is provided in the Web-based format, printed copies for class assignments and activities should be furnished only upon request.
4. Protocols for online postings and/or discussion need to be well established.
5. Online discussions and the effectiveness of online protocols need to be continuously monitored and changes rendered as necessary.
6. Synchronous rather than asynchronous discussions should be considered, in order to reduce the anxiety level of having to go online several times per week and to encourage real-time interaction.
7. Expert modeling and interaction with experts on relevant topics should be included in the design of courses aimed at teaching WBI. This may be conducted in face-to-face settings, if feasible, or incorporated as an online activity through some form of computer mediated communication.
8. Engage students in higher order thinking skills through the evaluation and synthesis of existing online courses and by posting their own work on the Web.
9. Encourage students to use electronic communication for teamwork to help alleviate the difficulty of scheduling group meetings outside of class time.
10. Instructors should take a significant role in facilitating and monitoring teamwork, and should model group communications.

References

Australian National Training Authority (ANTA). 1998. "Teaching and Learning Styles that Facilitate Online Learning." (http://Web.tafe.sa.edu.au/lsrsc/one/natproj/tal/)

Bannan, B., and W.D. Milheim. 1997. "Existing Web-Based Instruction Courses and Their Design." Pp. 381–387 in *Web-Based Instruction*, ed. B.H. Khan. Englewood Cliffs, New Jersey: Educational Technology Publications.

Bannan-Ritland, B., D. Harvey, and W. Milheim. 1998. "A General Framework for the Development of Web-Based Instruction." *Educational Media International* 35(2), 77–81.

Dabbagh, N.H., and J.Schmitt. 1998. "Redesigning Instruction Through Web-Based Course Authoring Tools." *Educational Media International* 35(2), 106–110.

Denzin, N. K. 1978. *The Research Act: A Theoretic Introduction to Sociological Methods*. New York: McGraw-Hill.

Goldberg, M. 1997. "Communication and Collaboration Tools in WebCT." Proceedings of the Conference Enabling Network-Based Learning, Espoo, Finland, May 28–30. (http://homebrew.cs.ubc.ca/Webct/docs)

Jones, M.G., and J.D. Farquhar. 1997. "User Interface Design for Web-Based Instruction." Pp. 239–244 in *Web-Based Instruction*, ed. B.H. Khan. Englewood Cliffs, New Jersey: Educational Technology Publications.

Khan, B.H. 1997. "Web-Based Instruction (WBI): What Is It and Why Is It?" Pp. 5–18 in *Web-Based Instruction*, ed. B.H. Khan. Englewood Cliffs, New Jersey: Educational Technology Publications.

Khan, B.H. 1998. "A Framework for Web-Based Learning." (http://Web.gwu.edu/~etlkhan/keynote/dimensions/framework1.html)

Patton, M.Q. 1990. *Qualitative Evaluation and Research Methods*. Newbury Park, California: Sage Publications.

Reeves, T.C., and P.M. Reeves. 1997. "Effective Dimensions of Interactive Learning on the World Wide Web." Pp. 59–66 in *Web-Based Instruction*, ed. B.H. Khan. Englewood Cliffs, New Jersey: Educational Technology Publications.

Ritchie, D.C., and B. Hoffman. 1997. "Incorporating Instructional Design Principles with the World Wide Web." Pp. 59–66 in *Web-Based Instruction*, ed. B.H. Khan. Englewood Cliffs, New Jersey: Educational Technology Publications.

Welsh, T.M. 1997. "An Event-Oriented Design Model for Web-Based Instruction." Pp. 59–66 in *Web-Based Instruction*, ed. B.H. Khan. Englewood Cliffs, New Jersey: Educational Technology Publications.

CHAPTER 15

Rubrics and a Strategy for Integrating Traditional Instruction and Distributed Learning

Pamela Havice, William Havice, and Clint Isbell
Clemson University
U.S.A.

Advances in information technology have created new possibilities for innovative and flexible learning by crossing the boundaries of time and place. With the advancement of computer networks, desktop videoconferencing, and the World Wide Web, learning modalities have greatly expanded, allowing for increased interactivity between the instructor and the learner, and also among learners. These advances in technology are helping to create new forms of electronic interactive education, such as Web-supported courses, that allow people to learn almost anything from anywhere at anytime, creating opportunities for lifelong learning (Heinich et al., 1999). Furthermore, the accountability and assessment of student achievement in these evolving learning environments will remain central in the development of interactive learning and in the instructor's paradigm shift from teaching to learning (Roblyer, 1997).

The Traditional Environment

The traditional learning environment, wherein a teacher stands in front of students in a classroom talking and writing with chalk on a blackboard has been defined by Kim and Kellough (1987) as "a didactic mode where knowledge is passed on to the learners via the teacher, or from content reading in a textbook, or both" (p. 202). Zenger and Zenger (1990) defined the traditional lecture as "an oral presentation given to a class by the teacher" (p. 31). Similarly, Ericson (1960) stated that the lecture, or "telling" method, is a teaching strategy without requirements for manipulative work. Teachers are comfortable with traditional methods of instruction because (Kim and Kellough, 1987)

1. The instructor controls the content.
2. The instructor controls time scheduling.
3. Student learning is predictable and manageable.

These three strengths may also be seen as weaknesses of the traditional mode in the following ways:

1. It stifles creative thinking.
2. Students' self-concepts are not addressed.
3. There is little student involvement in decision making.
4. There is a lack of intrinsic sources for student motivation.

Learning and Instruction

New media and theories of instruction and learning have been added to accommodate changes in technology. Cobb (1997) redefined learning with new instructional media as "a highly interactive set of events shared between a learner and various human/nonhuman agents, tools, and media..." (p. 24). With the development of more interactive learning opportunities, educators are experimenting with constructivism theory and distributed learning concepts. These concepts beg for different approaches/strategies in assessment methodologies to appropriately assess learning outcomes.

Distributed Learning

Recent developments in telecommunications have provided expanded opportunities for delivery of education and training. Distributed learning has become a popular term used to describe the use of telecommunications to deliver synchronous and asynchronous instruction. Distributed learning includes technologies delivered in part through electronic media such as videoconferencing, videotape, interactive television, electronic mail, and Web-based instruction for the distant learner as well as the traditional on-campus learner.

The concept of distributed learning integrates the interactive capabilities of networking, computing, multimedia, and hypermedia with teaching approaches such as collaboration, discovery learning, problem solving, and active learning. Hirschbuhl and Bishop (1996) stress the importance of the two kinds of interaction with regard to learning. Within a technology-driven distributed learning environment, a student interacts with the content as well as with others about the content. "Both types of interaction are important for efficient, effective, and affective learning" (p. 202).

Distributed learning is becoming a vital component of on-campus instruction at Clemson University. Clemson University has designed and implemented an innovative approach to course management and delivery through a collaborative learning environment (CLE). A Web-based system has been developed to facilitate active learning and collaboration for students enrolled on- and off-campus. The goal of the CLE is to provide technology-based services to enhance instruction. This includes network space that faculty and students can use to share resources, to communicate, and to post and retrieve class assignments. Additionally, the CLE class workspace includes user tools to facilitate instructional and learning tasks, as well as tools for assessment.

Distributed learning is a learner-based approach that integrates a number of different technologies to enable opportunities for activities and interaction in an asynchronous environment. With the proliferation of newer technologies, it is possible to experience place-shifted instruction with a wide variety of auditory and visual stimuli, more rapidly and with a deeper range of interaction. For example, students can interact with instructors and other students by posting comments to a discussion area on a Web site. With a synchronous learning environment, participants can log on to a Web site and interact with each other in real time. These systems enable us to develop new ways to use instructional technologies and to create more effective learning experiences for learners at any time and in any place.

Distance education is a part of the distributed learning model. The terms distance education, remote learning, and distance learning all refer to learning environments whereby place and/or time separate the student and instructor; thus the student learns independent of contact with the instructor and, often, other students. One of the greatest advantages offered by modern information technologies is the ability for *time-shifting* instruction—experiencing instruction at some other time after the live lesson—and *place-shifting* instruction—experiencing instruction at some place away from the teacher (Heinich et al., 1999).

The distributed learning model described above is based on blending appropriate technologies with aspects of open learning systems and distance education. This model gives educators the flexibility to customize learning environments to meet the needs of the learners, while providing both high quality and cost-effective learning. Regardless of which technology-based method is used to deliver education, a transition must be made from the traditional classroom environment to the technology-based distributive learning environment.

Changing Paradigms

Changes brought about by innovative technology can offer new and exciting opportunities for enhancing the learning and teaching environments within education and training environments. Along with these opportunities are challenges for improved interactivity and communication among the participants in the learning process. These changes, however, necessitate changes in paradigms from the traditional modes of instruction to distributed delivery for all involved. This paradigm shift will be most evident in the areas of delivery methods and assessment strategies.

According to some (Smith and Ragan, 1999), the instructional design process remains more or less the same for traditional-based learning and distributed learning environments. The major challenge is to make the transition from traditional to distance and distributed learning while providing the most effective delivery and assessment models.

Distributed Environments

Two examples for integrating and delivering content from a traditional classroom environment to a distributed learning environment can be found at Clemson University and at the Miramichi Community College in New Brunswick, Canada. For the past decade, traditional distance learning courses at Clemson University were offered through satellite technology and the use of videotaped lectures, either mailed to the student or offered on local television networks. In all of these methods of delivery, the assessment of learning has been very traditional. Now, using stand-alone Web sites and the collaborative learning environment offered in WebCT (Goldberg, 1997), faculty at Clemson University are shifting their course content and delivery methods out of the traditional classroom. Faculty are enhancing traditional courses with such features as online threaded discussions, online testing, video/teleconferencing, online worksheets, team and group assignments, and chat rooms.

Shifting course delivery and content from a traditional classroom environment required new assessment strategies. One example of this was using a faculty home page and WebCT (Goldberg, 1997) to support students and deliver content for a graduate course during the summer of 1999. The graduate-level course was revised to integrate the use of Web-based technology in an effort to enhance the course requirements and to provide greater distance learning flexibility for students. The majority of students taking the course worked full time, with varying job schedules that limited their participation in traditional classes. In addition, many of the students would have had to travel quite a distance to take the course on-campus. Traditionally taught one night each week during the fall and spring semesters, the course was revised to a four-month period beginning during the spring and concluding in August.

This particular course utilized a variety of distributed learning strategies including online team discussion groups, team projects, online quizzes, online resources, and online supporting worksheets. Through team evaluation projects, students were encouraged to use online discussion groups, teleconference, fax, and e-mail for communication during the course. Logs of team meetings were recorded and submitted throughout the course as a means of documentation.

Three different online course development applications were used to help support the course. The primary support was the department/faculty Web site that was used to provide worksheets and lecture material for preparation of in-class exams, the course syllabi, and the schedule. WebCT was used primarily for online quizzes, team discussions, bulletin board postings, course management, and calendar listings. The collaborative learning environment was used as a course management tool to submit course materials in lieu of e-mail and other student activities. As previously mentioned, the CLE is an integrated management and course development program developed at Clemson University for support of online courses.

Even though traditional assessment approaches (for example, exams and projects) were still utilized to evaluate student assignments, the addition of team meetings, team discussion, and meeting logs required a different approach to assessment.

To assist faculty in the ongoing improvement and future development of this course for online delivery, a survey was developed and administered to the twenty-eight students enrolled at the end of the course to determine their perceptions of the various activities and the online learning applications. It was generally found that using technology-based instruction not only allowed students to become more interactive with each other and the faculty during the course, but also increased student participation in team activities.

Students were asked to indicate components of the course that might be most desired if the course were to be delivered totally on line. The majority of the students indicated that online exams, team projects, worksheets to support the course readings, online discussion and conferencing, and links to related resources were all important components if the course were to be offered totally online. The students also indicated, however, that one or more required on-site (face-to-face) meetings would be desirable. Students were also surveyed to determine their preference of available technology that could be used to enhance the course. The majority of the students felt that the use of e-mail, chat/NetMeeting among class participants and the instructor, teleconference, and the use of CD-ROM with course content and interactive activities would be valuable. It was interesting to note that only seven of the twenty-eight students recommended the use of videotaped lectures received by mail as a mode of instruction.

Another example of integrating traditional course content into a distributed learning environment is the Trainer Certification Program developed by HRD Canada and delivered by the Distributed Learning Centre, Miramichi Community College. This is a self-directed program whereby the student is teamed with a mentor and support staff at the community college and utilizes the Internet, telephone, mail, fax, workbook assignments, and audio- and videotapes. Expectations of the course include development of needs assessments and instructional programs developed and delivered at the participant's work area. The programs are videotaped and submitted for evaluation. The success of the program has centred on the support personnel and mentor, along with the regular feedback and assessment of the submitted activities.

As student assignments and expectations change as a result of innovative distributed learning strategies, the assessment methods and strategies will need to change as well. Class assignments (such as the online projects), team evaluation and presentations, and individual participation requirements will require innovative assessment strategies to effectively and efficiently evaluate student performance and competencies.

Assessment

According to Gordon (1987) and Airasian (1991), assessment involves collecting, synthesizing, and interpreting information. In an online learning environment, numerous issues (accretion, negotiation, and interaction) involving individual learning and active participation in group discussions and conferencing become more important considerations in the assessment process. Gunawardena, Lowe, and Anderson (1997) describe the analysis of group interaction as a gradual evolution in the construction of knowledge. For example, when assessing group or individual interaction, the assessment process could include individual assignments, dialog, and collaborative teamwork. Each student may be evaluated using multiple sources of data, including both quantity and quality of student participation in online activities to determine the levels of learning.

With the increased availability of technology-based learning applications and delivery methods, innovative assessment models will be needed. For educators to develop a successful online course, multiple forms for assessing student work and/or performance must be created. These forms for assessment must take into account the paradigm shift occurring with the distributed learning environment. This paradigm shift increases the accountability for learning upon the student (Roblyer et al., 1997). To facilitate this shift of accountability, educators must continue to develop and refine assessment methods such as *rubrics*. Rubrics can provide students with a sense of empowerment for meeting learning objectives. Further discussion of rubrics as an assessment tool will be presented later in this chapter. The following section describes several online instruction systems requiring alternative assessment approaches.

Using Dialog

Through the use of structured Web-based dialog, many students who would not ordinarily participate in a traditional class discussion become more willing to participate. The dialog generated in an online course can be a rich source of formative evaluation material if the instructor is aware of this source.

As online discussion tools, such as chat rooms, threaded discussion, bulletin boards, and listservs, become more common for both individual and group interaction, dialog will develop into a more valid learning assessment approach. These online discussion tools can be used to encourage student participation in critiquing journal articles, facilitating team discussions, debating posted issues, and responding to online reference material. As faculty and students become increasingly interactive within the online learning environment, the dialog will become a more important component of the instructional process. As mentioned in the case study at Clemson University, student discussions and reactions to questions posted in the online discussion area were used to evaluate student learning.

Collaboration

Within the distributive learning environment, collaborative activities involving teams and groups can be effective strategies for enhancing the learning process. In our experience we have found that the interaction of geographically dispersed teams was enhanced when provided with technology-based communication, for example, e-mail and Web discussion areas. The following is a sample of a real-time team discussion using the bulletin board technology in WebCT.

Figure 15.1 Sample of student dialog

Joe connected at: Tue May 25 1999 17:49:53
Joe >>Hello!
Betty connected at: Tue May 25 1999 17:57:58
Ann connected at: Tue May 25 1999 17:57:59
Betty >>Hi Joe
Joe >>Hey Betty
Joe >>Hey Ann
Ann >>Please bear with me...this is my first chat room experience.
Betty >>Are we ready to discuss Stage 2?
Joe >>Yes!
Ann >>Joe, did you get a chance to ask our instructor about the meeting notes/logs from Stage One?
Joe >>Not yet, I was in Columbia again today and was working all day yesterday. I should be able to call him tomorrow.
Betty >>Be sure to ask him about Stage 1
Joe >>I will
Joe >>I got your e-mail attachment of the notes Betty, Thanks
Betty >>Now, for stage II — The design itself. My thoughts are: only one real strength with current program and that was that it was offered at several different times.
Joe >>Yes, but I think that even that could have been toned down a bit, maybe a more strategic approach to the timing.
Betty >>I agree — not very efficient, huh?
Joe >>Nope
Betty >> Joe, what do you suggest for alternatives?

Ann >>The question is did everyone need the same type of training?
Joe >>A time schedule laid out by the presenter requiring the employees to be there. Not a random method for presenting.
Betty >>I think everyone needed that same training but maybe not in the same way — definite different educational levels throughout the hospital (housekeeping to physicians)
Ann >>I think the hospital may have been better served to investigate what designs would have been more effective for certain types of learners. IE...housekeeping vs. doctors
Betty >>We didn't mean that — great minds....
Betty >>Or could have presented by departments
Joe >>I agree
Ann >>Possibly a pilot study could have been done on one dept to see what did and didn't work?
Betty >>Great Idea, Ann
Betty >>I think the facilities could have been more conducive to learning — not an auditorium with everyone spaced out (mentally and geographically) :-)
Joe >>Considering the number of times he presented, you would think that he would have improved with time, but it does not sound like it.
Betty >>I think he had a canned presentation and stuck with it no matter what
Joe >>Not very dynamic?
Ann >>Definitely. Also the audience might have identified better with the subject of the training if someone from their dept had conducted the training. That would have made it more specialized too.

With the expanded use of dialog in the distributed learning environment, group and team activities utilizing the real-time chat areas and threaded discussion will increase the need for innovative assessment strategies.

Rubrics: Enhancing Online Assessment

As educators, we are constantly making judgments about students and student performance. One of the major concerns for both faculty and students when using Web-based technology is the integrity of the course. This includes the integrity of both content and student participation. When a course has been well designed, is learner-centred, and promotes learner empowerment and self-reflection, online course integrity is maintained.

Rubrics provide an alternative to assessing or evaluating online student work and performance while fostering a sense of learner empowerment. Rubrics are simply a set of formal guidelines, scoring guides, or rating tools used to rate examples of student work or performance. The use of rubrics allows the educator to clarify the assessment criteria by which the student's work or performance will be judged. Furthermore, rubrics are designed to provide a fair and reliable means of scoring products, behaviours, assignments, and other activities that are subjective in nature. These guidelines can be extremely helpful in scoring everything from writing samples, collaborative team activities, and dialog samples to multimedia projects in Web-based courses. Table 15.1 shows a sample of a rubric created for evaluating presentations: This activity has been established to challenge the student to develop, deliver, and evaluate topic-appropriate presentations.

Rubrics provide a number of important advantages in the assessment process. Not only do they allow the assessment process to be more objective and consistent, but they also help the educator focus attention on important learning outcomes. This forces the educator to clarify the assessment criteria in specific terms. Rubrics help to demystify or take the guesswork out of the expectations for a project, therefore empowering the student to focus on weak areas while emphasizing the strengths in his or her own work. Rubrics encourage students to develop a consciousness about the criteria they use to assess their own abilities and performances, as well as to assess the performance of their peers. They also provide benchmarks against which to measure and document progress. In other words, rubrics emphasize the use of formative as well as summative evaluations.

Typically, rubrics consist of guideline grids or matrices with performance levels in the top row and performance dimensions along the left column. Each cell holds specific and objective criteria against which the selected performance standards can be assessed, resulting in a given score in a given dimension. Rubrics characteristically provide two to five performance levels.

When developing a useful rubric, there are several tips to keep in mind:

1. Create a general rubric that can be easily adapted to different activities.
2. Limit the number of dimensions. Limiting the number to four or five will allow the evaluator to do a more thorough job of developing each dimension.
3. Develop concrete, measurable, and teachable assessment criteria.
4. Create an "interval" rubric scale. This will provide a stronger, sounder rubric.
5. Include students in the creation or adaptation of the rubric.

The first tip is to create a more general rubric, not task-specific, which can be used in more than one application or project. To develop a sound rubric takes a lot of thought and work. Therefore, a general rubric is a more efficient use of time and makes it possible to track student improvement on successive projects. While being careful to avoid developing a task-specific rubric, the educator must also not be too general.

The dimensions of the rubric tell us "where to look." When creating a rubric, it is important to focus on a limited number of dimensions. Limiting the number to four or five will allow the evaluator to set priorities for what is really important.

Criteria tell us "what to look for" in a rubric. The criteria need to specify those things that matter most for each dimension. The criteria must also be concrete, measurable, and teachable. It is questionable as to whether one can teach a student to be creative, imaginative, or inventive. Furthermore, try to choose criteria that can be counted or marked as "present" or "not present." In striving to make criteria measurable, the educator needs to be careful in selecting descriptors. Try to avoid relative terms such as *poor*, *fair*, *good*, and *excellent*. To avoid discouraging students with value-laden terms

Table 15.1
A sample of a rubric created for evaluating presentations

Presentation Content and Delivery				
	Acceptable 1 point	**Exemplary 2 points**	**Self-Evaluation**	**Teacher Evaluation**
Topic Content	Presentation focuses on appropriate content for the topic. Identifies appropriate objectives for presentation.	Presentation focuses on appropriate content for the topic. Identifies and states appropriate objectives for presentation to meet the class needs.		
Organization	Meets time specifications. Is prepared and organized. Able to follow presentation.	Meets time specifications. Is prepared and organized. Able to follow presentation. Logical flow. Smooth transitions between content areas. Provides a summary of the presentation.		
Subject Knowledge	Demonstrates knowledge of topic by answering class questions.	Demonstrates knowledge of the topic by answering class questions with explanations and elaboration.		
Instructional Media	Uses two different types of instructional media to deliver presentation. Is prepared and familiar with use of media.	Demonstrates awareness of appropriate media for presentation. Is prepared and familiar with at least two		

	Acceptable 1 point	Exemplary 2 points	Self-Evaluation	Teacher Evaluation
		different types of instructional media in delivering presentation.		
Mechanics	The presentation has no misspellings or grammatical errors.	The presentation has no misspellings or grammatical errors. Text is clear and logical, and promotes viewer understanding. Follows the "6 x 6" rule for visual aids.		
Eye Contact	Presenter does not read from notes. Returns to notes frequently, moderate eye contact with audience.	Presenter does not read from notes. Maintains eye contact with audience, seldom returning to notes.		
Poise and Appearance	Presenter is poised and appropriately dressed for the presentation.	Presenter is poised and appropriately dressed for the presentation. Demonstrates self-confidence and promotes comfort of audience.		
Voice	Minimal use of fluctuation in voice. Some noticeable distractions.	Presenter uses a firm, clear, sincere voice. Varies pitch and pace. Avoids distractions ("uh," "oh," "ok").		
Scale: 16–13 = Exemplary, 12–8 = Acceptable, 7–0 = Not Acceptable				

such as *boring* or *poorly presented*, provide specific feedback on the actual traits that constitute a good versus poor performance.

In developing the rating scale in a rubric, it is important to keep the distance between the different levels equal. In other words, the difference between a mark of 1 and 2 should represent the same amount of improvement as the difference between 2 and 3. Statisticians call this type of scale an interval scale. In the real world of the classroom, this type of perfection in a rating system is often not possible. Educators often create *ordinal scales* whereby one project or performance is rated better than another. The bottom line is to create a rubric scale that is as interval-like as possible. This is believed to provide a stronger rubric.

Finally, in developing a rubric it is often helpful to include students in creating or adapting the rubric. This will accomplish several things. First, by involving students in the construction process they will better understand the expectations of the project. They will also be more likely to "buy in" to the work. Second, the students' good ideas will likely add to the quality of the rubric

Conclusion

The links for learning include course delivery systems; communication among educators, students, and others; and locating and consulting with people and information resources (Roblyer et al., 1997). These three activities are made possible with new information technology and can be improved with the development and advancement of distributed learning environments. For example, videoconferencing allows students and instructors at different locations to communicate through live video/audio, thus providing two-way communication (Kemp and Smellie, 1994). As band width and technology improve, new opportunities will be provided for simulation and videoconferencing as means of assessment. With this technology, educators and students are able to reach beyond their classrooms to interact with people and material resources in many parts of the world.

References

Airasian, P.W. 1991. *Classroom Assessment*. New York: McGraw-Hill.

Cobb, T. 1997. "Cognitive Efficiency: Toward a Revised Theory of Media." *Educational Technology and Research Development* 45(4), 21–35.

Ericson, E.E. 1960. *Teaching the Industrial Arts* (3rd edition) Peoria, Illinois: Chas. A. Bennett Co., Inc.

Goldberg, M. 1997. "Communication and Collaboration Tools in WebCT." Proceedings of the Conference Enabling Network-Based Learning, Espoo, Finland. May 28–30. (http://Aslnx1.Asb.Uah.Edu:8900/)

Gordon, M. 1987. *Nursing Diagnosis: Process and Application*. New York: McGraw-Hill.

Gunawardena, C., C. Lowe, and T. Anderson. 1997. "Analysis of a Global Debate and the Development of an Interaction Analysis Model for Examining Social Construction of Knowledge in Computer Conferencing." *Journal of Educational Computing Research* 17(4), 397–431.

Heinich, R., M. Molenda, J.D. Russell, and S.E. Smaldino. 1999. *Instructional Media and Technologies for Learning*. Upper Saddle River, New Jersey: Prentice-Hall, Inc.

Hensen, K.T. 1988. *Methods and Strategies for Teaching Secondary and Middle Schools*. New York: Longman.

Hirschbuhl, J.J., and D. Bishop, eds. 1996. *Computers in Education*. Guilford, Connecticut: Dushkin Publishing Group/Brown and Benchmark Publishers.

Kemp, J.E., and D.C. Smellie. 1994. *Planning, Producing and Using Instructional Technologies*. New York: HarperCollins College Publishers.

Kim, E.C., and R.D. Kellough. 1987. *A Resource Guide for Secondary School Teaching: Planning for Competence* (4th edition). New York: Macmillan.

Missouri Department of Elementary and Secondary Education, Division of Vocational and Adult Education. 1994. *Performance-Based Education: Implementation Handbook*. Columbia, Missouri: University of Missouri-Columbia, Instructional Materials Laboratory.

Negroponte, N. 1995. *Being Digital*. New York: Alfred A. Knopf.

Roblyer, M.D., J. Edwards, and M.J. Havriluk. 1997. *Integrating Education Technology into Teaching*. Upper Saddle River, New Jersey: Prentice-Hall, Inc.

Smith, P., and T. Ragan. 1999. *Instructional Design* (2nd edition). Toronto: Maxwell Macmillian.

Zenger, S.K., and W.F. Zenger. 1990. *Strategies and Techniques for Teaching*. Saratoga, California: R&E Publishers, Inc.

CHAPTER 16

Professors' Experiences in Commercial Web Course Management Systems

Lynn McAlpine, Robert J. Bracewell, and Terry Gandell
McGill University
Canada

As faculty developers, our primary concern rests in knowing how professors learn and improve their instruction, and how we can support their development. Of increasing interest to us, given these concerns, is the effect of new technology[1] on professors' thinking and actions related to teaching. In particular, we are interested in what professors undertake to change and why, what their actual experiences are with technology, and how they interpret the impact of technology on their teaching.

Studies of online learning in higher education suggest that, across disciplines, the greater the knowledge a professor has about computer-assisted instruction, the more positive the perception is of computers, as well as the willingness to use them (for example, Todd, 1993; Inoue, 1998). Studies (for example, Boddy, 1997) also report that lack of knowledge, software, and hardware, as well as a belief that undertaking such initiatives is time consuming, are barriers to using technology. These survey studies present the perceptions of relatively large numbers of professors in different countries.

In this chapter, we provide two grounded case studies to provide insight into the implementation process. These are profiles of professors' thoughts as they undertake what for them are new uses of technology. For those interested in understanding or undertaking such initiatives, these cases provide valuable in-depth information.

As a framework to organize our case data, we draw upon Schwab's (1973) "curriculum commonplaces." Schwab noted that in any situation in which teaching and learning were presumed to be occurring one could understand the process by considering four constituents and their relationship: the teacher, the student, the subject matter, and the context. We have elaborated on each of these commonplaces in specific ways to gain understanding of the role and outcomes of using Web-based technology in higher education (see also Bracewell et al., 1998):

- The role that each professor foresees for the use of Web-based technologies in the course that each is teaching together with the professor's rationale for this role;
- The extent of (and expectations for) students' access to and use of the Web-based technologies;

- How the subject matter shapes the use of Web-based technologies;
- The sources and degree of support that the university provides for the implementation and use of Web-based technologies.

The Setting: McGill University

McGill University in Montreal, Canada, is a multidisciplinary research-intensive university. The vision of the university is a quest for excellence in teaching and research. Within the past few years, there has been increasing institutional support for integrating instructional uses of the Web into teaching activities.

The Computing Centre, for example, provides the university with technical expertise and hardware that support the computing infrastructure at McGill. In conjunction with the Instructional Communications Centre, the Computing Centre recently began providing consultation and workshops on the technical aspects of Web course management systems. Furthermore, the Centre for University Teaching and Learning, also mandated to support professors' efforts to enhance teaching, has been offering a series of teaching and technology workshops (for example, use of online discussion, practice, and feedback). Further, competitive teaching and learning improvement grants are available through the Centre. Both professors of this study have benefited from these grants.

The Cases[2]

The professors, Allison and David, are experienced academics who have each been teaching at the university level for over fifteen years. They were interviewed, using a structured interview protocol, before and after the course they had taught through a Web course management system.

Allison is a professor in the Faculty of Education and an accredited teacher whose scholarly interests are in literacy instruction with a focus on writing. Her pedagogical perspective (as can be seen below) focuses on the importance of students engaging in interaction with their instructor and with each other to assume control of their learning. At the time of our interviews she was using Lotus LearningSpace (see the description of LearningSpace elsewhere in this book) for the first time as a resource in a course on the use of language across the curriculum. Students in the course had already attained an undergraduate degree, but were otherwise a heterogeneous group at various stages in their pre-service program (second to fourth year) and in a range of specializations (for example, history and mathematics).

David is a professor in the Faculty of Science whose scholarly interests are in computer science with a focus on software and programming. He is highly committed to instruction in higher education that integrates both the content and the skills required to achieve competence in computer science. At the time of our interview he was using WebCT (see the description in Chapter 12, "Managing Large Classes in WebCT") for the first time as a resource in teaching a large, entry-level, undergraduate class on computer systems. Most students in the course were beginning their specialization in computer science.

Professors' Perspectives on the Use of Web-Based Technologies

Both professors were using Web-based technologies to enhance the quality of instruction in their courses. For Allison, the learning outcomes of the course dictated her use of LearningSpace functions. These outcomes endeavoured

> to establish what promotes active student learning through student language use, looking at all the language, listening, speaking, reading, writing, obviously, but also thinking skills and of course connecting the parts of the curriculum.

To advance her students' treatment of language across the curriculum, Allison initially used a response log method in which students wrote hard copy responses to readings and ideas from the class and she responded. She found that this modelling transferred to student interaction using LearningSpace.

> They moved easily from that [hard copy] into doing the same thing on Lotus with each other...and now they don't seem to need me at all...it's been internalized.

A major reason David adopted WebCT was that it provided a straightforward way to input and organize the fairly substantial content of the course that he was teaching (he had previously used standard HTML format to present course content). Another reason was that WebCT gave the students ready access to course materials in a way that was appropriate to the discipline of computer science.

> ...[The course] covered a lot of very technical detailed information and all the details are available to them online. From that point of view, I'm certain that they will achieve the learning outcomes...the technology really makes it easy, because this is a computer course and the students have to get used to using the Web and downloading and moving files around.

Both professors viewed the use of these Web technologies as a tool for helping to realize worthwhile instructional activities. For example, Allison commented on the activity supported by the threaded discussion capability of LearningSpace.

> The students who have really taken this [on] as part of their classroom tools have used it to extend discussions enormously. [In] one-hour classes we would get cut off just where things were getting interesting. And they have been able to go onto the online discussion in the Lotus Course Room area where they can begin discussions, contribute to other people's topics, and...build up quite elaborate threads. They have extended the discussion...on many topics of interest to them, including some that I wouldn't have thought of as central myself.

Further, the students were

> extraordinarily open and quite eloquent in many cases in using personal narratives. They have put online things, I think, that took quite a lot of courage to do. So, the technology seems to have allowed people in a way to be both open and intimate. They really do feel more comfortable putting thoughts online. Plus, of course, they can revise their text as they go. It's not quite as risky as talking...you can pull something back as you say it and then rewrite it in a different way.

It seems that the experience confirmed the potential for the technology to preserve and even to enhance what she believes characterizes good teaching: interactivity and dialogue among the students to the extent that they "take on more and more central space and more power." David noted that many kinds of interaction are essential to learning.

> ...having the material is one thing, but it has to be part of a structure, an environment, where students can interact with teaching assistants, with [each other], with the professors, and make certain that they really learn the materials. So, having great computer technology to support you is useful but it's not the whole story.[3]

From these comments, it is clear that both professors viewed the technology as just one component of a course implementation that promoted content- and instructor-focused interaction among students. They achieved a dual mode of interaction based on both remote communication via the Web and more traditional face-to-face communication (Bracewell et al., 1998). Residing behind these perspectives on the use of Web technology are the professors' assumptions about the nature of learning—both can be characterized as constructivist in that they emphasise the importance of the learner's activity, both mental and social, in achieving understanding and learning (compare Spivey, 1997). As Allison comments,

> I like very interactive classrooms, very dialogic classrooms, where students...usually take on more and more central space and more power...so that students feel that their knowledge and their learning are centred and coherent rather than fragmented and incoherent.

For Allison, the Web technology was validated as an instrument to realize learning. When asked how her use of LearningSpace was related to learning outcomes, she responded,

> Very, very directly, I think it essential to my courses in general...the shared construction of new knowledge among the student group, so that they become in a sense creators and definers of what it is they learn.... There's a very practical element where the computer, the thread of discussions, and the connections (that I hope they will have) will allow them, if they use it, to keep on with what [they] would have

> here at McGill when they're not at McGill. So that there's continuity, there's connection, there's the dialogic rapport.

Likewise, David viewed learning as active and interactive.

> You learn things by doing them.... You can't just sit there passively and let all this information flow over you. You have to be involved and get your hands dirty and roll up your sleeves.... As I said on the Web site, it's the students' course; they're responsible for their learning and we are the catalysts who supply the information and tell them where the thing is, but they have to be actively involved with the learning process.

As mentioned above, one of David's principal reasons for using WebCT was the ready access to course material that was provided to students. Another reason, linked to his constructivist view of learning, was that it was a vehicle for feedback to students.

> The assignments are submitted by e-mail.... I have a copy of every assignment every student did during the course. So I [can] throw it up on the screen and I discuss exactly what they did and why they've got the grade they've got.

Of course, the assumption that learning is constructivist in nature, and that student activity and interaction are necessary for learning, immediately raises the issue for the professor of how to cope with the interaction, especially in situations like the ones examined in this chapter where the technology has been adopted in large part because it promotes interaction. Allison and David dealt with this problem in different ways, reflecting the different structure of content that they were teaching.

In Allison's Language Across the Curriculum course, which had an enrollment of about forty-five, the threaded discussion feature of LearningSpace provided a means of dealing with interaction by having students dialogue with each other. As mentioned previously, at the beginning of the course Allison modelled this task by having students address an issue and then responded to their comments in the class. This modelling and the subsequent transition of the activity to LearningSpace led to a reduction in Allison's monitoring of student interaction.

> I am a bit guilty about this. What I have realized is the first two or three weeks with Lotus, I was scrupulously going into Lotus...and checking how they were doing.... More recently, in the last four weeks, I just kind of let them go to it because they are doing so beautifully and I sort of just look in. But as I have said before, I almost feel my presence is no longer required.

For David's larger course (about 120 students) the problem of dealing with interaction was solved by the subject matter, so to speak. The subject matter (see below) was substantial and highly structured, lending itself to a style of interaction that was structured and focused on the completion of specific assignments.

> The [student] assignments are submitted by e-mail, they go into a central filing system, the T.A. marks them, I capture the marks electronically, and assignments get returned to the students with comments, with a grade on them.

Indeed, the large enrollment of this course can be seen as a consequence of the high degree of structure afforded by the content and course organization.

Student Access to and Use of Web Technology

The expectation of both professors was that students ought to have access to Web-based technologies. This could be achieved through the use of computer labs, but the assumption was that the better situation was one in which students had access through personal computers. As Allison commented,

> ...as we know, people with up-to-date equipment are hugely advantaged.

David elaborated on student access.

> What they really need is a computer which is reasonably fast...and it should have a high-speed data line to an Internet service provider.... There's no doubt the students who have a computer at home do better than the ones who don't.

Because of a number of differences between the two cases,[4] Allison was more explicit than David about problems concerning student access to and use of the technology. Concerning access, she stated,

> If you're going to use the technology, it should be accessible to all. And of course there's issues of [social] class and economics.... Computers can divide rather than connect if people become computer haves and have-nots. It has strong gender implications because women have less money.

Moreover, Allison was aware that not all students used the technology even when they had access.

> Lotus LearningSpace or WebCT or whatever it is will not help, even in the objectives we've identified, if the student doesn't use it. And that to me is not an empty statement; it's an important statement. Even in a recent graduate class, I heard that [only] two-thirds of the students joined in the discussion online. As far as I'm concerned, ... one-third has been effectively silenced, for whatever reason. Why didn't they [join]? Did they not have equal access to both hardware and software? Are they not as confident? Do they not feel at home working with the computer yet? Do they [choose not] to use it? Did they not have time?

In summary, both professors felt that student access to Web technologies is important for fostering learning. Both showed an awareness of current problems faced by students in securing that access.

Relationship Between Subject Matter and Web Technologies

In determining their instructional approach, the subject matter of the courses was a major consideration for both professors. As Allison stated,

> I'm also interested…in content area excellence…. I think the way that can best be maintained…[is] if the teacher is a content knowledge specialist who cares, who is enthusiastic. So…they are never going to be so much focused on students they'll forget the subject, or so much focused on the subject they forget the students.

For David, good teaching involves

> …passing on your own enthusiasm for the subject to the students, who are genuinely interested in it and will go and study the subject out of their own interest as well.

This consideration of the subject matter applied as well to how both used their Web technology. For Allison, the subject matter was concerned with how teachers use language to integrate different curriculum content areas. However, this integration had to deal with the background of the students, which was limited to one or two content areas. Allison achieved the integrative aspect by forming interdisciplinary groups, whose members used the technology to extend their interaction (as noted above).

> They have been able to go onto the online discussion in the Lotus Course Room area where they can begin discussions, they can contribute to other people's discussion topics, and [they] can build up quite elaborate threads and threaded discussions.[5]

She contrasted this subject matter with other possible course content. If she had a "huge amount of information," she could use the Web technology to save on photocopying. Or, if it was a "much larger class with a heavy reading load," she could imagine using the technology to exchange documents and information efficiently. Thus, she saw the use of LearningSpace in this seminar course as a tool for the interactivity and dialogue required to cover a number of content areas.

For David, the subject matter of the computer course required bringing together and organizing a substantial amount of content on how hardware and software are structured and function, as well as providing an interactive system that could present and allow the students to submit laboratory exercises on programming. He dealt with the integration of content and skill by specifying explicit and detailed learning objectives for the students.

> ...notice that on the course that I've done, there are learning goals for the students, not only for the whole course.... We also have learning goals for each and every lecture...and these turn out to be well-defined, step-by-step, bite-sized chunks they should be able to understand.

With respect to presenting the content, in his view the technology worked well to engage the students and help them to learn.

> I think not only the fact that the course material at every lecture was there; there was [also] a huge amount of additional stuff that was available by link so we wrote five, six, seven hundred pages of material over the summer.

With respect to managing interaction with students around the laboratory exercises, the system that David implemented involved submission of electronic reports and feedback. It was his view that

> the technology helps you to look after the large classes and it's the course management aspects which I think are getting better as the years go by.

This differential use of Web technology by the professors shows the use of Web resources as a tool that is governed by the nature of the curriculum. Regardless of the medium selected, professorial attention to the content and structure of their subject matter is an essential aspect of a professor's thinking when planning instruction for high-level learning (also found in Jenkins, 1996).

Support from the University

Both professors have worked with computer-based technologies in their courses for many years, so they know about the resources and services at the university that are available to support their initiatives, and they make use of them as needed. They have taken workshops on the Web technologies they are using. In the past, David has acted as an adviser in the Computing Centre and has taught workshops on the use of computer-based technologies for instruction and management. Both reported making use of the typical kinds of support that are offered formally by the university in preparing for their courses.

One of the aspects that stands out with respect to support is the substantial amount of informal aid that the professors made use of, and indeed, created. Allison saw the need, given other demands on her time, to capitalize on the prior experience of colleagues who had used LearningSpace in their courses.

> I have been wanting to do this now for a year and a half, but it's a classic thing with computers. Last summer, [a colleague] was waiting for various software [in order to help me]...and it didn't arrive...early enough.... I'm more interested in things once they are a little bit

> established. That's perhaps a bit mean because it's saying someone else can do the dirty work.
>
> Josephine is a very old and dear friend and...she's already used the Lotus. She will, I hope, if she's got the time, just help me get into the nitty-gritty.

This strategy turned out to be a successful one.

> I think that it was very fortunate for me, though very hard on other people, that other people [had] all of the teething troubles... By the time I arrived at it, many of the kinks had been worked out.

She also recognized the role of knowledgeable students in supporting the successful implementation of the Web technology.

> I've been very, very pleasantly surprised in general by the level of the students' competence with the computers.... Where there was a student who was struggling, there was almost always some other student in the class who was willing to help.

And more generally,

> A professor has to be willing to admit ignorance and that they can learn from the students. Much [of] what I've learned about computers in education I've learned from students actually, or with students perhaps.

David also made use of relevant experience that existed in the immediate university milieu. After securing an innovation grant, he recruited students to help with inputting and organizing the substantial content of the course.

> During the summer I hired three students, in fact, three students who had taken the course and were among the very best students in the class.... I supplied the course content, the actual material, and what they did was taking that material and getting it into a form which could be put on the Web site, and what they also did was surfing the Web to find other related interesting sites.

This use of informal sources extended to the students currently enrolled in the course.

> ...the first term when [the Web site]'s used, we encourage the students to tell us about the areas where they had difficulty. If they're simple things like typos, they get corrected. But if somebody says, "Oh I didn't understand what you mean by memory address register then we can go [put] in that extra section.... If you have 100, 150 students proofreading the site, for sure they're going to tell you what's wrong with it. So the next term is part of the sort of step-wise refinement process.

Another aspect that stands out with respect to informal means of support is the role of the professor's own knowledge about the use of Web technology (and computer technology generally) for instruction. This knowledge, the result of active and long-term use of computer-based technologies for instruction, allows the professors to network and to make judicious use of resources, both formal and informal, that are present in the university. This knowledge also serves as an important resource in determining how to implement particular aspects of the technology for specific courses. In fact, this is probably essential, given that the professor is responsible for organizing the content of the course. As David stated eloquently, the fair apportionment of institutional and personal support for these initiatives is an ongoing issue.

> But essentially the course content is the professor's responsibility and [the professor] has to know exactly what's going to go into the course, what goes into every lecture, how it's going to be set up and structured, and then in many cases it's the typing and detail, the layout... If the professors are in any way computer literate, they should be able to do it themselves. But whether they should be doing that is the other question. That's why I prefer to have some students work under my supervision to do it.

Higher education studies (for example, Boddy, 1997; Roberts and Ferris, 1994) suggest that professors often perceive a need for more knowledge and time in undertaking instructional initiatives with technology. Regarding time, both professors perceived it as an important university and personal resource. Although prepared to make the necessary time commitment, they both queried whether professors should be expending so much time, given their other responsibilities. As we have seen, both had developed strategies for economizing on their time commitments (as well as obtaining the knowledge they needed) by drawing on different resources within the university.

Recommendations

We make three recommendations about the effective use of Web technology from the professors' experiences documented in these two case studies. First, how these technologies are used for instruction should depend on an elaborated and explicit description of the content of the course and the professor's objectives for student learning in the course. We see in these two studies rather different content and objectives and, hence, different uses of the technology. A common aspect of the use of the technology, however, is that they have the effect of extending and enhancing the interaction initiated within the formal meeting time of the class to times and places outside of it.[6] This extension and enhancement applies both to social interaction with other participants in the course, whether fellow students, teaching assistants, or instructor, and to the content of the course as seen in Web-based information resources. In other words, these uses create the potential for formal instruction to be ongoing in the student's life and for information delivery to be just-in-time.

Second, informal means of support should be considered for the implementation and use of Web-based resources for instruction. We distinguish between formal and informal when considering the resources available. Formal resources are those that are commonly recognized and named within a university infrastructure (for example, a university computing centre, faculty computer technicians). On the other hand, informal resources, such as knowledgeable colleagues and students, are rarely recognized as part of the university infrastructure, and, in fact, may be largely invisible to others. In analyzing what is needed for successful implementation, these informal resources (colleagues, students, the professor's own experience) should be treated in a more explicit way.

Third, the changes made when using Web-based technology should be seen as incremental. These changes follow the pattern of modifications that experienced faculty have made in their instructional practice (McAlpine, Weston, C. Beauchamp, J. Beauchamp, and Wiseman, 1999). A professor's own knowledge and experience plays an important role in implementing the technology. To an outside observer, the uses of these Web technologies constitute a substantial change of instructional practice from the traditional one; but from the inside perspective of the professor, they simply build on prior experience. From the inside perspective, the well-known call to "start small" can be extended to "start small and continue as you began, making progress with small steps."

Notes

1 These technologies often consist of a number of commercially packaged Web-based tools for managing a course, which taken together constitute a system. Hence the phrase in our title, "Web course management system" (also see the Preface of this volume).

2 We were interested in these two professors' experiences because they provide information that may inform others who are considering the use of Web technologies in their instructional practice. (Indeed, this is the main objective of all the contributors to this volume.) Thus, our use of the case method is instrumental and collective (see Stake, 1995), and we have presented the cases in a manner that will bring the similarities and differences to the fore.

3 It was a concern with interaction that provided David with his principle criticism of WebCT. "WebCT has an e-mail package, but that e-mail package is internal to WebCT...so the student needs to have two different accounts, two different codes and passwords.... If it was a really totally integrated system, it would be easier for both the instructor and the students to use." Since this course, he has found a way to resolve this problem, which he successfully implemented in the fall of 1999. (The report on this solution is the content of another paper.)

4 A structured course on computer science places a high affordance on access to and use of web technology. University-provided lab facilities are comparatively extensive, and the proportion of students with advanced equipment is high. In contrast, such technology is more of an adjunct in education courses, one that brings to the fore issues about student access.

5 It is important to remember that the relationship between subject matter and the use of technology can be a two-way street, and technology can constrain the subject matter. Allison noted that previously in the same course, students had published a hard copy version of the work they had done and that they later had reported to her, "the package was the most useful thing." In the course this time, they created an online version, but, "no one got it...in their hand to take away.... I think there is a net loss rather than a gain."

6 This highlights one of the principal differences that we see between the use of these technologies in the public school and at the postsecondary level. In the public school, they change the nature of the interaction during formal instructional time because the hardware is present in the classroom. In the university, the hardware is rarely present in the classroom, so students use it outside of formal instructional time (see also Grégoire, Bracewell, and Laferriére, 1996)

References

Boddy, G. 1997. "Tertiary Educators' Perceptions of and Attitudes Toward Emerging Educational Technologies." *Higher Education Research and Development* 16, 343–357.

Bracewell, R.J., A. Breuleux, T. Laferrière, J. Benoit, and M. Abdous. 1998. *The Emerging Contribution of Online Resources and Tools to Classroom Learning and Teaching*. Report prepared for Schoolnet/Reschol by Telelearning Inc. (http://www.telelearn.ca/g_access/news/review.html)

Grégoire, R., R.J. Bracewell, and T. Laferriére. 1996. *The Contribution of New Technologies to Learning and Teaching in the Classroom: A Documentary Review*. Report prepared for the Advisory Committee on Research, Schoolnet/Reschol. (http://www.fse.ulaval.ca/fac/tact/fr/html/apport/impact96.html)

Inoue, Y. 1998. *University Teachers' Perceived Usefulness of Computer-Assisted Instruction*. ED420308.

Jenkins, A. 1996. "Discipline-Based Educational Development." *The International Journal for Academic Development* 1, 50–62.

McAlpine, L., C. Weston, J. Beauchamp, C. Beauchamp, and C. Wiseman. 1999. "Building a Model of Reflection." *Higher Education* 37, 105–131.

Roberts, N., and A. Ferris. 1994. "Integrating Technology into a Teacher Education Program." *Journal of Technology and Teacher Education* 2, 215–225.

Schwab, J.J. 1973. "The Practical: Translation into Curriculum." *School Review* 7(81), 501–522.

Spivey, N.N. 1997. *The Constructivist Metaphor: Reading, Writing and the Making of Meaning*. San Diego: Academic Press.

Stake, R.E. 1995. *The Art of Case Study Research*. Thousand Oaks, California: Sage Publications.

Todd, N. 1993. "Faculty Concerns as Gateways to Teacher Competency with Computer Technologies." ED362209.

Author Note: Preparation of this chapter was supported by the TeleLearning/Network of Centres of Excellence Program, Ottawa, Canada.

Part E

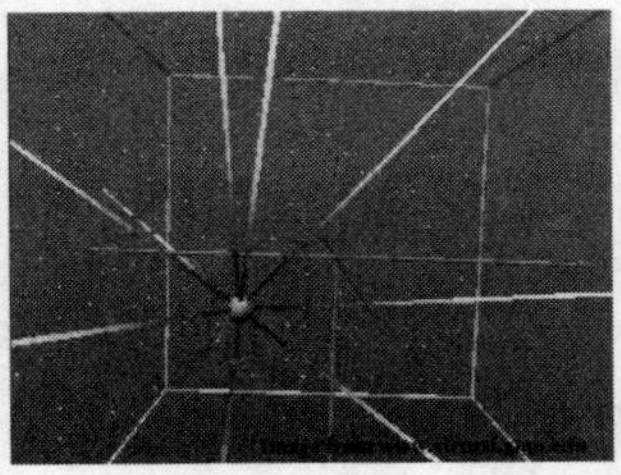

Applications of Web Course Management

CHAPTER 17

Lessons to Consider: Online Learning from Student and Faculty Perspectives

Lynne Schrum and Angela Benson
University of Georgia (Athens)
U.S.A.

The global education community is facing a complex problem. Learners in every location are required to gain new skills, and react to constantly changing situations. Around the world, learners are demanding anytime and anywhere education, and institutions are responding by committing substantial resources to provide online distance learning through courses and full degree programs at postsecondary and high school levels.

Distance education has been viewed as a way to offer lifelong learning to those who are geographically separated from traditional institutions, have obligations that limit their ability to attend regular courses, or prefer to learn in new ways. The challenge has always been to balance the need for intense and personal interaction with the reality of limited financial and other resources. Although for a long time individuals have requested distance learning that meets these needs, earlier attempts (satellite delivery, for example) met with spotty results (Greco, 1999; Westbrook and Moon, 1997). Now organizations and universities have turned to technology that has evolved to the point where it can provide the needed experiences through electronic networks and groupware (Gerencher, 1998; Mangan, 1999; Schrum, 1998).

This chapter discusses the trend toward electronic distance learning, and the management of online courses and programs, through the perspectives of faculty and students who have experienced them. We have many years of experience in researching and teaching through distance learning as well as designing and teaching online courses. The ideas in this chapter are drawn from those experiences, reviews of pertinent literature, and interviews with instructors, potential instructors, and students of online courses, particularly lessons learned through investigating an online MBA program.

Perspectives from the Literature

Distance learning in various forms has been around for a long time. Traditional distance learning environments were based on correspondence through passive media (paper, audio and video broadcast). These courses were conducted as independent experiences, with each learner corresponding only with the instructor. Recent developments in technology have offered the opportunity to improve these environments through increased communication, interactivity among participants, and incorporation of collaborative pedagogical models. Some of these courses are traditional subject matter courses, often undergraduate, while others are geared more to ongoing professional work activity. In some circumstances the technology is only a repository, and merely holds materials (Boston, 1992; Schrum, 1995), and in others there is evidence that the technology itself assists in a paradigm shift so that it becomes the environment for learning (Dede, 1995). In this transformed model of distance learning, individuals expect interactivity close to that provided in face-to-face classroom-based education.

The demand for online courses, enhanced by the ease of access, media attention, and interest from the private sector, has accelerated the rush toward online learning activities. These activities include informal courses, professional development tutorials, and even full degree programs; however, much uncertainty exists about the conditions that are essential to create a successful venture. Examples of face-to-face courses offered using a variety of telecommunications methods (for example, electronic mail, computer conferencing, two-way audio/video, satellite delivery) have been discussed in the literature (Benson, 1998; Harasim, 1993; Hiltz, 1990; Rice-Lively, 1994; Schrum, 1992; Sproull and Kiesler, 1991). In the majority of these courses, instruction was delivered entirely or principally via computer mediated communications (CMC). Studies have concluded that this form of education is effective for well-motivated students. More importantly, the studies make clear that instructors should not simply take a traditional course and place it on any type of educational network (Schrum, 1996; Wagner, 1993).

Figures 17.1 and 17.2 show the high and low ends of the technologies used for online learning. Figure 17.1 shows the "high-tech" videoconferencing learning environment, while Figure 17.2 shows the "low-tech" e-mail environment.

Online Learning Environments

Development of an online educational environment is not a trivial task. Faculty have had an especially difficult time changing the ways in which they teach, regardless of their own personal use of electronic media (Candiotti and Clarke, 1998). In an electronic environment the role of faculty changes in many ways, and, in particular, they must give up some control of the classroom environment. They are required to develop and design their activities and interactions in new ways, and they may be frustrated without the ability to recognize students' furrowed brows (Schrum and Berge, 1998). Kember (1995) urged designers to work toward deep learning, which requires moving away from excessive assignments, shallow assessments, and lack of freedom in activities. Heeren and Lewis (1997) suggested matching the media with the task, and keeping lean media for tasks that do not require much interaction—for example, electronic mail—and reserve rich media for things that require more interaction and a broader spectrum of activity. These challenges go far beyond the need to be comfortable with the reliance on technology to support their courses (Schrum, 1998). Wiesenberg and Hutton (1996) identified three major challenges for the designer to consider: increasing time for delivery of the course (they estimate two or three times what is necessary for a traditional course); creating a community online; and encouraging students to become independent learners.

Reid and Woolf (1997) discussed the benefits of integrating online components into traditional classes, such as accessibility, learner control, heightened communication, access

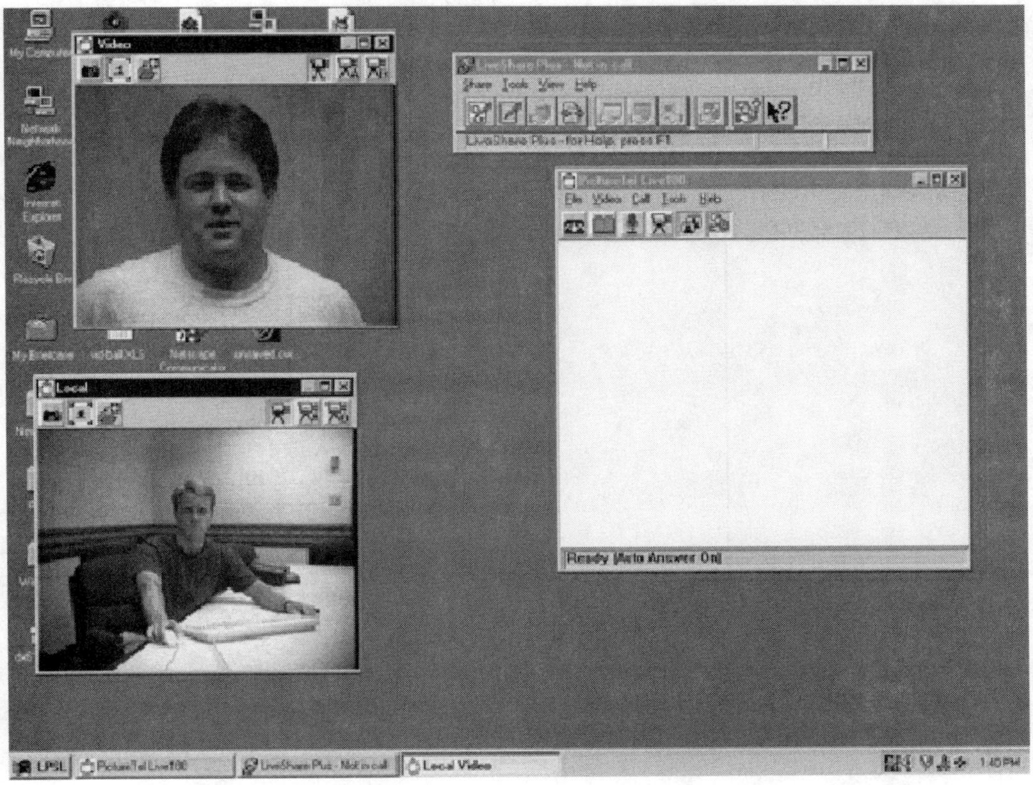

Figure 17.1
High-tech videoconferencing used in online learning

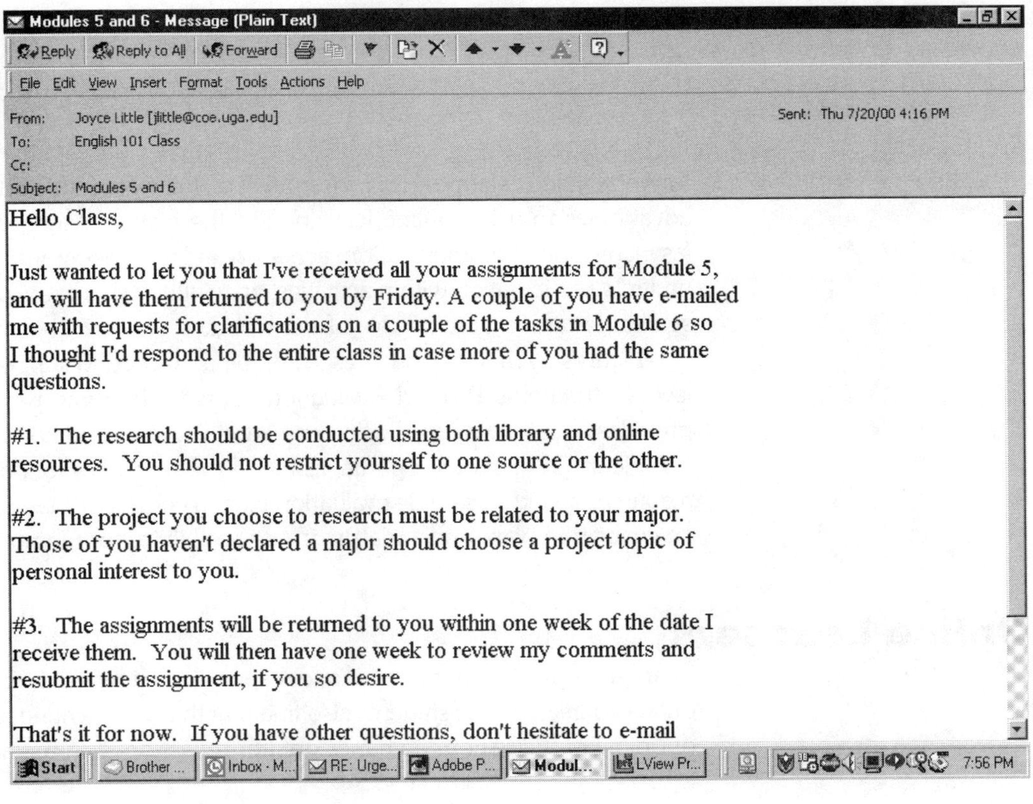

Figure 17.2
Mail message from a course delivered via e-mail

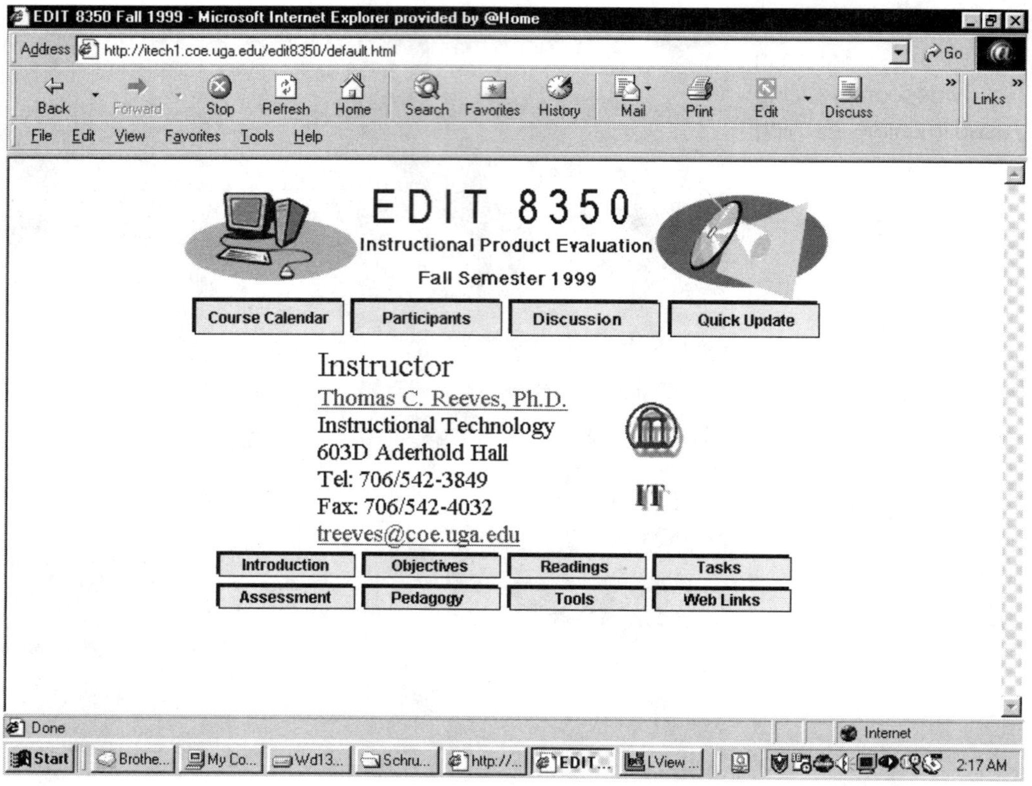

Figure 17.3 The home page from the online component of a face-to-face course shows administration and resources

to worldwide resources, and the potential for a student-centered environment. Other advantages to using online learning are the instantaneous (synchronous) and delayed (asynchronous) communication, access to and from geographically isolated communities, multiple participation within activities, and cultural sharing of diversity and recognition of similarities among the people of our world.

Figures 17.3 and 17.4 present Web pages used to support a face-to-face graduate-level Instructional Product Evaluation course. The main page, shown in Figure 17.3, provides access to a range of course administrative and content resources.

Figure 17.4 shows a partial listing of the resources found on the tools page. These resources include a sample evaluation plan, a checklist of tasks to perform when creating an evaluation plan, and a matrix of responsibilities for members of the evaluation team.

Online Learners

Learners report greater control and responsibility toward their learning when enrolled in online courses. These students also find that the act of writing, which constitutes the basis of online participation, demands greater reflection than the act of speaking required in

Figure 17.4
Tools page shows a partial listing of the resources

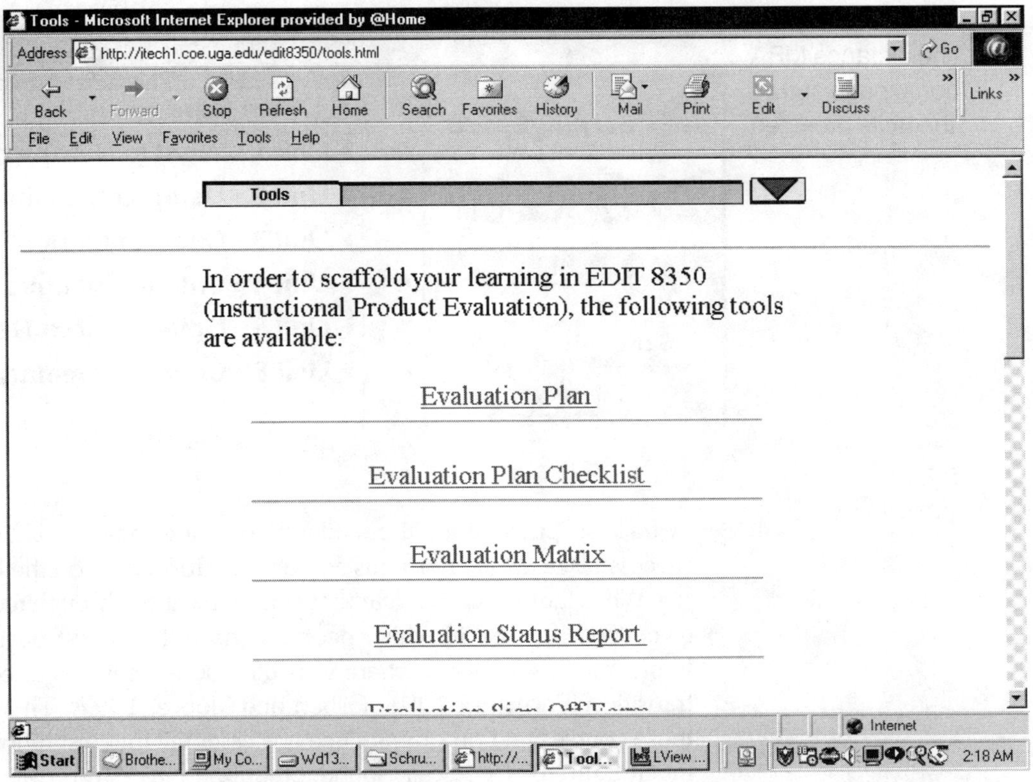

the traditional classroom. (Harasim, 1990; Rohfeld and Hiemstra, 1995). Several research and anecdotal studies looked at online components of traditional courses and concluded that these components substantially increase the communication between the teacher and the students, and among the students, when compared with similar classes without the computer communication component (Hartman et al., 1994).

Learners have to make a significant conceptual leap in order to benefit from online learning. Cognitive scientists and software engineers suggest that individuals must create mental models to understand and internalize what is happening in this new environment (Brandt, 1997). One study suggested that students had to take time to move through the initial efforts of learning the tools before they began constructing new knowledge (Yakimovicz and Murphy, 1995). Another study confirms the necessity for learners to have support to learn and act out their roles in these situations (Olson and Bly, 1991).

One graduate course demonstrated that even with independent online lessons, it was useful to add a component that requires students to interact with their colleagues in some way (Dehler and Poirras-Hernandez, 1998). Eastmond (1995) found that students reported feelings of isolation if they didn't keep up with the interactions, and must be taught to take personal responsibility for involving themselves. Similarly, it is important

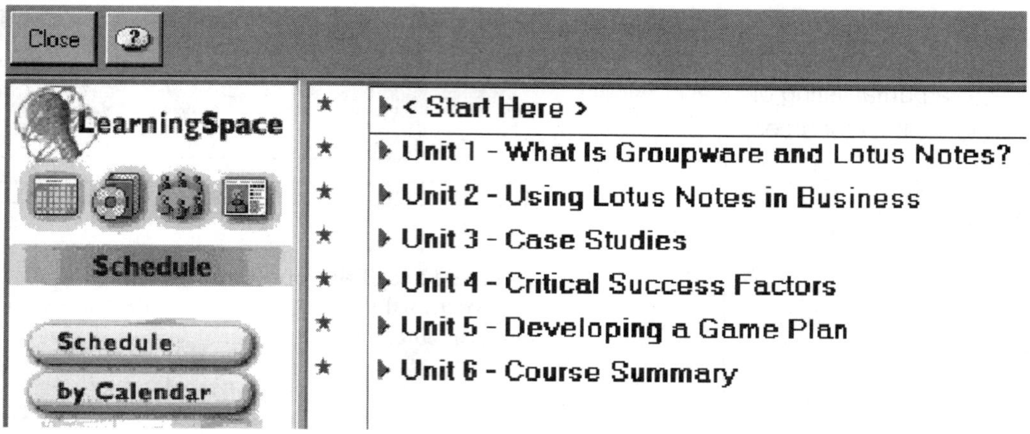

Figure 17.5
The distance MBA home page shows the units provided

to build in practice for the students to refine their evaluative and analytical skills to successfully use the enormous amount of information on the Internet (King, 1998).

While it has become clear that communication through technology has the potential to change the way in which people behave (Lea and Spears, 1991), institutions are frequently unsure about where to begin and what issues to consider as they make this transition (Ehrmann, 1995; Gilbert and Moore, 1997). Therefore, it is timely to study these courses and programs since it is essential that institutions take the lead to ensure that they are pedagogically sound, organizationally strong, and institutionally supported.

Case Study

Recently, a large corporation began working to create a distance MBA degree program at a southeastern university College of Business. Ten faculty members of the college collaborated with the corporation's Head of Corporate Education to design a program that would allow a cohort of forty-six successful executives to obtain an MBA in an intensive two-year format. The result was an integrated, multimedia, combined-format, online MBA program. Faculty worked in teams to integrate assignments and plan projects. Students met face to face with faculty for short and intense initial two-week and weekend sessions, but all other work was conducted through electronic communications using company-provided laptops. Substantial resources were devoted to a technological support team to assist faculty, design materials, and support students.

Five key decisions were made during the planning phase of the project that positively impacted its implementation in October 1998. First, it was agreed that the distance MBA program would include face-to-face time and distance time. The distance component was accomplished via Lotus LearningSpace and Lotus Notes, e-mail, and the telephone. Figure 17.5 shows a LearningSpace course home page for the distance MBA. The course was delivered in six easily accessible units.

Second, the business school and the company agreed on a specialized curriculum to meet the specific needs of its employees, while maintaining program and content accreditation standards.

Third, the business school and the company tried to balance the school and work demands of the students, who remained full-time employees. Faculty agreed to keep the students' school study time to fifteen hours a week when they were off-campus and the company agreed to limit the normal workweek to forty hours.

Fourth, the program maintained a support staff of three full-time employees and nine graduate assistants. The support team was responsible for initial training and ongoing support for both faculty and students.

Fifth, students provided weekly, anonymous online feedback of their experiences. Program faculty and administrators viewed these data each week and decided how to best respond to the concerns. For example, to deal with student complaints that assignments were grossly exceeding the specified time parameters, the program employed an on-campus MBA student to benchmark course assignments by completing the assignments and reporting the time required.

Faculty Planning

The faculty involved in this project had enormous energy and enthusiasm. In this program, unlike some implementations of innovative practice, time was devoted to issues of support prior to the launch of the program. Planning began the spring preceding a fall implementation with selection of faculty and support personnel. From an early survey, 75 percent of those chosen had little to no experience with online learning, either as a teacher or a learner. Those who volunteered, or who were chosen, had reputations as excellent teachers, and had demonstrated some characteristics of collaboration and willingness to accept a challenge in the past. The rewards for their participation included summer financial support, new laptop computers, valuable technological support and assistance, and course reduction during the first year. In exchange, each faculty member was expected to commit time and energy toward the reconceptualization of his/her course.

First, a month-long seminar was designed to learn about the software, from student and faculty perspectives, and to transform their subject matter and traditional teaching experiences to an online format. A consultant was brought in to offer assistance in online pedagogical issues, and faculty had time to work with technical support personnel on the specifics of their courses. One hundred percent of the faculty felt that they received more personal and technical support than they had anticipated.

At the same time, a weekly meeting was established for the entire faculty team. These meetings, called "customer quality assurance" meetings, allowed faculty sufficient time to discuss current issues, to collaborate on course experiences, and to address student concerns that had surfaced during weekly feedback. They also used these meetings as a checkpoint to identify students who were having problems in one or more courses.

Figure 17.6 shows the profiles component of the distance MBA course. This utility maintains the contact information for the online students and faculty. This figure lists the online faculty.

Faculty Concerns

The concern for providing appropriate and useful instructional experiences overshadowed all the other faculty concerns. Faculty members were unsure about the best way to proceed in creating the online experience. Some tried hard to convert as much as

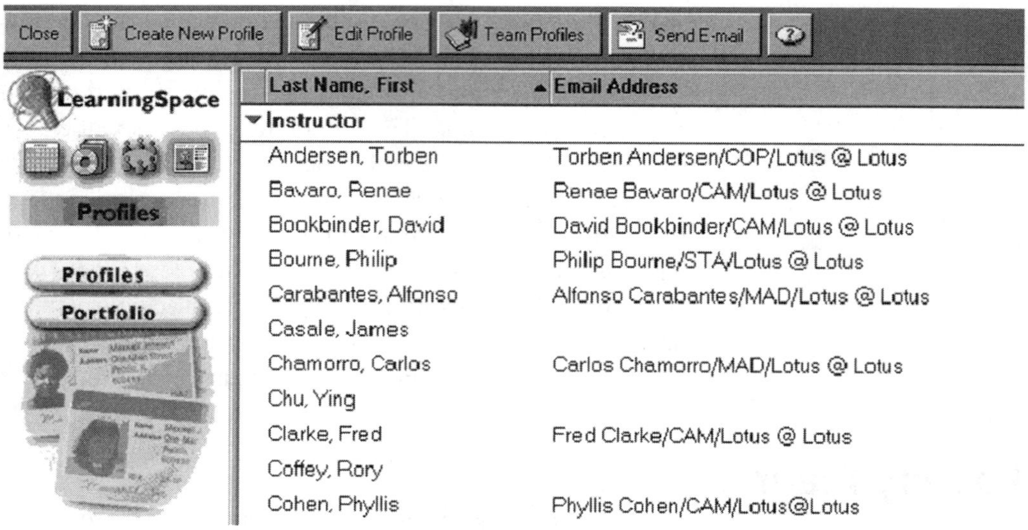

Figure 17.6
The profiles page lists e-mail addresses of online instructors

possible their existing class. Others approached it differently, and found themselves rethinking the course and their role. They were more interested in creating learning opportunities than sharing their knowledge. Additionally, some content areas were viewed as more appropriate than others for the online environment.

As quickly as a difficulty was identified, the faculty began to think about solutions. For example, "One of the biggest challenges was that the class had to be 'one size fits all' so it was too basic for several students but probably too challenging for a few. Perhaps we need to allow some students to [pretest] out of [some] classes...."

Overall, the reaction to teaching their courses online was extremely positive. One member of the faculty said, "The fifteen hours I had were the most fun I've had teaching. I believe this is because of the experience base of these students and the fact that they have the commonality of being from the same company."

One major goal of the faculty was to foster interaction between themselves and the students and among the students themselves. The initial two-week face-to-face session was considered a chance to get to know each other and to establish relationships. It was decided that they would all use threaded discussion rooms as a way to promote thoughtful and reflective discussion. This did not produce the desired results in every circumstance. Professors commented that students often read their questions, and then responded without reading the responses of other students, resulting in a linear commentary, rather than a discussion. It was decided that this tool was only useful for some activities and some subjects. Figure 17.7 shows a LearningSpace courseroom where the threaded discussions occurred.

The number one concern of all faculty members was the amount of time that it took to do a good job. One professor said, "I think it worked better than I would have ever expected. However, I have to say it was not without a cost, and the cost was that I spent forty to sixty hours a week for a two-hour course." Many of the others were concerned that they simply could not expend that amount of time on any one of their many daily responsibilities.

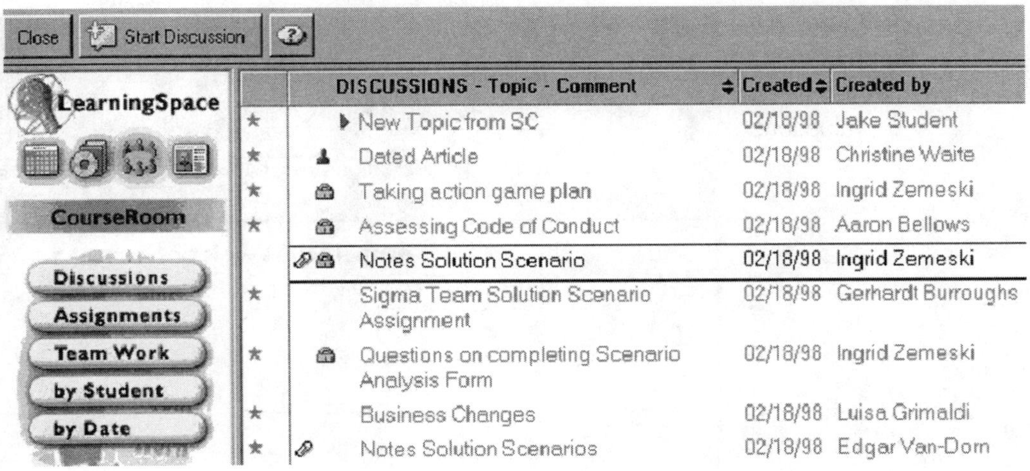

Figure 17.7
A threaded discussion area in the distance MBA courseroom

Student Concerns

Though more than 75 percent of the students thought they could handle the fifteen-hour a week course load, they entered the program concerned about their ability to be successful. Of the forty-six students surveyed, thirty-five expressed concern with their ability to balance schoolwork, the job, and their personal lives. As one student said, "[My concern is] balancing work responsibilities (for example, various committees, coaching, etc.) and this program and still have time for some sort of 'life.'" Fear of isolation, loss of student and instructor interaction, level of academic rigor, and level of personal preparation for the program, to a much lesser degree, were also cited as concerns.

The students, who were divided into eleven teams and given individual as well as team assignments, found their concerns proven valid within the first month of the program. The expected fifteen-hour weekly coursework turned into twenty to thirty hours for many students. As one student said, "The fifteen hours required, generally that's not enough to keep you up. The people that seem to be keeping up are generally running a little over twenty, twenty-five hours." The unexpected time requirement impacted their work and family lives, and caused the students much personal stress. Students found that they had to "make choices to do things and not do other things." As one student said, "My priorities are family, work, and school, in that order. If I have to turn in an assignment late, that is okay if I am working on one of the higher-priority areas." The one area in which students felt they could not cut back was on their teamwork. "I find that I pay more attention to anything that is team-oriented because I don't want to let my team down.... I'm willing to let my own thing [individual assignments] go, but not the team thing."

These students adopted various strategies to deal with the course load. They found study time while waiting in airports and riding in cars, and between meetings. As one student said, "I actually commute an hour a day in the car. So a coping strategy for me is to stick my computer in the passenger seat and listen to [the professor's] lecture while driving in." Students also found leveraging individual team member strengths when completing team assignments an effective strategy.

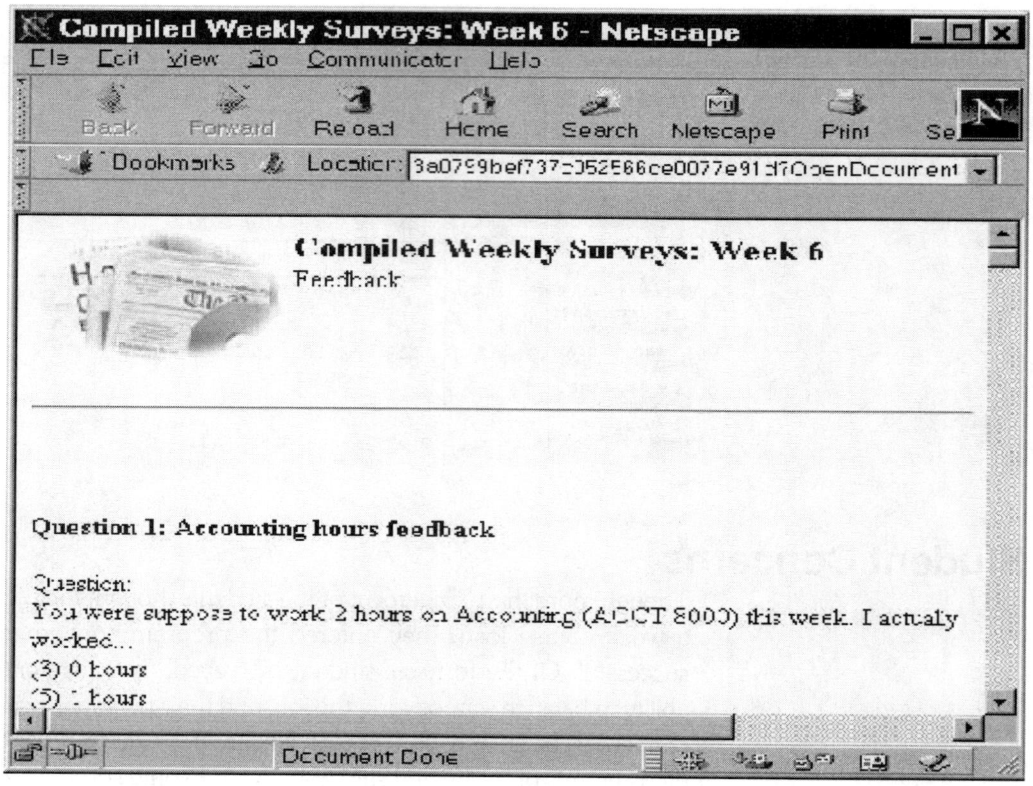

Figure 17.8
Survey results from weekly evaluations

Student Conclusions

Overall, the students felt that the teams were very effective. When asked about the most effective component of the program, one student said, "Group work—getting a different perspective on group assignments has been very valuable. Also, I can't imagine doing this program without the emotional and spiritual support of my team."

Most students cited faculty responsiveness as a positive component of the program. "The professors and staff have been absolutely wonderful about adjusting the workload and assignments" in response to student reports in the weekly online program evaluations. Figure 17.8 presents a partial listing of the summary of one week's evaluation. The students reported the number of hours spent on each course taken, and those numbers were compared to the program hours allotted for the courses.

In general, the students felt that some courses worked better as distance courses than others. They felt that Statistics was particularly difficult, while Legal was perfect for case-based team activities. As one explained, "Legal [was] great for teams because you get on a conference call and in twenty minutes you could talk about the issues. Someone would take minutes and then summarize and then give you feedback on their summary."

For the most part, students found the course content directly applicable to their daily work lives. "The assignments and topics of study are very relevant to my day-to-day work. Many of the issues that I deal with at work every day are similar to the things I am studying," says one student. Even those who didn't find direct application of the content found their "awareness raised" by the courses they took.

Lessons Learned

The results of research on this MBA program confirmed results from other research and other implementations of educational innovations. It appears clear that support—from faculty, administration, and technical teams—is essential. This program's commitment to providing support and ongoing improvement was identified by faculty and students as crucial to its success. The ability of the students to react honestly to their experiences and, most particularly, the willingness of the faculty to respond and adapt, were two of the most important aspects of the program.

Teaching in new ways has always been a challenge for faculty, especially when the new paradigm requires team teaching, reallocation of limited resources, ongoing dialogue for planning, and translating the group processes used for student work to that of faculty (Schlesinger, 1996; Watkins, 1996). The experience of the faculty in the MBA program provided insight for other faculty moving to the world of online teaching and learning. Because their support needs were met satisfactorily, they were able to direct their energies to providing effective learning experiences for the distant students. With appropriate technical and pedagogical support, they were able to experiment with course design and to allow course design to evolve as they received feedback from their students. Some faculty found value in translating attributes of their online course design to their traditional face-to-face courses. While faculty considered their online experience a positive one, the experience came with a high cost. The first cost was the time required to support the courses and the students. Second, they were unhappy at the loss of traditional classroom cues and feedback.

Several common threads emerged from the students' perspectives and experiences. First, students struggled to balance their course work with full-time jobs and personal lives. They learned to convert any down time in their daily schedule into study time. Many made short-term sacrifices in their personal and professional lives so that they would be able to reap the long-term benefits of having an MBA degree.

Second, the students had to adapt to a distance learning environment. The individual courserooms, which had been expected to promote student interaction, did not have that effect for the students, who cited their team members as their greatest source of support and interaction. In addition, students recognized that some courses worked better in a distance environment than did others, just as they found that some activities were better completed as a team while others were much more easily and appropriately accomplished individually.

Conclusions

This chapter presented current research about the essential conditions necessary to succeed in creating and managing online educational experiences, and specifically described the efforts of one business school to move to a hybrid model of MBA programming. While it is clear that most institutions will consider offering various options for learning to potential students—and for many, the online option is an excellent one—

this chapter demonstrates that many pedagogical, organizational, and institutional systems, policies, and resources must be dedicated to ensure that the experiences will be positive for students and faculty alike. Clearly, more research is needed to continue to inform the efforts of these institutions, and it is essential that those involved continue to share their challenges and experiences.

References

Benson, A.D. 1998. Focus: "From Face-to-Face Lecture to Asynchronous Online Collaboration." *Open Learning Systems News* 65, 1–4.

Boston, R.L. 1992. "Remote Delivery of Instruction via the PC and Modem: What Have We Learned?" *The American Journal of Distance Education* 6(3), 45–57.

Brandt, D.S. 1997. "Constructivism: Teaching for Understanding of the Internet." *Communication of the ACM* 40(10), 112–117.

Candiotti, A., and N. Clarke. 1998. Combining Universal Access with Faculty Development and Academic Facilities. *Communications of the ACM* 41(1), 36–41.

Dede, C. 1995. "The Transformation of Distance Education to Distributed Learning." *InTRO* July (http://129.7.160.78/InTRO.html)

Dehler, C., and L.H. Poirras-Hernandez. 1998. "Using Computer Mediated Communication (CMC) to Promote Experiential Learning in Graduate Studies." *Educational Technology* 38(5), 52–55.

Eastmond, D.V. 1995. *Alone but Together: Adult Distance Study Through Computer Conferencing*. Cresskill, New York: Hampton Press, Inc.

Ehrmann, S.C. 1995. "Asking the Right Questions: What Does Research Tell Us About Technology and Higher Learning?" *Change: The Magazine of Higher Learning* 27(2), 20–27.

Gerencher, K. 1998. "MBA Programs Go Online." *InfoWorld* 20, 71–72.

Gilbert, L., and D.R. Moore. 1997. "Building Interactivity into Web Courses: Is Commercial Groupware or Design with Web Tools the Solution?" (http://star.ucc.nau.edu/~nauweb97/papers/gilbert/gilbert.html)

Greco, J. 1999. "Going the Distance for MBA Candidates." *Journal of Business Strategy 20*(3), 30–34.

Harasim, L.M., ed. 1990. *Online Education: Perspectives on a New Environment*. New York: Praeger.

Harasim, L.M., ed. 1993. *Global Networks: Computers and International Communication*. Cambridge, Massachusetts: The MIT Press.

Hartman, K., C.M. Neuwirth, S. Kiesler, L. Sproull, C. Cochran, M. Palmquist, and D. Zubrow. 1994. Patterns of Social Interaction and Learning to Write: Some Effects of Network Technologies. Pp. 47–78 in *Computer Mediated Communication and the Online Classroom*, eds. Z.L. Berge and M.P. Collins. Cresskill, New York: Hampton Press, Inc.

Heeren, E., and R. Lewis. 1997. "Selecting Communication Media for Distributed Communities." *Journal of Computer Assisted Learning* 13(2), 85–98.

Hiltz, R.S. 1990. "Evaluating the Virtual Classroom." Pp. 133–184) in *Online Education: Perspectives on a New Environment*, ed. L. Harasim. New York: Praeger.

Kember, D. 1995. *Open Learning Courses for Adults: a Model of Student Progress*. Englewood Cliffs, New Jersey: Educational Technology Publications.

King, K.P. 1998. "Course Development on the World Wide Web." Pp. 25–32 in *Adult Learning and the Internet* (Vol. 78), ed. B. Cahoon. San Francisco: Jossey-Bass Publishers.

Lea, M., and R. Spears. 1991. "Computer Mediated Communication, De-Individuation and Group Decision Making." Pp. 155–173 in *Computer Supported Collaborative Work and Groupware*, ed. S. Greenberg. San Diego, California: Academic Press, Inc.

Mangan, K.S. 1999. "Top Business Schools Seek to Ride a Bull Market in Online MBA's." *The Chronicle of Higher Education* 45(19), A27–A28.

Olson, M.H., and S.A. Bly. 1991. "The Portland Experience: a Report on a Distributed Research Group." Pp. 81–98 in *Computer Supported Cooperative Work and Groupware*, ed. S. Greenberg. San Diego, California: Academic Press, Inc.

Reid, J.E., and P. Woolf. 1997. "Online Curriculum Development at Shorter College: A Report from the Field." (http://www.caso.com/iu/articles/reid02.html)

Rice-Lively, M.L. 1994. "Wired Warp and Woof: An Ethnographic Study of a Networking Class." *Internet Research* 4(4), 20–35.

Rohfeld, R.W., and R. Hiemstra. 1995. "Moderating Discussions in the Electronic Classroom." Pp. 91–104 in *Computer Mediated Communication and the Online Classroom*, eds. Z.L. Berge and M.P. Collins. Cresskill, New York: Hampton Press, Inc.

Schlesinger, P.F. 1996. "Teaching and Evaluation in an Integrative Curriculum." *Journal of Management Education* 20(4), 479–499.

Schrum, L. 1992. "Professional Development in the Information Age: An Online Experience." *Educational Technology* 32(12), 49–53.

Schrum, L. 1995. "Educators and the Internet: a Case Study of Professional Development." *Computers and Education* 24(3), 221–228.

Schrum, L. 1996. Teaching at a Distance: Strategies for Successful Planning and Development. Learning and Leading With Technology, 23(6), 30-33.

Schrum, L. 1998. "Online Education in the Information Age: A Study of Emerging Pedagogy." Pp. 53–61 in *Adult Learning and The Internet*, ed. B. Cahoon. San Francisco: Jossey-Bass, Inc.

Schrum, L., and Z.L. Berge. 1998. "Creating Student Interaction Within the Educational Experience: A Challenge for Online Teachers." *Canadian Journal of Educational Communication* 26(3), 133–144.

Schrum, L., and T. Lamb. 1997. "Computer Networks as Instructional and Collaborative Distance Learning Environments." *Educational Technology* 37(4), 26–28.

Sproull, L., and S. Kiesler. 1991. *Connections: New Ways of Working in the Networked Organization*. Cambridge, Masachusetts: MIT Press.

Wagner, E.D. 1993. "Variables Affecting Distance Educational Program Success." *Educational Technology* 33(4), 28–32.

Watkins, T.L. 1996. "Stage One: Creating a New MBA Core with Team Teaching." *Journal of Management Education* 20(4), 411–421.

Westbrook, T.S., and D.K. Moon. 1997. "Lessons Learned from the Delivery of a Graduate Business Degree Program Utilizing Interactive Television." *Journal of Continuing Higher Education* 45(2), 25–33.

Wiesenberg, F., and S. Hutton. 1996. "A Graduate Program Using Computer Mediated Conferencing Software." *Journal of Distance Education* 11(1), 83–100.

Yakimovicz, A.D., and K.L. Murphy. 1995. "Constructivism and Collaboration on the Internet: Case Study of a Graduate Class Experience." *Computers and Education* 24(3), 203–209.

CHAPTER 18

Learning to Teach Online: The Experiences of Two University Teachers

Susan Gibson and Dianne Oberg
University of Alberta
Canada

Both of us teach in the Faculty of Education at the University of Alberta. Our stories of learning to teach online differ in context but share some common themes, which others may find useful in learning to be virtual educators. Dianne developed a graduate-level distance education program in teacher-librarianship, while Sue developed a Web component for an undergraduate teacher education course in social studies education. We both chose WebCT as our course development software at a time before it was selected as a standard course design tool for the University of Alberta.

Our stories of learning to become virtual educators very much represent the unique experiences of two faculty members at the time. Others may have quite different stories to tell. Our stories are shaped by the fact that we teach within a large research-intensive university that is primarily focused on face-to-face instruction. An important consideration is that the University of Alberta is a comparative newcomer to distance learning, and lacks much of the infrastructure that facilitates the development of online courses. Dianne is the only faculty member at the University of Alberta in teacher-librarianship. Sue is the only faculty member in her department using a combination of virtual and face-to-face learning activities to teach an undergraduate education course.

Dianne's Story

Setting the Context

My interest in distance education did not come from a personal desire to develop learning-at-a-distance programs, but from my realization in the early 1990s that the opportunities for teachers to access education in teacher-librarianship were diminishing. They were diminishing in terms of both the availability of educational leave for teachers and in the number of university faculty teaching in this field across Canada. Through the 1990s, drastic cuts were made to the public and separate school sector in Alberta. Cuts were made to school library services generally, and to teacher-librarian time allotments specifically. Pessimism about the future of teacher-librarianship resulted in plummeting enrollment numbers in the on-campus courses in teacher-librarianship. As a faculty member I had two options: I could either change my area of teaching and research, or find more students. I was reluctant to adopt the first option, and since there had been regular calls in the profession for more accessible education programs, I decided to adopt the second, and explore the possibilities of distance learning.

Initial Steps

My initial entry into online education was a long process. It included taking a study leave to Australia in 1993 to investigate programs there (Oberg, 1994); experimenting with teaching by videoconferencing; and making two unsuccessful attempts to obtain funding for a distance learning project.

In 1997, the Teacher-Librarianship by Distance Learning project began at the University of Alberta, with the financial support of Learning Enhancement Envelope (LEE) grants from the provincial Alberta Advanced Education and through release from teaching one course through an Academic Technologies for Learning (ATL) partnership. From the outset, ATL's mandate has been to support the use of technology in teaching and learning initiatives at the University of Alberta. ATL provides training and consultation in instructional design, multimedia, and Web course production and evaluation on the most effective applications of these technologies. To encourage faculty use of technology in teaching, ATL offers a partnership program that supports promising technology-based projects by providing time, space, tools, and support (ATL Web Site, 1999).

The Plan

The Teacher-Librarianship by Distance Learning project proposed the redevelopment for distance learning of eight graduate-level courses. The project designers—including myself, five sessional instructors with experience in school library education, and a former Masters in Library Information Science student as research and technical assistant—worked together and planned the project to meet the needs of our students. From prior experience, we knew that our students would be primarily female teachers, working full time and taking one course at a time. We believed that most teachers would be new to distance learning and unaccustomed to taking university courses without the structure of a regularly scheduled weekly class. During my study leave in Australia, I learned that successful programs featured both "high structure" and "high dialogue." That is, student completion rates, student achievement, and student satisfaction were highest where the courses had clear guidelines and timelines and where there were many opportunities for student and faculty interaction.

At the University of Alberta, our primary goal was to develop an online program for school library education, characterized by professional relevance and academic integrity. We also hoped that the program would model for our students the use of technology appropriate to school settings.

Professional Development

Throughout the development of the project, there have been regular meetings of the Teacher-Librarianship by the Distance Learning project team ("tl-dl" team). The tl-dl team collaboratively developed the framework that would be used for all courses, including the number of topics or units and the maximum number of pages for reading packages. We included professional development as a regular part of the tl-dl team meeting, which included sessions with an instructional designer to help us "think outside the box" in selecting instructional strategies, demonstrations of software for course delivery, and critiques of courses that had been designed by ourselves and others. We reviewed conference facilitation strategies and discussed how to ensure that students had the opportunity to shape the learning experiences to meet their needs and interests.

The tl-dl Project

The tl-dl project will be completed by the end of the 1999–2000 academic year. With nine courses offered online, students are scattered across Canada's western provinces and territories. Online access provides these students with the opportunity to earn a post-baccalaureate Diploma in Education in the School Libraries. Many students continue to take individual courses in the program as part of M.Ed. and MLIS programs or for continuing education purposes.

The tl-dl program uses a mixed technologies approach: Web pages, computer conferencing, video, and print. The courses are mounted on the Internet using the course development and delivery software, WebCT, which has a very flexible and powerful conferencing system. Students in these courses access the library catalogue and many online databases through the University of Alberta's Web pages, and they use the resources of the Web to conduct research. All courses include some materials that are mailed to the students, such as textbooks, audiovisual materials, and readings.

Participating students say that they like the flexibility of the courses—being able to work at their own pace, being able to schedule their study around their work and family commitments, and being able to take a course they need without travelling, without leaving their families, and without losing income. At the beginning of each session, some students have difficulties in accessing and using e-mail. Many feel disadvantaged by the lack of face-to-face discussions; and for some, the lack of ready access to research resources is a constant concern. However, most students eventually complete course requirements successfully (course completion rates have averaged well over 90 per cent).

The online courses have been evaluated as required by the University of Alberta. In addition, we have examined in a systematic way the long-term impact of online coursework on professional practice (Oberg, 1998). Students are asked by questionnaire to assess the impact of the courses they completed in the previous year. Overall, the results showed that the coursework offered through the Teacher-Librarianship by Distance Learning program is having a positive impact on students' knowledge of communication technologies and on their professional practice in schools.

Sue's Story

Setting the Context

I have been teaching an elementary social studies course to undergraduate education students for twelve years. Because I believe that active learning and direct school-based experience are essential to learning to teach, I have consistently tried to teach this course through a school partnership. This involved having my university students work directly with small groups of children and their teachers as they experienced social studies in Grades 1 to 6 classrooms. These school-based experiences have always been highly rated by the university students, teachers, and children involved; however, they have become increasingly more complicated to arrange. Many of our education students work full time and attend classes full time. Our programs have become more complex, allowing for little freedom and flexibility in students' timetable scheduling. There is no space in students' lives to provide sufficient time in the school for maximum learning. This was the catalyst for my interest in designing some form of virtual school experience.

The Plan

I too applied to ATL for support for my virtual school project. I was given a three-course release (four months of teaching time), a fully equipped multimedia computer work station in the studio, and access to a wide range of technical and design services. My project involved the development of a Web site that featured a series of virtual field trips to elementary social studies classrooms in which teachers would talk about their practice and children would share their experiences and their understandings about social studies. It would also provide Web links to useful social studies sites for teaching ideas, materials, and resources as well as opportunities to discuss issues related to the teaching of social studies with experts across the country.

My overall goals for this project were to enhance students' confidence and competence in using and applying computer technology to the teaching and learning of social studies; to allow the students and myself to participate at different levels and from different locations; and to help me develop and test the ways in which learning can be enhanced by technology.

Professional Development

Another reason for initiating this project was to assist me in acquiring new skills to use technology more effectively in my teaching. I looked on the ATL partnership as an opportunity to upgrade my computer skills, particularly in terms of effective use of the Internet. I needed to learn some specific skills such as HTML coding, video capturing, and streaming and scanning. I wanted to learn more about evaluating Web-based learning resources, how to use a computer mediated conferencing system, and how to design interfaces that were aesthetically and pedagogically appropriate.

The Design

Throughout the fall of 1998 and winter of 1999, a great deal of time was spent in designing the architecture of the virtual field trip, deciding on a Web design program, and filming classroom sequences. I began the design process by articulating my personal goals for my course in consultation with the ATL instructional designer. As I revisited my beliefs about teaching and learning, I began to clarify what I felt would be important to include in this Web-based experience for students. My personal goals were based on a view of the adult learner as a constructivist learner (Brooks and Brooks, 1993).

First, because adult learners need opportunities to learn from real-life problems and practice, I wanted students to be able to see teachers and children in action and to listen to them talk about their experiences as they worked with social studies. Second, because adult learners learn from opportunities to reflect, I also wanted there to be built-in checkpoints to engage students in reflection-in-action. Third, since adult learners make meaning through collaboration, I wanted students to experience a community-of-learners approach to learning about teaching where they could interact regularly with me, their peers, and others. Lastly, I wanted the learning experiences—not the technology—to be the focus of the course.

Next, a decision was made about which virtual experiences would most authentically immerse students in learning to be a social studies teacher. Based on my beliefs about teacher learning, the instructional designer and I examined a constructivist approach to the use of the technology as described in Jonassen (1996). We felt that this design would support meaningful learning with technology by using the cognitive tools that these future teachers would use with their students. A problem-based learning approach would present students with authentic problems from practice while requiring them to become immersed in the real situated process of thinking through key teaching questions. Five key questions were considered when organizing the content of the course:

1. Why is social studies taught in elementary schools?
2. How do you choose content and plan for instruction based on your goals?
3. What resources are available to support your teaching of social studies?
4. What approaches to social studies teaching would best help you to meet your goals?
5. How do you assess children in order to enhance their learning in social studies?

The virtual field trip would provide a variety of multimedia experiences, as well as Web links and access to outside experts. WebCT was selected as the Web construction tool for the virtual field trip because it provided everything that students and I would need in one computer environment. WebCT provided both public conversational space in the form of conferencing, as well as private reflection space for students in the Notes section. Also WebCT provides security by allowing the site to be password-accessible only to students.

The next step was to design the interface. Here we had to consider questions about what the home page would look like; what visual identifiers, buttons, and icons would need to go on it; and what students would need to be able to do. To provide an authentic appearance, the home page was designed as a conventional bulletin board typically found in elementary schools.

Videotaping during school visits captured the school experiences that we needed for Web site development. Permission had to be sought from school personnel and parents of the children who were to be videotaped. The logistics of filming in a busy classroom with substantial background noise had to be addressed. Since I was not involved in the videotaping, shooting matrixes had to be prepared for the camera operator to capture the segments that I felt we would need. Some video eventually had to be scripted because of poor sound quality. A video database was set up to categorize all of the footage. Video then had to be edited to suit our Web site. Frequent debate occurred over whether to stream the video or to use CD-ROMs, because of the large amount of video. Eventually

Figure 18.1
Home page of the Social Studies Education course

we decided to have both CD-ROMs and video streamed from the university server so that there was a backup in case of server malfunction.

As the design process was unfolding, there were many questions that needed to be addressed related to the user-friendliness of the virtual field trip. I had to consider students' comfort level in terms of their familiarity with computers and their prior knowledge of features offered in WebCT, including conferencing, e-mail, and home page design, as well as their perceptions of the importance of computers as a tool in their future teaching careers. A questionnaire was distributed on the first day of class to determine the students' needs. Due to the number of novice users in the class, we decided to make the introduction to the Web site a scavenger hunt through the virtual field trip. This proved to be a wise decision since everyone enjoyed the experience and left feeling less intimidated about the computer afterwards. A paper manual was provided that walked users through all aspects of the virtual field trip to provide further support for the novice users. A lab assistant was also hired to assist with the class and to offer one-on-one help whenever it was needed.

I also had to be aware of the possibility of the increase in students' time spent on aspects of the course because of the masses of information available through the Web site. Careful tracking of students' hits per page using the WebCT course management function helped me to determine what aspects of the site were taking the longest for students to complete.

Booking the lab space was an issue that had to be addressed early because lab space in our faculty is at a premium and has to be booked a year in advance. We needed to ensure that students had both class time and extra time outside of class to complete the required components.

We also needed to consider the fact that many students might want to access the site from home. Internet connections over phone lines from home were affected by the size of large video files, so instead the students were permitted to borrow a copy of the CD-ROM version to work on the site outside of the university labs.

When I began this project, I had hoped that a virtual field trip would be perceived by students as stimulating, productive, and supportive of the development of valuable knowledge and new skills relating to teaching and learning in elementary schools. I also hoped that the site would increase students' opportunities to interact and learn from others through electronic means, and provide greater flexibility for them to learn from diverse locations. Finally, I hoped that using the Web site would assist students in developing acceptance of new tools for teaching and learning and in acquiring skills they will need for their future teaching careers.

Evaluation

In the spring of 1999, a small component of the virtual field trip Web site was piloted with one class over a condensed thirteen-day version of the social studies course. An evaluation specialist from the ATL Studio administered a pre- and post-course questionnaire to the class and conducted an hour-long focus group discussion with them at the midpoint of the course. The evaluator was impressed with students' enthusiasm for the Website, and with their interest in having more applications of technology used in their education courses. The evaluator also noted that students said they were able to access all of the information provided in the virtual field trip. Students also said that they had enjoyed the video of the teachers and children, as well as the opportunity to e-mail experts across the country and receive their thoughtful responses.

Then in the fall of 1999, a research assistant was hired to document students' learning about teaching social studies from their experiences in the virtual environment over a regular thirteen-week course. This study is currently in progress under the direction of an independent evaluator. Data are being collected using introductory and exit questionnaires with the whole class, and bimonthly interviews with four volunteers from the participants. From the early feedback, it seems that the virtual field trip was well received. I can now see evidence in the students' reflective papers that they are rethinking their initial responses to the five key questions based on the evidence they are collecting through the virtual field trip. They are also thinking carefully about the use of technology in their future teaching of social studies as they design Web-based projects for the major course assignment.

Emerging Themes

Learning New Skills

One of the greatest challenges for both of us in the design and implementation of online courses has been learning new technical skills. This was particularly true for Sue because her course includes more graphic and video materials. Both instructors began with basic e-mail and word processing skills. We had used the Internet for information seeking, but neither of us had built a Web page, let alone a course. We found ourselves evaluating course delivery software options. When we began the project, we had little idea how to visualize the architecture of an online course. At the time, there were few models available to help us make decisions.

Learning Project Design and Management

Faculty members usually design their courses on their own. But in our case, we collaborated with instructional designers, WebCT specialists, video specialists, graphic artists, Webmasters, and evaluation researchers. Dianne also had the responsibility of coordinating a team of instructors to establish consistent design guidelines. We found ourselves involved in other aspects of the projects, such as providing financial management; hiring student assistants and technical assistants; and dealing with budgeting, and reporting that information to the funding agencies.

Time Considerations

Even though we both had some course release, the time demands for course design were much higher than we anticipated, and much higher than was provided for in the course release agreement. The time invested was so large that spinoffs were essential in order to compensate. Nevertheless, we found research opportunities from the projects, which subsequently resulted in academic publication and presentations.

Student Satisfaction and Achievement

Research suggests that student learning in distance learning courses can be as good as or better than learning in traditional face-to-face courses (see, for example, Cheng, Lehman, and Armstrong, 1991; Haynes and Dillon, 1992; Suter and Perry, 1997; Weingand, 1984). Although initially students in Dianne's online program were unsatisfied with their learning experience, this changed as instructors became more skillful at facilitating class interaction and as the level of students' technical knowledge increased.

Initial responses from students in Sue's virtual field trip course were positive, though research data are not yet available on the impact of online resources integrated into traditional face-to-face learning (as they were in the virtual field trip). Students liked the self-paced approach to learning, and that different learning styles were accommodated, and were pleased that the course was not as "difficult and scary" as they had anticipated.

Technical problems continue to frustrate Sue, Dianne, and their students. In the fall of 1999, the Web server went down on the first week of class, a hacker gained access to the faculty server, authentication problems arose, and some students had problems with their passwords. Furthermore, the on-campus labs were overbooked, making it impossible for students to get extra lab time. As usual, solving these problems required the involvement of others (such as lab technicians or server managers) who were often not immediately available when the problems occurred.

Contributions to Faculty Development

As a consequence of the development of our technological and pedagogical skills and the encouragement of others in presentations and discussions of the project throughout the University, our Web-based projects constitute a modest contribution to the innovation capacity of the University of Alberta. For example, Dianne presented the distance program for University Teaching Services and the ATL Leaders in Learning Symposium. Sue presented her course at the New Faculty Orientation and at an ATL ShowTime. Both have spent numerous hours demonstrating and discussing their projects with colleagues in Education and other faculties at the University.

Closing Thoughts

For Dianne, the benefits of the Teacher-Librarianship by Distance Learning project have begun to match the time and energy invested. Student achievement levels have begun to match student satisfaction levels. Instructor satisfaction is increasing as well, as a result of the positive responses from students and from colleagues. The team approach has been very successful in supporting instructor learning and in encouraging innovation and risk-taking in teaching. Sue is still dealing with a number of unanticipated problems, many of which have to do with students' lack of technological skill. However, she sees improvement in their confidence and competence with each new lab session. Overall, both Sue and Dianne can say that they have personally grown a great deal in their understanding of technological and pedagogical issues as a result of their work on these Web-based projects. As is usual with innovation, being early adopters of WebCT has had its drawbacks. One drawback is that few people have much appreciation for the struggles and the difficulties that early adoption engenders. Having each other for support and encouragement has made the experience less daunting and more rewarding.

References

Branch, J.L. 1999. "Distance Education: What's Best for Learning?" *Teacher-Librarian Today* 5(2), 29–32.

Brooks, J., and M. Brooks. 1993. *In Search of Understanding: The Case for Constructivist Classrooms.* Alexandria, Virginia: Association for Supervision and Curriculum Development.

Cheng, H.C., J. Lehman, and P. Armstrong. 1991. "Comparison of Performance and Attitude in Traditional and Computer Conferencing Classes." *American Journal of Distance Education* 5(3), 51–64.

Haynes, K.J.M., and C. Dillon. 1992. "Distance Education: Learning Outcomes, Interaction and Attitudes." *Journal of Education for Library and Information Science* 33(1), 35–45.

Jonassen, D. 1996. *Computers in the Classroom: Mindtools for Critical Thinking*. Englewood Cliffs, New Jersey: Merrill Pub.

Oberg, D. 1994. "Distance Education for Teacher-Librarianship: Learning from Programs in Australia." Pp. 104–111 in *School Library Media Annual* (Vol. 12), eds. C.C. Kuhlthau, M.E. Goodin, and M.J. McNally. Englewood, Colorado: Libraries Unlimited.

Oberg, D. 1998. "The Impact of Distance Learning on Professional Practice." *Teacher-Librarian Today* 4(2), 32-34.

Suter, W.N., and M.K. Perry. 1997. "Evaluation by Electronic Mail." Paper presented at the 26th annual meeting of the Mid-South Educational Research Association, Memphis, Tennessee, November 12–14.

Weingand, D.E. 1984. "Telecommunications Delivery of Education: A Comparison with the Traditional Classroom." *Journal of Education for Library and Information Science* 25(1), 3–12.

CHAPTER 19

Integrating Virtual and Traditional Instruction

Coral Mitchell and Jim Kerr
Brock University
Canada

In recent years, the use of the Internet to offer university-level courses has been at the top of the research agenda in education. Student learning does not appear to be adversely affected by Web course management if careful attention has been paid to pedagogic issues during the design and its implementation. Furthermore, students in online courses seem to enjoy greater autonomy and flexibility than students in traditional settings relative to the completion of course requirements. Web courses are also useful for affording access to individuals who may be unable to attend traditional settings because of time, distance, physical, or family constraints.

In spite of what appears to be the situation, however, the picture is incomplete. Little has been written about student perceptions of Internet-based Web course management; and even less has been said regarding the integration of Internet-based and traditional instructional systems. In this chapter, we address these two issues by presenting the results of a study that tracked the initiation of a pre-service Technology Methods course through two modes of instruction, one being traditional face-to-face instruction, the other a series of Internet-facilitated discussion and activity sessions.

Methodology

Participants

Participants in the research included the course instructor and forty-three of the eighty-nine students enrolled in a pre-service Education course entitled Junior/ Intermediate Mathematics, Science, and Technology (EDUC 8P21) offered during the fall–winter 1998–99 term at Brock University.

Design and Materials

The study was undertaken to compare the effectiveness of two instructional approaches in the course. One approach was a face-to-face model of in-class instruction and interaction, with classes held on campus. The other approach was a combination of computer-based instruction and interaction through a majordomo discussion list and Internet Web site for threaded conferencing. While there has been some opposition to comparative media research of this kind—contrasting Medium A vs. Medium B (for example, Clark, 1994; Mayer, 1997)—there is still strong support for studies of this kind (see, for example, Seel and Winn, 1997).

Our study was intended to investigate student and instructor comparisons of face-to-face versus Internet-based course activities and instructor-student communication. Students were asked to compare their experiences of the course activities and the comparative effectiveness of their learning, and to investigate their perceptions of the challenges and benefits associated with online learning. Further, the study set out to explore the perceptions of the instructor regarding the instructional niches for face-to-face and online environments and the challenges associated with online teaching.

Procedure

The course was offered between September and March within one academic year. Course topics included electronic mail, computer conferencing systems, electronic report cards, Internet resource searches, electronic text discovery and manipulation, databases and spreadsheets, desktop publishing, electronic utilities, packaged software application and evaluation, and social implications and issues. The eighty-nine students in the course were divided into four instructional groups, each of which met with the instructor at different times on the same day for a period of 80 minutes.

The course consisted of nine face-to-face sessions and five online sessions. For the face-to-face sessions, course activities varied among instructor mini-lectures and demonstrations, instructor-directed computer activities, student-directed seminar presentations, and instructor-initiated discovery activities. Instructor-directed information and procedures were also posted on the course Web page. The online sessions consisted of small-group discussions to define a computer-related issue or question, electronic posting of these group products to the majordomo or to the threaded conference on the Web page, and whole-class discussions posted to the majordomo in relation to the small-group postings. From time to time, the instructor also posted relevant information to the majordomo listserv. In several face-to-face sessions, the instructor provided detailed information regarding the procedures for accessing and completing the online activities. Furthermore, he arranged several opportunities in the face-to-face sessions to deal with issues relative to the online component and to debrief the online activities.

Data Collection

Because we were interested in student perceptions about the course, we chose to collect qualitative data. A variety of data collection strategies were used to collect information from students and instructor. First, students were asked to complete a questionnaire regarding their ability to use electronic technology and their general perceptions of the usefulness of Internet Web course management. In order to note changes in students' perceptions over time, questionnaires were completed at the beginning of the course and again at the end. Open-ended questions gave students an opportunity to describe the value they believed the Internet held for instructional purposes.

Table 19.1
Class schedule

Date	Topic	Activity	Environment
September 15	Electronic mail	Instructor demonstration and mini-lecture; computer practice	Face-to-face
September 29	Computer conferencing	Demonstration and mini-lecture; computer practice	Face-to-face
October 6	Internet data search	Demonstration and mini-lecture; student discovery	Face-to-face
October 20	Internet uses in the classroom	Small group discussion	Online
October 27	Measurement and spreadsheets	Demonstration and mini-lecture; student discovery	Face-to-face
November 3	Electronic publishing	Mini-lecture; student discovery	Face-to-face
December 8	Teacher use of technology	Small group discussion; posting to large group	Online
December 14	Teacher skill levels and preparation	Small group discussion; posting to large group	Online
December 17	Educational utilities	Demonstration and mini-lecture; computer practice	Face-to-face
January 5	Internet-based software	Instructor demonstration and mini-lecture	Face-to-face
January 12	Corporate contributions of classroom computers	Small group discussion; posting to large group	Online
March 2	Software evaluation	Virtual seminar	Online
March 9	Software evaluation	Student presentations	Face-to-face
March 30	Software evaluation	Student presentations	Face-to-face

In the second type of data collection, students were asked to submit two electronic logs in which they recorded ongoing perceptions of specific attributes of the course. The logs were sent to the students via e-mail after the first and third online sessions. Students sent their responses through e-mail.

The third data collection instrument consisted of student submissions to online discussions that were submitted periodically throughout the duration of the course.

Finally, the researcher conducted electronic interviews with the students after the fourth face-to-face session. Of the forty-three participating students, all completed the first survey, seventeen completed the second survey, forty completed the first log, ten completed the second log, and thirteen completed the electronic interview. Forty participating students submitted messages to the online discussions, with a range of from two to thirty-five messages per person.

Data from the instructor were collected periodically during the course in the form of formal and informal reflections and conversations with the researcher. Data collection took the form of unstructured interviews, with the instructor determining the direction of the conversation. In each case, the researcher began the conversation by asking the instructor to talk about his experiences with the course. Once the conversation started, the researcher asked occasional questions for clarification or extension, but the instructor maintained control over the way in which the conversations unfolded.

Data Analyses

The data from the students were subjected to constant comparative analysis and thematic presentation. The data were then unitized and sorted into categories. A category was considered to be a theme if it included comments from more than five participants or if it were found in more than two data collection sources. Major themes emerging from this analysis included general uses of online learning activities, value of course activities, instructional imperatives, degree of computer competence and confidence, access to technology, and personal preferences and motivation.

Data from the instructor were subjected to constant comparison analysis by the researcher, followed by a discussion with the instructor regarding the completeness and appropriateness of the emergent themes. The instructor determined whether or not a set of data was sufficiently compelling to qualify as a theme. From this discussion, the initial themes developed by the researcher were refined to include three major themes: student characteristics, instructional imperatives, and instructional niches. These themes are discussed later in this chapter.

Students' Perceptions

The open-ended questions in the data collection instruments gave students an opportunity to share their perceptions in their own words. The thematic analysis of the qualitative data yielded six themes: general uses of online learning activities, value of course activities, degree of computer proficiency, instructional imperatives, access to technology, and personal preferences and motivation.

General Uses of Online Learning Activities

In the pre-course and post-course surveys, students were asked to describe the educational purposes that they thought the Internet and e-mail could serve. Responses in the pre-course survey fell into five categories. The category that received the greatest number of responses (n=30) was *communications and quick information access*. Examples of uses in this category were for keeping in touch with other educational colleagues, for submitting questions and requests for information to other sources, and for staying abreast of general information. The next most frequently cited category (n=12) was *research*. This category differed from the previous one in that it related information searches and data downloads to specific topics of study rather than to general information. Other categories, each of which received one or two responses, were *entertainment*, *job searches*, and *electronic commerce*. In the post-course survey, the only uses cited were *communication* and *research*. In this case, research received the highest number of responses (n=12) and communications the lowest (n=3). A notable difference in the second survey was that the students did not differentiate between collecting general information and conducting specific research, as they had in the first survey. Also noteworthy was the fact that the noneducational purposes listed in the first survey were not cited in the second survey.

Value of Course Activities

One aspect of interest in this study was the perception of students regarding the relative value of online and face-to-face learning activities. The data indicated that students found the greatest value in the face-to-face component of the course. Although students reported that they enjoyed learning about the computer and the Internet, they also stated that online activities should be secondary to face-to-face activities. As one individual put it, "I prefer face-to-face. Although I do recognize the relevance of the Internet, I feel the Internet removes the personal aspect of learning." In the post-course survey, most students (n=11) evaluated the online activities negatively. A number of reasons for this evaluation were cited: excessive e-mail submissions (n=3); narrow focus of online discussions (n=1); repetition in online discussions (n=2); lack of participation in online discussions (n=1); difficulty of access (n=1); and technical confusion (n=1). Four students saw value in the online activities, for the following reasons: opportunity for ongoing communication (n=2); increased e-mail and computer proficiency (n=2); and interesting discussions (n=1). When asked in the post-course survey about an effective blend of face-to-face and online activities, five students chose mostly face-to-face, one chose mostly online, one chose an equal mix, and five were unsure. In the electronic interview, one student noted that the online discussion had been useful for considering possible negative impact of computers. However, the data yielded few compelling stories of the value of the online activities and several passionate pleas to eliminate that part of the course.

The activities most frequently mentioned as beneficial were those that gave the students first-hand experience with computer and Internet functions that they could apply in their own classrooms. Students commented specifically on activities where the instructor had led them through programs and applications that were currently being used in school systems, such as the provincial report card. In the first electronic log, one student reported that there appeared to be little connection between course activities and teacher preparation, but the same individual also said, "I love the tips offered in class, that is, how to copy pictures from the Internet."

Degree of Computer Proficiency

The trend in perceptions about the value of online and face-to-face activities was repeated in perceptions about students' learning. For the most part, students related their learning to the activities that had taken place in the classroom with the instructor and students present. Two exceptions to this trend can be noted. Two students indicated that they had improved their technological capability as a result of the online activities, and one student had gained an understanding of the social impacts of computers as a consequence of the online discussions. All other students (n=14) cited learning that had taken place in face-to-face activities.

Regardless of the venue, two kinds of learning were noted. First, the students reported an increase in computer proficiency. Second, they reported an increase in application capability. That is, students were learning how to use computers, and they were learning how to apply computer programs to professional practice.

A confounding factor relative to computer competence was the differing skill levels. This difference became apparent in the first electronic log, where submissions indicated that the students with limited competence had failed to access the online activities. In their submissions, these students noted two reasons for this failure: a lack of confidence with the technology and a lack of understanding about the online activities. These concerns diminished over time, although the different levels of computer competence were evident throughout the course. For example, in the second log, concerns over personal competence were not evident, and only three students were concerned over expectations for the online activities. In the electronic interview, two individuals noted a continuing lack of computer competence, and four students commented on having achieved considerably greater technological skills. Four students noted that the technological aspects of the course appeared to be at a rather basic level, with no substantial skill levels being expected or needed. In the final survey, no concerns over competence were presented, two students noted an increase in their proficiency with computers and technology, and two students indicated that students who demonstrated a sufficient level of computer competence should have been exempted from the course.

The second kind of learning, that is, school classroom applications of computer programs and Internet functions, was cited as valuable most often by the students who had come into the course with computer skills already in place. In the first log, one student expressed a concern that the bulk of the course content was devoted to learning about the computer rather than about teaching with the computer. Similarly, submissions to the electronic interview relative to classroom-specific applications came from those students with pre-existing computer skills. In the final survey, four students indicated that they were still not proficient enough with computers or the Internet to be able to apply them to classroom practice or to their own learning.

In summary, in the early stages of the course, concerns were common in relation to computer competence and online course activities, but the concerns diminished over time. The data indicated that some students perceived growth in their computer competence and confidence during the course, but that those students who came into the course with well-developed computer skills did not benefit as much from the course. Finally, students with sufficient computer skills were ready to learn ways to apply computer and Internet technology to their professional practice, while computer-novice students required additional technological practice before they could advance to application activities.

Instructional Imperatives

The theme that yielded the most comments overall was that of the necessity of good instruction. Data in this regard focused on the need for structured expectations, explicit procedures, and clear instructions. The first log yielded the bulk of complaints in this regard, with eleven students indicating at least some level of confusion with course expectations or procedures for completing course activities. By the time of the second log, these concerns had abated considerably, with only two of the eleven students expressing concerns over unclear instructions or expectations. In the electronic interview, all the comments regarding the instructor (n=11) were positive and indicated that the instructor had been helpful, accessible, and knowledgeable. However, one individual noted that the course lacked structure, and seven students noted that they had no clear understanding of course expectations. The final survey yielded no comments about instruction and only two comments about unclear course expectations. In summary, although concerns over instruction diminished as the course progressed, students continued to note the importance of good instruction, especially for the online aspect.

Access to Technology

Although no specific questions were asked about access, this issue emerged in all data collection instruments. In the pre-course survey, three students noted that access must be ensured if the use of computers and the Internet is to be encouraged in university courses. In the first log, one student noted that access to course activities was problematic because of an overused computer lab at the university. This problem was repeated by another student in the second log and again by two other students in the electronic interview. In the final survey, three individuals noted that access to computers had been a problem for them throughout the course. In all, seven different students noted problems with access. This theme was noteworthy not because of the number of individuals commenting on it but because of the recurrence of such comments over time and between different evaluations.

Personal Preferences and Motivation

As with access, no questions had been asked specifically about personal preferences. Instead, the theme emerged from inductive analysis to account for the tendency of students to embed their submissions in accounts of personal desires, learning styles, and motivational sets. Clustering of the data indicated that students fell into two distinct categories. In the first category, there were those individuals who needed direction and guidance from the instructor in order to engage in course activities or to complete course assignments and who were motivated by external forces such as the allocation of marks or the instructor's requests. In the second category were those students who expressed a desire for personal autonomy and flexibility in completing course activities and who were motivated by internal forces such as curiosity, personal gratification and accomplishment, and the desire to learn more.

When individuals in the first category were asked to evaluate their performance in the course, they talked in terms of course marks or completed assignments. In response to the same questions, individuals in the second category spoke in terms of personal effort, participation, and understanding. Furthermore, individuals in the first category noted that they found the online activities easy to ignore because "they have the feeling of being optional." That is, individuals who were externally motivated also found the online aspect of the course easier to avoid than did the individuals who were internally motivated. Differences between an internal and an external locus of control were evident in all data collection instruments except the pre-course survey.

Instructor's Perceptions

In order to track the perceptions of the instructor, the instructor and the researcher talked formally and informally at various times during the course. The structure for these conversations, and for the informal reflections of the instructor, emerged in response to pressing issues, concerns, or successes that characterised the progress of the course. Inductive data analysis and discussions between the researcher and the instructor yielded three themes: student characteristics, instructional imperatives, and instructional niches.

Student Characteristics

A particularly compelling conversation was held shortly after the first log submission, when it became evident that less than half the class had participated in the previous online session. In that conversation, the instructor indicated that he had only gradually become aware of student concerns regarding course expectations. He noted that, in the face-to-face session prior to the start of the online activities, he had provided detailed instructions to the students regarding the online sessions and had assumed that all students were familiar with the procedures for accessing the activities. When he realized that so many students were not engaged in the online session, he conducted a face-to-face session to resolve the problem. He called the students' attention to the online activities, set up a tutor system that paired students who had been engaged with students who had not been active, and walked the whole group through the procedures for accessing the online sessions. Next he sent out test messages and verified that all students were subscribed to the majordomo and knew the procedures for online activities. This intervention was repeated three times.

Halfway into the course, the instructor was still not sure if all students were accessing the online sessions. At a subsequent face-to-face session at least one student asked again why she was not receiving any information through the majordomo. The instructor wondered, "If the course [had been] 100 per cent online, how would I have known this was a problem and how would I have resolved it, when they needed face-to-face help?"

The instructor noted that, in his interactions with the students, he had become aware of differences among the students on two fronts. First, there were those who were comfortable with the technology and those who were not. Second, there were students who were self-directed and those who were not. These differences led him to categorize the students into four groups: (1) self-directed and technically competent; (2) self-directed and technically unskilled; (3) other-directed and technically competent; and (4) other-directed and technically unskilled. The instructor had observed marked differences in the responses of students in each of the four categories relative to the level of work, level of performance, and attitude toward class activities and technology. These responses are summarized in Table 19.2.

Table 19.2
Student responses to technical tasks

	Technically skilled	Technically unskilled
Self-directed	1. Participate consistently and effectively	2. Find the necessary help to participate
Other-directed	3. Can participate but often avoid class activities	4. Avoid both the computer and the activities

According to the instructor, students in the first category (self-directed and technically competent) were consistently online and produced the bulk of the majordomo and small-group discussions. These students were eager to find online activities, information, and resources; were able to impose personal deadlines; and were willing to inject personal comments, attitudes, values, and understandings into online discussion and activities. They appeared to be comfortable with taking chances in the online environment, both in terms of learning and in terms of using the technology.

This level of activity was not found in students who fell within the other three categories. Students in categories 2 and 4, who were technically unskilled, needed considerable technological help from the instructor and had participated only marginally, if at all, in the online activities. Students in category 2, self-directed but technologically unskilled, participated after receiving help from a tutor or from the instructor. Students in category 3, technologically competent and other-directed, participated only occasionally and submitted marginal entries to the online discussions. These entries met the required assessment expectations, but were not as extensive or as thoughtful as the entries provided by students in the first category. Students in category 4, other-directed and technologically unskilled, failed to engage in online activities until they were reminded that such engagement was a course requirement and would constitute part of their final grade.

Instructional Imperatives

When the students "got lost" for the online component, the instructor wondered if it was partly his fault. He commented, "I had no idea how much of my instruction I take for granted. I just assume students have understood me when it looks like, here, they haven't." He indicated that he had expected the students to be computer literate enough to access the online component without detailed procedures. This assumption turned out to be inaccurate. In his mind, the assumption was reasonable because it was based on his observations of an increase in technological capacity among students over the past four years. He said, "Everyone now uses e-mail and knows all about the Internet, don't they?" He found out that, in fact, some of these students did not. He concluded that his instruction had not been sufficiently detailed because it was based on a faulty assumption.

In a conversation at the conclusion of the course, the instructor noted that the differences in the students had led him to think about different instructional needs. For example, he noted that those students who were involved because it was a requirement of the course only went online when they were directly instructed to do so. They felt comfortable when tasks were well defined and clearly directed by the instructor but were not comfortable injecting ideas or comments into online discussions or experimenting with the technology. Unless the instructor told them specifically and directly to go to a certain Web site or electronic forum, they did not engage in class activities. He indicated that he had never found a way to elicit more thoughtful or consistent contributions from this group of students.

The instructor also noted that the students who were technologically unskilled failed to contribute not because they did not want to but because they did not have the technical skills to use the computers or the Internet functions. As their level of computer proficiency increased, so, too, did their contributions to electronic class activities. He observed that he had incorrectly assumed that all students had some level of computer competence and that he could move quickly into applications. He soon noticed, however, that certain students became frustrated when he failed to provide sufficient technical guidance or support. He noted that the presence of the computer had made the problems of the computer-novice students more obvious than they might have been in a more traditional discipline. As the course progressed, he discovered that the kinds of instruction and activities that suited computer-competent students were qualitatively different from the kinds of instruction and activities that served the novice students. In other words, he had discovered a need for different instructional imperatives depending on the skill sets and the motivation sets of the students.

Instructional Niches

The instructor noted that there appeared to be particular instructional niches for online and face-to-face course components. The online environment had proved to be more suitable for large-group discussions about such philosophical issues as the social and educational impacts of computers. It was also acceptable for small-group conversations about course projects, for access to external information, and for communication links beyond class time.

By contrast, the face-to-face environment proved to be more suitable for skill-building exercises and for demonstration of software applications. As a result of his experience with this course, the instructor believed that a useful mix would be a repeated cycle of face-to-face and online sessions. An initial face-to-face session would serve to establish student competencies, to demonstrate course procedures, and to guide student practice. The online session would serve as practice, discourse, or research, depending on the course objectives. The subsequent face-to-face session would serve to "iron out the bugs" in the previous online component, to demonstrate the next set of course requirements, and to introduce the next round of online activities.

Finally, the instructor commented that, in subsequent years, he would do certain things differently. First, he would try to group students according to computer skill level, and establish course content, objectives, and assignments to address either literacy skills or application skills. Additionally, the computer-competent group would work more online, while the computer-novice group would work more with the instructor or a lab assistant. Second, he would focus application activities on educational computer software approved and licensed by the Ontario Ministry of Education and on the software used in school systems. Third, he would limit the virtual environment to an e-mail system and one conferencing system such as WebCT. Fourth, he would expect a student product, with clearly established criteria for quantity and quality, to be offered at the end of each online session.

In conclusion, the instructor noted that some of the problems encountered in this experience were perhaps temporary and could be expected to evaporate as students began arriving in teacher education programs with computer skills already in place.

Some problems, however, could only be solved by paying careful attention to the instructional imperatives of the moment. That is, in any learning environment, whether online or face-to-face, the instructor needed to clearly articulate course objectives and requirements and to throw away assumptions about the students. What is obvious to the instructor, he said, is not necessarily obvious to the students, and the instructional imperative is to make everything obvious to the students.

Implications

Reflections on the results of this study cause us to suspect that the problems encountered in Web-based instruction are, at least to some extent, similar to problems faced by students and instructors in traditional modes of instruction. That is, if left alone, students will probably still behave in the same manner as they do in traditional courses. Unless intrinsic motivation is in place, they are not likely to benefit from online instruction any more than they would from face-to-face instruction. Furthermore, if left alone, instructors will probably still teach as they have done in traditional courses. Unless they pay careful attention to directions and procedures, their students are not likely to benefit from Web-based instruction any more than from face-to-face instruction.

The results of this study suggest that students need to be self-directed, self-regulating, and self-disciplined for virtual instruction to be effective. Alternatively, extrinsic controls and directions must be extremely well defined in order to provide explicit directions and controls. In short, an instructor cannot assume that students are engaged in the online sessions. Instead, the instructor should check with individuals prior to, during, and after each online session. Although this is a huge investment of time for the instructor, it is probably necessary to offset the potential of students being "lost."

The categories developed in this study provide a framework for predicting student engagement relative to online activity. Our hypothesis is that those in category 1 will participate because they can and they want to, and they will reap benefits, in spite of the instruction. Those in category 2 will probably find others (instructor or classmates) who will help them overcome technical problems, and they can be expected to participate when they become technologically capable. By contrast, those in category 3 may participate if there is enough extrinsic motivation to entice them, but may avoid the activities in favour of computer entertainment. The greatest difficulty is with the students who fall into category 4. They are likely to avoid the computer and, consequently, miss out on all online learning opportunities.

The difficulties experienced by the computer-novice students in this study are not qualitatively different from the difficulties experienced by students who come to other disciplines, such as Mathematics or English, with an underdeveloped skill set. The presence of the computer may have made their problems more obvious but not necessarily more difficult. In traditional disciplines, students may have simply found ways to hide their problems, and instructors may have found ways to ignore the problems. But in traditional disciplines and in the technological environment, the issue of the skill set is at the heart of the instructional imperative. This phenomenon suggests that each time instructors develop a new instructional environment that is grounded in a new skill set, they inadvertently redefine the "at-risk" population. That is, whether or not a student will be "at risk" is at least partially a function of the kinds of skills they are expected or assumed to possess.

Adult students, such as the ones in this study, are perhaps not as likely as children to say, "I don't get it." If so, then instructors, when designing and implementing online courses or, for that matter, face-to-face courses, should assume nothing about their students. Instead, they should check everything. Although this is common pedagogic knowledge, it is not necessarily common instructional practice. It bears repeating: one of the most important instructional imperatives, whether in an online or a face-to-face environment, is to know your students and then to plan your instruction with their needs, skill sets, and motivation levels clearly in mind.

Recommendations

Our experience with this course has opened our eyes to some of the more hidden problems of Web-based course management. We believe that the issues are surmountable, but we also believe that they deserve careful, explicit, ongoing attention. Our experience has also indicated the importance of professional development for instructors who are launching online courses. Instructors cannot give students what the instructors do not possess. With that in mind, we make the following recommendations.

1. Never take a face-to-face lecture course and place it, unmodified, into an online environment. Always examine the methods and materials that are used in the face-to-face course. Think about what they would look like to someone who only has access to text or graphics. Translate them into strategically designed methods and materials that make sense in a text/graphic environment. As an example, a face-to-face setting allows and even encourages "free-wheeling" discussion that often includes diverse changes in topics. Participants learn to develop an understanding of the conversational landscape and are able to mentally manipulate the various paths. In an online environment, by contrast, it becomes essential for someone to moderate the conversation and to explicitly differentiate the paths.
2. Consider the implications of the skill level of the students, and be prepared to offer assistance and encouragement. Never assume that the students know how to access the online materials.
3. Never assume that all students are engaged in the process. Always find a way to determine if any participants have failed to join the conversation or the activities. Never assume that all students are engaged in the process. Keep track of the students to ensure that no one becomes disassociated from the group.
4. Never allow the course to be dominated by pages and pages of text. Limit the amount of text that any participant, including the instructor, posts at any one time. A couple of well-structured paragraphs are likely enough to stimulate thoughts and subsequent dialogue.
5. Discourage submissions that contain little or no substance. Insist that students elucidate their thoughts and arguments. Provide examples of unacceptable submissions (for example, "I agree with Suzy," or "Check out the Web site at www.trythis.com."). Give explicit directions as well as implicit modelling for acceptable submissions.
6. Always find ways to provide some kind of human touch. Because of the nature of the text/graphic environment, this may be one of the most daunting tasks,

but it is also one of the most important. Something as minor as the electronic happy face (**:-)**) will let the downline readers get some sense of your emotional state. Spontaneous, unedited text, with grammatical colloquialisms and spelling errors, also offers a bit of a human touch. We have not yet found a satisfactory set of strategies for this purpose, but we continue to try. Above all, teaching and learning is a human process that demands human interaction. The online environment cannot be allowed to circumvent the humanness of this enterprise.

References

Clark, R. 1994. "Media and Method." *Educational Technology Research and Development* 42(3), 1042–1629.

Dede, C. 1996. "Distance Learning–Distributed Learning: Making the Transformation." *Learning and Leading with Technology: The ISTE Journal of Educational Technology Practice and Policy* 23(7), 25–30.

D'Souza, P.V. 1991. "The Use of Electronic Mail as an Instructional Aid: An Exploratory Study." *Journal of Computer-Based Instruction* 18(3), 106–110.

Gillard, G. 1993. "Deconstructing Contiguity." Pp. 182–195 in *Reforming Open and Distance Education: Critical Reflections from Practice*, eds. T. Evans and D. Nations. London: Kogan Page.

Gladieux, L.E., and W.S. Swail. 1999. *The Virtual University and Educational* Opportunity: Issues of Equity and Access for the Next Generation. Washington: College Entrance Examination Board. (http://www.collegeboard.org/policy/html/virtual.html)

Harasim, L., ed. 1993. *Global Networks: Computers and International Communication*. Cambridge: MIT Press.

Hiltz, S.R. 1988. "Collaborative Learning in a Virtual Classroom." CSCW 88: Proceedings of the Conference On Computer-Supported Cooperative Work (pp. 282–290), Portland, Oregon.

Mason, R. 1998. "Models of Online Courses." *Journal of Asynchronous Learning Networks* (http://www.aln.org/alnweb/magazine/vol2_issue2/masonfinal.htm)

Mayer, R. 1997. "Multimedia Learning: Are We Asking the Right Questions?" *Educational Psychologist* 32(1), 1–19.

Murray, B. 1999. "Technology Invigorates Teaching, But Is the Pizzazz Worth the Price?" *APA Monitor* 30(4), 1, 36–37.

Phipps, R., and J. Merisotis. 1999. *What's the Difference? A Review of Contemporary Research on the Effectiveness of Distance Learning in Higher Education*. Washington: The Institute for Higher Education Policy. (http://www.ihep.com)

Robin, B., J, Tellez, and R. Miller. 1998. "A Comparison of Text-Based and Graphical Internet Tools in Pre-Service Teacher Training." *Journal of Technology and Teacher Education* 6(4), 259–272.

Roddy, M. 1999. "Using the Internet to Unite Student Teaching and Teacher Education." *Journal of Technology and Teacher Education* 7(3), 257–267.

Seel, N., and W. Winn. 1997. "Research on Media and Learning: Distributed Cognition and Semiotics." Pp. 293–324 in *Instructional Design: International Perspectives*, eds. R. Tennyson, F. Schott, N. Seel, and S. Dijkstra. Mahwah, New Jersey: Lawrence Erlbaum and Associates.

Windschitl, M. 1998. "The WWW and Classroom Research: What Path Should We Take?" *Educational Researcher* 27(1), 28–33.

CHAPTER 20

International Collaborative Group Interaction: An Online Experience

Diane P. Janes
University of British Columbia
Canada

This chapter[1] is an evaluation/case study of an online course and, in particular, observations in the area of online collaborative group work and interaction. Using a quasi-Stake Responsive Model and participant-observation for data gathering, this chapter will review the design of the course, discuss student reactions to several key questions, and end with recommendations for online collaboration and future research.

Background

In 1996, the Monterrey Institute of Technology (ITESM) began looking for international partners and strategic alliances with other universities. ITESM is modelled on the Massachusetts Institute of Technology (MIT), and has twenty-seven campuses in Mexico, a number of local centres in other cities and Latin American countries, and a Virtual University component. "ITESM sought out UBC [University of British Columbia] for several reasons. These included its strong link with the Asia Pacific [area], its attractiveness as an opportunity for faculty and student research and exchange, and its expertise in distance education, especially in the area of interactive technologies" (Bates, 1995, p. 51). At the same time, UBC was looking to widen its international activities and ITESM offered strong ties with Mexican and Latin American communities, with many research and exchange possibilities. The result was a strategic partnership in several areas, with one of the elements being distance education. On June 21, 1997, the Distance Education and Technology unit of Continuing Studies at UBC signed a partnership with the Virtual University of ITESM to develop and offer a five-course postgraduate Certificate in Technology-Based Distributed Learning (Bates and de los Santos, 1997). The author has been involved in the design and implementation of all five courses.

Course Design

Figure 20.1 shows the home page for the Web course Social Issues in Technology-Based Distributed Learning, the fourth course in the Certificate program. Social Issues was

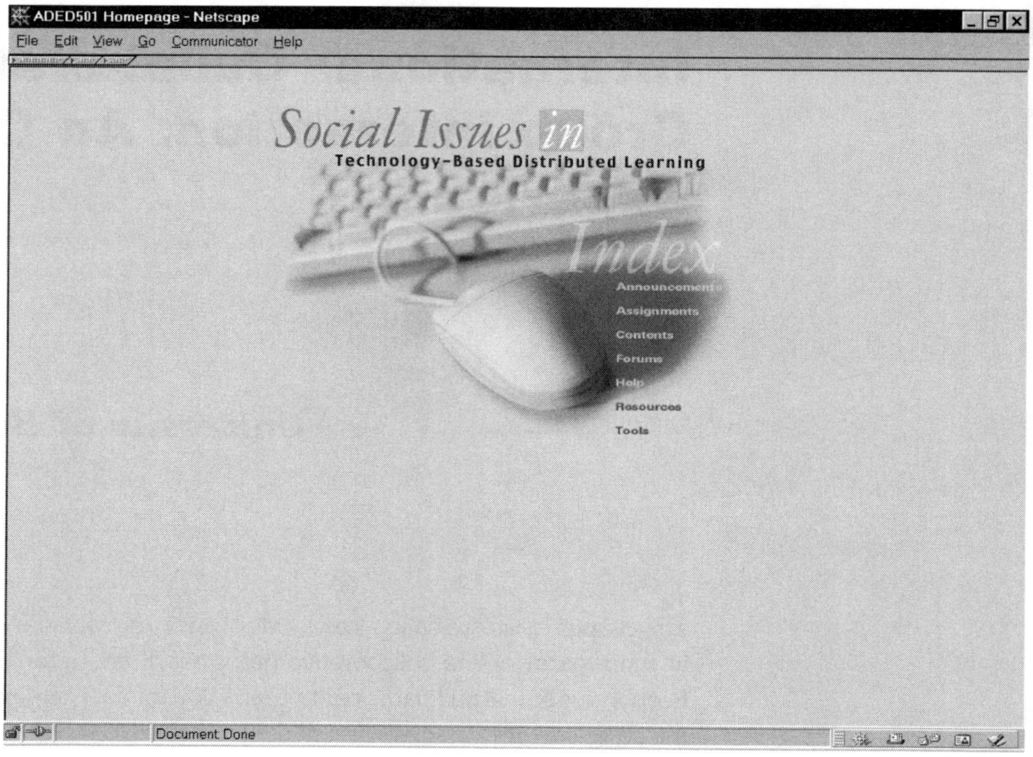

Figure 20.1 Home page for the Web course Social Issues in Technology-Based Distributed Learning

offered to students for the first time in the winter of 1999, with an enrollment of thirty-eight students from ten countries.[2]

The students enrolled in the course fell into three categories: masters/Ph.D., certificate, and audit.[3] The certificate and graduate students engaged in the discussions and collaborative work under the same standards for evaluation. The audit students participated as they felt able. Concurrently, ITESM's Virtual University had an enrollment of over one hundred students from Mexico, Chile, and Venezuela. Over the thirteen weeks of the course, the students engaged in a number of online activities designed to enhance their online interaction. After preliminary introductions and online posting of personal and professional biographies, the course began formally with the student submission of three short individual analyses of writings from the field of distributed learning and distance education. Figure 20.2 shows the course outline for the Social Issues Web course.

These short papers discussed the social questions and technology-based learning problems raised in the Book of Readings,[4] provided through online URLs (collected by the course authors), or produced by the student's own research. These 500-word papers encouraged students to begin systematic argument in preparation for the brainstorming. About halfway through their work on the small papers, the online brainstorming session began. Students were asked to choose discussion topics for the course. Although the instructors had ideas about topics considered "hot" in published work on distance education, they designed the course so that students would select core topics. At the end of the brainstorm session, the instructor summarized the key topics:

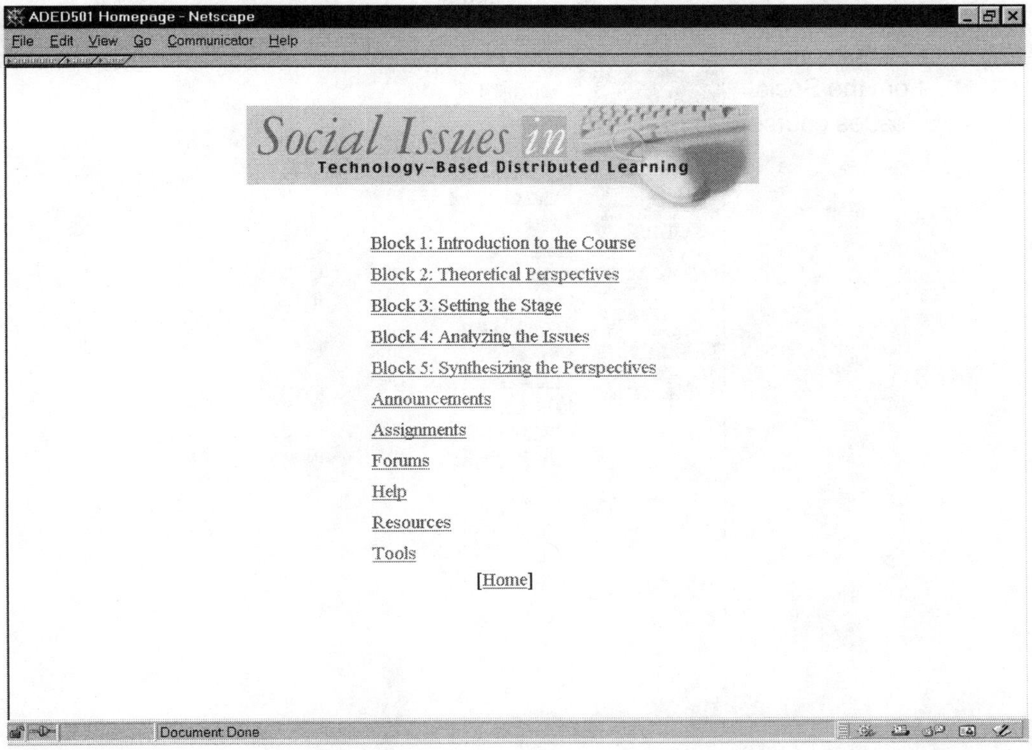

Figure 20.2 Course outline for the Social Issues Web course

Education. Topics included the effects of technology in teaching/learning; dehumanization, de-skilling; the impact on purpose; functional/emancipatory issues; and cultural asymmetry.

Access. Topics included technological access; "psychological" access; learning styles; social access; disparity, gender, class, etc.; disparity between developed/developing countries.

Globalization. Topics included cultural imperialism.

Whose interests are being served? Topics included copyright; commodification; militarization; economics.

Course instructors then created a framework for the next phase of the course—the online, small group presentation. Immediately after the brainstorming period, the graduate and certificate students were divided first into two groups (A and B) and then into six smaller groups within an A or B section (A1, A2, A3, B1, B2, and B3). Each subgroup (with five to six members per group) was assigned the task of deciding which issue to research and present. A formal presentation was to be written via consensus in each of the online private group fora. Each small group assigned a presenter, moderator, and summarizer, and led the discussion about their chosen topic with the main group they belonged to (A or B). Specific criteria were in place for the assignment of tasks within the group and these criteria were used to evaluate the work of the group.

Several fora were set up in WebCT (the Web course management system) to facilitate this round of collaboration. The procedure for group interaction went as follows. First,

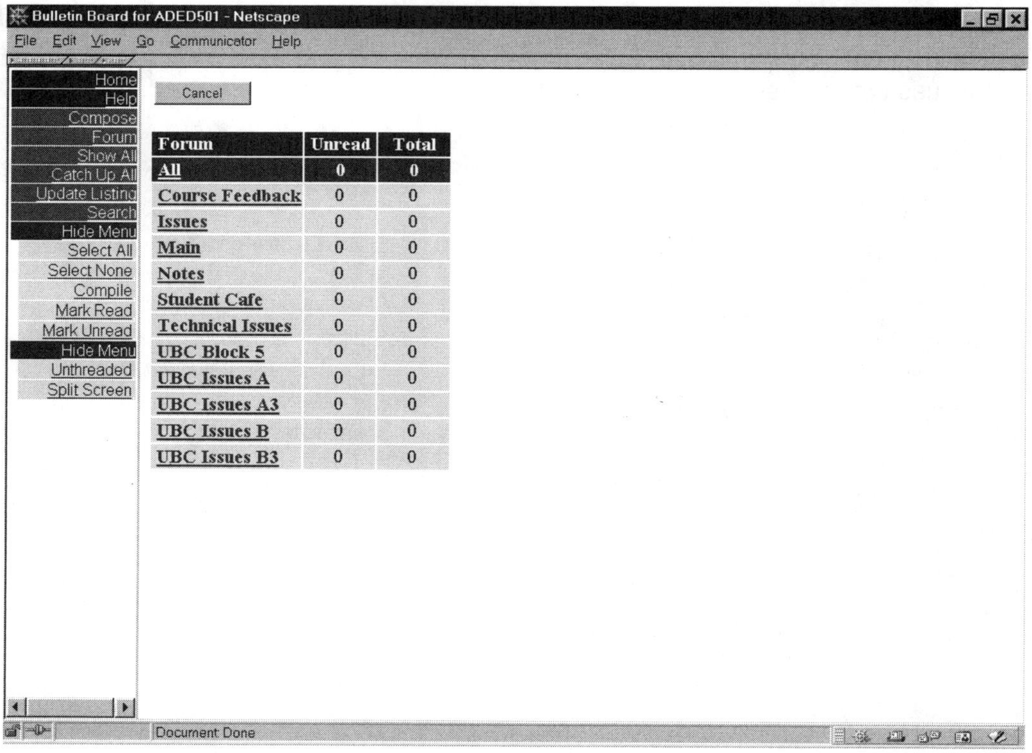

Figure 20.3 Sample of fora from the Social Issues course

the Canadian, Mexican, and international students were randomly assigned to groups. Second, each group was assigned its own "members-only space" to plan their presentation in private. Only the instructors had access to all of these private spaces. Third, students were advised that they could use any communication method available to them to move the group process along: e-mail, real-time chat, asynchronous discussion, fax, telephone, desktop video, or in-person contact, if time and place allowed. At the end of the term, with the formal presentations complete, the students rejoined the larger forum to debrief and discuss their experiences. In setting up the debriefing, one of the instructors posted the following instructions:

> In the "Issues" thread, we'd like you to try to make some final comments that synthesize the various perspectives on a particular issue. By this we mean "the combining of diverse conceptions into a coherent whole or the dialectic combination of thesis and antithesis into a higher stage of truth." It can be the issue that your group focused on or it can be some other issue. In this thread you might also suggest issues that did not get covered that you felt should have. We'd also like you think about and comment on how you think you can affect change. What power do we, as individuals and in our professional capacities, have to influence the way in which technology-based distributed learning unfolds and its social impact? What are our responsibilities as educators with regards to the social impact of technology-based distributed learning? (Instructor Z)

The last assignment of the course was a final formal paper, submitted individually by each student. The formal paper required discussion, analysis, and reflection on an issue raised within the course, and from their own experiences pertinent to the issue within the course.

Methodology

The Social Issues course was chosen as a case study because of the intensive interaction and student control/decision making that was part of the course. The course designers felt that this was an opportunity for intensive Web-supported collaborative learning.

Design of the Study

A participant-oriented evaluation was initiated to examine the first offering of the Social Issues in Technology-Based Distributed Learning course. "Participant-oriented evaluation" has been included under the responsive model of evaluation approach, as described in Worthen, Sanders and Fitzpatrick (1997). "Participant-oriented evaluation tries to portray an activity or program around which clear boundaries have been placed" (p. 156). Participant-oriented evaluation has several distinguishing characteristics: namely, inductive reasoning is used; a multiplicity of data are examined; the evaluations do not follow a standard plan; and the data are understood to record a multiple rather than a single reality (Worthen et al., 1997). Moreover, participant-oriented evaluation readily conforms to the case study model, delineated in Stake (1978):

> ...most case studies feature: descriptions that are complex, holistic and involving a myriad of not highly isolated variables; data that are likely to be gathered at least partly by personalistic observational and a writing style that is informal, perhaps narrative, possibly with verbatim quotation, illustration, and even allusion and metaphor. (p. 7)

Participants

As mentioned above, the students (n=38) from ten countries enrolled in the Social Issues course were masters/Ph.D. students, certificate students, and audit students. ITESM's Virtual University enrollment included over a hundred students from Mexico, Chile, and Venezuela. These students ranged in age from early twenties to late sixties. They were from various backgrounds, including university professor, lecturer, software developer, multimedia coordinator/developer, community college instructor, librarian, distance education specialist, TV/film producer, K–12 program developer, consultant, self-employed person, clinical psychologist, student, K-12 teacher, director of training, retired person, artist, international project manager, engineer, and computer programmer.

Data Collection and Analysis

Observations on Student Interaction

In the thirteen weeks of this course, the participant-observers (instructors) concluded that this was an active and interactive experience for most of the students. In all, the students and instructors exchanged 2018 postings to the online fora in WebCT, and approximately 1400 e-mails were received by the two instructors.

Peer Moderation of Discussions

The case study reported on several tasks, including student reactions to peer-moderated discussions; online participation; language; project and time management; and collaboration and leadership in international groups. From the outset, each of the six groups dealt with these tasks in various ways. Many of their choices stemmed from their work or experiences in face-to-face settings. From the beginning, there was a need to interact online and via other modes of communication to achieve consensus. Agreement varied from group to group. In the smallest interaction, a presentation with online moderation and facilitation was created with just forty-two messages. The longest interaction peaked at 230 messages. Both of the last groups to present their work noted a lack of participation no matter what they tried, with acknowledgement by those who participated in the debriefing that they were, by that time in the course, exhausted.

> I'm a little unsure of how to express what I'm feeling or sensing, so the easiest thing is to just come out with it! Perhaps everyone (our own group, and our peers as well) is tired or a little burned out, or overwhelmed. Or just that they have lives. However, I'm a little disappointed with how our discussion forum is going. It appears as though there may be some difficulty in others "getting" what we're trying to draw out in discussion. Don't get me wrong; there have been a few good contributions. But it feels like pulling teeth to me. Any suggestions? (Student K)

> Learning in a constructivist mode is meaningful, but it takes time and hands-on experience to make this possible. I really enjoyed working with members of my small group and the energetic participation. We were disappointed at the low level of involvement in our discussion and we wondered how much could be attributed to being third, spring break, the topic, or the way we posed the question. In any case the best way to learn how to moderate and present is to do it. But feedback is also necessary/helpful from the participants and the tutors. (Student Y)

Yet those who presented first and experienced the highest interaction by fellow students over the three- to four-week discussion series, expressed some trepidation about going first.

> I must say that I found it a bit tough to be out there blazing the trail. I now think of a thousand things I may have done differently as moderator to help steer and form the discussion. My tendency was to let people talk and only interrupt if I thought they were getting out of hand. Sorry if I failed you all there. In the end, though, I thought that most people seem to be more polite and stuck to the topic more so than they would have in a f2f [face-to-face] discussion. Do you agree? (Student F)

Throughout the experience, students questioned within the groups their own reactions and choices. With respect to this, a number of students felt they left the process with more questions than they had when they began.

> Again, when I think back to the experience that our [smaller] B group had, I wonder how the construction of abstract thinking can be addressed in an online medium? How does it differ from FTF [face-to-face] approaches? The scenario building approach of our presentation was modeled after the successful FTF group experience of one of our members. Obviously, this type of exercise requires participants to take some risks and cope with a certain amount of ambiguity. Is this more difficult for students in an online learning environment? Are there specific strategies with online teaching to facilitate and support the uncertainties of learning? (Student X)

Online Participation

Online participation in this course varied and was dependent on the personal circumstances of each student at that time. This finding was consistent with our experiences in face-to-face settings in other courses. Three important observations emerged during this course: "balancing," "lurking," and "trying to experience all." Some examples are listed here.

> As with the other participants that have posted, I too enjoyed the interactive nature of this course. Both tutors' input and encouragement to collaborate were paramount to the course's success—without it, it would have failed, I think. I agree with [student] (above) when she refers to the quantity (and length, for me) of the discussions and presentations—exhausting at times, but very interesting nonetheless. I felt as though I had to play a careful balancing act when coming down to what I should read, research, say, discuss, do online vs. off-line, etc. As there are only so many hours in a day, and I, like many others, put in a bursting "day-at-the-office." (Student A)

> I am not sure if some of my colleagues realize that, while there may not have been actual participation in some of their discussions, that didn't mean we weren't "listening" (I believe they call it "lurking" here in the online world.). For while some have an easy time writing their responses, it takes others longer. And the longer it takes, the more time one has to reflect about hitting the Cancel button instead of the Post button. (You don't capture "cancels," do you?—It's the same effect as having [a] hand up in class—but by the time the teacher gets to you, someone has already voiced your thought, but better.) (Student F)

> ...felt I cheated some of the group discussions. There were so many good topics and things going on, but found it quite exhausting. Sometimes I felt I couldn't keep up. I wanted to focus on ALL of them. (Does anyone else relate to this?).... (Student K)

Irrespective of the instructor cautions about balancing reading with online discussions, for some students, choosing which conversation to participate in, and which to avoid, took some time and experience. Even then, the cautions went unheeded by some students.

Language

The language of instruction for this course was English (at the request of the Mexican partners). While the ITESM-registered students and the UBC-registered students read in English, the discussion groups were either conducted in Spanish with Spanish-speaking instructors (for ITESM) or in English with English-speaking instructors (for UBC). Although there were many opportunities for students in both concurrent sessions to interact, it was only during the collaborative activities in the course that they were required to work together. These collaborative activities were voluntary on the part of the students, although it was encouraged. English was the language used most often to do the work in these collaborative exercises. However, any other mutually agreed upon working language was also acceptable.

In one of the early posts in the course, a student used an online translator to try to assist him in communicating with his Spanish-speaking colleagues. He questioned his colleagues after this attempt:

> Do you think that this could allow people to feel that they have a greater connectedness with the help of these translation sites? (Student G)

The response of his colleagues, although encouraging the concept and his efforts, noted that the software did little to assist in the communication.

> Actually the translation is pretty bad. Although I can make some sense of [it] your post is barely understandable, but we (at least I) appreciate the effort. (Student D)

> I agree with [Student D] in that the translation is pretty bad, but it is the intention that counts. Do you know how to write any Spanish without any help? You may do better. I find that most of the times these official translators usually use very formal language. (Student L)

Beyond talking about language as a societal issue in the theoretical sense, no other conversations took place online regarding language use. This particular thread continued with several more posts of an intense discussion on the limitations of translator software and on other language and technology issues.

Project and Time Management

For several students with older machines, especially those who appeared to identify themselves as early adopters of technology, time commitment became an issue.

> I enjoyed this course although I have to admit that it took its toll in respect to time spent. Much of this alas was dealing with my tired old machine.... (Student B)

The design experience on the part of the authors of the course certainly suggested that group work, especially when the membership is kept small, provided many opportunities for interaction and collaboration not found in a larger group format. Even so, students found the work of the small group, while effective, very time consuming.

> I appreciate the variety of materials you presented to us at the beginning—to start the thinking process. The process of breaking us into smaller groups and having us make presentations and hold discussions was effective—though very time consuming. (Student F)

Bartolic-Zlomislic and Bates (1999) have been conducting a two-year study entitled "Developing and Applying a Cost-Benefit Model for Assessing Tele-Learning." Their research has resulted in six Canadian case studies—it includes the first offering of the Technology-Based Distributed Learning Certificate—and makes the suggestion that

> when comparing student estimates of their time spent working on the course to actual course requirements, students generally fell within the desired range of time.... While the actual time spent was similar to that spent in a face-to-face course, it *seemed* to take more work. This is possibly due to the sequential and more intense nature of the discussion fora. (p. 61)

The issue of perception versus the reality of time commitment was echoed by students in the course.

> Looking back at my time log, and in spite of a late start, I spent about 40 hours in discussion between 5 Mar[ch] and 19 Mar[ch]. Reading was in addition to this. Because of other commitments, I find it really difficult to get on the list every day, and that's important for continuity of discussion. I appreciate the need for a long discussion period to allow a reasonable number of people to interact a number of times, but it is difficult to visit the list frequently for an extended period. The flexibility of time online is both a blessing and a curse. (Student M)

The comment of Student M sums up the two-sided coin of technology-based distributed learning. The flexibility of time committed to working online was beneficial and intrusive.

Collaboration and Leadership in International Groups

The observation of this course and its students with respect to collaboration and leadership within international groups was valuable. Overall, the students met the challenges presented by international collaboration without hesitation. Yet, the issues that seemed to be prevalent could also be considered prevalent in face-to-face collaboration, in some respects. Issues of concern included the following:

- The "disappearance" and "silence" of team members for long periods of time when decisions were necessary within the group;

- The encouragement of some of the more quiet group members by some of the more vocal ones;
- The recognition that lurking did not mean lack of engagement with the ideas or the learning;
- The need to respect the time it took to collaborate online to achieve consensus without having met the person or persons with whom you were working;
- The need to respect, at all times, the points of view of the group and to create a safe environment for discussion, disagreement, and compromise.

> I learned a lot about the collaborative learning process and about the values and opinions of my peers. This certainly has been important for me and dramatically extended my understanding of the complexity of TBDL [technology-based distributed learning] in the real world. (Student T)

> ...Groups. Again, a completely different experience than other ones! It's amazing the juggling that goes on. In a way, I rather liked that we were assigned to groups because it's more true to life. It's very time-consuming to organize groups virtually. Personalities came through which humanized the process for me. Two things were difficult for me. (i) Some members didn't make contact for ages, so I even wondered if they were still there; (ii) Sometimes feedback was needed asap and some group members seemed to vanish just then. We resorted to a lot of communication via e-mail as some of us had difficulty with Web and interaction was critical.... (Student K)

Recommendations

A Template for Collaboration

A number of interesting design ideas emerged from the development and student reaction to the activities and tasks throughout the thirteen weeks of interaction. These ideas might hold some promise for future online group work in other courses and projects.

Careful Design, Preparation, and Organization

There are a number of complicated issues with respect to collaborative online learning. To ignore them is like ignoring the perceptual differences of objects refracting above and below a water line. Perceived effects of technology on teaching and learning can no more be ignored than the effects of water on objects. For example, technology exaggerates what normally happens in a face-to-face setting. The problems associated with face-to-face collaboration also exist in online settings, but with the feeling somehow that it is bigger, stronger, and more difficult to overcome in the latter context. Counteraction of these perceptions must be incorporated in the design of the activity, the preparation of the students and instructors, and the organization of the overall course. Thoughtful anticipation of student and instructor needs can reduce feelings of anxiety associated with exhaustion or frustration.

Different Groups of Two or Three

Although sorting students into groups appears to be a simple idea, one of the hidden complexities of online learning and interaction is the time needed to form relationships and to create the groups that are able to function without reliance on face-to-face contact. Using only written text to transfer meaning can open a group to misinterpretation. Observation seems to indicate that the smaller the group, the quicker its members are able to find common ground and to take command of their assigned collaborative activity. Smaller groups encourage everyone to participate and contribute, and to take into account language and cultural issues through high levels of interaction.

There are several ways in which an instructor can create small groups. One way is to randomly assign participants to a group without participant involvement in the selection. When working online in a collaborative environment, consider using participant self-selection. If you choose this option, consider the time delay involved. Finding one's own group online takes time and requires the instructor, in advance, to have set up some mechanism (participant biographies or an online e-mail listing of participants) by which participants can contact each other freely and easily.

Brainstorm: An Online Collaborative Activity

Especially for postgraduate work in online collaboration, it is important that participants have some control over their learning. One way this course tried to accommodate learner control was to require brainstorming as an online collaborative activity. The project defined brainstorming as the contribution of at least one idea to the brainstorm session. Individuals could contribute more than one idea, but the intention was to get everyone to post at least once. Each idea had to have a reference point or context (for example, derived from one's work, experience, reading, or observations). Each idea had to be accepted without judgment by other participants. Finally, the brainstorm had a distinct beginning and end date for the interaction, with postings limited to one hundred words.

Once the brainstorm was finished, the participants and, later, the instructors worked together to form a framework or a context in which the issues identified could be expanded upon through research and discussion. This type of activity permits learner control, and can make a course more timely and relevant for the participants. Learners should be involved in setting the agenda for this and any activity.

Assessment and Specificity

Be specific on assessment. How will the students interact with each other? With the instructor? What is the purpose of the assignment? What problems might be anticipated? With international group work taking place online, participants are without many of the tools and coping strategies that can be assumed in graduate work in a face-to-face or traditional classroom setting. Therefore, it is very important to provide clear guidelines to students on how to interact, how to adapt traditional coping skills to this new learning environment, and how they will be assessed in their group activities. Any information you can provide to the learners to assist them in planning their interaction with each other will most likely result in collaborative work that will have both depth and thoughtfulness. Clear criteria for assessment must be established and related to both process and product.

Finally, it is always useful to require some tangible product or "deliverable" as an outcome of the process.

Criterion Checklist

Make a checklist of criteria that you think would be a useful guide for students as they participate in online group work. Another complexity of online learning is the feeling of being alone and of missing something, even with many opportunities to interact with one another. These negative feelings can be alleviated to some extent with comprehensive and thoughtful criteria for learner interaction with each other and with instructors. By anticipating some of the areas of conflict or insecurity, an online teacher can facilitate online collaborative activities without structuring the uniqueness and creativity out of the activity.

Participation

Consider the scope of participation in a Web course: It can be local, regional, national, or even international. What are some of the differences in various types of participation under these varying conditions? Groups are more easily formed when the participants have common interests and experiences, and when they are located in the same time and place. Groups that share a common time and place can often share many common interests and experiences. However, participants in an online interactive collaborative environment may or may not have common interests and experiences. They may have a common language or they may not. They may live across the street from each other in the same city or they may live a whole world away. Given the global village concept of online learning, it is important to consider who is participating and where they are located. A group working collaboratively online for the first time, with members in different time zones, speaking different languages, with different cultural touchstones, might need more assistance from an instructor or participants than a group that meets face to face for the first time.

Summary

The chapter described the complex organization, design, and evaluation of Social Issues in Technology-Based Distributed Learning, the first offering of an international online course. From the discussion evolved a template for collaborative online learning. However, this case study is intended as a beginning of a series of opportunities for future research. The potential of Web-based instruction is enormous. There is a need for more research into collaborative online learning. Online learning has been called a new paradigm, one that facilitates collaboration and critical thinking. Yet the ideal is not always realized in many of the uses of this new media. There is a tendency to use new technologies to replicate older technologies. Much of the present-day Web-based instruction is limited to content transmission. There must be recognition on the part of teachers and designers that developing collaborative activities presents both practical and logistical problems. More work is needed to help educators to fully utilize the online collaborative opportunities that exist in networked online learning.

Notes

1 The author would like to acknowledge the support of the ITESM and UBC instructors and students of ADED 501; Dr. Mark Bullen, Dr. Tony Bates, and the members of the Distance Education and Technology team; and the 602 Doctoral Seminar, Faculty of Education at the University of British Columbia, in the preparation of this work.

2 The ten countries represented are Australia, Botswana, Canada, China (Hong Kong), Finland, France, Germany, Mexico, the United States, Yugoslavia.

3 Audit students register for the courses and pay full tuition but are not required to submit assignments or participate in any of the online discussions.

4 The Book of Readings is a copyright-cleared collection of journal articles and book chapters chosen by the course instructors.

References

Bartolic-Zlomislic, Silvia, and A.W. Bates. 1999. "Investing in Online Learning: Potential Benefits and Limitations." *Canadian Journal of Communications* 24 (3), 50–78.

Bates, A.W. 1995. *Technology, Open Learning and Distance Education*. London: Routledge.

Bates, A.W., and J.G. Escamilla de los Santos. 1997. "Crossing Boundaries: Making Global Distance Education a Reality." *Journal of Distance Education* (12)1/2, 49–66.

Berge, Z.L. 1998. "Concerns of Teachers in Higher Education." Pp. 29–31 in paper presented at the ISTE Conference TEL-ED '98, New Orleans, Lousiana.

Boshier, R. 1996. *Aims of Adult Education: Introduction to Adult Education*. Course manual for ADED 412, pp. 55–117. Vancouver: University of British Columbia.

Bullen, M. 1998. "Participation and Critical Thinking in Online University Distance Education." *Journal of Distance Education* 13(2), 1–32.

Bullen, M., and D. Janes. 1998. "Tutor and Student: Online Graduate Teaching and Learning in an International Context." Pp. 191–192 in *Proceedings of the 14th Annual Conference of the Canadian Association for Distance Education*, eds. J. Baggaley, T. Anderson, and M. Haughey. Athabasca, Alberta: Athabasca University.

Gayol, Y., and F.M. Schied. 1997. "Cultural Imperialism in the Virtual Classroom: Critical Pedagogy in Transnational Distance Education." Paper presented to the 18th Conference of the International Council for Distance Education, State College, Pennsylvania.

Harasim, L., S.R. Hiltz, L. Teles, and M. Turoff. 1995. *Learning Networks: A Field Guide to Teaching and Learning Online*. Cambridge, Massachusetts: MIT Press.

Janes, D. 1999. "Techniques and Strategies for International Group Work: An Online Experience." Paper presented at the 5th International NAWeb'99 Conference, Fredricton, New Brunswick.

Jones, S.G., ed. 1998. *Cybersociety 2.0: Revisiting Computer-Mediated Communication and Community*. Thousand Oaks, California: Sage.

Mason, R. 1991. "Moderating Educational Computer Conferences." *DEOSNEWS* 1(19).

Rheingold, H. 1993. *The Virtual Community: Homesteading on the Electronic Frontier*. Reading, Massachusetts: Addison-Wesley.

Rohfeld, R.W., and R. Hiemstra. 1995. "Moderating Discussions in the Electronic Classroom." In *Computer-Mediated Communication and the Online Classroom in Distance Education*, eds. Z.L. Berge and M.P. Collins. Cresskill, New Jersey: Hampton Press.

Stake, R.E. 1978. "The Case Study Method in Social Inquiry." *Educational Researcher* 7, 5–8.

Sullivan, E.V. 1983. "Computers, Culture, and Educational Futures: A Critical Appraisal." *Interchange* 14(3), 17–31.

Worthen, B.R., J.R. Sanders, and J.L. Fitzpatrick. 1997. *Program Evaluation: Alternative Approaches and Practical Guidelines* (2nd edition). New York: Longman.

APPENDIX

Links and Startups

Examples of Web-Based Instruction, Web Course Management Teaching, Learning, Instructional Design, CBI

Advanced Web design
http://home.earthlink.net/~robertstephens/class.html

Seven steps to success: Designing online courses
http://www.sit.ecu.edu/FacultyResources/designingonline/

Java: Nothing to fear
http://www.ibm.com/java/education/buildapplet/index.htm

The Web Academy
http://www.webacademy.com/

Web course management tools
http://linus.umd.edu/lectures/wit/index.htm

Web course management system: A masters thesis
http://guthrie.hunter.cuny.edu/oicit/main/itg/wcms.html

The creators of the first Web course management system
http://www.madduck.com/madduck.html

Course management tools
http://www.sonoma.edu/IT/ITS/Course_Management/

Indiana State University: Web course management tools
http://fcrc.indstate.edu/fcrc/pages/tools.html

Evaluation and selection of Web course management tools
http://evaonline.euro.org/News/19990329123013_24.html

WEB III: Web-based distance education course
http://www.nr.cc.va.us/ITI/ITI_1998/web3.htm

Assessment and evaluation of Web-based courses
http://edtech.clas.pdx.edu/PSUedtech/Documents/web_courses/web_course_assessment.html

Faculty resource kit at the Ohio State University
http://telr.ohio-state.edu/faculty/de/resources/faculty_resource_kit.cfm

Course/test management and delivery
http://www.thomtech.com/mmedia/becker/assess.html

Introducing and supporting a Web course management tool (Cornell University)
http://www.cit.cornell.edu/atc/cst/SyllabusWeb/sld001.htm

Course management software
http://www.ati.swt.edu/agenda/course_manager.html

Testing Web course management software
http://fog.ccsf.cc.ca.us/~kfrizler/webmgmt.html

Web course management
http://www.cedarville.edu/dept/ca/cic/tool_management.html

Course management systems
http://illinois.online.uillinois.edu/stovall/fsi99/cms/

Commercial course managment software
http://www.ssc.msu.edu/~oit/tools.html

Course management
http://www.upenn.edu/computing/help/collab/course-mgmt.html

WWW course management software
http://saber.towson.edu/~schmitt/courseware/

Introducing Web Course in a Box
http://www.rider.edu/oit/wcb/info.htm

Instructional Development Center: Virginia government showcase
http://www.sotech.state.va.us/govnnow.htm

WebCT: Web course tools
http://www.mcg.edu/ecss/webct.htm

How to start (and further develop) your Web course page: A primer
http://maxweber.hunter.cuny.edu/~mkuechle/webpage_primer.htm

Integrated course management software
http://online.parkland.cc.il.us/presentations/ISU/icmt.htm

Integrated Web-based course delivery tools
http://www.cfl.mq.edu.au/cfl/resource/revcom.html

WebCT is another online course option
http://web.cc.iastate.edu/newsletter/199904/article4.html

Faculty Internet Service Center: Web-based instruction tools review
http://socrates.berkeley.edu:7521/wbi-tools/wbi-tools-review.html

Online training for the automotive industry
http://www.autotrain.org/auto-home/developement.html

Comparing WebCT and TLM
http://webct.laurentian.ca/webct/robinson.htm

Course server software for online teaching
http://wwwtlc1.murdoch.edu.au/teach/guide/res/examples/course-servers.html

Web course case study: Oregon State University, Challenging Students' Paradigms
http://nova.umuc.edu/ide/potentialweb97/dorbolo.html

More on Web Course Management

Web course tool selection committee report (July 1998)
http://www.utexas.edu/cc/cit/tools/index.html

Practical Web management (HTML writers' guide)
http://hwg.org/services/classes/w201.2.html

Teaching through the Web reference
http://www.teachonweb.org/reference.shtml

Evaluation and selection of Web course management tools
http://sunil.umd.edu/webct/

Web Course in a Box
http://www.saida.org.lb/wcbweb.htm

Web Course in a Box (Virginia Commonwealth University)
http://www.vcu.edu/mdcweb/iat/iat.html

Web Course in a Box
http://www.fln.vcu.edu/demo/demo.html

Creating a library Web course (Central Oregon Community College)
http://www.cocc.edu/cfinney/classes/lib127i/create.htm

Audiographic telecourses for the Web: An experiment (Michigan State University)
http://www.ascusc.org/jcmc/vol4/issue2/larose.html

Writing Web pages with Web Course in a Box (Queen's University)
http://www.queensu.ca/wcb/schools/QU/its/nberndt/1/

WebTeach: Running a Web-based course
http://www.comp.lancs.ac.uk/webteach/course.html

High-end Web authoring courseware shells and other authoring software
Bob Jensen at Trinity University
http://www.trinity.edu/rjensen/245soft1.htm

Web Course in a Box: All you add is students
http://www.uwm.edu/IMT/IOT/IOTsprg-sum97/wcb.html

WebCT articles library
http://www.webct.com/library/

Web-based instruction resource site (main menu)
http://www.personal.psu.edu/faculty/w/d/wdm2/main.htm

Web-based instruction resource site (HTML guides)
http://www.personal.psu.edu/faculty/w/d/wdm2/htmlguid.htm

Course server software for online teaching (software comparisons)
http://cleo.murdoch.edu.au/teach/guide/res/examples/course-servers.html

Web-based instruction resources (theory, evaluation, and design;Utah State University)
http://english.usu.edu/jcurry/wbi.html

Online teaching and learning resources (National Education Association)
http://www.nea.org/he/abouthe/techip.html

Welcome to the Web developer's virtual library! (DHTML, HTML, CGI, JAVA, etc.)
http://wdvl.internet.com/WDVL/

Sample Startups

Interesting opportunities are opening up that could influence how professors teach and how they get paid for their teaching. Check out some of these startups.

Figure A.1
Tutor.com

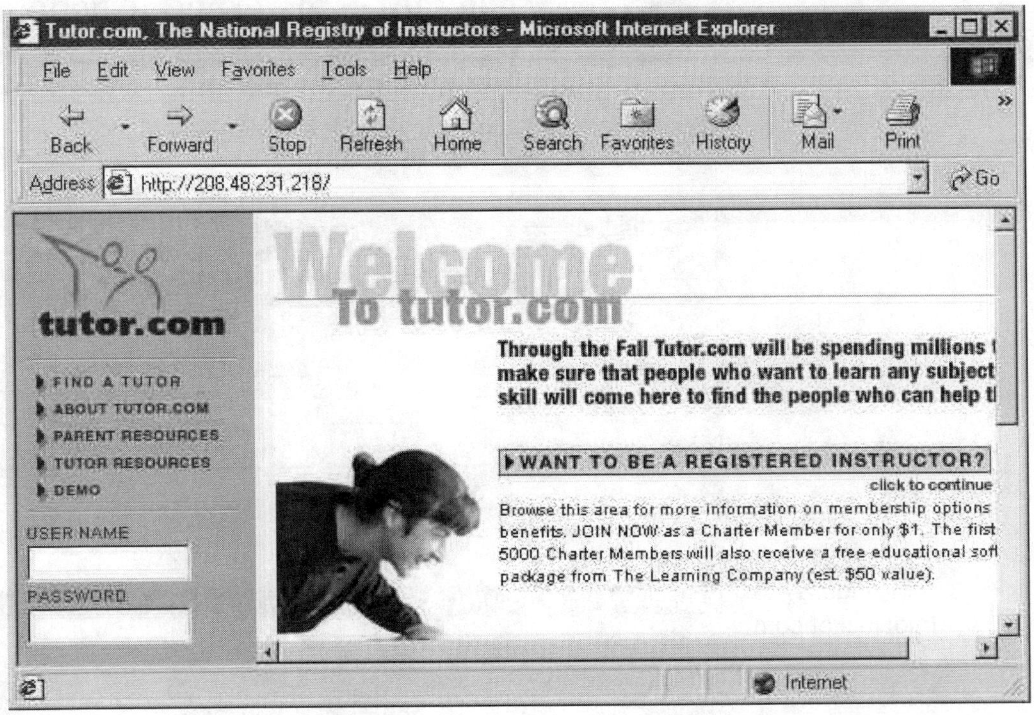

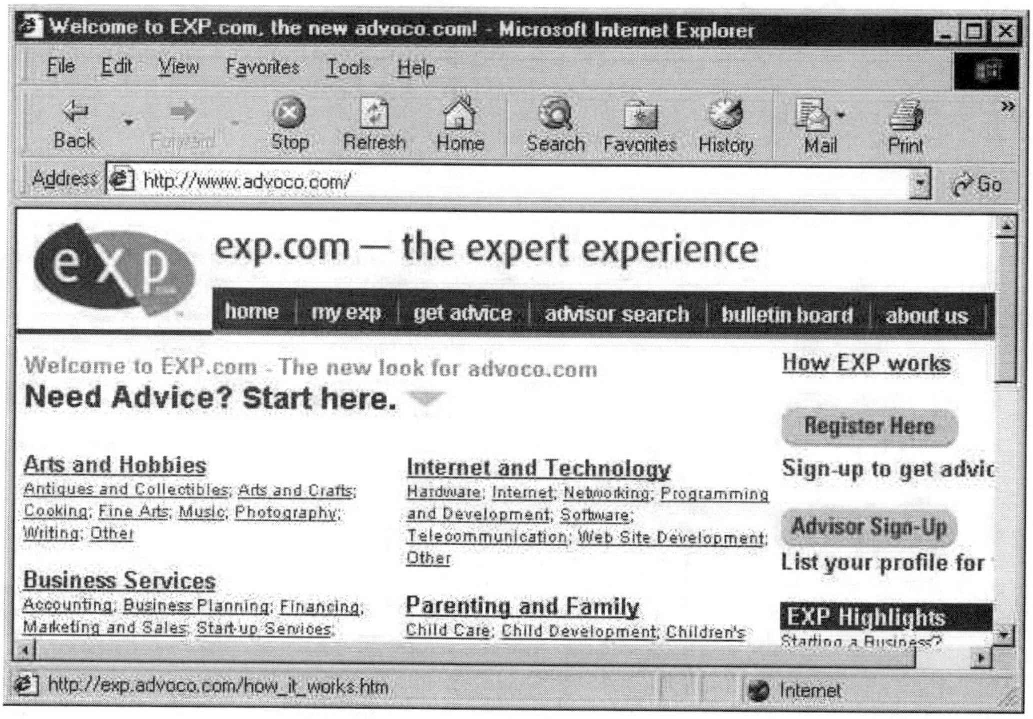

Figure A.2
EXP.com

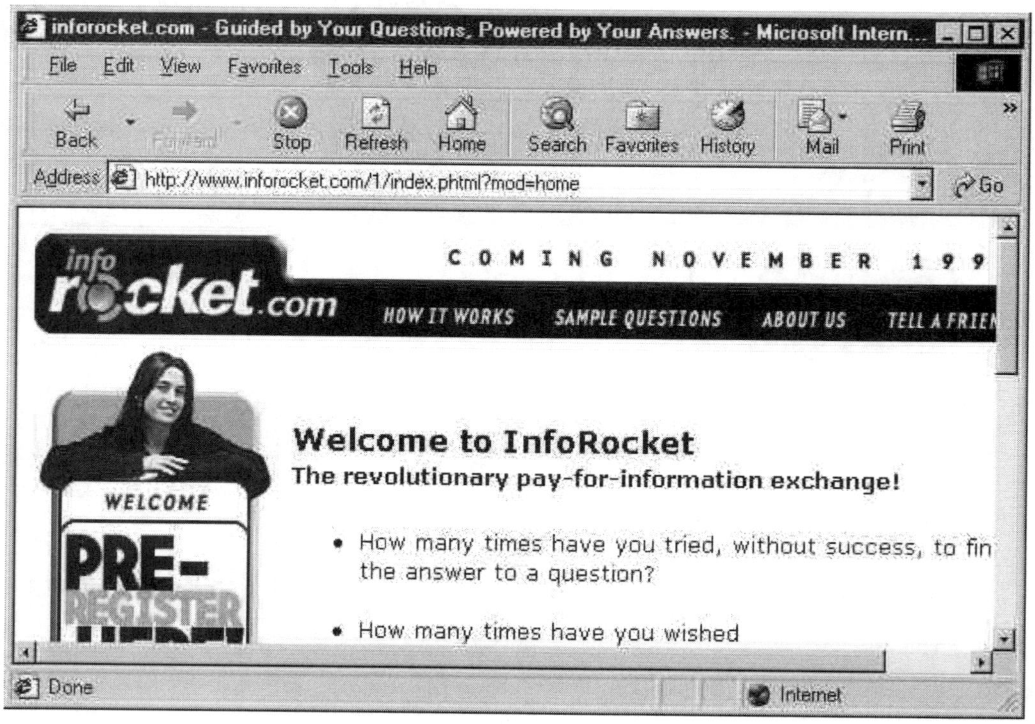

Figure A.3
InfoRocket.com

Figure A.4
ExpertCentral.com

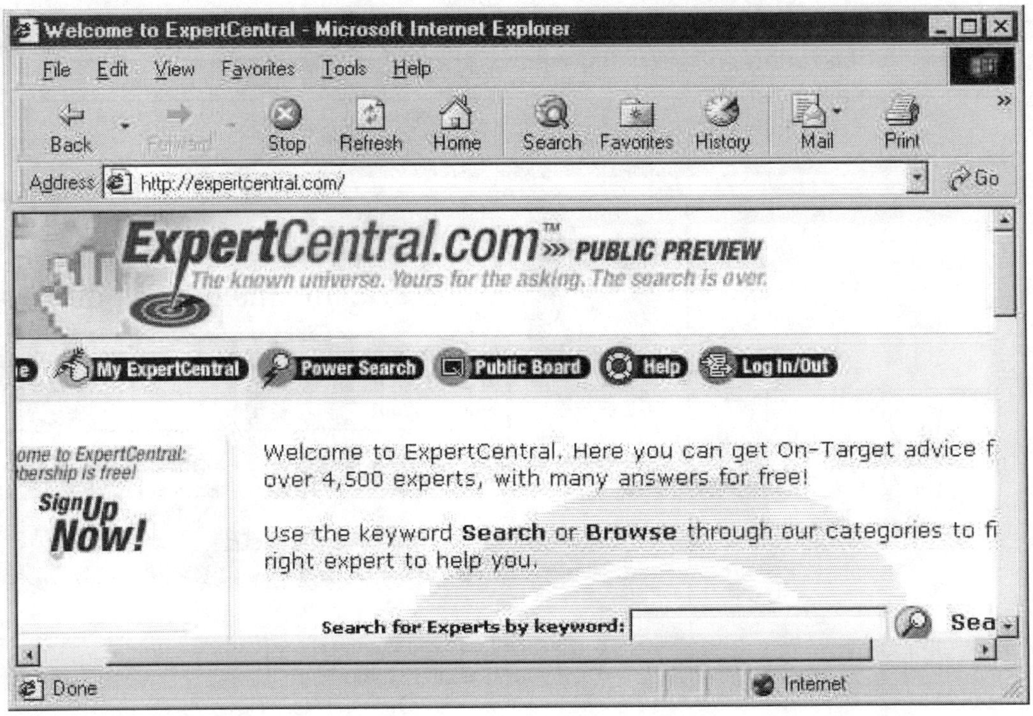

Figure A.5
Deja.com

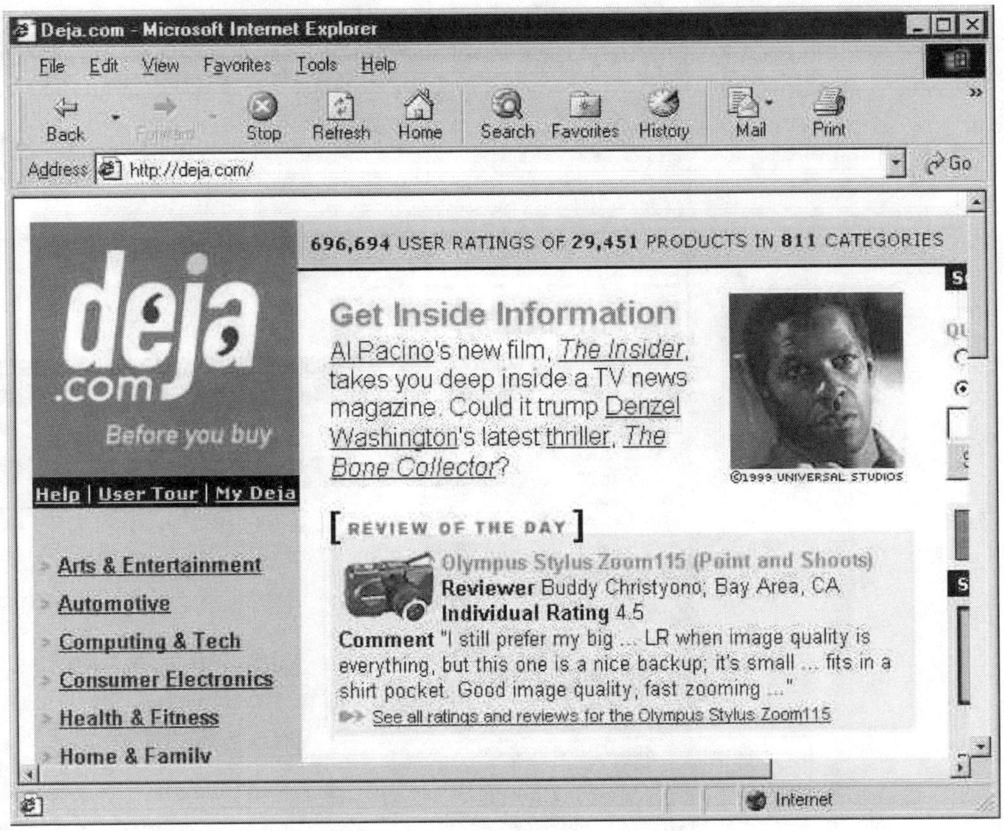

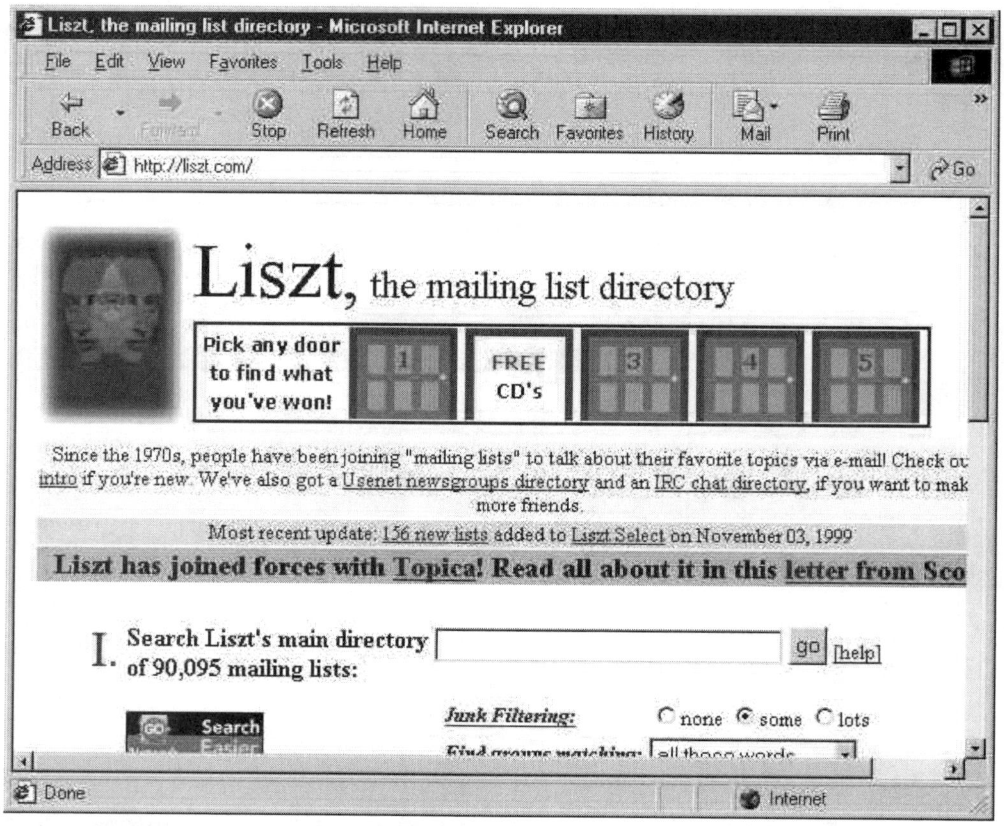

Figure A.6
Liszt, the mailing list directory

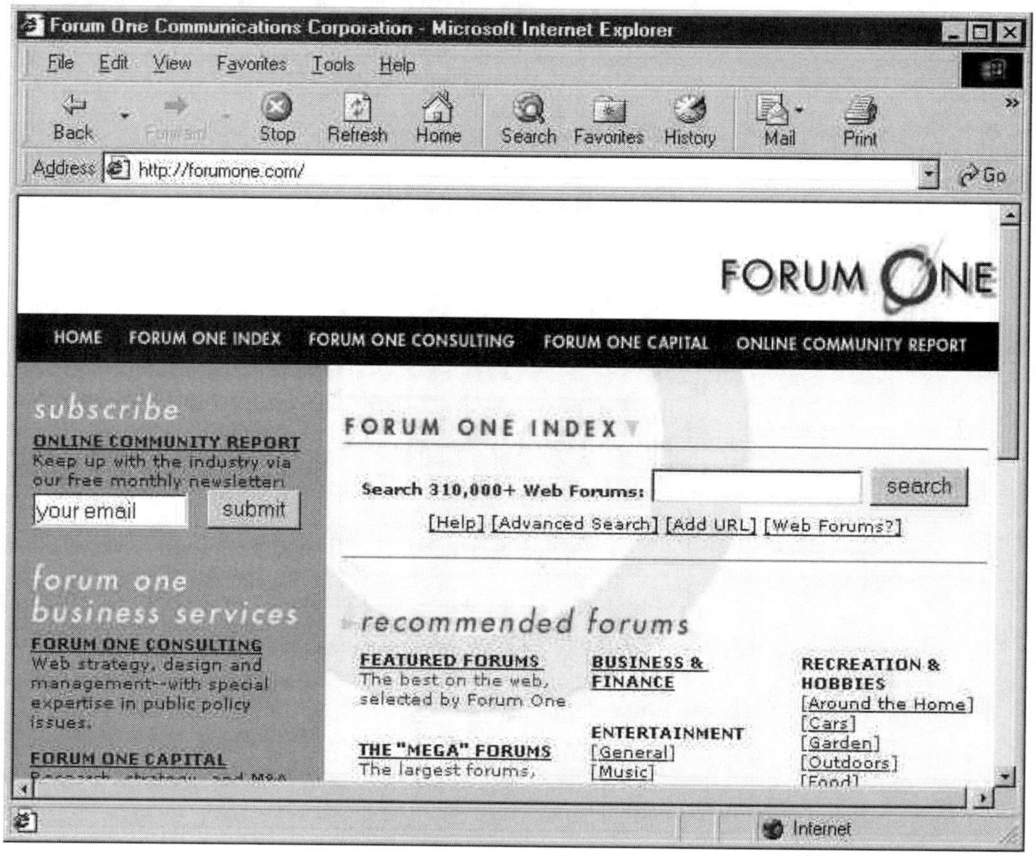

Figure A.7
Forum One

Figure A.8
About.com

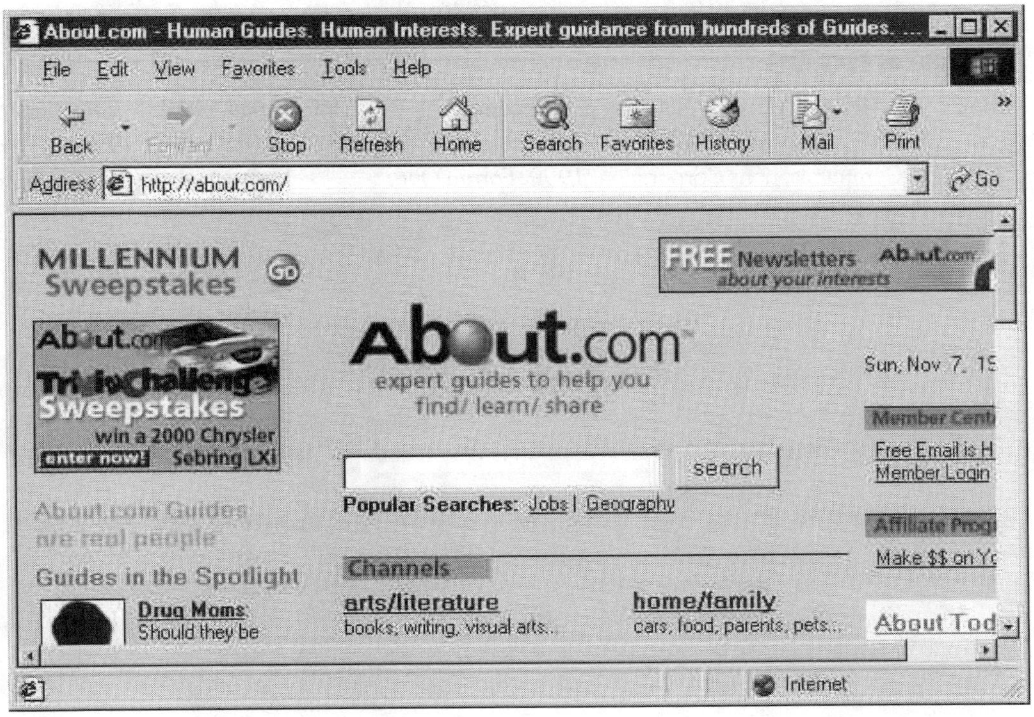

Figure A.9
iSyndicate.com

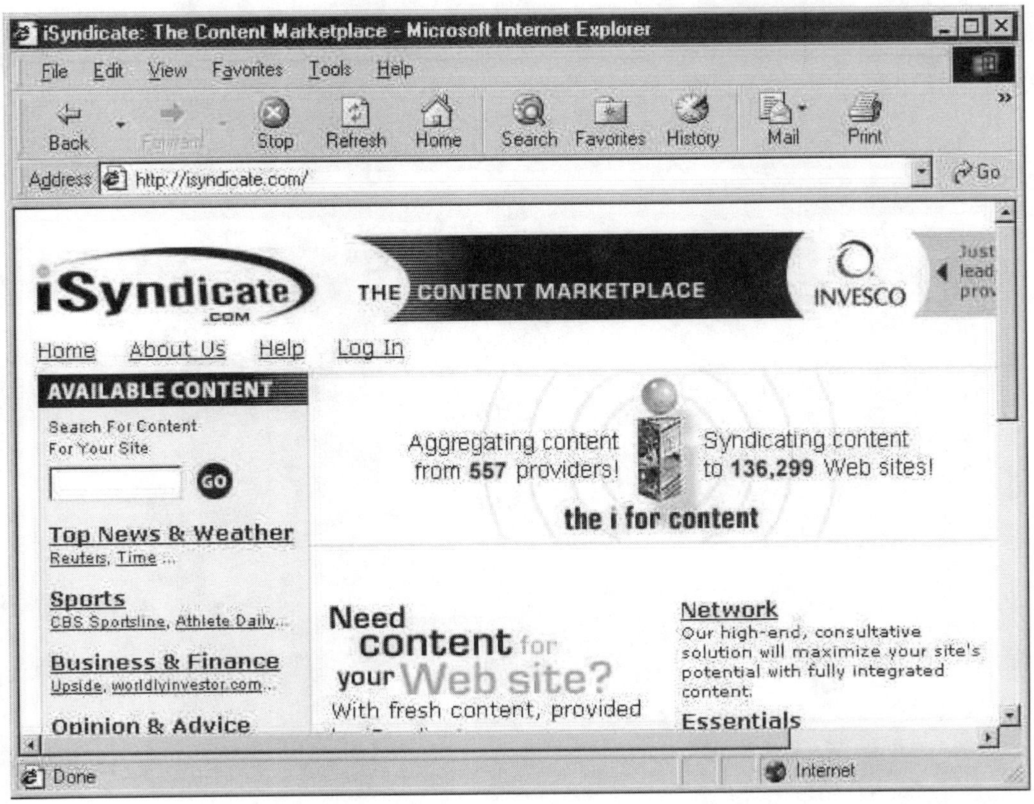

References

Benning, M. 1999. *EXP.com.* New York: EXP.com Inc.

Cigale, G. 1999. *Tutor.com*. New York: Tutor.com, Inc.

Forum One Communications Corporation. 1999. *Forum One*. The Forum One Index.

InfoRocket 1999. *InfoRocket.com*. New York: Silicon Alley.

Schmergel, G. 1999. *Expertcentral.com*. Needham, Massachusetts: ExpertCentral.com, Inc.

INDEX

J–K

L

M

N

O

P

Q

R

X–Z

AGMV Marquis
MEMBRE DU GROUPE SCABRINI
Québec, Canada
2000